Hope for the earth

Vistas on a new century

Ernst M. Conradie

Wipf & Stock
PUBLISHERS
Eugene, Oregon

Wipf and Stock Publishers
199 W 8th Ave, Suite 3
Eugene, OR 97401

Hope for the Earth
Vistas for a New Century
By Conradie, Ernst M.

ISBN: 1-59752-209-0
Publication date 5/18/2005
Previously published by University of the Western Cape,
South Africa, 2000.

Contents

Preface to the 2005 edition

Hope for the earth: Vistas on a new century was first published in 2000 through the University of the Western Cape in South Africa. It appeared as the eighth volume in the series "Text and Context". The new edition of this publication through *Wipf and Stock* allows for a wider distribution since the UWC edition was quite limited in this regard.

The Wipf and Stock edition contains some minor changes compared to the previous edition. These changes pertain to the page layout and formatting of the manuscript and some minor corrections. This also implies that the page numbering of the two editions are not the same.

This edition should not be understood as a revised edition though. Such a revised edition would have to take into account a large corpus of publications on Christian eschatology which appeared since 1999, especially around the turn of the millennium. These publications include a number of important new contributions within the context of ongoing dialogues between Christian theology and the various sciences. A revised edition would therefore require a significant updating especially of Chapter 14.

In addition, there has been a steady stream of new publications in the field of ecological theology. I have given an account of the state of the debate in this regard in two publications published at the University of the Western Cape in 2001, namely *Ecological theology: An indexed bibliography* and *Ecological theology: A guide for further research.* I have also offered a future agenda for ecological theology in an article entitled "An agenda for ecological theology: Some reformed perspectives from the South African context" (published in *Interface* 7/1, 14-29).

Since the publication of *Hope for the Earth* I registered a long-term, cooperative research project at the University of the Western Cape entitled "Ecology and constructive theology: Reflections on Christian doctrine". The purpose of this larger project is to engage in a series of full-length academic studies on particular aspects of Christian doctrine in the light of the emergence of ecological theology as a distinct mode of theological discourse. The hope is that such theological reflections will help to support an environmental praxis, ethos and spirituality in Christian communities in the Southern African context. *Hope for the earth* may now be understood as the first major study within the context of this larger project. I have now also completed a project on anthropology which was published by Ashgate (Aldershot, UK) in 2005 under the title *An ecological Christian anthropology: At home on earth?* My friend and research associate David Field is working on a similar project in the field of ecclesiology. Several others have contributed similar studies on specific aspects of Christian doctrine from within different contexts and theological traditions. One example is the excellent recent study entitled *Breath of Life: A theology of the Creator Spirit* by Denis Edwards (Orbis Books, 2004).

Sadly, since 1999 some of the projects described in Chapter 20 have lost their impetus. For similar stories and a guide for Christian earthkeeping in the South African context, see also the book *A rainbow over the Land: A South African guide of the church and environmental justice* by Ernst Conradie & David Field (published by the Western Cape Provincial Council of Churches, 2000). An important new development in 2002 saw the emergence of the Network of Earthkeeping Christian Communities in South Africa (NECCSA) with the aim of collecting further examples of stories of earthkeeping in a Christian context. It serves as a network between Christians already engaged in earthkeeping. These stories are available from the NECCSA website at www.neccsa.org.za.

There has also been a steady stream of new publications on Christianity and the environment from within the African context by authors such as Marthinus Daneel, David Field, Mary Getui, Samson Gitau., and Jesse Mugambi. An important document was published by the Ecumenical Foundation of Southern Africa under the title *The land is crying for justice: A discussion document on Christianity and environmental justice in South Africa* (2002). The publication of this document coincided with the World Summit on Sustainable Development which was held in Johannesburg in August 2002. See also the edition of the *Bulletin for Contextual theology in Africa* on "Church, environment and the World Summit on Sustainable Development (WSSD)" (Volume 8, No. 2-3, 2002) which contains several similar statements and a number of excellent articles.

Despite these considerations, I maintain that the main argument of *Hope for the earth* and the analysis of the structure of eschatological discourse (see Chapter 1-4) remain valid. What has become slightly dated is the situatedness of the discourse within the context of the new century that was dawning when the book was first published. The desperate need for a message of hope for the whole earth has certainly not become dated.

Ernst Conradie
April 2005

Introduction

A few introductory comments are necessary on the contexts from which this study on *Hope for the earth* emerged and within which it is rooted.

1. This study is the product of a research project registered at the University of the Western Cape, South Africa and entitled *Hope for the earth? Eschatology, cosmology, and ecology*. The aim of this research project is to explore the viability of an eschatological approach to an ecological theology, spirituality and praxis in the South African context.

The basic intuition of an eschatological approach is that a Christian environmental praxis can only be empowered on the basis of an adequate understanding of Christian hope. It is hardly possible to motivate ourselves to care for the earth unless we are convinced that there is indeed a future for ourselves and for the earth.[1] Despair in the face of environmental destruction will inevitably lead to a spirit of resignation.[2] Without any hope, without any vision of a future for the earth itself, an environmental praxis will soon lose its impetus. It will consciously be fighting a loosing battle. If life becomes a struggle for basic survival, as is often the case in Africa, it will be increasingly difficult to resist environmental destruction. Only where there is hope, can life become meaningful.[3]

The notion of an eschatological approach to ecological theology is based on a very helpful typology suggested by John Haught.[4] He identified three major approaches to ecological theology, namely an apologetic, a sacramental and an eschatological approach. Let us look briefly at this typology.[5]

a) An *apologetic approach* relates to an attempt to retrieve the notion of a more harmonious relationship between humanity and nature from the Biblical roots and the subsequent history of Christianity. It is apologetic in the sense that it defends the value of the Bible and the Christian faith for an environmental praxis against

---

1 See Haught (1995:196).

2 Haught (1993:24) may well ask: "If this final wreck and absolute extinction is the last word about the universe, then why seek now to preserve it against the inevitable void that seems to be its destiny?"

3 Images of the future have long been recognized as the one of the crucial building blocks of comprehensive worldviews. In portraying the place of human beings in the world, religious cosmologies not only describe the origins of the universe but also its destiny. These images of the future express that which has ultimate significance for people and form the basis of values and attitudes and the choices people make. Images of hope for the future are crucial for the kind of choice orientated behavior needed for environmental praxis. See Olivier (1989:29).

4 Haught (1993).

5 See my more detailed discussion (Conradie 1998) of the typologies of Haught and others.

the famous criticism of Lynn White and others that Christianity bears a "huge burden of guilt" for the ecological crisis.[6] The thrust of this model is to move beyond a theology of dominion understood as domination towards a theology of stewardship. Human beings should be regarded as the stewards,[7] caretakers, priests, custodians or guardians[8] of creation who have the task of "tending the garden"[9] with wisdom and respect. Haught comments that the vast majority of Christian theologians follow such an apologetic approach.

This theology of stewardship has often come under criticism. The notion of stewardship is regarded as a too managerial and androcentric concept to support the ecological ethos and vision of the place of humanity in creation which is needed today.[10] The managerial steward is a sanctified version of the technocrat![11] According to the metaphor of stewardship, God seems to be viewed as an absentee landlord who has put human beings in charge of the master's property.[12] Alternatively, this task to govern and order nature wisely is modeled on that of a benevolent monarch or patriarch. Furthermore, it assumes human supremacy among the species. Even though the emphasis is on responsibility instead of domination, the management model assumes that we as (male) human beings know best. The theology of dominion or stewardship fails to accentuate that we belong to the earth more than it belongs to us, that we are more dependent on it than it is on us, that we are *of* the earth and not living *on* the earth.[13] Or, in the words of Thomas Berry, "The human is less a being on earth or in the universe than a dimension of the earth and indeed the universe itself."[14] The history of humanity is nothing but an episode in the larger history of the cosmos.

Despite this criticism, the value of the notion of stewardship should not be denied. Nash insists that an ecological commitment is far more important than verbal purity.[15] Rasmussen also senses that there is at least a shared consensus in the debates on the motif of stewardship that 1) human beings do not own the earth and 2) that "the earth is the Lord's."[16]

b) A *sacramental approach* explores the inter-relatedness of human beings and

---

6 See White (1967).

7 See, especially Hall (1990), Wilkinson (1991).

8 See Osborn (1994).

9 Granberg-Michaelson (1987).

10 Granberg-Michaelson (1990:12).

11 See Hall (1990:234f) who acknowledges this danger of overestimating our managerial skills. Hall argues that the symbol of stewardship is nevertheless more appropriate than any other available metaphors.

12 McDonagh (1994:130).

13 Haught (1993:101).

14 Berry (1988:195).

15 Nash (1991:107).

16 Rasmussen (1996:236).

nature. Whereas the apologetic approach would emphasize the relationship between human beings and nature, the sacramental approach sacralizes the unity of humanity with nature. It regards nature as something sacred, a place where the presence of the divine may be experienced (thus sacramental).[17] Human beings are called to respect and celebrate this sacredness. Haught cites the creation spirituality of Thomas Berry and Matthew Fox, various expressions of ecofeminism, indigenous theologies and deep ecology as examples of such a sacramental approach.

Although this sacramental approach to ecological theology is theologically often quite radical, its environmental ethos remains curiously conservative. Its main thrust is to retrieve and to return to a sacralization of nature. This seems to be regarded as the last best hope for the preservation of ecosystems amidst the onslaught of the late capitalist industrial economic order.

Haught also points out that societies, for whom nature was or still is sacred, have nonetheless destroyed their natural habitation throughout the centuries. In this sense a sacramental approach can be somewhat naive and perhaps too romantic. According to Haught, a purely sacramental approach cannot easily accommodate the shadow side of nature (including the sins of humanity as a particular part of nature).[18] The model of sacramentalism may mask the unequal and corrupted relations of power within ecosystems.

c) Haught proposes an *eschatological approach* to ecological theology. Instead of a retrieval of ecological wisdom from former cultures, he calls for a transformation of an ecological vision towards the future. Any adequate ecological theology must be future orientated. An environmental ethos is not so much aimed at the preservation of the created order, but inspired by a vision of creation as the prototype of the new creation.[19] Haught cites the theology of Jürgen Moltmann, the evolutionary cosmology of Teilhard de Chardin and (his own notion of) process theology as examples of such an eschatological approach to ecological theology.

One may argue that, despite the (valid) criticisms that could be raised against the apologetic and sacramental approaches, these three approaches to ecological theology may be compatible with one another. All three these models provide a distinct theological rationale for caring for the earth, but the temporal focus of each approach is different. The sacramental approach emphasizes that the earth is a sacred gift from God (in the *past*) which should therefore be treated with due

---

17 Pannenberg (1994:138) comments that this terminology is too general and imprecise. He adds that the notion of a sacramental universe generally omits the eschatological dimension that is decisive for understanding nature according to Romans 8:19f.

18 Haught (1993:111). McFague (1993:71) and Ruether (1992:242) argue from an ecofeminist point of view that the creation spirituality of Berry and Fox cannot do justice to the sense of oppression and injustice that is part of the awesome mystery of life on earth. There is an ungrounded evolutionary optimism which is perhaps due to the attempt to replace the hegemony of a fall / redemption theology by an emphasis on creation theology (only). Nevertheless, creation spirituality presents a utopian, eschatological vision not of how things are but how they should be.

19 Bridger (1990:291).

respect. The eschatological approach emphasizes a vision of the *future* of the earth in God's presence. This vision serves as an inspiration for an environmental praxis in the *present*. Such an environmental praxis is guided by the conviction that "the earth is the Lord's" and may be described with concepts like stewardship, gardening or earthkeeping. This study will nevertheless focus, in terms of Haught's typology, on the value of an eschatological approach to an ecological theology, spirituality and praxis.

One of the results of the environmental crisis is that it has led to a widespread sense of despair. David Hallman comments that, "The problems of ecological destruction and global poverty are certainly of a magnitude and intractability to elicit unmitigated despair."[20] Indeed, "Hopelessness is the greatest killer – of joy, of initiative, of loving concern, of social and ecological responsibility, even of physical life".[21] Despair can certainly become a "sickness unto death" (Kierkegaard). Furthermore, despair becomes a self-fulfilling prophecy when it leads people to think that action is futile.[22] Only a persistent hope that can continue to care for the earth amidst environmental degradation can therefore energize an environmental praxis.

Hope is indeed a precious commodity. The question therefore seems to be: Where can a vision of hope amidst such a sense of environmental despair be found? In what way could this hope include a sense of hope for the earth itself? Is the Christian hope one of salvation for human beings *from* the earth or does it include some vision of hope *for* the earth itself?[23] How could a vision of hope for a new earth be made intelligible within the parameters of modern cosmology that indicates the radical finitude of the earth itself? And how can such a vision of Christian hope inform and empower an environmental praxis and spirituality - especially on the African continent?

2. These questions set the agenda that this study seeks to address. It has to do so by integrating the concerns of eschatology, cosmology and ecology (the subtitle of the above mentioned research project). It investigates the viability of such an eschatological approach to an ecological theology in more detail. More specifically, it explores the value of such an eschatological approach to an environmental spirituality and praxis in the South African context. This specification raises the thorny issue of Christian eschatology in an African context.

---

20 Hallman (1994:8). He immediately adds that what emerges from literature on the environment is often not resignation but an astonishing conviction, vision, celebration, humor and hope. For one example of such a vibrant sense of hope in a context of poverty and misery, see Ortega (1989).

21 Nürnberger (1994:148).

22 Barbour (1993:266).

23 See Moltmann (1996:259): "Christian eschatology must be broadened out into cosmic eschatology, for otherwise it becomes a Gnostic doctrine of redemption, and is bound to teach, no longer the redemption of the world but a redemption from the world, no longer the redemption of the body but a deliverance of the soul from the body."

This has been a controversial issue ever since the publication of John Mbiti's study on *New Testament eschatology in an African background* (1971). Mbiti suggested that traditional African cosmology has "virtually no concept of the future" (beyond a few years at most).[24] He argues that the language structure of some cultures (he focuses on the Akamba of Kenya) does not even make provision for the future tense. It has a two-dimensional concept of time, an indefinite past and an intensely active present.[25] The center of temporal gravity lies in the past. There is virtually no future dimension or general notion of the end of the world. Mbiti concludes that eschatology remains somewhat foreign to traditional African culture. Whatever eschatology Christianity in Africa internalizes has to be adopted from the Jewish-Christian tradition.

The generalizations in Mbiti's thesis have often been criticized.[26] However, the legitimacy of Mbiti's arguments does not need to deter us here. The stark contrast between his suggestions and the strong futurist emphasis in many recent Western eschatologies is nevertheless noteworthy. In the work of scholars like Moltmann, Pannenberg and Haught a strong orientation towards the future is regarded as a defining characteristic of Christianity. They develop a metaphysics of the future where the future becomes the very paradigm to comprehend God's transcendence.[27] The contrast with Mbiti can scarcely be starker.

This does raise some serious questions though. Sharply formulated: Do Africans have to adopt a typically Western (?) orientation towards the future before they can become Christians? Is the future consciousness in the Western world the necessary product of the Jewish-Christian (prophetic) tradition? Or is a futurist metaphysics perhaps a one-sided view of Christian eschatology? How does an orientation towards the future in Christian eschatology relate to the unleashing of the dream of progress in the Western world – with its devastating ecological consequences? Alternatively: Is Mbiti's assessment of traditional African culture perhaps one-sided? Is a consciousness of the future not also present in traditionalist societies in the form of a narrative notion of time? In addition: How should one interpret the increasing cultural, racial, ethnic and religious plurality of contemporary culture in African cities? What is still "African" about an urbanizing and industrializing Africa? How should Christianity in Africa relate to the intoxification of African youth with the same dream of material progress? More poignantly: How should one fathom the paradox that a sense of disorientation, resignation, nihilism and cynicism prevails in the affluent industrial societies of the Western world (despite its future consciousness),[28] whereas a vibrant sense of hope prevails

---

24 Mbiti (1969:17, 1971:30).

25 Mbiti (1971:24f).

26 See chapter 15 for more detail in this regard.

27 See chapter 13 for more detail in this regard.

28 A global survey by the Angus Reid Group constructed a "Hope Index" in 1998, asking people how optimistic they felt about the future. According to this survey, pessimism reigned supreme in the affluent countries of Europe. They are healthy, wealthy and unhappy. In Germany (per capita GDP $28 000) only 18% of the respondents were

in many African communities – despite the desperate plight of Africa and its supposed lack of long-term planning and an orientation towards the future?[29]

This interesting and extremely complex set of questions will not and cannot be answered in this study. They will not even be addressed directly. Hopefully, this task will soon be taken up with far more competence and perceptiveness by some of my African colleagues and students. However, these questions will remain present to shape the horizon within which this study is approached. This horizon does account for the numerous occasions in the text where debates in eschatology, ecology and cosmology are specifically related to the (South) African context.

3. In an essay on the future of the cosmos, Paul Santmire (1984, 1989) perceives the need to integrate the concerns of ecology, cosmology and eschatology and notes that "... no single theologian has yet explored the implications of the theology of hope substantively for the 'theology of the earth,' that is, the biophysical world, the cosmos, or nature."[30] In an article published in 1990, Bridger also calls the link between ecology and eschatology the "neglected dimension".[31]

Fortunately, in the last decade a number of contributions have been published which explored this link between ecology and eschatology on the basis of the work of Moltmann, process theology or ecofeminism.[32] Haught argues, for example, that the eschatological dimension of the prophetic tradition in Christianity and its characteristic emphasis on hope may perhaps form the distinctive contribution of Christianity to a global ecological vision since most other religious traditions also emphasize the sacredness of nature. The orientation towards a vision of the future in the light of God's promises in the Christian (prophetic) tradition may indeed be vital for an ecological spirituality and praxis.

However, an eschatological approach to an ecological theology is not without some serious pitfalls. The track record of the history of Christianity in providing a form of hope that could empower an environmental praxis has not been too promising. Christian hope has often focused on the world to come, thus fostering and endorsing a sense of escapism and a lack of concern for this earth. Reinforced by apocalyptic images of the imminent destruction of the world in the Biblical roots of Christianity, Christian hope has often been understood as redemption *from* the earth and not *of* the earth itself. Catherine Keller comments that this eschatological distraction from the earth complies with the ecological destruction of the earth. The tendency in Christianity has been to hope for an afterlife rather than for life itself. She says: "Does not Christian eschatology gather under its wings precisely that array of doctrinal symbols that has drawn interest away from the earth,

---

upbeat about the future, and in France ($26 000) it was 17%. By comparison, South Africa ($3 500) scored 42% whereas Brazil ($4 400) scored 64% on the Hope Index. See Behrens (1999).

29 See also Metz & Moltmann (1995:168).

30 Santmire (1989:267).

31 See Bridger (1990:291).

32 See my indexed bibliography (Conradie 1998) for numerous references in this regard.

from natural conditions, from finitude and flesh?"[33] Keller adds that the same tendency is evident in Christian eschatology:

> Christendom is surely not accidentally the culture whose holy book happens to culminate in a vision of the imminent devastation of the earth, the culture that has developed the technology and politics capable of Armageddon, nuclear or greenhouse.[34]

Moreover, biblical eschatology, with its unleashing of a dream of future perfection, is for many inimical to environmental concerns. It harbors the danger of strengthening the myth of progress.[35] Some critics therefore sense in the prophetic vision of a better future an ecologically dangerous feature of Christianity.[36] Thomas Berry argues, for example, that the Bible's looking toward a future messianic age has set loose a drive toward progress and limitless development that is draining the earth of its natural resources at a calamitous rate.[37] It is the biblical injunction to transform the world that has inspired and legitimated ecological recklessness. In the Western world, especially (but not only), there is indeed a deeply ingrained faith in progress and continual material prosperity and the ability of science and technology to satisfy the insatiable wants of humanity.[38]

There is a clear need for an ecological reinterpretation of Christian eschatology. An escapist eschatology, perhaps along with a worldless notion of God's transcendence, and a personalist reduction of the cosmic scope of salvation, constitutes three crucial areas where Christian piety has often inhibited an environmental ethos, spirituality and praxis. Any ecological theology will remain shallow unless an adequate response to these three problems can be provided. Ecological theology has to be more than a revisited theology of creation.

How, then, should the vision of Christian hope be understood in such a way that it will not destroy, but bring healing for the earth and all its creatures? This question will be addressed with reference to each of the above mentioned three areas, namely the cosmic scope of God's salvation from evil (Chapter 16), the hope for life beyond death (Chapter 17) and the hope for eternal life with God (Chapter 18).

4. This project on "Hope for the earth?" is to some extent a sequel to my earlier work, *Rus vir die hele aarde* ("Rest for the whole earth").[39] In this work I explored the ecological significance of the Biblical theme of the Sabbath. The various chapters of this book dealt with various aspects of the content of the Christian faith

---

33 Keller (1997:86).

34 Keller (1997:95-6).

35 See especially Brunner (1954) for a sustained emphasis on the need for a clear distinction between Christian hope and the ideology of progress.

36 See Cowdin (1994), Haught (1993:106, 1996:49).

37 See Berry (1988:204-6), Haught 1993:16).

38 Olivier (1989:32).

39 Published in Afrikaans (only) by Lux Verbi (1996).

(the gospel, creation theology and anthropology, soteriology, Christology, Pneumatology, eschatology and ethics). Each of these aspects was investigated through the lens of the Sabbath and its ecological significance. The present work explores not so much the content of Christian faith but of hope. At the same time, it acknowledges that rest for the earth is, in the words of the Dutch theologian Bram van de Beek "ver te zoeken" (hard to come by).[40] The drama of the history of the cosmos is, as Haught also argues, characterized by restlessness:

> For nature too, as we know from science, is and always has been restless. The cosmos itself appears now as the story of an adventurous quest. We can no longer idealize nature as a haven from the adventure of history. For it too is now seen to be fundamentally a story of restless searching. ... We can now accommodate the cosmos itself to the theme of homeless wandering. If we are faithful to nature and our continuity with it, we must accept its inherent "insecurity" ... [41]

The present work therefore wishes to explore the question whether there is, from a Christian perspective, ultimately hope for this restless earth.

As the subtitle of the project indicates, this study seeks to integrate an interest in eschatology, ecology and cosmology. The focus though will be on eschatology, simply understood as a reflection on Christian hope, an account of "the hope that is in us" (1 Peter 3:15). The concern of the study is to investigate the content of Christian hope with a newly found ecological sensitivity. The ecological crisis thus serves as a stimulus for a reinterpretation of eschatology. The hope is that this may provide us with a luring vista, a vista that may focus the eyes of Christian faith on but also beyond the threats to life awaiting us in the new century. While an interest in the cosmic scope of Christian hope will prevail throughout this study, a concern with modern cosmology is less dominant. An explicit discussion of cosmological parameters is only found in Chapters 6, 7 and 14.

This focus on eschatology does not imply that all the classic themes in Christian eschatology can or will be discussed. All the other Christian doctrines are certainly of importance to eschatology, but many of these will unfortunately have to remain underdeveloped, for example a focus on Christ as the Eschatos,[42] the work of the Spirit in God's new creation, the relationship between justification, sanctification and hope (e.g. the notion of universal salvation), the church as an eschatological community,[43] the eschatological significance of the sacraments,[44] etc.

---

40 Van de Beek (1989).

41 Haught (1990:173).

42 See the South African contribution by König (1989) in this regard. Sauter (1999:50) formulates the inextricable link between eschatology and Christology concisely: "Eschatology does not add a conclusive chapter to Christology, but contributes to the expectation of Jesus Christ as the one to come. ... The task of eschatology is to keep alive the question, 'Are you the one who is to come?'"

43 See the South African contribution by Theron (1978) on the unity of the church as a concrete sign of the eschaton for the cosmos. Also cf. Braaten (1969:110) on the church

Relatively little attention will be given to many of the classic eschatological symbols, including the kingdom of God, the resurrection of Christ and of the dead, the coming of Christ, and divine judgment. The relation between eschatology and apocalypticism (or millennialism), that is clearly of importance to an ecological ethos, is also not discussed in this study.[45]

5. As a white, middle-class, male, Afrikaans-speaking, reformed South African I cannot help but be sensitive to my own social location. The right to speak and to be listened to – and therefore to write and to have one's deliberations published – cannot be assumed. In an all too wordy, word-impoverished culture (David Tracy), infested with the ideologies of colonialism, capitalism, classism, racism, androcentrism, linguistic imperialism, and anthropocentrism, words have to be chosen carefully. Several questions have to be addressed. Why does one write? On which topic? For whom? With what pretension? To achieve what purpose?

Perhaps the safest route is to argue that I am simply writing for myself. I am writing to understand myself and to gain clarity on the many discourses that influence my life and thought. I write to clear my own mind and in the hope that a few others may recognize some of these discourses, that they experience the same problems and hopefully that they can identify themselves with some of the perspectives and arguments offered.

These reflections require a few autobiographical comments. These not only reflect my conversation partners but may also serve as an opportunity to express a word of gratitude towards some of the formative influences behind the present text.

My Conradie ancestors came to South Africa from Germany in 1686. This implies that I am a Euro-African of the tenth generation, born and raised from the soil of Africa and shaped by the cultures of its colonizers. I grew up in the quaint town of Stellenbosch, near Cape Town and close to the Jonkershoek valley with its towering and rugged peaks. My childhood experience was one of learning to appreciate the exquisite beauty of these surroundings. The reformed tradition in which I was later trained as a minister, guided me to see such beauty as God's creation. Much of my life as a teenager and a young adult helped me to realize that the larger world is not as beautiful as Jonkershoek. I was gradually exposed to the South African realities of poverty, apartheid and naked racism and oppression. The contrast between so much beauty and repugnant ugliness also helped me to understand the pervasive influence of Afrikaner intellectual elitism, a colonialist mentality, patriarchy, and consumerist greed on the South African society. The evangelical pietism of my reformed world brought me to believe that Jesus loves the world. But how does this relate to the forces of ugliness that surround us?

My training at the University of Stellenbosch exposed me to three enduring

---

as "the place where the world has become conscious of its future destiny in the kingdom of God's freedom and love."

44 See, especially Wainwright (1988), Barns (1998).

45 See the contribution by Keller (1996) in this regard.

pillars of modernity.[46] My philosophical training (in hermeneutical phenomenology, philosophy of religion, linguistic analysis, critical theory) exposed me to the quest of the (German) Enlightenment for critical inquiry and intellectual honesty – and to the tensions that may harbor for received Christian piety. With numerous friends, too many to name, I had the opportunity to debate the political values of the French and American revolutions (liberty, fraternity, equality) and their relevance for the brutal South African realities of the 1980's. With more friends, I continued to explore the beauty of South Africa's mountain and coastal scenery and to see the ambiguity of the impact of the (English) industrial revolution on the modern world.

My theological training at the University of Stellenbosch exposed me to the world of reformed theology. From Augustine, Calvin, and Luther, Bavinck and Kuyper I learned to acknowledge the pervasiveness of sin (*corruptio totalis*) and subsequently our dependence on God's grace (*sola gratia*). An array of Dutch and German reformed theologians from an earlier generation – Berkouwer, Hendrikus Berkhof, Miskotte, Noordmans, Van Ruler, Barth, Bonhoeffer, Brunner, Thielicke – continues to remind me of the danger of natural theology, of a theological scheme based on nature and grace instead of sin and grace. Mentors such as David Bosch, Jaap Durand, Willie Jonker, Dirkie Smit, Johann Kinghorn, Carel Anthonissen and others helped me to integrate these insights within the South African situation.

My doctoral studies on the amazingly rich work of David Tracy helped me to appreciate and assess plurality, ambiguity and otherness. His imaginative integration of the discourse of mystics and prophets, of the Catholic language of analogy and the Protestant language of dialectic, of the continuation of a Platonic and Gadamerian conversation with interruptive and argumentative conversation partners (including deconstruction, critical theory) continues to challenge me.

Since the completion of my dissertation I maintained a keen interest in theological hermeneutics. However, I was increasingly attracted to the field of ecological theology (a much broader term than environmental ethics). This opened up a new wealth of literature from all around the world and provided a fresh angle to approach some of the more traditional literature. The impact of authors like Jürgen Moltmann,[47] Wolfhart Pannenberg, Bram van de Beek, Leonardo Boff, Sallie McFague, Rosemary Ruether, Larry Rasmussen, Wesley Granberg-Michaelson, Sean McDonagh, Thomas Berry, John Haught and numerous others will be evident throughout this study.

Since 1993, I have had the privilege to teach theology at the University of the Western Cape. With its turbulent political history and the rich diversity of students

---

46 See David Tracy's assessment (1994) of the lasting importance of these pillars of modernity in a postmodern culture. He does not include the impact of the industrial revolution in his analysis.

47 If some of the sections in the text below may read almost like extended book reviews on Moltmann's major works on cosmic eschatology, this indicates my gratitude and indebtedness to his rich and groundbreaking contributions to this field.

and colleagues it provides one of the most interesting contexts anywhere in the world to do theology in. This context frames the agendas of political democracy, economic justice, social reconciliation, gender equality, religious and cultural diversity and environmental degradation with an uncanny acuteness and urgency. I am grateful to my students for their numerous questions and raw enthusiasm for theology. Teaching in a cross-cultural context has also helped me to realize the intricacies of rooting theology in an African context. Indeed, there is no purely "African" context; most of us are the product of different contexts and therefore have to learn how to cope with the conflict between these contexts, with "walking in two worlds." This may explain the earlier comment that I cannot write theology "for" anyone. One can only write in the hope that your conversation partners may recognize some of their own questions and perspectives in your deliberations. Maybe this may help them to reconstruct their own questions and answers. If my friends, colleagues, students and more distant conversation partners find my deliberations of any value in this regard, I would be most grateful.

5. A project like this could never have been completed without the help and encouragement of friends and colleagues. Allow me to express a word of gratitude to the following persons for their very specific contributions.

- Several of my colleagues in the Western Cape region participated in a colloquium investigating Biblical perspectives on "hope for the earth". The contributions of Danie van Zyl, Louis Jonker, Douglas Lawrie, Johann Cook, Roger Arendse, Jan Botha and Niek Pretorius were invaluable in shaping my understanding on the eschatological trajectories in the Bible. These contributions have been published in Volume 66 of *Scriptura* (1998:3) on "Biblical perspectives on cosmic eschatology."
- The University of the Western Cape granted me study leave in the second semester of 1998 to work on this project. This proved to be one of the turbulent periods in the history of this university. This also implied an additional workload for several of my colleagues for which I am most grateful. The privilege of enjoying study leave during such a painful period was almost embarrassing.
- The financial assistance of the Centre for Science Development (Human Sciences Research Council) towards this research is hereby acknowledged. Opinions expressed and conclusions arrived at are those of the author and are not necessarily to be attributed to the Centre for Science Development.
- This financial assistance enabled me to visit the Center for Theology and the Natural Sciences in Berkeley, California to work on specific aspects of the larger research project. This not only opened up the world of science and religion for me. It also provided me with numerous conversation partners from which new friendships could emerge. I am most grateful to the hospitality that my wife and I received from Bob Russell, Ted Peters, Richard Randolph, Mark Richardson, Bonnie Johnston, Kathryn Smith, Lou Ann Trost, Philip Clayton, and others.
- Several friends were willing to read and comment on sections of the manuscript. The many helpful suggestions from David Whiting, Christo Lombard,

Humphrey Mogashua, Douglas Lawrie, Robert Vosloo and others are highly appreciated.

- Some sections of this text have previously been published, in a different form, elsewhere. Chapters 5 & 6 draws from an article entitled, "Hope for the earth? Discerning the cosmic depths of despair" (*Scriptura* 66, 1998:3, 279-308). Chapter 7 draws on an article entitled, "Reconstructing an ecological cosmology: A South African contribution" (*Scriptura* 61, 213-230). An edited version of chapter 13 also appeared as an article entitled "In search of a vision of hope for a new century" in the *Journal of Religion & Society* (Creighton University) 1, par 1-58. Some of the material for Chapter 20 was published as "Living in hope: Some examples from our Southern African neighbours" (*Faith & Earthkeeping* 1997:11, 6-7).
- The text follows the American instead of the British conventions of spelling. Some sections of the manuscript were prepared for publication in American journals, following the period of study leave in Berkeley.
- This work is dedicated to the son that my wife, Marietjie, and I expect in June this year and who will grow up in a new and demanding century. May God, the Source of all hope (Rom 15:13), open new vistas to guide him during this century.

Ernst Conradie
March 2000

Part A: The need for a clear vision of hope

1. Hope at the dawn of a new century

In her novel, *The infinite plan*, Isabel Allende tells the story of an itinerant evangelist, James Reeves who saw his mission as that of "selling hope" to his audiences. At the dawn of a new century, the world is evidently in need of a clear vision of hope. But where can such a vision of hope, hope for us and for the whole earth be found? It is evidently not for sale!

As expected, the turn of the millennium has provided us with abundant images of the future. These images range from optimistic visions of increasing global affluence through education and technological sophistication to catastrophic images of the end of the world which can only breed despair.[1] In the new century it will gradually dawn on us that the next one hundred years will not simply be a continuation of the status quo of this century. We will have to shift our vision further ahead in order to take full responsibility for the shaping of the new century.

In South Africa, many young black students still believe that the future is indeed rosy. For them, education, health services, housing conditions are slowly but surely improving. Education will provide them and their children with better opportunities for employment. The future can only be better than the apartheid past. On the other hand, many other South Africans have already become disillusioned. For the poorest on the economic periphery, the Reconstruction and Development Programme (RDP) promised much but delivered little. Economic power remains entrenched in the hands of the elite. Some long back for an Africa unspoiled by colonialism and industrialization while others fear what the future will bring for their grandchildren. They see apocalyptic images of imminent catastrophe. Those in the economic center fear the deterioration of social services and rampant crime. They become more and more security conscious and entrench themselves in lush pockets of affluence. Others are simply marginalized in the political power game.

The same tension between optimistic hope and despair epitomized the transition from the nineteenth to the twentieth century in Europe. The twentieth century dawned with the legacy of the nineteenth century intact: dramatic advances in science and technology seemed to ensure a bright future. The twentieth century witnessed the collapse in Europe of the Enlightenment visions of an age of freedom from toil, slavery, poverty, ignorance and superstition.[2] This was epitomized by the numerous crises that shocked the twentieth century: the Russian revolution, two world wars, the Holocaust, the threat of nuclear disaster, the Cold War, the fights against colonialism, the failure of development and the growth of poverty,

---

1 See Raiser's (1997:ix) illuminating comments on the coming of the new millennium.

2 See Cochrane (1999:30).

escalating ethnic and religious conflicts and, in South Africa, the struggle against apartheid. We arrived at the end of the twentieth century with a highly ambiguous legacy in which "fragility rather than confidence, doubt rather than certainty, fragmentation rather than integration predominates."[3]

This shift from the nineteenth to the twentieth century was also reflected in Christian theology and, more specifically, in eschatology.

In the nineteenth century eschatology became a "pale reflection of the social ideals of a secularized European society."[4] Ernst Troeltsch commented just before World War I that: "The eschatological bureau is closed these days."[5] By contrast, in the twentieth century, eschatology became the "storm center" of theology (Von Balthasar). It moved from a "perfectly harmless chapter at the end of Christian dogmatics" to the center stage of theological reflection (Barth).[6] The twentieth century became, as James Orr predicted, the age of eschatology.[7] The whole of Christian theology could now be regarded as eschatological since the eschaton is no longer understood as the "End" but in terms of God's presence. Every statement about God is eschatological since, as Tillich has argued, it has to deal with "ultimate concerns."[8] Eschatology is therefore not only one element of Christianity; hope is the medium of Christian faith as such.[9] Eschatology is not a discipline besides other disciplines, but "that basic discipline which determines, forms, and shapes every theological statement" (Metz).[10] The eschatological outlook, Moltmann argues, "... is characteristic of all Christian proclamation, of every Christian existence and of the whole church."[11] Indeed, eschatology is the center that holds the whole web of Christian doctrines together.[12] This turn to eschatology became at the same time the key to the renewal of Christian theology in the twentieth

---

3 Cochrane (1999:32).

4 Braaten (1985:343).

5 Quoted in Braaten (1985:343).

6 See Barth's *Epistle to the Romans* (1933:500).

7 See Runia (1997:105). He refers to Orr's book, *The progress of dogma* (1901:345).

8 Tillich (1951:11-15, 1957:1-12).

9 See Moltmann (1967:16): "From first to last, and not merely in epilogue, Christianity is eschatology, is hope, forward looking and forward moving ... The eschatological is not one element of Christianity, but it is the medium of Christian faith as such, the key in which everything is set." Reflecting back on his project since the publication of *Theology of hope*, Moltmann (1996:xii) explains that a theology of hope had to formulate a new fundamental category for theology to replace the theology of love in the middle ages and the theology of faith at the time of the reformation. See also Moltmann (1967:33).

10 Metz (1969:90).

11 Moltmann (1967:16).

12 Volf (1995:138). Volf distinguishes this illuminating notion of the primacy of eschatology (as the center of the web of doctrines) from the view that eschatology is the *basis* on which one builds everything else.

century.[13] *Fides quaerens intellectum* may become *spes quaerens intellectum* and *credo ut intellegam* may become *spero ut intellegam*.[14]

Given this shift, it is hardly surprising that eschatology has become as disparate as twentieth century theology itself. This is reflected in the numerous schools of eschatology that have emerged in this century. The confusing and sometimes contradictory interpretations of Christian hope in the twentieth century have obscured the content and meaning of eschatological concepts.[15]

As a result of the myriad of approaches, conflicts and suggested typologies,[16] eschatology is often perceived to be a highly complex and demanding discipline.[17] This has inhibited a clear and inspiring vision of hope in an age of growing (ecological) anxiety. It also led to a paradoxical tension between hope, the central theme of any Christian eschatology, and eschatological reflection itself. We do not know what we hope, only that we hope or, even worse, that to hope is very important. "Perhaps it is time to admit", Carl Braaten comments, "as in the story about the emperor's new clothes, that for all the talk about eschatology ... the theological mind has denuded itself of any symbols of the future that can inspire hope and action."[18] Tragically, this leaves room for the over-confident apostles of technological progress or for apocalyptic prophets of doom to dominate the market of producing visions that inspire hope, or install anxiety and despair.

In this context, the aim of this study is to formulate, in an age of ecological anxiety and despair, a vision of hope that includes hope for the earth. At the same time, in order to elicit a vision of hope that can indeed inspire people (in South Africa) to respond to the realities of environmental degradation, this vision must be formulated with sufficient clarity and preferably in language and metaphors that can be recognized and appropriated from within Christian communities. But a metaphorical wealth of eschatological images will remain purely intra-linguistic[19] unless this clarity is reached in critical dialogue with contributions emerging from the astrophysical and biological sciences. The purpose of such dialogue is to find an appropriate sounding board for Christian theologians to clarify, if only for themselves, the cosmic scope of their own eschatological assertions. The purpose need not be to baptize modern cosmology or to test theological truth claims in

---

13 See also the following prophetic comment by the Dutch theologian JH Gunning (1888): "We are deeply convinced that, as in the first century the confession of faith was formed by a backward movement that had its starting point in the eschatology, so the renewal of our systematic theology and preaching, which we need very much in our day, also has to issue from eschatology" (translated and quoted in Runia 1997).

14 See Moltmann (1967:33).

15 See also Nolan's (1987:61) assessment (from the point of view of liberation theology) that modern eschatology seems to be moving in a world of ideas that is quite different from the world of the Bible.

16 See Chapter 13 for a more detailed discussion of such typologies.

17 See also Hall (1996:456).

18 Braaten (1972:52).

19 Drees (1990:121).

terms of scientific criteria.

The task of formulating a clear and intelligible vision of hope for the earth is truly daunting! To attain something of the necessary clarity, I will defend a somewhat bold proposal in this study, namely *that Christian hope responds to especially three aspects of the human predicament*:

1) The predicament of sin and its effects in various manifestations of evil in the world,
2) The predicament of (human) finitude (in time), and
3) The predicament of the limitations of human power and knowledge (in space).

Since this analysis will be used throughout the argument, the following two chapters will analyze the three predicaments (Chapter 2) and show how Christian hope has traditionally responded to these predicaments (Chapter 3). Chapter 4 provides a brief summary of the "eschatological road map" which will be used and further developed in subsequent chapters.

Part B will investigate the ecological depths of despair in order to guard against the temptation of selling cheap forms of hope. It will follow the analysis of the three human predicaments in Part A to investigate a sense of despair at three levels, namely the ecological impact of evil (Chapter 5); the ecological dimensions of finitude (Chapter 6); the absence of God on earth (Chapter 7). A short fourth Chapter (8) is added to comment on some South African dimensions of despair.

Part C will briefly note the historical trajectories of Christian hope in the First Testament (Chapter 9), the New Testament (Chapter 10), the history of the Christian tradition (Chapter 11) and the impact of modernity (Chapter 12). Part D then investigates three contemporary manifestations of hope in more detail, namely manifestations of hope in twentieth century Christian theology (Chapter 13), manifestations of hope in the context of science and religion debates (Chapter 14) and three South African manifestations of hope (Chapter 15).

The task of Part E is to develop a vision of hope more systematically. In response to each of the three predicaments, the category of "a theology of life" (World Council of Churches) will be used to express a Christian vision of hope for life amidst the forces of death (Chapter 16), for life beyond death (Chapter 17) and for eternal life with God (Chapter 18).

Part F reflects on the ethical implications of this vision of Christian hope. It discusses the social impact of hope in terms of the notions of inspiration, preparation and responsibility (Chapter 19). This is concretized in the final chapter (20) that looks at some examples of Christian communities that embody and practise a vision of hope for the earth.

2. Three human predicaments

2.1 The roots of human hope: the predicament of an unacceptable present

In an instructive essay on eschatology in a South African textbook on Systematic Theology entitled, *Doing theology in context*, Klaus Nürnberger explains the "inner logic" of human hope in the following way:

> At the root of eschatology lies the common human awareness that what reality is, does not correspond to what reality ought to be. Such an awareness emerges and grows in times of suffering and need ... The orientation of faith towards the future was instigated by an unacceptable present.[1]

Nürnberger then argues that Christian faith identifies certain redemptive experiences in which God is believed to act in history, to intervene in concrete predicaments by changing what is into what ought to be. These redemptive experiences always remain partial and provisional, never comprehensive and final, establishing merely signs of what reality ought to be. At the same time, God's redemptive acts in history provide a promise of something greater, of something that will go beyond the fulfillment of earlier promises. Faith therefore incites hope and expectation. Hope is manifested as a trust in God, a trust that is by definition oriented towards the future.[2]

While soteriology focuses on these redemptive experiences (with specific reference to the person and work of Christ), eschatology articulates the conviction that reality will eventually be transformed into what it ought to be.[3]

I find Nürnberger's identification of the "inner logic" of eschatology quite illuminating. Significantly, he roots hope in immediately accessible present human experiences – and not in a somewhat abstract metaphysics of the future.[4] I also find the connection between soteriology and eschatology convincing.[5] I would, however, want to take his analysis a few steps further:

As Nürnberger argues, the orientation of faith towards the future is indeed instigated by an unacceptable present. Hope as the anticipation of a new and different future is born from experiences of suffering and thus has its *Sitz im Leben*

---

1 Nürnberger (1994:139, 140). See also Braaten (1985:329): "Eschatology promises fulfillment; hope presupposes something lacking. Human beings hope for what they lack."

2 Nürnberger (1994:140).

3 Nürnberger (1994:139).

4 See Chapter 13.4 for a more detailed discussion in this regard.

5 Braaten (1974:9) notes that the re-emergence of eschatology in modern theology can be seen as a legitimate reaction against a splitting of eschatology from soteriology (i.e. as a doctrine of the last things). See the comments on the structural *differences* between soteriology and eschatology below.

among the suffering and oppressed (Moltmann).[6] Hope is born from the subversive memory of suffering (Metz). Suffering is therefore the mother of hope (Alves).[7] Hope lives in the tension from the negative to the positive, from the sufferings of this present time towards a redemption that is longed for (Braaten).[8] This feature of hope is not only typical of Christian faith; it is, in fact, a common human response to problems experienced in ordinary life.[9] Arguably, the rudimentary desire of most people is not aimed at lofty social, economic or political ideals or the quest for immortality, but simply for a prolongation of their current situation – *without* some of the present problems that they experience. We would preferably like to remain part of this world, not another.[10] We hope for a world in which we can continue to live a humane life without serious problems, without hunger, homelessness, oppression, sickness, loneliness or frustrations. Within the context of everyday life, we hope to do well in exams, we hope that our children will cope in life, we hope for an improvement in health, for a cure for cancer, we pray for an end to violent conflict.[11] And we may harbor some dreams, aspirations and visions for a better life for ourselves and our children.

This orientation towards the future is characteristic also of most traditionalistic cultures. Indeed, an orientation towards the (immediate) future is not only typical of Western Christianity and its roots in the prophetic tradition. There seems to be an indomitable human spirit of hope that maintains, even against all odds and expectations, the possibility of something different. It keeps saying: "Who knows, perhaps ..."[12] Ernst Bloch's observation that the most fundamental characteristic of human existence is that we are beings who hope, may, in this sense, also apply to traditional communities in Africa.

One may therefore conclude that the human predisposition of hope is indeed instigated by an unacceptable or an unsatisfactory present. In his analysis, Nürnberger focuses on experiences of injustice, suffering, death and despair.[13] Again, these are typical human predicaments. However, these predicaments are not quite similar. They are also interpreted in different ways in different religious traditions.

I propose that three distinct aspects of the (human) predicament, to which Christian eschatology has traditionally responded, may be identified:

---

6 Moltmann (1972:91), also Galilea (1988).

7 Alves (1969:120).

8 Braaten (1969:39).

9 See Braaten (1969:33f), Macquarrie (1978), Hayes (1989:87) for contributions to a phenomenological discussion of the "universal phenomenon of hope."

10 Van de Beek (1996:192).

11 Hentz (1997:7).

12 Berkhof (1967:20). Berkhof adds that the common human disposition of hope is characterized by a deficiency and an uncertainty while the Christian faith is a "well-founded hope" (the English title of his work on eschatology), based on what has already been given – in the resurrection of Christ.

13 Nürnberger (1994:139).

- The predicament of human self-enclosure due to the effects of sin in various manifestations of evil: injustice, slavery, oppression, conflict, corruption, destruction, degradation, suffering, and untimely death;
- The predicament of (human) finitude in time: mortality and transitoriness;
- The predicament of (human) finitude in space: the inability of human beings to transcend the limitations of human knowledge and power.

The need for a distinction between *three* human predicaments was prompted (for me) by a reading of Augustine's *Confessions* with post-graduate students at the University of the Western Cape in 1997. I was struck by Augustine's sustained attempt to grapple, as a Christian theologian, with the Manicheist dualism of good and evil, on the one hand, and the Platonic duality of ideas and the material world on the other. For Manicheism the human predicament is that of coming to terms with *evil* (or sin) whereas the escape from *ignorance* (of the One) is the quest of Platonic and neo-Platonic philosophy. Augustine shared the Manicheist awareness of the pervasive problem of evil, rejected its dualism by appropriating an integrated Platonic worldview but, against the thrust of neo-Platonism, also affirmed the goodness of the created order together with the Jewish-Christian tradition.

Before we investigate these predicaments in more detail, a few brief observations are important:

- There are, of course, many similar analyses of the human condition. One example is the classic analysis by Kant of the three human quests (What can I know? What must I do? What may I hope for?). Hannah Arendt presented a somewhat similar analysis of three aspects of the human condition, commenting on our relationships with the earth, with time itself and with social life in all its plurality and ambiguity.[14] Paul Tillich's classic description of the relationship between finitude and sin also wrestles with similar distinctions.[15]
- The notion of "human predicament" is not used here merely as a synonym for "worldview", "horizon", or "life experience". The three predicaments suggest more concrete, material and therefore to some extent *fixed* restrictions to human life. These limitations will, of course, be interpreted in different ways in different historic periods and in different contexts.
- This analysis, and the eschatological "road map" that will be based on it, shares with any other model or typology certain inherent limitations. Two of these limitations may be acknowledged from the very beginning. a) The distinction between human finitude in space and in time remains somewhat arbitrary. Especially in Chapters 17 and 18 it will become evident that an eschatological

---

14 Arendt (1959).

15 Tillich (1951:184-202, 1957:33f, 66f). Tillich defines finitude as being, limited by non-being (i.e. not-yet being and being no-longer) (1951:189). Tillich (1957:39-44) is careful not to associate the emergence of sin with the predicament of finitude. Sin is not ontologically necessary. In his typical terminology, Tillich only locates the inexplicable emergence of evil in the "transition from essence to existence" (1957:29f).

response to these two dimensions of finitude necessitates an integrated approach. b) Readers will have to judge for themselves whether the analysis of human knowledge and power – which relates to spatial limitations and is correlated to the eschatological significance of knowledge of God – is convincing. Perhaps the contribution of this study should be understood as an attempt to test and develop the *relative* fruitfulness of this suggested eschatological road map.

- A specifically Christian hope is, in my view, certainly "rooted" in the ordinary human experience of an unacceptable present. It also "responds" to such predicaments. This does not necessarily imply that Christian hope can be "based" anthropologically on the "universal phenomenon of hope". Christian eschatology is not based on any anthropology.[16] The Christian "hope against all hope" (Rom 4:18) is not something that we "possess". It is a sign of redemption of those who lived with no hope and without God in the world (Eph 2:12). Subsequently, we do not "have" hope, we are "grasped by hope and now live "in" hope.[17] Christian eschatology may have a structural correspondence to hope in ordinary life (based on the continuity between creation and eschaton),[18] but it radicalizes both an assessment of and a response to the human predicament.
- The term "respond" that is used here does not suggest that an analysis of the human predicament could first be made – to which Christian eschatology then has to respond "afterwards" – that is in the way Tillich formulated (but not practiced) his correlation method.[19] Instead, it suggests that an analysis of eschatological discourse will indicate that different aspects of the human predicament are presupposed and addressed in such texts. The identification and description of these predicaments therefore emerge together with an eschatological vision. In the traditional language of Christian piety, sin is only recognized through the knowledge of God, not through a semi-autonomous analysis of the human condition. The depths of the predicament of sin is only uncovered in the experience of God's grace. It is only when the strong light of grace penetrates our lives that we can clearly see the long shadow cast by our past sins.[20] The limitations of human existence are only realized in confrontation with a transcendent God.

2.2 The predicament of evil: the devastating effects of sin

We as human beings are confronted with the effects of sin through the many manifestations of evil in the world:[21] injustice, slavery, oppression, enslavement,

---

[16] See Pannenberg (1984:120f) for a discussion of this tension between an eschatology based on the divine promise or on anthropology.

[17] Sauter (1999:20-21).

[18] See Braaten (1985:329) and the discussion in chapter 13.3.

[19] See Tillich (1951:59f).

[20] McClendon (1994:122).

[21] It is clearly not possible to present a fully developed doctrine of sin within the present

hatred, alienation, conflict, corruption, destruction, degradation, cruelty, induced suffering, and untimely death.[22] These problems are caused by human beings themselves. Unlike the predicaments of temporal and spatial finitude, the predicament of evil is the effect of a self-inflicted act of human *self*-enclosure (cf. sin as *incurvatus in se*).[23]

These problems are often manifested in the form of the devastating effects of one's own sins, for example on one's body, one's family, one's community, one's immediate environment. It can also be manifested in the form of "being sinned against".[24] People often endure suffering as a result of sins directly or indirectly inflicted on them by other individuals or groups. This applies especially to the sins of the powerful, not because they are necessarily more sinful, but because their sins may have more devastating effects.[25] The consequences of structural violence are often even more serious. This is the result of an accumulative institutionalization of insensitive decisions, unsustainable habits, and dangerous practices. It leads to societal structures that are unjust because they are used to enforce domination, exploitation and alienation. Within these structures violence is practiced not directly and personally, but indirectly through laws, customs and institutions. Through these structures violence is legitimated.[26] Structural evil manifests itself, to name only a few obvious examples, in the global problems of patriarchal oppression, economic exploitation and injustice, impoverishment, ethnic and religious conflict, environmental degradation and, more specifically, environmental injustice: the devastating effects of the material greed of some on both the environment and on other human beings.

The seriousness of the predicament of evil can be assessed in quite different ways. Throughout the centuries the pendulum has swung to and fro between optimists and pessimists. Some believe in the essential goodness of the human person (and of the natural order) while others speak of the "total depravity" of humanity. Yet others opt for a (Manicheist) dualism between the forces of good and evil.

This pendulum movement has also characterized the twentieth century. Some believe that human problems are simply the result of ignorance and that education,

---

discussion. My concern in this section is not so much with the nature or origin of sin but with the devastating and restrictive effects of sin, understood as evil. For the notion of evil as the effects of sin, see Tillich (1957:59f), Gutiérrez (1973:173f), Peters (1994:8).

22 For Welch (1990:159), untimely death ("death cause by human folly or evil, by torture, environmentally induced cancer, war, occupational hazards or malnutrition"), needs to be resisted, not death itself.

23 If sin is linked to self-enclosure (see Moltmann 1979:122), then God's salvific activity in history may be conceived as "opening up systems which are closed in themselves" (Moltmann 1985:211). Through God's indwelling presence all finite life systems are opened for the fullness of life (1985:214).

24 See Moltmann (1996:90) and Volf (1996:81-85, 114f) for a discussion of the complexities involved in this distinction.

25 Gilkey (1976:259, 286).

26 Moltmann (1996:95).

scientific progress, technological innovation, economic growth and a democratic order will ultimately ensure a better future. Others, often the victims of these very processes, realize the pervasiveness of evil lurking beneath patriarchy, increasing global poverty, religious and ethnic conflicts, and environmental degradation.

Christianity, like other religious traditions, has grappled with the causes and effects of sin and has indicated a way towards salvation from sin and victory over evil. In the rich tradition of reflection on sin, sin has, for example, been described as pride, selfishness, the negation of the good and alienation from a relationship with God.[27] An assessment of the seriousness of the predicament of sin and evil has been radicalized in some Christian traditions, most notably the Pauline, Augustinian and reformed traditions, through the notions of original sin and the "total depravity" (*corruptio totalis*) of humanity. This radicalization of the predicament of sin is balanced by an emphasis on the abundant grace of God. Salvation from sin and victory over evil is possible only through the grace of God shown to us in Jesus Christ.

2.3 The predicament of finitude in time

We human beings are not only confronted, directly or indirectly, by the evil effects of sin in the world. We also experience transitoriness and have to face the always imminent possibility of death. We are nothing but dust, grass which withers away and dies (Gen 3:19, Ps 90:5-6, Is 40:6-7). We live for seventy or eighty years and these pass by in quick succession (Ps 90:10). We can control neither our own futures and destinies, nor those of society after our deaths (see Eccl 2). Unlike God, our existence is in time; not in eternity. The time allotted to us therefore remains limited.[28]

A closer investigation discloses different dimensions of this predicament of (human) finitude in time. The most obvious manifestation of finitude is the moment of eventual death that each individual human being has to confront. The mystery and finality of death is the subject of numerous reflections and cannot be investigated here in any detail - except to remind ourselves of the futile attempt in most modern societies to hide the reality of age, illness, dying, death, and mourning from everyday life.[29] Death is, of course, also experienced by all other living organisms. Moreover, the biological sciences have helped us to appreciate the finitude of whole species and not only of individual specimens. This also applies to the human species itself. We are nothing more than a brief episode in the cosmic and planetary drama. Even mountains, rivers, ecosystems, oceans, and whole continents are exposed to the arrow of time. Many of the earth's prominent topographi-

---

27 See Peters (1994) for a recent study of these manifestations of sin.

28 See Barth's classic analysis of allotted time (*CD* 3.4, 553-640). Barth identifies two limitations, the limits of time in contrast to eternity and the limitations of time itself; the time that has been given to us is a time that will irrevocably come to an end. It is of the essence of human existence to be limited.

29 See, for example, Moltmann (1996:50-56).

cal features have emerged relatively recent in geological time. Likewise, the astrophysical sciences have helped us to understand the finite life span of the earth, the solar system, whole galaxies and possibly of the universe itself.[30] The experience of finitude is therefore not limited to human beings; it has cosmic dimensions. The world itself is destined to pass away.[31]

While life endures amidst the always imminent threat of death, the predicament of finitude is experienced in the form of transitoriness, or "perpetual perishing" (Whitehead).[32] The predicament of transitoriness is related to the not lingering of the present moment and the inability of humans to return to what has once been.[33] It therefore always implies a sense of loss – of every precious moment and each opportunity just gone by. It also applies to the cycles of weeks and seasons, the passing of each Christmas and each birthday celebration. This awareness of transitoriness is exemplified precisely by experiences of "kairotic time"[34] where time "seems to stand still" – in celebrations of the liturgy, in myths and rituals, or in a walk through the forest on a day of rest.[35]

The predicament of finitude (in time) is addressed in Western philosophy in terms of the classic problem of coming to terms with change (transience). It is radicalized in numerous religious traditions[36] where it provides the stimulus behind the ultimate quest to transcend the boundaries of time itself. It manifests itself most visibly in the quest for immortality or life beyond death.

2.4 The predicament of limitedness in space

We as human beings have to come to terms with the spatial limitations set by our bodily rootedness. All living beings strive for space, a physical location, a body, a piece of soil, a home, a city, a country, a planet. The need for space also has social dimensions, namely a sphere of influence in a family, a community, a vocation, the

---

30 See Chapter 6 for a more detailed analysis of these dimensions of finitude.

31 Brunner (1954:202). Körtner (1995) argues that an apocalyptic anxiety for the "end of the world" is the result of the perception of finitude as inescapability; as a situation from which there is no way out (1995:94). Apocalyptic itself is an attempt at overcoming world anxiety through world negation (1995:99).

32 Cobb & Griffin (1976:120) argue that this problem of "perpetual perishing" is even more acute than injustice, physical suffering, mental anguish or untimely death itself. They say: "What destroys in our maturity the zest of our youth is not so much the discovery that injustice, suffering and anguish are all part of life; it is the realization that the moments of joy in which these evils are overcome fade into dim memories and are finally lost altogether" (1976:120).

33 Brunner (1954:43).

34 See Petersen's (1995) study on kairotic time with specific reference to the African Initiated Churches.

35 See my analysis (Conradie 1996) of the experience of time during the Sabbath rest.

36 Macquarrie (1978:20) argues that a preoccupation with death together with a hope that transcends death has indeed been characteristic of all cultures.

institutions of social society, etc.[37] The limitations of these social dimensions of space constitutes the finitude of human freedom.[38] This also has important implications for human *power* and *knowledge*.

We experience restrictions to the spatial territory that we are able to exert an influence on. There are therefore limitations to human power. We may extend our physical power and control through social institutions, political authority, organized labor and improved technologies, but such power finally remains limited. Unlike God, we are not omnipotent.

Likewise, human knowledge remains limited due to the restrictions set by our bodiliness. Our physical locatedness in space and the limited size and abilities of the human brain imply limits to the knowledge that we can assimilate and accumulate. We simply cannot know everything. We may extend the frontiers of knowledge through the wisdom accumulated in human history, through cooperative research projects and advanced information technologies, but such knowledge ultimately remains limited. Unlike God, we are not omniscient.

Human wisdom may be born from an acceptance of these restrictions. However, such an acceptance also leads to a sense of insecurity and anxiety.[39] Together with other living organisms, human beings therefore create systems of security to protect and increase their space.[40] This is not only the result of a fear for what may happen to me in future. It is a more vague anxiety for the unknown, for powers beyond my control.[41] The assessment of Qohelet is that we as human beings have

---

37 Tillich (1951:194).

38 Gilkey (1976:255).

39 The notion of anxiety or *Angst* (derived from the Latin for "narrows" *angustiae*) implies, as analyzed by Kierkegaard and in existential philosophy, not only finitude but also an awareness of this finitude. For Tillich (1952:35), anxiety "is the state in which a being is aware of its possible nonbeing." Tillich (1952:32f, 1957:34) also distinguishes between fear and anxiety. Fear has a definite object which can be faced, analyzed, confronted, endured. Anxiety has no such object because its source is not so much the unknown, but the threat of nothingness.

40 Tillich (1951:195).

41 See Körtner's (1995) detailed discussion of what he calls "world anxiety." He describes this as a feeling of longing, the "experience of being lonely and abandoned in the middle of finitude." This anxiety is caused by the enormous, immeasurable element of cosmic space as well as the equally immeasurable element of cosmic time. However, the focus of world anxiety is not the threat of imminent death, but the notion of non-being. Körtner quotes descriptions by Pascal and Kierkegaard of this sense of world anxiety. Both Pascal and Kierkegaard use explicitly spatial metaphors and address a lack of power and of knowledge. For example:

> "The eternal silence of these infinite spaces frightens me" (*Penseés* 206)
>
> "When I consider the short duration of my life, swallowed up in the eternity before and after, the little space which I fill, and even can see, engulfed in the infinite immensity of spaces of which I am ignorant, and which know me not, I am frightened, and am astonished at being here rather than there; for there is no reason why here rather than there, why now rather than then" (*Penseés* 205).

received a glimpse of the '*olam*, of eternity (Eccl 3:16). We cannot help but to ask questions about that which transcends us. But at the same time we also know that we will never be able to find satisfactory answers to our quest for insight. This adequately describes the pathos of the human predicament of spatial limitations.

Despite the recent emphasis in the natural sciences on the space-time continuum, the predicaments of finite human space and time remain, at least to some degree, distinct on an experiential level. The predicament of limited knowledge and power leads to insecurity, to anxiety for the unknown, for powers beyond one's control. The predicament of temporal finitude leads to anxiety for what may happen to me in future and to the realization that there will come a time when we shall no longer be here.[42] A perfectly healthy human being can neither know everything, nor do everything. At the same time, the power of the powerful is quickly eroded by human mortality.

The pursuit of philosophy, history,[43] the arts, and the sciences has been to transcend the limitations of knowledge (and power) as far as possible. The quest of neo-Platonic philosophy is, for example, to transcend these limitations in order (through the powers of reason, memory and insight) to comprehend the One. This quest is radicalized in numerous religious traditions to gain insight in the ultimate mysteries of the cosmos and whatever may transcend the cosmos. Likewise, the aspiration of many exponents of the mystical tradition is to reach beyond the qualitative difference between the finite world and God in order to attain, if for one fleeting moment, the *visio Dei beatifica*.[44]

In a Christian context the predicament of human limitedness in space therefore often manifests itself in the search for reliable knowledge of God. Since such knowledge of God includes an interest in God's transcendence, this quest has often led to an element of other-worldliness – to reach out to God in a realm beyond this world.

"Where am I? What does it mean to say: the world? What is the meaning of that world? Who tricked me into this whole thing and leaves me standing here? Who am I? How did I get into the world? Why was I not asked about it ...?" (*Fear and trembling*, 200)

42 See Tillich's (1951:194) classic exposition of this anxiety.

43 According to Barth (*CD* 3.2, 1960:701), the irresistible compulsion to historical study, the "passionate storming of the gates of time as it has taken form in history", is the result of the contrast of human existence in time with God's eternity.

44 For the Augustinian notions of the *visio Dei*, see the *Confessions* Book 7.xvii and 9.x.

3. Christian hope and the three predicaments

The analysis of the three (human) predicaments in the previous chapter may help to illuminate an important structural difference between Christian soteriology and eschatology, between the content of faith and of hope. While soteriology focuses on salvation from sin (the first predicament), Christian eschatology has traditionally responded to all three these aspects of the (human) predicament.[1] The roots of Christian eschatology remain soteriological. The primordial Christian hope is for salvation from sin. However, this hope can and has historically been extrapolated to respond to the predicaments of finitude in time and also in space.

Let us follow this development in more detail.

3.1 Christian hope for salvation from sin

In the Biblical roots of Christianity, hope is predominantly expressed as a hope for salvation from sin, liberation from oppression and an ultimate victory over evil. In this sense, Christian hope is indeed, as Nürnberger argues, instigated by an unacceptable present. The future is often conceived of not so much in terms of positive anticipations and aspirations but in the negative terms of present suffering. In criticizing the evils causing such suffering, people seek and hope for another and better future.[2] Or, as Alves observes, "By radically negating what is, on account of the suffering it causes, history is forced to look for a new tomorrow."[3]

To this observation Moltmann adds the proviso that Christian hope is both a "negation of the negative" and an anticipation of the positive.[4] This anticipation is rooted in God's promises and expects the fulfillment of these promises. It is based on the promises of God that sin, suffering, oppression and evil will not have the final word. Moltmann explains that a promise is a declaration that announces the coming of a reality that does not yet exist. A promise pledges a new future and the *word* of the promise itself already creates something new, stimulating a new expectation. It directs us towards the future fulfillment of such a promise.[5]

---

1 Compare this with Nürnberger's assumption that the structural difference between soteriology and eschatology is that the former focus on partial and provisional redemptive experiences while eschatology points to a more comprehensive consummation of these redemptive experiences. My proposal is that eschatology responds to more than experiences of redemption from sin, evil and injustice.

2 Moltmann (1970:113-114).

3 Alves (1969:120).

4 Moltmann (1979:125). See also Moltmann (1977:193): "The first mediating category which must be mentioned in the messianic sphere is anticipation. An anticipation is not yet fulfillment. But it is already the presence of the future in the conditions of history. It is a fragment of the coming whole."

5 Moltmann (1967:103). Pannenberg (1998:175-6) argues that Moltmann's earlier work one-sidedly emphasized the element of contradiction. A promise can only be recognized

These promises are regarded as trustworthy because Godself is reliable.[6] The hope of Israel was born from the confession of the faithfulness (*hesed*) of Yahweh, projected onto the screen of the future.[7] The basis of Christian hope is therefore not human self-transcendence or latent natural processes but in the God of promise. The close link between Christian hope and faith give it its unique character in distinction from ordinary human hopes.[8] This trust in God is strengthened by present experiences of redemption and thus anticipates the more comprehensive *fulfillment* of these promises.[9] Hope becomes unsteadfast unless it is based on past and present events that provide the grounds for trusting in a future fulfillment. The grounds for Christian hope is depicted in stories, songs and celebrations of how God has *already*, time and again, acted faithfully.[10] Only this already allows us to say anything meaningful about the still unknown future.[11] As Edward Schillebeeckx explains:

> Because Israel remembered certain meaningful events from the past and associated them with new events of the present, both past and present illuminated each other, and thus it experienced and interpreted its history as the gradual fulfillment of a divine promise. Within this concept of history the present itself was seen as a new promise, a new door opening to a new future. And ultimately the whole earthly history becomes the unfolding of an eschatological expectation.[12]

This trust in the fulfillment of God's promises is expressed in powerful *visions of a future* with God where justice and peace will prevail, "on earth as it is in heaven."

---

as such if a certain correspondence between protology and eschatology, between creation and consummation is assumed.

6 See the letter to the Hebrews 10:23. "Let us hold fast the confession of our hope without wavering, for he who promised is faithful." Pannenberg (1998:539) argues that grounding eschatology in the concept of promise is correct inasmuch Christian hope can only rest in Godself. However, a mere emphasis on the category of promise or the claim that promises are from God remains insufficient for a Christian eschatology unless the God of the promise can be recognized as such. In this sense eschatology is a function of the doctrine of God and rests on the soil of the knowledge of God.

7 Berkhof (1967:16-17).

8 Pannenberg (1998:174).

9 For Moltmann, the promises of an eschaton are indeed fulfilled, but this does not imply the presence of the eschaton in history. Fulfillment is not the presence of what is promised; it is the extension of the promise itself. In this sense the eschaton contradicts present reality and bursts open all worldly cohesions (see Schuurman 1991:95).

10 Haught (1993b:178).

11 Schillebeeckx (1969:49) in criticism of Moltmann's one-sided emphasis on the radical *novum* anticipated in Christian hope.

12 Schillebeeckx (1969:48). See also Berkhof's similar comments: The cumulative experiences of Israel with Yahweh in history convinced them that this God will lead them to a new future in which God will establish a dispensation of comprehensive *shalom* (1985:510).

This is epitomized by the vision of *shalom* in the prophetic tradition. The scope of this salvation is not merely personal or societal but indeed cosmic. Carl Braaten describes this prophetic vision eloquently:

> The coming kingdom, which Yahweh was to establish for his people, enjoyed the same material reality as the promised land. It would be a land flowing with milk and honey. The faithful remnant of Israel would be drawn to the holy mountain at their dwelling place. There is no specific hope for heaven or life after death. Salvation will be something to see; the earth will be extremely fruitful, people will be inwardly renewed, society will become righteous, and the nations will be at peace. Israel, the least of the nations, will be exalted above all the others, provided the people remain faithful to the ancient covenant.[13]

According to the apostolic witnesses included in the New Testament, this trust in the fulfillment of God's promises received a new depth through the incarnation, life, ministry, death and resurrection of Jesus, the Christ and through the powerful presence of the Holy Spirit in the early church.[14] The resurrection of Christ validated the promises of the First Testament. It provided a pledge, a deposit of God's promises of salvation. Moltmann explains the eschatological significance of the resurrection:

> The resurrection has set in motion an eschatologically determined process of history whose goal is the annihilation of death in the victory of the life of the resurrection, and which ends in that righteousness in which God receives in all things his due and the creature thereby finds salvation.[15]

The apostolic witness to the resurrection of Christ soon became the basis of the Christian hope that God's promises of an all-encompassing *shalom* will indeed be fulfilled in future. Christian hope is therefore indeed *mediated* hope.[16]

This New Testament hope for salvation from sin was expressed in a number of well-known and powerful images, for example the great banquet, the wedding feast of the lamb, the new Jerusalem, the new earth and, especially, the coming kingdom of God. The history of interpretation of these images and visions of the future with God has been characterized by both plurality and ambiguity (Tracy). The sense of hope expressed in these metaphors is nevertheless characterized not by somberness but by exalted joy.[17]

---

13 Braaten (1985:331).

14 See Berkhof (1985) for an emphasis on the eschatological significance of the relationship between Christ and the Spirit. Both Christ and the Spirit anticipates the future.

15 Moltmann (1967:46). Note that Moltmann responds here both to the predicament of sin and of death.

16 Moltmann (1979:22) adds: "Christian thought is certainly mediated hope - hope, that is to say, for the resurrection and eternal life through the cross of the risen Christ."

17 Berkouwer (1972:22f).

3.2 Christian hope for life beyond death

In the history of the Christian tradition, the scope of Christian hope has often been extrapolated (for better or for worse!) from its soteriological core to incorporate a response to the predicament of temporal finitude; to the problem of death and mortality.[18]

What will happen to me after I have died? In religious traditions around the world a reflection on this question is seldom completely absent. Some may be content with the ideal of a blessed longevity in this life, with little concern for one's own infinite self-perpetuation.[19] Some may hope to survive, not as isolated individuals in a distant heaven, but in the collective soul of the tribe, in communion with its present members who continue to venerate their ancestors.[20] Others may count on an "objective" sense of immortality: the presence of our genes will continue physically through future generations or in their memories of us. Yet others hope for a continuation of life after death in a personal form, for example through reincarnation, an immortal soul or a resurrected body.[21]

In the early history of the Jewish-Christian tradition the problem of human finitude received relatively little attention.[22] According to the Biblical narratives, the patriarchs expected a shadowy existence in She'ol after their deaths, withdrawn from communion with God. This image is also reflected in several of the Psalms (e.g. 88:10-12, 115:17). Death implies a severance from life.[23] Furthermore, the vision of *shalom* in the pre-apocalyptic prophetic tradition was a thoroughly this-worldly vision for the foreseeable future of a society where pervasive evil will be

---

18 The belief in some form of life after death was widespread in the Ancient Near East and in Israel also before the Persian period. However, such earlier notions of life after death were reinterpreted through the emergence of Jewish apocalypticism (see McDannell & Lang 1988:15f, also Ruether 1983:237f). See also Moltmann's view (1967:132) that it was an intensification of God's promise that led the prophets to regard even death itself as a transformable possibility.

19 Ruether (1983:235f) suggests that this is, typically, an all too male concern.

20 See Ruether (1983:251) for a similar description of the hope beyond death in Native American culture and religion.

21 See Kuitert (1993:241) for a somewhat similar analysis of various cultural views on life after death, namely veneration of ancestors continuing to be present, continued existence in a shadowy realm of the dead, death as a fiction, a journey continued elsewhere, the ritual and magic call by shamans to allow the dead to return (if temporarily) to the realm of the living, continued existence in the collective memory of the group, personal victory over death through reincarnation, an immortal soul or a resurrected body.

22 See Chapter 9 for more detail in this regard.

23 Many scholars conclude from this emphasis on death as the severance from life that Israel knew no real hope or expectation for the life to come. Death, the end of one's human lifetime was the final horizon. By contrast, Berkouwer (1972:173f) argues that Israel maintained that Yahweh was Lord also over death from an early period (see e.g. Ezek 37, Is 25:7f, Dan 12:2). The expectation of the resurrection is therefore more than a foreign influence on Israel.

restrained, transformed and conquered. This prophetic vision (e.g. the expected new earth in Isaiah 65) is concerned with the future of life on this earth, a new golden age of shalom, and not with a world beyond the annihilation of this one.[24]

For some time, the pious in Israel may have had some inkling that even death has no power over them whom God loves. The communion with God will prevail not only in death, but also after death.[25] It was somewhere during the Persian period that the scope of a hope, that was still focused on the predicament of sin, was extrapolated to include the promise of life after death. Otherworldly eschatological traits were gradually associated with hope for salvation from sin as Israel came into contact with Persian and Hellenistic influences.[26] By the time of Jesus, this hope was formulated by the Pharisees as the belief in the resurrection of the dead.

This belief in resurrection was radically transformed by the resurrection of Christ. This became the basis for the Christian belief in the resurrection of the dead. The focus of Christian hope for life beyond the boundaries of human finitude was no longer based on what God could do, but on what God had done in Jesus Christ.[27] Through the resurrection, Christ conquered not only the power of sin and evil but also death itself. The victory of Christ over death became the foundation of Christian hope.

In the theology of Paul the predicaments of sin and of mortality could therefore be merged into one another, because "death itself is regarded as the wage of sin" (Rom 6:23). If sin is the root cause of death, salvation from sin necessarily implies victory over death. Paul could therefore develop a notion of Christian hope that includes life beyond death.

This integration of the predicaments of sin and finitude was a crucial development in Christian eschatology. Since then, and until very recently, the view that human beings would not have been mortal – if the fall did not take place – dominated the Christian tradition. Death (the predicament of finitude) affects the human condition only as a result of sin. Subsequently, Christian hope anticipated salvation from sin *and* victory over death *simultaneously*.[28] Hope for life beyond death (a response to the predicament of finitude) was based on hope for the fulfillment of God's promised salvation (the predicament of sin).

This hope for life beyond death was classically expressed in the images of the resurrection of the body, the continued existence of the soul, eternal life and heaven awaiting believers after their deaths. In the popular imagination (especially since the medieval period), Christian hope is often almost exclusively understood as the hope for life beyond death.

---

[24] Moltmann (1996:275), Braaten (1985:331).

[25] Schillebeeckx (1969:50).

[26] Braaten (1985:331).

[27] Berkouwer (1972:180).

[28] Ruether (1983:239) identifies a "double scenario" here: a historical millennium fulfilling the demand of justice and a subsequent dispensation of life everlasting where the righteous can achieve immortality.

This integration of the predicament of sin with the predicament of finitude (death) on an individual level was paralleled by a similar development in the Judaeo-Christian tradition which responded to the finitude of society and the world as such (i.e. not merely to individual finitude).

According to the prophetic tradition, the sins of society would lead to God's judgment and untold suffering, death and the destruction of society. But if death is a sign of God's judgment, then God's power must also extend beyond death. The prophetic vision could thus be extended to address a catastrophe such as the Babylonian exile. God's promises remained valid despite the worst catastrophes.[29]

In the imagery of Jewish apocalypticism the seriousness of this predicament was radicalized to anticipate the imminent annihilation of the world.[30] Sin was expected to have cosmic ramifications. The prophetic "Day of the Lord" became an event with apocalyptic proportions. Behind this sense of crisis were particular experiences of tyranny, oppression and persecution from which no escape seemed possible. Extinction seemed inevitable. This sense of crisis also thrived in a context of widespread mass anxiety over the imminent "end of the world."[31] In this way, the cosmic dimensions of evil and cosmic finitude were integrated with one another.[32]

In such a hopeless context, the focus of hope shifted to a glorious new world instead of a return to an ancient ideal.[33] The function of eschatology was to provide consolation in a context of injustice. Beyond this catastrophic event, a completely new age, a new cosmic dispensation, was envisioned in which both the power of societal evil *and* of death would be conquered. Ultimately, beyond the present era, all will be well, justice will prevail, there will be no more tears.[34] The forces of evil will *finally* be eradicated. This new age would be discontinuous rather than continuous with present history.[35] In his study on the "End of time", Thompson comments on this shift in eschatological thinking:

> ... early Christianity presents a radical new twist to the belief in the imminence of the End of the World which permeated the first-century Middle East. It is the first religion to offer its adherents the possibility of escaping the flames in which the rest of the world

---

29 Moltmann (1967:131f). Moltmann identifies on this basis a universalization and "intensification" of God's promises within the prophetic tradition.

30 See, for example, the historical context of apocalyptic texts like Daniel and Revelation.

31 Thompson (1996:18f).

32 Martin Buber argues that Christianity has lost it Jewish roots and its attachment to this world in this shift from prophecy to apocalypticism. Prophetic religion believes in the idea of the redemption of the earth; apocalyptic religion abandons the earth as hopelessly lost. See also Berkouwer (1972:229).

33 Thompson (1996:13).

34 Nürnberger (1987:108). This apocalyptic assessment that this world has been abandoned by God, often constitutes a form of escapism which expects salvation only in the coming age (Peters 1978:47).

35 Macquarrie (1978:39).

will perish.[36]

Although most Christians are no longer inclined to pray, "Let grace come, and let this world pass away" (Didache 10:6),[37] this awareness of the coming end of history and of the world as such remained prevalent throughout the history of Christianity. Prophetic and apocalyptic Biblical texts were (and often still are) simply read as predictions of events leading to the end of the world. The details of these events are debated with more or often with less sophistication in millennialist, Adventist, and dispensationalist circles.

3.3 Christian hope and the knowledge of God

The scope of Christian hope has often been extrapolated even further to incorporate a response to the predicament of human limitedness (in space), with specific reference to the limits of human knowledge and power. In the presence of an omniscient, omnipotent and benevolent God these limitations can be transcended. The hope and yearning of many is therefore to come into the presence of God.

According to the witness of several Biblical texts, the separation between God and the world is not an ontological separation. It is our sins that have separated us from God (e.g. Is 59:2, Ps 14, 53, Rom 3). If the problem of sin can be addressed, the people of God will be able to experience God's presence in their midst. The restrictions to our knowledge of God are therefore not due to the predicament of limited human knowledge and power but to the predicament of sin. Conversely, a growing in the knowledge of God is closely related to the process of sanctification. Holiness is the ultimate requirement for the beatific vision.

Furthermore, the immanence of God is stressed in the Biblical roots of the Christian tradition. God is present in the Sabbath, in the created order, in events of salvation and liberation, in the temple, in Jesus Christ, in the church as the body of Christ, in the gifts of the Spirit, etc. The eschatological image of Revelation 21:3 is also directed at God's immanence and not at an ultimate transcending of human limitations. Humans have to accept the limitations of their existence but can still live their earthly lives in the presence of God (*coram Deo*). This is the theme of numerous psalms and of the wisdom literature.

This immanence of God is often coupled with an equally strong emphasis on God's transcendence. God is in heaven and human beings are restricted to the earth (Is 55:8f, Eccl 5:1). God is therefore not separated from the world; God does transcend the limitations of the world. God simply remains beyond human grasp. To "see" God face to face is impossible (1 Tim 6:16) and fraught with deadly dangers.

Despite these Biblical witnesses, the scope of Christian hope is often broadened to address the predicament of the limitations of human knowledge and power. This is partly the logical consequence of the hope to overcome the predicament of

---

36 Thompson (1996:20).

37 See Moltmann (1979:18) for this perceptive comment on the Didache.

finitude. If one can share in the victory over death and experience eternal life in the presence of God, does this not also imply the attainment of an encompassing vision? In this dispensation we may only see in a mirror dimly, but in a next dispensation we will comprehend fully (1 Cor 13:12). We will see God face to face. The pure of heart are called happy because they will indeed see God (Mat 5:8)! When Christ comes and everything is revealed, we shall see Christ as he really is (1 John 3:2).[38] To be in God's presence is the ultimate goal of human existence: "One thing I ask of the Lord, and only this I seek: that I might dwell in the house of the Lord all the days of my life" (Ps 127:9).

This dimension of Christian hope became more prominent due to the influence of Platonism, neo-Platonic philosophy and Gnosticism on Christianity.[39] The Greek notion of *theoria*, the contemplation of eternal ideas, "shining in pure light," was easily fused with the contemplation of the divine.[40] However, these ideas no longer belonged to the encompassing realm of the cosmos, but to the transcendent realm of God (adapted from the Jewish emphasis on the uniqueness of God).

The distinction between humanity (incarcerated in the material world) and God thus became an ontological separation.[41] In order to know the truth as God knows it, we must escape from the finite limits of bodily existence.[42] In this form, the quest for the beatific vision assumes that the separation, the alienation of human beings from the presence of God, is due to ignorance and not to sin. The limitations of finite knowledge are what prevent us from having fellowship with God. What would heal the rift is infinite knowing – a merging of the human and divine into a single union of intellect.[43] The beatific vision thus implies a supra-sensible and ecstatic knowing, a form of participatory knowledge, a seeing from the point of

---

38 Küng (1984:218) notes that seeing God – which according to the Old Testament is fatal for human beings on earth – becomes, according to the New Testament, remarkably the main content of the consummation.

39 Moltmann (1967:156) argues that the Greek notion of the timeless epiphany of the eternal presence of God presented itself as the fulfillment of eschatological expectations: "The eschatological expectation of what has 'not yet' happened becomes a noetic expectation of the universal disclosure and glorification of what has already happened in heaven" (1967:159).

40 Berkhof (1967:61).

41 Van Hoogstraten (1999:70f) argues that neither Judaism nor Greek philosophy assumed a dualist worldview. The Greek logos was reflected in the natural order. Likewise, the God of Israel was involved in nature and in history. The Christian dualism between God and the world, heaven and earth, the spiritual and the material world was the result of an integration of the Greek (cosmic and static) and Hebrew (historical, dynamic) worldviews. The Greek logos prevailed but it lost its connection with *cosmos* and *physis*. To "save" the God of Israel an early dualism between God and the world was introduced.

42 Peters (1992:320).

43 Peters (1992:320). In response, Peters insists that, "The problem of the human condition is not essentially one of ignorance. Ignorance is only a symptom. The real problem is sin" (1992:320).

view of eternity.[44] The quest for the knowledge of God therefore had to follow the neo-Platonic route of transcending the material world to attain the ultimate *visio Dei beatifica*, "an intuitive vision and face-to-face experience of the divine essence which is not mediated by any created reality" (Benedict XII).[45]

Christian hope thus became the quest to return to the eternal presence of an omniscient and omnipresent God. To be in the presence of God, together with Christ who has ascended to heaven, is to experience the eschaton. For countless believers through the centuries, the climax of seeing God face to face has been at the center of their hopes and expectations.[46] While the Scotists perceived the beatific vision as a form of mystic love, the Scholastic (Thomistic) tradition understood it in terms of a purely intellectual enjoyment of the divine substance – which thus responds more directly to the limitations of human knowledge.[47] In this exclusive concentration on God there seems to be little room for relationships with other human beings or with the earth itself.[48] It is a heaven for aesthetes and ascetics only.[49] This has led to the dominance of what Paul Santmire has called the "metaphor of ascent": the other-worldly quest to escape from the confines of the material world in order to experience the presence of God.[50]

3.4 Concluding comments

Christian responses to all three these predicaments were integrated with one another at least since the medieval period. The Christian hope was understood as

---

44 Peters (1992:320).

45 Hayes (1989:197). Christianity also transformed some aspects of Greek cosmology. According to Greek philosophy, the cosmos was eternal; everything that exists had to exist from eternity. The cosmos followed the cycles of endless repetition where everything basically always remained the same. In Christianity the doctrines of creation and eschatology required a more dynamic worldview where, in the end, there will be a consummation of everything. The glory of the end will surpass that of the beginning (Braaten 1985:335). The tension between Greek and Christian worldviews was resolved through the notion of an immortal soul that participates in and will return to the realm of God. While Christianity maintained a belief in the resurrection of the body, this was expected only in the distant future. The dualism of body and soul therefore postponed any immediate need to respond to material aspects of salvation and Christian hope (see Braaten 1985:336).

46 Berkhof (1967:60). This is perhaps epitomized in Dante's *Divina Comedia* which reaches its climax when the poet ascends to see the Trinity.

47 Hayes (1989:197).

48 See Berkouwer's (1972:359f) thorough discussion of the *visio Dei* in which he argues that the *visio Dei* and a *visio mundi* should be closely related to one another.

49 Küng (1984:217).

50 Santmire (1985:17f). The motif of ascent is well illustrated in the popular chorus: "Turn your eyes upon Jesus, look full in his wonderful face, and the things of the earth will go strangely dim, in the light of his glory and grace."

"going to heaven one day".[51]

This implied, firstly, an escape from the material world, the earth and a transcending of the ontological separation between God and humanity in order to reunite the soul with God. Secondly, the predicament of human finitude is finally overcome in heaven where the immortal soul enjoys everlasting life in the presence of God. In the medieval synthesis, the immortal soul is to be reunited with the body (through the resurrection of the body), but necessarily only in a very vague sense. The finitude of history and the earth itself is acknowledged and resolved through an apocalyptic and very graphic vision of the "end of time" when both evil and death will finally be conquered. Thirdly, heaven also provides a final escape from the miseries and suffering of earthly existence (the predicament of sin). It also confers a just reward for those who were sinned against, who have suffered injustices and oppression.[52]

Such an eschatological synthesis cannot be avoided. In my view, any adequate eschatology should indeed respond to all three these predicaments and has to provide some degree of integration. Nevertheless, I argue that a conflation of these predicaments often leads to some confusion in Christian eschatology, typically obscuring its soteriological core.

A response to the predicaments of human finitude in space and in time should perhaps be approached only on the basis of a response to the predicament of sin and evil (thus following the trajectories in the Biblical roots of Christianity). A preoccupation with the predicament of finitude all too easily leads to rampant speculation about the long-term future and thus remains distant to our everyday concerns. A preoccupation with the predicament of the limitations of human knowledge and power leads all too easily to an abstract, intellectualist and elitist form of eschatology.[53]

It may therefore be helpful to discuss an eschatological response to each of these predicaments separately before investigating the need for a more adequate synthesis in later chapters.

---

51 Moltmann (1985:181) comments: "The prayer for the coming of the kingdom 'on earth as it is in heaven' was replaced by the longing to 'go to heaven oneself.'' For a detailed and more sophisticated historical survey of Christian notions of "heaven", see McDannell & Lang (1988).

52 See Berkhof (1985:521-2) for a similar analysis of various connotations of eternal life.

53 See Tillich's (1963:86) perceptive comments on the intrinsic exclusiveness of the humanist ideal of education. He says: "The intrinsic exclusiveness of the humanist ideal prevents it from being the final aim of human culture. It is the ambiguity of humanistic education that it isolates individuals and groups from the masses, and the more it isolates them, the more successful it is."

4. An eschatological road map

The aim of this brief chapter is to provide a summary of the argument thus far. It will also provide an indication of the way in which the analysis of the three human predicaments will be developed in subsequent chapters. In this way it will provide a road map for the journey that will follow.

a) The human predicament

In Chapter 2 we noted the following three dimensions of the human predicament:

- The predicament of the effects of sin as this becomes evident in the many manifestations of evil in the world: injustice, slavery, oppression, conflict, corruption, destruction, degradation, suffering, and untimely death;
- The predicament of the various dimensions of finitude, transitoriness and mortality (in time);
- The inability of human beings to transcend the limitations of human knowledge and power (in space).

b) Ecological dimensions of despair

In Chapters 5-7 we will investigate three ecological dimensions of despair on the basis of this analysis of the three human predicaments.

- The ecological dimension of the evil effects of sin is obviously manifested in the ecological crisis itself. More specifically, it is manifested in environmental injustice: the devastating effects of the material greed of some on both the environment and on other human beings.
- The predicament of temporal finitude has various ecological dimensions which are manifested, for example, in the extinction of species, the loss of biodiversity, and the limited life span of the human species, ecosystems, the earth and possibly the universe itself.
- The quest for human knowledge and power also has important ecological dimensions. This is manifested in the desacralization of nature (through deist notions of God, coupled with a positivist notion of science) and the devastating effects of technocracy within the context of industrial capitalism.

c) Christian hope as a response

In Chapter 3 we noted that Christian eschatology has traditionally responded to all three these dimensions of the (human) predicament:

- Christian hope promises salvation from sin, liberation from oppression and an ultimate victory over evil. The hope for victory over evil is born from the promises of God and based on the resurrection of Jesus, the Christ. The trust that God's promises will be fulfilled anew is expressed in the prophetic vision of *shalom* and in the proclamation of the coming of God's kingdom.

- Christian hope can be extrapolated to respond to the predicament of (human) finitude in time. The hope for life beyond death is expressed in personal images such as the resurrection of the body, in historical images such as the *parousia* of Christ, and in cosmic images such as the expectation of a new earth.
- Christian hope can be extrapolated further to respond to the predicament of the limitations of human knowledge and power. These limitations can be transcended in the presence of an omniscient and omnipotent God. This hope is structured on the basis of the Ascension of Christ and is often expressed in the quest for a beatific vision.

In subsequent chapters, this argument will be further developed in especially two steps. These developments are simply stated in summary form below.

d) Some typical eschatological tensions

A typical eschatological tension can be identified in each of these responses to the (human) predicament (see Chapter 13). An exclusive emphasis on one pole within this tension will lead to a distortion of Christian hope. On the basis of this tension, some criteria may be identified to detect distortions in accounts of Christian hope.

- Christian hope for salvation from sin, liberation from oppression and victory over evil maintains a tension between the "already" and the "not yet" of the fulfillment of God's promises.
- Christian hope for life beyond death maintains a tension between the continuity and discontinuity of this life and eternal life, this dispensation and the next, this earth and the new earth.
- Christian hope for being in the presence of God maintains a tension between the immanent and the transcendent, between God and the world, between the dimensions of space-time and eternity.

e) A vision of hope for the earth

The fruitfulness of this eschatological grid, which was stated here in summary form, will have to prove itself by serving as an appropriate road map to guide the journey in subsequent chapters. It will also provide a point of departure to formulate a vision of hope for the earth in Chapters 16-18.

- In response to the environmental effects of sin, Christianity may proclaim and practise a vision of hope for the liberation of the earth itself. This is expressed, for example, in the context of the ecumenical movement, in the notion of a sustainable community, in the vision for Justice, Peace and the Integrity of Creation, and in the program for a "theology of life."

This vision of hope will become utopian and shallow without a prophetic reminder of God's judgment on unsustainable practices. No civilization built on a legacy of colonialism, slavery, imperialism, capitalism and consumerism will be able to escape God's judgment. No hope for the victory over evil epitomized by Christ's resurrection is possible without the exposure of sin through the cross.

- In response to the reality of death, Christianity may proclaim a vision of life beyond death – for humans and other animals, for extinct species and for the earth itself. A contemporary expression of this hope may use the images of God's loving memory, a cosmic pilgrimage and a homecoming banquet. Every moment of our earthly pilgrimage may be lived in preparation of the banquet feast of eternal life.

  This vision of life beyond death will become superficial without an acknowledgement of finitude, including the finitude of the human species and of the earth itself. Death (and suffering!) is not only the result of sin but is also an inescapable aspect of the existence of creation in time.
- In response to the limitations of human knowledge and power, Christianity may proclaim the vision that we live our lives within the realm of God's creative and nurturing love. A responsible exercising of human knowledge and power may participate in this creative and nurturing love. A Christian life is lived in anticipation of the revelation of God's glory, when God will come to live with us (Rev 21:3). This vision requires a clearer understanding of the relationship between our existence in time and space and God's presence in the realm of eternity.

  This vision will become dangerously arrogant without a recognition of the limitations of human knowledge and power.

f) The social impact of Christian hope

Some eschatological tensions are also evident in the social impact of Christian hope (see Chapter 19). An inability to maintain the above mentioned eschatological tensions will lead to distortions in Christian hope which become evident in the social impact of such hope:

- Hope for the fulfillment of God's promises of salvation from sin / evil is characterized by a critique of the present (a negation of the negative) and the anticipation of a promised *novum*. It thus leads to *inspiration*, expectation and resistance but also to patience and perseverance.

  This hope is distorted by an exclusive emphasis on the already of God's salvation, leading to either *triumphalism* or *resignation* (depending on one's present position of power). A denial of the possibility of something new will soon lead to despair. By contrast, an exclusive emphasis on the "not-yet" of God's salvation may degenerate into wishful thinking or *utopian fantasies*.
- Hope for life beyond death is characterized by a life of *preparation*. The significance of every moment of this life is reinterpreted within the context of the

dimensions of eternity.

This hope is distorted by an exclusive emphasis on the discontinuity between this life and the next – which may easily degenerate into a form of *escapism* from an unacceptable present. By contrast, an exclusive emphasis on the continuity between this life and the next may again lead to either *triumphalism* or *resignation* (depending on one's present position of power). More specifically, a denial of life beyond death may encourage a spirit of *hedonism* and *consumerism*.

- Hope for and an awareness of being in the presence of God is characterized by a life of *responsibility*. To express this in typically reformed language: An appropriate response to God's gracious presence is a life of gratitude.

  This hope is distorted by an exclusive emphasis on God's immanence, implying the need to rely on material forces and innate human abilities for the future. Again, this may encourage either *triumphalism* (activism) or *resignation*. A denial of God's transcendence will have a similar effect. By contrast, an exclusive emphasis on God's transcendence may encourage a spirit of *quietism* that expects everything from God without taking responsibility for human power and knowledge.

In each case the eschatological tension should not imply a leveling of this tension. Instead, it requires a dialectic where both poles are given their full weight.

- A full acknowledgment of the "not yet" is necessary precisely to provide inspiration to resist the forces of evil.
- A full acknowledgment of the discontinuity of life beyond death is important to put the present life into a broader perspective and thus to encourage a commitment towards this life.
- A full recognition of God's transcendence is important in order to acknowledge and to accept responsibility for both the limitations and the potential of human power and knowledge.

An eschatological road map

Three predicaments	**The evil effects of sin**	**Finitude in time**	**Finitude in space**
	Injustice, conflict, hatred, alienation, oppression, corruption, environmental degradation	Death as the end for each individual, for species, for the planet itself The transitoriness of each moment, each opportunity	The limitations of human knowledge and power
Ecological impact / Dimensions of despair	The ecological crisis itself Eco-injustices	Extinction of species The limited life span of ecosystems and the earth	Deism in theology Positivism in science Technocracy

Christian hope	Salvation from sin Liberation from oppression Reconciliation amidst alienation Victory over evil	Life beyond death: in its personal, historical and cosmic dimensions	The presence of an omniscient, omnipotent God
Biblical images	Shalom The reign of God God's judgment	Personal: Resurrection of the dead Historical: Parousia of Christ Cosmic: the new earth	God's presence in the Sabbath, the temple, in the incarnation and Ascension of Christ, in the church The beatific vision
Eschatological tensions	Already / not-yet Promise - fulfillment	Continuity / discontinuity; this body / the resurrected body; this life / everlasting life; this earth / the new earth	Immanence / transcendence World / God Space-time / eternity
Social impact	Triumphalism Or: resignation Critical inspiration Utopian fantasies	Hedonism & consumerism Or: resignation Preparation Escapism	Activism Or: resignation Responsibility Quietism
Hope for the earth / Resurrection hope	Life amidst death Sustainable community JPIC Theology of life	Life beyond death God's loving memory A cosmic pilgrimage A homecoming banquet	Eternal life Being in Christ God's Shekinah
Prophetic reminders / The cross of Christ	Unsustainability Judgment on evil	Suffering and death as inevitable	Accepting human limitations

Part B: Images of despair

How should a vision of Christian hope for the earth be articulated at the dawn of a new century? It does not require a prophet to realize that we will have to come to terms with increasing and systemic environmental predicaments in the coming century. Where, then, can a vision of hope that includes hope for the earth be found?

In order to address these questions, one is perhaps well advised to first investigate the ecological depths of despair in more detail. Christian eschatology should guard against the temptation of selling cheap forms of hope.[1] Whereas cheap grace (Bonhoeffer) may undermine the integrity of the gospel, cheap hope will undermine its plausibility. This happens whenever Christian hope becomes unrelated to the actual future of the earth, society and individual human beings, and therefore uninspiring for the present. Such hope may provide ultimate assurance that nothing can separate us from the love of God (Rom 8:39), but does not encourage a responsibility towards the environment. Such forms of hope cannot empower an environmental praxis in the world in which we live. It may elicit some form of hope, but such hope will remain futile, in vain, and escapist.

The following four chapters will therefore focus on an assessment of the problem of despair, with specific reference to the environmental dimensions of such despair. It will follow the analysis of the three human predicaments in the previous two chapters to investigate a sense of despair at three levels:

- The ecological impact of evil (Chapter 5);
- The ecological dimensions of finitude (Chapter 6);
- The absence of God on earth (Chapter 7).

A fourth chapter (8) is added to comment briefly on some South African dimensions of despair.

The discussion will remain deliberately one-sided insofar as it will only focus on the available evidence supporting a sense of despair. A more optimistic construction of the evidence would also be possible.

---

1 For the notion of "cheap hope", see also Beker (1994:28, 30); Hall (1996:466).

5. The ecological impact of evil

5.1 The environmental crisis

At the dawn of a new century a sense of despair, of hopelessness in the face of pervasive and apparently overpowering evil, is exemplified in the environmental crisis. The fear of many is that the twenty-first century will end in an ecological nightmare.

This does not discount the many other burning issues that will dominate the social agenda of the new century. Indeed, global poverty, unemployment, social services, malnutrition, famine, AIDS, crime and brutality, the breakdown of moral values and social cohesion, ethnic and religious tensions and a host of other issues will all require our dedicated attention. But most if not all of these issues are intertwined with aspects of the social and natural environment.

Especially since the early 1970's, numerous studies, too many to recall here, have accumulated evidence of regional and global environmental disasters. The earlier emphasis was on a variety of problems, including the following:

- The world's increasing human population;
- The scarcity of resources and energy supplies (this was particularly important in the light of the oil crisis in the 1970's);
- The potential danger of nuclear war (e.g. during the years of the "cold war");
- The protection of endangered plant and animal species;
- The problem of soil erosion;
- The problem of (industrial) pollution in its more visual forms;
- The management of urban waste.

These environmental problems intensified during the decades that followed. Not only have the number and extent of these ecological problems increased, but also their "quality", that is, their potential danger for the future of life on earth.[2] The range of environmental hazards now includes the following:

- The environmental impact of global population and its threat to the carrying capacity of the earth (a function of growth of human population, consumption and the use of technology);
- The salination and toxification of soil in the first world, overgrazing and deforestation in the third world, the collapse of fishing industries due to persistent over-fishing, the virtual destruction of the rainforests and other ecosystems, often leading to desertification;
- Atmospheric pollution: the threats of ozone depletion, global warming, acid

---

2 Kroh (1991:79f).

rain, and changing weather patterns;[3]

- The pollution of water supplies through highly toxic forms of waste (including the problem of the disposal of nuclear waste);
- The loss of biodiversity.

The hiddenness and slowness of the environmental crisis remains a major obstacle in raising a public awareness of the seriousness of this crisis. The cumulative effect of environmental degradation should nonetheless not be underestimated. The survival of the human and other species at the top of the food chain is indeed at stake. The earth's ecosystems have lost their equilibrium and may be, through a process of slow poisoning, on the way to ecological death. "We are", says Larry Rasmussen, "violating the basic law of life itself: exchange and reciprocity, giving and receiving, living and dying and dying to live, in some relatively fair measure".[4] The very building blocks of life: soil, water and air are being poisoned in this process (see the categories in the list above). In the words of Thomas Berry and of Brian Swimme:

> Our entire society is caught in a closed cycle of production and consumption that can go on until the natural resources are exhausted or until the poisons inserted into the environment are fed back into the system.[5]

> We are soaking all life forms with poisons, changing rivers into lethal sewage, and hurling million tons of noxious gases into the respiratory system of the Earth.[6]

The extent of the environmental crisis is often expressed and explained in the form of ominous statistics. An alarmist use of such statistics unfortunately lasts only as long as people remain feeling scared. A more penetrating analysis of the environmental crisis requires a thorough analysis of the global political economy, taking a wide variety of economic, social, political, demographic, philosophical and reli-

---

3 Keller (1997:84f). She argues that allusion to changing weather patterns have taken on ominous and even apocalyptic proportions. Apocalyptic thinking is being colored green.

4 Rasmussen (1991:358). Perhaps the basic problem remains the acceptance of planetary limits. The famous report on *Limits to growth* (1972) expressed the first reservations concerning the viability of sustained economic growth. Unlimited growth is simply not possible on a finite planet. A finite planet cannot sustain continuous, expanding demands on its resources. We are indeed living beyond our means! See Larry Rasmussen's (1975) still helpful explanation of the economic, social and biospheric dimensions of this notion of "limits to growth". The notion of limits to growth is explained in a quite lucid way in the following story about Ghandi:

> After Ghandi led India to independence someone asked him whether India will now try to reach the same standard of living as England. His answer was: "It took Britain half the resources of the planet to achieve its prosperity; how many planets will a country like India require?" (quoted in Granberg-Michaelson 1992:17).

5 Berry (1988:57).

6 Swimme (1995:74).

gious factors into account.[7] Such an analysis is beyond the scope of this chapter.

In the need to raise a public awareness of environmental issues, the contributions of those with a poetic sensibility – alongside scientists and social analysts – deserve special notice. Artists are indeed the antennae of society (Ezra Pound). They seem to be able to register and express the pain impulses of the environmental crisis. A few random examples from around the world may illustrate this aesthetic environmental sensibility.[8]

> I am concerned about the wounds and bleeding sores on the naked body of the earth. Have we not seen the long-term effects of these bleeding sores? The famine? The poverty? The chemical and nuclear accidents? We are responsible directly or indirectly. We are strangling the earth (Wangari Maathai, the founder of the Kenya Green Belt Movement).[9]

> The means by which we live have outdistanced the ends for which we live. Our scientific power has outrun our spiritual power. We have guided missiles and misguided men (Martin Luther King Jr.).[10]

> In the excitement over the unfolding of his scientific and technical powers, modern man has built a system of production that ravishes nature and a type of society that mutilates man (Ernst Schumacher).[11]

> When the last tree has been felled, and when the last river has been seized, only then will we finally realize that we cannot eat money (Mohandas Ghandi).[12]

> The unleashed power of the atom has changed everything except our way of thinking. Thus we are drifting towards a catastrophe beyond comparison. We shall require a substantially new manner of thinking if the human is to survive (Albert Einstein).[13]

> We are the termination, not the fulfillment of the earth process. If there were a parliament of creatures, its first decision might well be to vote humans out of the community, too deadly a presence to tolerate any further (Thomas Berry).[14]

> My name is Anna. I am from the Marshall islands in the Pacific Ocean. My people have traditionally treasured our lands and lagoons - sources of our food. Now ... our land no longer feeds us. The more we eat of its fruit and the fish in our waters the sicker we

---

7 See the excellent study by Rasmussen (1996) for one exemplary attempt to incorporate these aspects in a theological assessment of the environmental crisis.

8 On the link between beauty and an ecological sensibility see Haught (1990, 1993), also Boff (1995).

9 Quoted in Scharper & Cunningham (1993:7).

10 Quoted in Scharper & Cunningham (1993:56).

11 Schumacher (1973:246).

12 Quoted in Boff (1995:35).

13 Quoted in Scharper & Cunningham (1993:26).

14 Berry (1988:209).

become. ... From 1946 to 1958 nuclear tests were held in our atolls. Some of our atolls have simply disappeared. Others are still slowly releasing radio-activity into our waters. While our older people are still suffering from radiation sickness many of our children have genetic effects. We women feel this particularly; we think of our children (from an International Consultation on "The integrity of Creation", World Council of Churches, Norway, 1988).[15]

Particularly in the speeches of the chiefs the theme of the barren earth keeps recurring, reflecting a growing awareness of the seriousness of environmental degradation. During the planting ceremonies in the Gutu district in 1988 Chief Gutu expressed concern about the absence of many species of wild life formerly found on his lands. He complained about the chopping down of the densely wooded holy groves of the ancestors. As a result, he insisted, one could no longer hear the drumbeat of the spirit of Mount Jerimanda at the onset of the rains - formerly a sign of the country's well-being.

In such comments one detects a note of desperation, almost of fatalism in the face of a situation virtually beyond repair. Lament finds comfort in a nostalgic return to the past of abundance. There is a yearning for the thickly wooded forests where the ancestral drums heralded the onset of the good rains; the time when Mwari, the Shona creator god, was apparently satisfied with his people and showed his approval of their observance of ancient custom by sending them plentiful rains (Inus Daneel on deforestation in Zimbabwe).[16]

Apartheid not only degrades the inhabitants of our country. It degrades the earth, the air and the streams ... we are calling for the restoration of the land, the forest and the atmosphere. The greening of our country is basic to its healing. There is a lot of healing to be done in South Africa (Albie Sachs).[17]

5.2 Environmental degradation and the popular imagination

In spite of the accumulating evidence, environmental issues are often still marginalized on public agendas and in the popular consciousness. We still speak of the environmental crisis as if it is distant, as if does not affect us directly, as if it will go away sometime or another.

In South Africa, the focus of the public debate has, understandably, shifted from the struggle for political liberation and democracy to economic liberation. Problems such as poverty, unemployment, education, housing, health services, crime and HIV/AIDS seem to demand far more urgent attention than the hidden, often indirect and all too long-term environmental problems. The focus of social concern is on the needs of the poor, the hungry, the homeless, the sick, the abused, the unemployed, the aged, the illiterate. The environment is simply not a dominant concern in the rhetoric of politicians, on the agenda of economists, or in the popular imagination. The need for a healthy environment is acknowledged in the new South African constitution but remains rather sidelined as an issue for critical

---

15 Quoted in Scharper & Cunningham (1993:50).

16 Daneel (1994:442).

17 Quoted in Cock (1994).

debate, practice and policy-making.

Many still view a concern for the environment as the hobby of an affluent, leisured minority who would like to preserve the environment for purely aesthetic reasons. Some conservationists seem more concerned about wildlife than about other human beings.[18] The nature conservation policies of the apartheid era provoked the suspicion that conservation boils down to the establishment of game reserves for a privileged few, often at the expense of the dislocation of local people.[19] Others fear that attention to environmental concerns may divert scarce human and financial resources from the more pressing issues of poverty, hunger and employment.[20] Finding employment now seems far more urgent than the long-term environmental impact of mining, manufacturing, farming, forestry or fishing. The conflict between "feeding people" (caring for immediate needs) and "saving nature" (protecting scarce resources) therefore remains all too real.

There is nevertheless a broad recognition, also amongst the poor and marginalized in South Africa, that human well-being is dependent on the well-being of the land. The destruction of the environment will necessarily affect human dignity. This recognition is indeed crucial since the victims of environmental degradation and injustice are often from the poorest part of the population. The problems that the poor and marginalized experience on a daily basis are often essentially environmental problems. The poor are driven to live in physical conditions which are of a bad environmental quality (and which are therefore "open" for occupation). The poorest often live (and work!) in urban waste dumps. Others accept employment in dreadful environmental conditions with grave risks to health (e.g. toxic gases, pesticides).

This link between poverty and environmental hazards has both urban and rural

---

18 Someone once commented that: "It sometimes appears as if it is easier to raise R2 million to save a rhinoceros than to save a human from a life of deprivation". Quoted in Cock & Koch (1991:46).

19 Ackermann & Joyner (1996:122).

20 In 1991, Frank Chikane expressed a similar concern about placing the environment on the social agenda of the church:

> To most of us who come from countries which are ravaged by senseless wars, characterized by gross violations of human rights and by massive poverty and unemployment, the introduction of the item of the integrity of creation on our agenda seemed like a conspiracy by those who benefit out of our poverty and oppression, to divert and diversify our struggle for justice in our situations. It seemed like some people wanted to keep us busy with seeming abstract concerns about the misuse of biotechnology rather than the real issues of land dispossession and racism, sexism, economic exploitation (classism), political oppression, and denial of the right of religious freedom and the use of religion as an instrument of oppression (quoted in Niles 1992:36).

Leonardo Boff (1995:12) quotes (but then also refutes) a similar argument:

> Ecology is a luxury of the rich. It is a product of the northern hemisphere. These people have despoiled nature in their own countries and have robbed the colonized peoples of the entire world, and after all that are now claiming a safe ambience and ecological reserve for the preservation of a species in the process of decline.

manifestations. South Africa's urban townships were often located precisely on environmentally degraded land that was therefore not in demand. People living in urban townships are often the victims of environmental degradation. They are confronted with a host of environmental problems on a daily basis, although this is usually not identified as such:[21]

- Air pollution, either through nearby industries or through the use of braziers and coal stoves (even in electrified houses);
- Pollution of water supplies by broken sewerage pipes, stagnant pools, or people doing their washing next to water taps to avoid walking characteristically long distances to reach a decent washing place, if one exists at all;
- The visual ugliness of pollution, leading to a lack of basic human dignity;
- Very high population densities, a localized form of overpopulation.
- Inadequate sanitation;
- A high incidence of contagious diseases;
- Regular floods or landslides;
- A lack of basic infrastructure;
- Cutting of trees for firewood in the neighborhood, where any are left;
- The struggle for political control over ever scarcer resources.

In rural areas, the scarcity of clean drinking water and firewood are environmental problems at their very roots – with serious human and economic consequences. Deportation or removals under apartheid[22] forced many South Africans to live in over-crowded conditions on land unable to support them effectively – resulting in extreme poverty. This process has reinforced environmental degradation through overgrazing, soil erosion and the exhaustion or depletion of water supplies. Many people have resorted to poaching and forms of deforestation as a survival strategy. These forms of environmental degradation are seldom deliberate, but an increasing number of humans in a limited area inevitably exact an environmental toll. This environmental damage increases poverty, leading to a vicious circle in which people are damaging the very fabric on which they depend for their survival.

Women and children often bear the brunt of coping with these environmental problems. As soil deteriorates, women have to work longer hours in backbreaking toil to harvest food from barren soil. Children suffer most from diseases like diarrhea due to a lack of drinkable water and inadequate sanitation. In deforested rural communities, girls and women spend increasing energy and time to collect firewood.[23] Women are often forced to work in environmentally hazardous condi-

---

[21] See the excellent article of Lawson, "The ghetto and the greenbelt" in Cock & Koch (1991:46-63) and, from a Latin-American perspective, Gudynas (1995).

[22] Numerous studies have indicated the adverse effect which apartheid policies have had on the environment in South Africa (see, for example, Cock & Koch 1991, Durning 1990, Ramphele & McDowell 1991).

[23] See the following telling observation (quoted in Wright & Kill 1993:10): "The boys have nothing to do. For girls it's different. We have to look after the family, collecting

tions for low wages. Women receive fewer financial rewards, work more hours, have less access to education, do more of the household work, and have to bear and provide for their children. Typically, mothers sleep last and rise first.[24]

By contrast, the middle class and elite members of the South African society enjoy first world standards of water, energy, sanitation, health care and education. Their lives display the consumerism and wastefulness that is characteristic of most of the first world with its devastating effect on the earth. Inadequate environmental legislation does little to mitigate this impact.

In the light of these observations, there is a growing need to recognize that concerns about economic injustice, social health and environmental degradation are inextricably linked and often reinforcing one another. This is expressed in the well-known notion of "Justice, Peace and the Integrity of Creation". The notion of eco-justice is also used with increasing frequency to indicate that systems of injustice have both an *eco*nomic and an *eco*logical dimension.[25] This also indicates the enormous complexity of the problem.

Understandably, most of us find ourselves unable to analyze and respond to this complex agenda. We simply continue with our often unsustainable lifestyles. Yet, there remains a deep-seated cognizance that environmental problems will not go away. In the popular consciousness, the environmental crisis therefore lurks beneath the surface as a silent but pervasive fear for the long term future of life on this planet. This sense of despair is reinforced by a loss of confidence in the ability of technology to ultimately remove human fear and anxiety amidst the threat of the overwhelming forces of nature. This is indeed an "age of diminishing expectations" (Christopher Lasch). The message from this mounting data has become increasingly clear to everyone in slogans such as: "The future isn't what it used to be." Or: "If current trends continue, we will not!"[26]

When ordinary people consider the long-term future, let us say the future for their grandchildren, they often see a very somber picture. We fear over-population, crime, poverty, rampant diseases, chaos, economic deficits, and increasing environmental hazards. Paul Santmire's summary of the cosmic depths of despair is worth quoting at length:

> The threat of mass catastrophe is now a commonplace of the popular mind. With the passing of each day, we are becoming more and more familiar with scenarios of global thermonuclear death and devastation, planetary ecological collapse, toxic pollution of our environment, vast blights of deforestation and soil erosion, constant economic crisis for the great majority of the earth's peoples, and rampant starvation in some regions of the world, all punctuated by the threats of nuclear accidents or terrorism and stories of increasingly capricious patterns of global weather. Hovering in our consciousness, as well, is the vague but dismal image of the end of cosmic history itself, ignominiously,

---

firewood as before, but we have to walk further each day to find any." (Sara, aged 14, an Ethiopian refugee living in a Somalian camp).

24 Wright & Kill (1993:10).

25 Hessel (1992).

26 Daniel Maguire, quoted in Rasmussen (1996:10).

> eons from now, through some kind of universal "heat death." It is existentially thinkable today, perhaps as never before, that the final word being written across the pages of the whole human drama, and across the pages of the cosmos itself, is *finis*, termination, death with terror, torment, and excruciating moments of pain. These are apocalyptic times indeed. And the dark clouds of a future which is no future often flood backward, as it were, into the present, producing a deep-seated and widespread spiritual anomie.[27]

There is a widespread sense of living in an end-time, drifting increasingly rapidly towards a catastrophe through human failure. While apocalyptic visions of the end of the world may also be found in Biblical literature, there is a much more recent awareness that such pervasive destruction is indeed possible.[28] This awareness is often expressed in apocalyptic images of the end of the world[29] ("Apocalypse now"). These may take the form of religious visions of the imminent judgment and destruction of the world. This is evident from the virtual explosion of apocalyptic and millennialist literature as the year 2000 is dawning upon us.[30]

More often these apocalyptic images are expressed in horror movies, cartoons, science fiction literature or heavy metal rock music. They are full of images of cosmic horrors, featuring, for example, vengeful insects or rats or machines taking over the world, frequently in the aftermath of a nuclear catastrophe.[31] In these latter-day apocalyptic portrayals of cosmic battles, the forces of the Light often save the day, but provide only temporary reprieve[32] from the daily fears, cosmic despair and spiritual anomie that pervade much of contemporary culture.[33]

Sallie McFague argues that these apocalyptic images of the future are barely accurate. Instead, she paints the following (perhaps more realistic) picture of the future (e.g. in 2100):

---

27 Santmire (1989:265-6).

28 Küng (1984:247) comments that: "While the end of the world appeared to the authors of the Old and New Testament wholly and entirely as an act of God, surprising and unexpected like a thief in the night, for modern authors the end of the world has been seen for a long time as a possibility open to man." (The exclusivist use of gender is *not* appropriate here).

29 See Thompson (1996) for a thorough discussion of apocalyptic notions of the "end of time."

30 See, e.g. Thompson (1996).

31 Santmire (1989:266).

32 Küng (1984:249) comments that an illustrious phalanx of superheroes, substitute-Messiahs and fantasy-redeemers (from James Bond to Superman) is produced by our imagination to protect us from the nightmare of the inferno and to give us the feeling that we can get away again.

33 Santmire (1989:266). In a chapter on "hope on a dying planet" John Cobb (1992:124) comments on the loss of a sense of hope amongst the (American) youth: "In much of our youth culture, hope is focused on short-term goals and easily shattered when these are not realized. The quest for kicks, or mystical meaning, or celebration of life in the present moment, is in part an expression of the loss of hope, a loss we older people have bequeathed to our children."

> It will, I suspect, generate a different, far more mundane, kind of horror: the struggle for food and water, the stench of pollution in the sky and ocean, the battle for decreasing parcels of arable land, the search for basic medical care and education. Succeeding generations will set their sights lower: they will not expect shade trees in the cities or forests in the country any more than they will expect a better future for their children. They will, among other things, learn to live with "much beauty irrevocably lost," but by then they may not even miss it. They will have grown used to a hotter, drier planet with many more people and many fewer trees, flowers and other animals.[34]

One may perhaps add that pockets of wealth, probably extreme wealth will continue to exist. Since this wealth will be based on ever scarcer resources, it will have to be protected by more than high walls, sophisticated alarm systems and barbed wire fences. The first instinct of the affluent will be to stave off demise by accelerating the exploitation of the earth and its poor, while maintaining their affluent life-style amidst dwindling resources.[35] To quote Sallie McFague again:

> As more of the earth becomes desert, water scarcer, air more polluted, food less plentiful, the lines between the "haves" and the "have-nots" will become even more sharply drawn. Justice for the oppressed will recede from view when resources become scarce. If the human population doubles in forty or fifty years, as seems likely, and the pressure on the planet for the basics of existence intensifies, those with power will do what is necessary to insure their own piece of the disappearing pie.[36]

Herman Daly and John Cobb paint a similar picture:

> On a hotter planet, with lost deltas and shrunken coastlines, under a more dangerous sun, with less arable land, more people, fewer species of living things, a legacy of poisonous wastes, and much beauty irrevocably lost, there is still the possibility that our children's children will learn at last to live as a community among communities. Perhaps they will learn also to forgive this generation its blind commitment to ever greater consumption.[37]

Is there any hope to prevent the global system from collapsing under its own logic of exploitation? Is there any hope that the process of environmental degradation can be turned around? Is there any hope for (human) life on earth? There are several reasons why a positive scenario seems unlikely:

- What makes an awareness of environmental poisoning rather disquieting, is the fact that it may literally be too late already. The effect of the current depletion of the ozone layer, greenhouse gases, nuclear spillage, and poisoning of water systems will only become visible after a number of years.
- The environmental crisis is the product of a civilization built originally on

[34] McFague (1993:8).

[35] Ruether (1992:257).

[36] McFague (1993:9).

[37] Cobb & Daly (1994:406).

Western scientific and technological expertise and colonial natural resources and labor. This has led to unparalleled levels of affluence for some in the economic center and abject poverty for others on the economic periphery. A concern for economic justice certainly demands that the poor receive their fair share of the world's resources. This is also an ecological necessity. Indira Ghandi's comment still remains valid: "Poverty is the biggest polluter. If you are interested in us not polluting, you must help us to get rid of our poverty."[38] However, as the notion of limits to growth clearly indicates, economic justice cannot be established only on the basis of an ever increasing *production* of wealth; it necessitates a more equitable *distribution* of wealth.

- The redistribution of wealth is a daunting task in an increasingly global culture of consumerism. There has been little sign of any impact on the materialism and consumerism that pervades industrialized countries.[39] Bill McKibben observes that affluence leads to inertia and that a voluntary simplification of one's lifestyle falls outside the desire of most Americans.[40] In fact, a culture of affluence seems to demand more and more. Through the use of technology it seeks to consume a finite nature infinitely.[41] This culture of consumerism is simply not sustainable. If everyone were to drive as many cars and pollute the air as much as Americans and Europeans do, humanity may already have been suffocated. Not surprisingly, the culture of consumerism has spread to become the dominant global culture. The hope and yearning of the world's poor is to achieve an equally affluent standard of living. But the lifestyle of the world's affluent center cannot be universalized and can be maintained only at the expense of the majority on the economic periphery.[42]
- The environmental crisis is a function of the current global economic order. Industrialized countries may try to preserve a clean environment in their own backyards, but the root of the problem remains their unsustainable level of consumption and pollution. The effects of these processes are often only visible elsewhere. The world market compels the Third World to abandon their own subsistence economy and plant monocultures for the world market's use, as well as to cut down the rainforests and to overgraze their grasslands.[43]

Moltmann therefore argues that the ecological crisis is not a temporary crisis: "It is a slow but sure and irreversible catastrophe, in which the weaker living things will be destroyed first, but then the stronger things too; and finally human beings as well."[44] Although there are still some optimists who envision technological and

---

[38] Quoted in Granberg-Michaelson (1992:9-10).

[39] Hallman (1994:5), McKibben (1989:150-154).

[40] McKibben (1989:193,204).

[41] Gilkey (1976:261).

[42] Moltmann (1996:209).

[43] Moltmann (1996:207f).

[44] Moltmann (1996:208).

social solutions to these daunting problems, the language used in films, drama, fiction and art to portray the future is predominantly one of anxiety and despair.[45] Or, in the poetic language of Karl Jaspers: "The lights are going out, and one feels oneself plunging into an abyss."[46]

This sense that we will probably not be able to do something about the environmental crisis can only result in resignation. Sallie McFague comments: "The decay of our planet is probably inevitable, so we might us well accept it. What real chance do we have of turning things around?" She adds: "All of this is probably true!"[47] McFague proceeds by referring to the people in Albert Camus' *The plague*, who did not expect to escape the plague but nevertheless decided to live a life of integrity, to live as if life mattered, despite the brutal reality that defined their world.

This is surely a form of hope and resistance. One has to make the best of a bad situation. One still has to get up in the morning and do something! One may put one's hope in hope itself, in the "power of positive thinking." But is this the vision of hope for the earth that can empower an environmental praxis? To tell ourselves to hope in order that there be hope will, in the long run, be futile. Hope has to rest on something other than its own usefulness.[48] The question therefore remains: Is there any hope for the earth in the wake of environmental despair?

The question on the mind and in the hearts of many people is whether it is still possible to counteract these destructive forces? How can we recognize the mortal danger in which we live and yet avoid falling into either disillusionment or fatalism?[49]

---

45 See already Berkhof (1967:82). For several examples from European literature, see Küng (1984:247-8).

46 Quoted in Körtner (1995:2).

47 McFague (1993:207).

48 Cobb (1992:124).

49 Béguin-Austin (1993:31).

6. Ecological dimensions of finitude

Christian eschatology has often been preoccupied with the predicament of human finitude at an individual level. In Chapter 2 we have seen that various dimensions of finitude can be identified. The environmental crisis and the extinction of numerous species have made us aware of the finitude, the mortality of whole species and not only of individual specimens. Indeed, the predicament of finitude includes the death of individual human beings, the deaths of specimens of other living organisms, the finitude of whole species, of ecosystems, of the earth, the solar system, whole galaxies and possibly of the universe itself.

In this chapter we will look at some of these dimensions of finitude in more detail.

6.1 The cosmic dimensions of finitude

The task of scientific and theological cosmologies alike is to reflect not only on the origins of the universe but also on its destiny.[1] The long term future of the universe has been the subject of an ongoing debate in scientific discourse.[2]

The debate hinges on the question whether the expansion of the universe which began with the Big Bang will go on permanently (to die a "cold death" of entropy), or whether it will one day come to a standstill through the forces of gravity, and then enter in a phase of contraction with increasingly hot temperatures that would finally bring it to a singularity similar to the beginning, a point of unlimited density and compression.[3] In other words: Will the universe eventually become *fried* or *frozen*?[4]

According to the first theory of an "open" universe, the generation of new galaxies, stars, "black holes" and "white dwarfs" will eventually come to an end. The final destiny of the universe is governed by the second law of thermodynamics: all forms of energy will eventually be reduced to a state of total entropy. Everything will finally burn to ashes. The present second generation of stars will come to an

---

1 David Tracy (1994:77) insists that: "The questions of cosmology are not properly understood as *only* concerned with the origin and natural structure of the world. Those cosmological questions include the destiny of the world as well – including the destiny of human beings, indeed of history itself – as 'inextricably bound up' with the destiny of the cosmos."

2 A number of popular books have recently been published on the future of the universe (i.e. "scientific eschatology"). See, e.g. the quite accessible overviews by Davies (1994), Hawking (1988:42f). See also the discussions from a theological perspective by Drees (1990:117-154), Haught (1993:11f), Körtner (1995:146f), Küng (1993:162f), Pannenberg (1997), Peacocke (1979:319f), Peters (1989:51f), Ruether (1992:40f), Worthing (1996:160-198).

3 Pannenberg (1994:158).

4 Russell (1994:559).

end. After 10^{12} years the sky will become dark. Russell comments: "Ours is perhaps the last generation of stars, a time which, when gone, will be followed by countless ages of darkening cosmic expansion and an unknown ending."[5] The protons and neutrons that make up all matter will become destabilized and will eventually disintegrate after 10^{32} years or more. Even galactic black holes will then "evaporate" through the emission of particles. Eventually, the universe would consist of a sea of radiation (photons, neutrinos), electrons and positrons that are hardly interacting.[6] Hans Küng comments: "Cold will slowly enter the cosmos: death, silence, absolute night."[7] The universe will end, not with a bang but with a whimper.[8] Paul Davies adds: "The final feeble resources of free energy will be exhausted, the whole cosmic machine will have run down to a standstill and the second law of thermodynamics will have claimed its last victims."[9] Or, in the words of James Trefil: "At some distant time in the future, the universe will be a cold, thin, expanding sea of radiation, with a few forlorn particles to break the monotony."[10]

According to the second theory of a "closed" universe, the expansion of the cosmic explosion of the Big Bang will eventually come to an end and then slowly turn into a contraction. In a process lasting billions of years, the universe will implode at an increasingly rapid pace and at ever-increasing temperatures. This will lead to the so-called "Big Crunch" during which a complete dissolution of atoms and atomic nuclei will take place. The time-scale of these events remains disputed and depends on the current density of the universe. Estimates range from 50 billion years to extremes similar to those predicted by the theory of an open universe.[11] The final outcome is nevertheless the same: the universe will come to an end in something like a cosmic black hole. Indeed, black holes provide a foretaste of this universal annihilation. Stephen Hawking's comment applies to such a cosmic catastrophe as well:

> One could well say of the event horizon what the poet Dante said of the entrance of Hell: "All hope abandon, ye who enter here." Anything or anyone who falls through the event horizon will soon reach the region of infinite density and the end of time.[12]

The highly speculative theory of an oscillating universe provides a variation on that of the closed universe. This theory, proposed amongst others by physicist John

---

5 Russell (1994:573).

6 See the helpful brief overview by Drees (1990:246f).

7 Küng (1984:251, 1993:164).

8 Ruether (1992:42).

9 Quoted in Peacocke (1979:327).

10 Quoted in Peters (1989:53).

11 Davies (1994:119f).

12 Hawking (1988:94). The reference to Dante's comment on the entrance to Hell reminds one of the stark contrast between this universal annihilation and any form of hope expressed in Christian eschatology.

Wheeler, suggests that a completely new world, perhaps with a new set of physical laws, may come into being after a Big Crunch (e.g. a "Big Bounce"). The Big Crunch for one cosmic epoch might be the Big Bang for another. Or perhaps, as some speculate, our universe may already be the product of a second or third "Big Crunch."[13] However, if this cycle of expansion and collapse continues *ad infinitum* (?!), these successive cycles of an oscillating universe may finally also die the cold death of entropy. If, on the other hand, these oscillating cycles of expansion and collapse are indeed endless, a comparison with the futility of the myth of Sisyphus will be in order: "Must Sisyphus for ever roll his stone up the hill only for it to roll down again every time it approaches the top? That was a description of Hell!"[14]

There is also a third possibility that the density of the universe may prove to be precisely the critical density. The universe will then be neither "open" nor "closed" but "flat". This implies that the universe is expanding at precisely the rate necessary to avoid eventual collapse. This would indeed require phenomenal precision! Insofar as the universe does not collapse, it is essentially similar to the model of an open universe. According to the standard open model, the galaxies will continue to expand although the rate of expansion will decrease until a relative stable rate is achieved as the galaxies become less and less restrained by their mutual gravitational attraction. According to the model of a "flat' universe, the galaxies would in the remote future appear to come to a relative standstill, moving away from another only at the rate necessary to prevent re-collapse.[15]

The critical factor in scientific discussions of these theories is the density of mass necessary to slow and stop the process of expansion. If, according to present calculations, the critical mass density exceeds 10^{-29} grams / cm^3, then gravitational pull will draw everything together again. The available scientific evidence indicates that the density of mass in the universe is too sparse by a factor of ten or a hundred. However, there may be a quantity of unseen matter (dead stars, interstellar dust, galactic holes, black holes, sub-atomic particles, etc). Recent investigations on inflationary models of the universe indicate that the density may be close to the critical density. The debate between these theories remains unresolved.[16]

Both the alternatives of a "cold" or a "hot" death to the universe are catastrophic and will indeed constitute the end of the universe as we know it. The unpalatable truth appears to be that the final disintegration of the universe is assured.[17] If the universe had a bright beginning, its conclusion is cast in a dark, nihilistic shadow. Whether fried or frozen, all life will end.[18] The basic thrust of these obser-

---

13 Worthing (1996:190) adds that the idea of a cyclic universe itself is very old, going back to the ancient civilizations in Greece, China and Egypt. It may also find early theological support in the writings of Origen.

14 Arthur Eddington, quoted in Worthing (1996:188).

15 Worthing (1996:184-5).

16 Peters (1989:52), Worthing (1996:162f).

17 Peacocke (1979:329).

18 Peters (1989:53).

vations is towards what John Haught has called "cosmic pessimism".[19] Cosmic pessimism is the conviction that the world has no transcendent origin and no divinely shaped destiny.[20] According to this worldview, the final destiny of the physical universe is the void of utter meaninglessness. We live in a pointless or tragic universe, one that lacks any telos, any ultimate purpose. The prevailing mood of "cosmic pessimism" is well expressed in a famous comment by Stephen Weinberg:

> It is very hard to realize that this all is just a tiny part of an overwhelmingly hostile universe. It is even harder to realize that this present universe has evolved from unspeakably unfamiliar condition, and faces a future extinction of endless cold or intolerable heat. The more the universe seems comprehensible, the more it also seems pointless.[21]

In a recent article, Haught quotes a number of scientists who echo this sentiment. Sandra Faber also finds that the universe is "completely pointless from a human perspective." Marc Davis agrees although he finds it "depressing". Margaret Geller indicates a disinterest in the subject: "... why should the universe have a point? What point? It's just a physical system, what point is there?"[22]

This sense of cosmic pessimism is exemplified by the apparent implications of the second law of thermodynamics when applied on a cosmic scale. The laws of thermodynamics form the basic household rules (= *oikos-logos*) governing our planetary home. They describe the basic energy processes on the planet. The first law states that while energy can be converted from one form to another, the *quantity* of energy in a closed system will remain the same. The second law holds that the *quality* of energy will decrease (or, at best, remain more or less the same) through any such conversions of heat to do useful work. The available energy will tend towards increasing randomness and disorder (entropy). While some areas within a system may temporarily become more ordered, this will be at the cost of more disorder somewhere else in the system.

Unlike the other basic laws of physics, the increase of entropy in a closed system is an asymmetrical, one-way process (the thermodynamic "arrow of time"). Entropy and decay is irreversible and unavoidable. The result is that everything will die the death of high entropy (sometimes referred to as the "heat death"). The second law therefore seems to confirm the most pessimistic of worldviews. Its cosmological consequences evoke complete hopelessness. It leads to an utter elimi-

---

[19] Haught (1993:14). He argues that this cosmic pessimism is rooted in a scientific materialism, namely the contention that everything is ultimately reducible to chemistry and physics, that "matter" (however mysteriously nuanced this concept may have become in modern physics) is alone the sole author and substance of all that is real. See Chapter 14 for more detail in this regard.

[20] Haught (1993:17).

[21] Weinberg (1977:154-155).

[22] Quoted in Haught (1998c:2).

nation of history, leaving no hope whatsoever.[23] Karl Heim writes that, ever since the formulation of the second law, "there has lowered over mankind, like a dark thundercloud which will one day shed its load, the picture of the heat death of the universe ... in which the whole sum of energy in the universe will have dissolved into masses with equal temperatures and equal radiation."[24]

It has to be noted that the laws of thermodynamics only apply within a closed system. The earth is, for example, not a closed system since it is constantly being penetrated by energy from the sun. This heat is, of course, extremely useful and through the processes of photosynthesis[25] provides the energy on which all forms of life on earth are based.[26] Nonetheless, the entropy of the whole earth-sun system is increasing. The more important question is whether the second law applies to the universe itself. The universe (*qua* universe) may or may not operate like a closed system. The cosmological applicability of the second law therefore remains disputed in scientific research.[27] It may be expected that many regions of the universe will continue to behave as open systems with fluctuations of energy and matter. However, there will be a tendency over increasingly wide tracts of the universe to reach thermal equilibrium ("heat death").[28]

Paradoxically, as Worthing notes, the apparent infinity of an endlessly expanding universe seems to be confronted with the problem of *finitude* at every turn.[29] And, as Eddington once explained, when the universe falls prey to the final heat death, "time will extend on and on, presumably to infinity, but there will be no definite sense in which it can be said to go on."[30] Ted Peters also links the second law to the predicament of finitude:

> The application of the second law of thermodynamics measured in terms of entropy to the macrocosmos leads to the notion of temporal finitude. If the universe in its entirety is moving irreversibly from order to disorder, from hot to cold, from high energy to dissipative equilibrium, then ... the universe will eventually die. Even though in far-from-equilibrium sectors or microcosms within the larger whole we will find creative activity and the emergence of new structures, the overall advance of the cosmos is in the

---

23 Körtner (1995:147). See also Chapter 14 for a discussion of the possibilities of a more optimistic interpretation of the second law of thermodynamics.

24 Quoted in Worthing (1996:179).

25 A new awareness of the dependency of human beings on plants has emerged in recent literature. As McFague (1993:106) puts it: "The plants can do very nicely without us, in fact better, but we would quickly perish without them."

26 This "good news" about a seemingly inexhaustible source of energy does not lessen the importance of the finitude of planetary resources and the limits to the planet's ability to absorb waste products. See Rasmussen (1975).

27 See the helpful overview of arguments against the cosmological applicability of the second law by Drees (1990:243f) and Toulmin (1982).

28 Peacocke (1993:64).

29 Worthing (1996:180).

30 Quoted in Worthing (1996:180).

> direction of eventual dissipation and heat death.[31]

Indeed, the pessimism, if not nihilism, associated to the second law seems to dominate the popular imagination concerning the destiny of the universe, namely that the universe will ultimately die a senseless death. There seems to be no basis for a steadfast Christian hope within the physical universe itself. Haught insists that such a worldview cannot support an environmental ethos and vision.[32] He comments: "If the final wreck and absolute extinction is the last word about the universe, then why seek now to preserve it against the inevitable void that seems to be its destiny?"[33] The question is therefore whether anything is worth saving and protecting if reality is, in the final analysis, devoid of any hope? Does it make any sense to care for nature if the cosmos itself seems to be intent on its own annihilation, if nature itself is relentlessly pulling all things into the pit of nothingness and death? Is there any virtue in caring for nature if this means little more than "building our paltry dams against the flow of entropy?"[34]

6.2 Planetary dimensions of finitude

While the ultimate destiny of the universe may be in dispute, the destiny of the earth itself can be predicted with more confidence: it will be destroyed together with the sun, our local star. Within a finite number of years (approximately five billion), the hydrogen in the sun's central regions will become depleted. The temperature of the sun will rise as it becomes a red giant star. In these final convulsions of heat, the oceans will evaporate, all forms of life on earth will whither away, and the earth itself will melt away.[35] The planet on which life as we know it evolved, will have disappeared for ever from the universe. The sun itself will eventually be reduced to a ball of burnt-out matter.[36] From the perspective of the astrophysical sciences there is therefore a very blunt answer to the question whether there is any

---

31 Quoted in Worthing (1996:180).

32 Haught (1990:166, 1993:24f) mentions the irony that many cosmic pessimists, scientists who despair about any meaningful cosmic destiny, are nevertheless ardent supporters of environmental reform. To these thinkers, the very indifference and precariousness of the universe at large makes the local domain of life on earth in all its perishability all the more worthy of preservation. In fact, Haught argues, "Too much trust in an ultimate cosmic purpose might diminish our spontaneous respect for the delicacy of living forms to which evolution has unconsciously and painfully given birth on our insignificant planet" (1990:167). However, such a tragic sense of cosmic pessimism seems to undermine a vision which could support an environmental praxis in the long run (Haught 1993:23f). If the advocates of cosmic nihilism support environmental causes it is probably on the basis of their moral and aesthetic sensitivity but despite their materialist worldview.

33 Haught (1993:24).

34 Haught (1993:115).

35 Haught (1993:115), Peacocke (1979:325).

36 Peacocke (1979:325).

hope for the earth: No! This constitutes the planetary dimension of finitude.

At first sight, these scientific predictions may seem to confirm the apocalyptic images of the earth's final destruction that remain alive in the popular imagination. Is the destiny of the earth not clearly predicted in Biblical texts such as Isaiah 51:6 and Matthew 24:6-8, 29? The sun will be darkened, the moon will not give its light, the stars will fall from heaven, the heavens will vanish like smoke and the earth will wear out like a garment.[37]

The adequacy of the exegesis of these texts is not of immediate concern here.[38] More importantly, and in terms of the ultimate destiny of the earth predicted by the astrophysical sciences, these apocalyptic images in the popular imagination contain only a half-truth. In apocalyptic visions of the annihilation of the cosmos, a new earth will rise on the other side of this destruction. The scientific predictions carry no such assurance of subsequent renewal.[39] Furthermore, these apocalyptic images usually expect the destruction of the earth, if not in the immediate future, at least within the imaginable future.[40] By contrast, the time frame suggested by the astrophysical sciences spans billions of years. Furthermore, even the worst possible nuclear catastrophe or collision with asteroids will not be able to "kill God's earth."[41] It may destroy virtually all forms of life on earth (some rudimentary forms of life will probably manage to survive such a catastrophe), but the earth itself seems destined to prevail for another few billion years.

Compared to the long-term fate *of* the planet earth, the future of any form of life *on* earth (or rather: *in* the earth's biosphere) is less predictable. If the history of the last billion years is anything to go by, planetary catastrophes will probably occur at regular intervals. In the great Cambrian extinction (540 million years ago) and again in the Permian extinction (245 million years ago) more than half of all forms of life on earth were destroyed. A similar catastrophe took place at the end of the Cretaceous era (67 million years ago).[42] Species have become extinct throughout the earth's evolutionary history.[43] This process is being accelerated through the current loss of biodiversity with thousands of species being driven to

---

[37] It must be added that these apocalyptic images are pale shadows of the far more dramatic predictions by the astrophysical sciences of end of the earth and of the universe itself. See Peacocke (1979:329).

[38] See Ruether (1993:61-84) for an insightful discussion of biblical apocalyptic from an ecological perspective.

[39] Ruether (1992:85).

[40] Although such a form of destruction is conceivable (e.g. through a collision between the earth and a comet) this remains, in terms of scientific calculations, extremely unlikely (Körtner 1995:140).

[41] Contra the suggestion of the title "Are we killing God's earth" (Vorster 1987).

[42] Rasmussen (1996:25f).

[43] In an article entitled "Rust is ver te zoeken" (Rest is hard to come by) Van de Beek (1989) comments that "God is continuously stirring the soup. Otherwise everything will come to a standstill. And then the whole lot will be burnt!" Evolutionary movement, with all the pain and suffering it implies, is necessary for the survival of ecosystems.

extinction each year. Barbour comments: "Their genetic libraries, built up over millions of years, are lost forever."[44] Nevertheless, some forms of life on earth seem to have the tenacity to endure even the worst catastrophes.

The future of human life is only slightly more predictable. The species *homo sapiens* will most probably disappear from the earth sooner or later. *Homo habilis* made its mark on earth about 2.6 million years ago while *homo erectus* emerged only 1.5 million years ago. Archaic forms of *homo sapiens* first appeared little more than 500,000 years ago. The Neanderthals were in Europe 100 000 years ago and evidence of religious rituals like burials date back only 30 000 years ago. The history of species suggests that the present proliferation of a (too?) highly specialized[45] human species cannot and will not endure forever. This, surely, should sober our natural anthropocentrism. We are nothing more than an episode in the cosmic and planetary drama. It is indeed possible that we will be succeeded by other, perhaps even more intelligent species on earth.[46]

How and when human life as we now know it will disappear from the earth is again much less predictable. While some forms of Christian apocalypticism may feel justified in seeing such an eventuality as the final day of God's judgment on the sins of humanity, it can hardly be linked to the expectation of the "imminent" return of Christ.[47] Christians are not only reminded to refrain from any such predictions. The end of human life on earth is simply not very predictable. Despite the worst nuclear and environmental scenarios the human species may survive for another few thousand or even a few million years.

Nonetheless, the nuclear era has brought one important difference compared to earlier expectations of the end of the world (read: the end of human life on earth). We are the first generation to know that such a catastrophe is not only an apocalyptic image; we know that and how it may be possible – and that it may occur at any time.[48] The danger of a major nuclear war was reduced considerably by the end of the Cold War but this has not and cannot undo the know-how of atomic warfare and atomic energy.[49] The ailing Russian economy, furthermore, only

---

44 Barbour (1997:278).

45 Van de Beek (1996:209-210).

46 Van de Beek (1996:192) regards the possibility of a *homo excelsior*, a species more intelligent than *homo sapiens*, as a terrifying prospect. Human hope longs for the continuation of human existence on earth, if only under better conditions.

47 Van de Beek (1996:215). He indicates that there is a tension between the popular Christian expectation of the destruction of the world at a future apocalyptic appearance of the risen Christ (which he refers to as "eschatological creationism"!) and scientific predictions, based on the available empirical evidence that the earth and the cosmos will endure much longer. Or, in the words of Hans Küng (1984:252): "... biblical eschatology is not a prognosis of end-events any more than the protology is a report of events at the beginning." To resolve this tension by separating Christian faith from empirical experience is not a legitimate escape route from the perspective of Christian apocalypticism itself.

48 Küng (1992:164).

49 Körtner (1995:174).

heightens the danger of nuclear spillage and of terrorism with nuclear weapons. Jürgen Moltmann therefore argues that we are living in the "last age" of humanity. His argument is worth quoting at length:

> The age in which we exist is the last age of humanity, for we are living at a time when the end of humanity can be brought about at any minute. The system of nuclear deterrence which has been built up and increasingly perfected has made it possible to end the life of a large part of the human race in a few hours. The nuclear winter which will follow a war with nuclear weapons will leave even the survivors no chance. This time of ours, when humanity can be brought to an end at any moment, is indeed, in a purely secular sense and without any apocalyptic images, the 'end-time'; for no one can expect that this nuclear era will be succeeded by another in which humanity's deadly threat to itself will cease to exist. The dream of 'a world without nuclear weapons' is certainly a necessary dream, but for the time being it is no more than wishful thinking. No one seriously expects that people will ever again be incapable of doing what they can do now. Anyone who has learnt the formula can never forget it again.
>
> If the nuclear age is the last age of humanity, then today the fight for humanity's survival means the fight for time. The struggle for life is the struggle against the nuclear end. We are trying to make our present end-time as end-less as possible, by giving threatened life on earth ever new time limits. This fight to stave off the end is a permanent fight for survival. It is a fight without victory, a fight without an end – at best. We can prolong this nuclear end-time, but it is an end-time in which we and all succeeding generations must live out our lives under the Damocles sword of the bomb.[50]

Sallie McFague identifies three important differences between the nuclear and the environment threats to life on earth: the environmental crisis is more subtle, more non-democratic and far more complex than the nuclear threat. Compared to the nuclear threat, ecological destruction is more hidden, imperceptible but equally deadly:

> The nuclear threat is clear and stark: it involves someone pushing the button to begin the process of annihilation. Ecological deterioration is subtle and gradual: it involves the daily, seemingly innocuous, activities of every person on the planet.[51]

6.3 Finitude as the ultimate hurdle?

One may argue that these all too long-term cosmic and planetary dimensions of finitude are not really relevant for environmental concerns in the immediate future. Most people are simply oblivious or not too bothered about gloomy scenarios concerning the long term future of the planet or even of the cosmos. It will scarcely impede or foster an environmental spirituality or praxis. There seems to be good enough reasons in the more immediate future to care for the environment (although these reasons usually remain purely anthropocentric). Likewise, the fact that I am inevitably going to die one day does not stop me from caring for that part of the

---

[50] Moltmann (1996:204-205).

[51] McFague (1993:2f).

environment which is my own body. Medical doctors spend their entire careers trying to extend the (quality) of life of their patients. These attempts are ultimately bound to fail because the eventual death of the patient is inevitable. However, this does not make the medical profession futile.[52] Where life prevails, there seems to be an imperative to nurture and protect it.

Indeed, a spirit of hope is not necessarily related to the possibility or inevitability of death. Many brave South Africans maintained a spirit of hope during the years of struggle against apartheid, often in desperate situations and despite humiliation and suffering. The inspiration behind such a spirit of hope was not deterred by the harsh reality of suffering, torture, and death. It was much less influenced by speculations about the long-term future of the cosmos.

A spirit of hope is therefore not necessarily linked to the possibility of an endless continuation of personal existence, the human species, the planet or the cosmos. Furthermore, not even the promise of some form of life beyond death seems to influence a spirit of hope directly. The promise of the resurrection of the body has seldom encouraged Christians to care for their bodies.[53] In fact, it may have caused a degree of neglect, since bodily harm will be restored in the life to come. Likewise, the promise of a new earth in the distant future will probably not inspire Christians to care for this earth.

These comments seem to indicate that the reality of finitude may be less serious for an environmental ethos and praxis. Many people are willing to accept finitude as a fact of life. This simply encourages them to enjoy life to the fullest in the here and now even though death then remains an always imminent threat. Several contemporary Christian theologians seem to think along a similar line. In fact, one may argue that the acceptance of finitude is a virtue because it acknowledges that, as human beings, we are not God. We cannot transcend the limits of our finite existence in space and time.

There is, in my view, a degree of legitimacy in these arguments. I have argued earlier that Christian eschatology should focus primarily on the predicament of sin and evil and not on the predicament of finitude. A preoccupation with finitude or life after death easily becomes speculative and remains distant from everyday concerns. A theology that focuses on the numerous and all too real dimensions of evil seems far more appropriate and less esoteric. A Christian ecological theology should focus on the present threats to life instead of the finitude of (life on) the planet somewhere in the distant future.

Does this imply that Christian eschatology may safely disregard the predicament of finitude? There are several reasons why it would be unwise to ignore the sense of despair emerging from the experience of finitude.

a) Death always implies a sense of separation. This is experienced by the loved ones who are left behind even more than by the one approaching death. The trauma of death is obviously more acute when death is caused directly (e.g. murder) or

---

52 This comment is derived from Samuel Ijsseling.

53 I am grateful to Brian Gaybba for this observation.

indirectly (e.g. car accidents) by the effects of human sin (the predicament of evil). It is nonetheless also present with death at a ripe old age.

b) Furthermore, the very real existential trauma of finitude is also experienced in the transience of each precious moment and each wasted opportunity just gone by. This sense of loss is also present in the saddening realization that a particular species has become extinct forever, or in the recollection of the earlier abundance of wildlife in a now "developed" area. That the end of human civilization may be equally traumatic is expressed in the words of Bertrand Russell:

> All the labors of the ages, all the devotion, all the inspiration, all the noon-day brightness of human genius are destined to extinction in the vast death of the solar system and the whole temple of man's achievement must inevitably be buried beneath the debris of the universe in ruins.[54]

c) The link between the predicament of evil and the predicament of finitude is even more crucial. Death implies an end to the possibility of experiencing salvation from sin or restitution from injustices. The experience of evil demands an end to unjust suffering, some form of compensation and some form of judgment on the wicked. This becomes impossible in this life when death intervenes.[55] This link between finitude and injustice will be discussed in more detail in Chapter 17.

d) The argument that a vision for the ultimate destiny of the universe has little impact on one's present ethos is less persuasive than it may appear at first sight. An encompassing vision is required to address the kind of ultimate questions about the meaning of life which religious traditions tend to grapple with. Indeed, what is the meaning of the short span of time allotted to this planet and life upon it, compared to the unimaginable duration of the universe?[56] It is the task of religious cosmologies to grapple with precisely these kind of questions (see the discussion in Chapter 7.2). Anthropocentric motivations for an environmental praxis cannot provide answers to these ultimate questions. They cannot install an ultimate vision of hope or inspire an environmental ethos. When hope disappears, life itself soon becomes meaningless. If nihilism can even lead people to destroy a healthy body (through suicide), it will certainly lead to neglect of the rest of the environment.[57]

The question therefore remains: What kind of hope is there for the earth and for ourselves? What, in the face of planetary and cosmic doom, is the significance and

---

54 Quoted in Russell (1997:196).

55 Van de Beek (1996:208) adds that the ameliorization of the world, even the quest for justice, peace and a healthy environment, simply cannot, in the light of the finitude of the history of humanity and perhaps the cosmos, be an end in itself.

56 Tillich (1963b:68).

57 See the comment by Körtner (1995:17): "Nihilism involves thinking the ambiguous sentence 'Nothing matters,' which with diabolic relentlessness steers toward global annihilation through nuclear war or through exploitation of the earth's resources."

purpose of our finite existence in space and time? Any hopes, dreams, and visions for the future are undermined by the radical finitude, not only of individual human life, but also of the earth itself and of the universe. The problem of despair thus remains closely linked to the predicament of finitude.

The question of finitude will simply have to be confronted anew. If this question is avoided the endless hope promise by the Christian gospel will soon become disillusionment by the realities of a hopeless end. That is, unless we wish to yield to the temptation of yearning for salvation *from* the earth (and not also *of* the earth), unless we wish to relinquish any continuity between my body and the resurrection of the dead, between this earth and the Christian hope for a new earth, between cosmos and eschaton. But then there remains little reason not to rejoice in the final destruction of the earth. Indeed, as Rosemary Ruether argues, "The apocalypticists may even oppose efforts to ameliorate poverty, prevent war, or clean up ecological damage, for this is to oppose God's will and retard the final deliverance!"[58]

---

[58] Ruether (1992:84).

7. The absence of God on earth

7.1 The ambiguity of human power and knowledge

The twentieth century has witnessed a breathtaking extension of the frontiers of human knowledge and power. The sciences uncovered the immeasurable expanses of the universe as well as the fathomless detail of sub-atomic particles. More importantly, the sciences managed to reconstruct, for the very first time, a single narrative of the history of the universe.

This vast extension of human knowledge has led to an equally spectacular increase in human power through technology and industry. Indeed, knowledge and education enhance power – as both the unemployed and the masses of students in South Africa realize quite clearly.[1] The impact of technical power has been multiplied through social and political organization, but more dramatically through the economic structures of business corporations, huge multi-national companies and lucrative trade agreements.

There is no need to deny the liberating benefits that (at least a certain segment of) humanity has reaped from modern science and technology. The average human life span has been extended by a generation or more, many diseases have been brought under control, enormous wealth has been produced and distributed to millions, so that human life and culture could extend beyond a mere struggle for survival. Consequently, there emerged, especially amongst the affluent, a deeply ingrained faith in the gospel of progress and continual material prosperity and in the ability of science and technology to satisfy the insatiable wants of humanity.[2]

At the same time, the extension of human knowledge and power also brought misery and despair instead of hope to the world. Scientific knowledge has become the preserve of an expert elite, leaving the general public subjected to the fascination and horror of science.[3] Furthermore, power is not only a function of technological know-how, but also of capital, ownership of the means of production, access to (cheap and well-trained) labor, access to and the control of markets, political leverage, military protection, socioeconomic contracts, and psychological willpower. In all these ways the exercise of knowledge and power can and has been contaminated by the pervasiveness of the predicament of evil, often manifested in colonialist arrogance and capitalist greed.

The achievements of science and technology have proved, as a result of this contamination, to be deeply ambiguous. As Bonhoeffer commented amidst the

---

1 Within the context of Western apathy to the many miseries that we see on television, Moltmann (1997:21) argues that knowledge does not mean power any longer: "Knowledge means powerlessness: 'after all, there's nothing we can do about it' - so we hold our tongues, and stay mute."

2 Olivier (1989:32).

3 Moltmann (1972:93).

destruction of war machinery: "The benefits of technology pale into insignificance beside its demoniacal properties."[4] The master of the machine becomes its slave. The demand for absolute liberty brings humanity to the depths of slavery.[5] There is no need to review the side-effects of technology and industry here. It has become quite evident that the yields of technology will prove to be short-lived unless they are ecologically sustainable.

The ambiguity of science and technology is the result of the domination of a particular set of values based on progress, development, production, competition and growth. The same ambiguity characterizes the drive toward progress. Although it remains the aspiration and dream of numerous people living in abject poverty to achieve a standard of living comparable to the world's affluent, once this affluence is obtained it often leads to anxiety and despair, not hope. Prosperity based on injustice can only lead to anxiety. It is impossible to be hopeful if one has to defend an island of prosperity in the midst of a continually rising sea of poverty.[6] Furthermore, as Jürgen Moltmann comments, "Progress is no longer an expression of hope, as it was in the nineteenth century. It is a fate to which people in the Industrial countries feel themselves condemned."[7] Walter Benjamin formulates it even more poignantly: "The angel of history sees the inexorable course of progress as it really is, as a heap of rubble rising toward heaven."[8] At the same time, hope has become one of the lost virtues of the Western world. Its loss infects every aspect of social and cultural life. And, as Jacques Ellul observes, "When we see hope die, death itself is present." Moltmann adds:

> Everywhere people feel deceived, abused, dispirited, exploited and estranged so that they no longer trust the inbuilt goals and hopes of our progressive societies, universities, churches and sciences. They refuse to live goal-orientated and future-conscious, since they refuse to freeze that future in its present image.[9]

This ambiguity of science and technology calls for an urgent reflection on its basic assumptions and aims. Despite the vehement protest of several of the dominant philosophical schools of the twentieth century (especially existentialism, neo-Marxism, structuralism, deconstruction) the world of technology, industry and finance remains, in terms of its basic assumptions, thoroughly secular if not positivist. This allows technocrats, bureaucrats and securocrats to determine the course of the global economy – with far-reaching consequences for the world's poor.

This dilemma is, at least in the Western world, the result of a long historical development in which a strict demarcation between science and (Christian) theology emerged. Until very recently, theology and science could coexist only on

---

4 Bonhoeffer (1995:99).

5 Bonhoeffer (1995:102).

6 Moltmann (1980:22-3).

7 Moltmann (1985:28).

8 Quoted in Sauter (1999:101).

9 Quoted in Peacocke (1979:319).

the basis of a tacit agreement to demarcate for each form of inquiry separate and non-overlapping spheres of authority.

In the discussion below we will look at the origins of the demarcation between religious and scientific cosmologies. I will show why this demarcation has devastating consequences for the self-understanding of science and technology as well as of Christian theology. Moreover, it has led to the apparent absence of God and the loss of any vibrant hope to transcend the limitations of human power and knowledge to obtain knowledge of God and of God's involvement in the world.

7.2 The retreat from cosmology in Western Christian theology

One of the classic tasks of cosmology[10] is to provide us with a story within which we can live.[11] Cosmologies provide us with a story of the origin and destiny of the universe and of the place of humanity within the cosmos.[12] They answer the questions asked by children and adults alike: Who am I? Where do I come from? What am I doing here? How should I live? Whom should I love? Where am I going? What will happen to me when I die? What must I do to be saved? Storytellers of all cultures seem to refuse to stop short of telling the cosmic story itself, however pretentious that may seem.[13]

The interest in cosmic origins may be partly speculative and explanatory but the main concern of such reflections is to understand who we are in a framework of larger significance. Cosmologies locate human life within a cosmic order across which the moral fabric of society is often woven.[14] Likewise, creation stories are

---

[10] I prefer to use the concept "cosmology" instead of "worldview" because the former clearly includes a notion of the origin and destiny of the cosmos. The concept "worldview" is often used in a more limited and anthropocentric sense, that is, with reference to views on the *human* world (society). "*Religious* cosmologies" (as distinct from *scientific* cosmologies) are usually based on religious narratives about the creation and destiny of the world (and of humanity) and sometimes develop these narratives more systematically. The discussion will focus on the legacy of the demarcation between religious and scientific cosmologies.

[11] Lindbeck (1989:95f) argues that paradigmatic stories (e.g. creation stories) play a vital role in the construction of a habitable social and religious "world" within which communities orientate themselves. These stories are not merely part of the culture of the community; the community lives within the "world" portrayed and created by these paradigmatic stories. These stories also structure the *nomos* and *ethos* of such a community and provide a frame of reference that enables people to cope with the demands of life.

[12] See the definition of cosmology by Brian Swimme (1996:98) who also distinguishes cosmology from science: "Cosmology is the story of the birth, development and destiny of the universe, told with the aim of assisting humans in their task of identifying their roles within the great drama. Science on the other hand is focused on obtaining a detailed understanding of the physical processes of the universe."

[13] Rasmussen (1994:176).

[14] Barbour (1989:128, 1997:203). There is no necessary relation between the order of nature (*cosmos*) and a particular (moral) order of society (*polis*). However, in most

recalled and celebrated in worship and ritual because they tell us who we are and how we can live in a meaningful world.[15] There seems, therefore, to be an inextricable link between cosmologies, a sense of identity and a system of moral values.[16] Or, in the words of Thomas Berry:

> For peoples, generally, their story of the universe and the human role in the universe is their primary source of intelligibility and value. Only through this story of how the universe came to be in the beginning and how it came to be as it is does, a person comes to appreciate the meaning of life or to derive the psychic energy needed to deal effectively with those crisis moments that occur in the life of the individual and in the life of the society. Such a story is the basis of ritual initiation throughout the world. It communicates the most sacred of mysteries. ... Our story not only interprets the past, it also guides and inspires our shaping the future.[17]

In the cosmology of medieval Christianity,[18] the Hebraic vision of creation was expressed within a neo-Platonic and a Ptolemaic worldview.[19] The synthesis of scholastic theology integrated the notions of God, the world and humanity in a geocentric system of harmonious relationships. Ian Barbour explains that this hierarchically ordered[20] scheme was easily visualized and corresponded to the commonsense experience of the solidity of the earth:

> Here *position* and *destiny* coincided. Humanity was unique and central in both location and importance; the divine was more perfect and comprehensive, separated both geographically and metaphysically from the created order. Within this overall pattern, every entity from greatest to least had its status and purpose in the graded *hierarchy of reality*: God, planets, angels, men, women, animals, and plants. Everything was in its

---

cultures these two aspects are merged into what Toulmin (1990:67) calls a single "cosmopolis".

15 Barbour (1989:146).

16 Rasmussen (1994:178). See also the very different assessment of the link between cosmology and ethics by Ellis & Murphy (1996).

17 Berry (1988:xi).

18 For a description of the medieval theological cosmology, see Wildiers (1982).

19 Toulmin (1990:68) argues that explicit cosmologies did not play any central role in medieval Christian theology. Since Augustine, the focus has been on the human failure to maintain the *moral* order. The spiritual disciplines and the message of salvation addressed this problem. It was only during the time of the Renaissance that the recovery of classical texts reawakened the concern with cosmology. However, my argument here is that the moral order of medieval theology was built on the foundation of a Ptolemaic cosmology. When this cosmology was undermined the moral order and the theology of salvation was also undermined.

20 According to Wildiers (1982:136f), theologians in the Middle Ages had no doubt that God created a perfect order in the universe. God is a God of perfect order. Cosmos is therefore synonymous with order. We simply need to look at the "book of nature" to discover this order. Sin may be regarded as the disturbance of this order and redemption and eschatology as the restoration of this order.

neatly arranged place in an integrated total plan. It was a law-abiding world, but the laws were moral and not mechanical.[21]

This cosmology provided some security and stability to the medieval *corpus Christianum.* Within this "symbolic universe" (Berger) the medieval social order received an ultimate theological justification, an absolute legitimacy and a universality of scope.[22] In this self-contained cosmology the whole world and its network of relationships could find ultimate meaning and security in a God who "holds the whole world in *his* hands."

If God was the supreme entity in the hierarchy of being, humanity was the center of the cosmic drama. Nature was subordinate to humanity. Nature provided the stage setting for the drama of God's interaction with humanity. In the medieval hierarchy lesser creatures were designed to serve human interests. While this scheme was ultimately theocentric, its portrayal of the world remained curiously anthropocentric.[23]

The story of the fragmentation of this theological cosmology is as complex as the history of Europe since that time.[24] Among the many factors contributing to this process, one may mention the following: the almost tangible sense of cosmic insecurity caused by the Black death,[25] the technological advances throughout the Middle Ages, the development of a Franciscan interest in observing the "book of nature", the purely theoretical postulate of the unlimited character of the universe (1440) by Cusanus,[26] the political and economic impact of the Reformation, the journeys of exploration and exploitation into new worlds by Columbus and others, the new astronomy of Copernicus,[27] Galileo and Kepler,[28] the new empirical mode

---

21 Barbour (1997:6).

22 See Berger & Luckmann's (1967:112f) classic analysis of symbolic universes. The universal scope and absolute validity of a symbolic universe is of special importance here. When these dimensions are undermined, a symbolic universe no longer defines the "whole" and thus becomes a symbolic sub-universe.

23 Barbour (1997:8-9).

24 Oberman (1986:25) describes the late Middle Ages (before the dawn of the protestant reformation) also as "the Age of Crisis" in every conceivable sphere. The synthesis provided by Scholastic theology was already beginning to crumble. See Oberman (1986:25-32).

25 According to Berry (1988:125), two distinct responses to the plague emerged: one looked towards a religious redemption from this tragic world and the other towards greater control of the physical world to escape its pain. These two approaches still exemplify modern tendencies (towards a purely religious community or towards scientific knowledge, technological control and industrial power).

26 This postulate sowed the seed of the fragmentation of the medieval cosmology. If the universe itself could be conceived of as unlimited (and not limited, closed, and hierarchical), its center is everywhere, its circumference nowhere and its relationship with an infinite God obscure (see Wildiers 1973:154-156).

27 The most revolutionary aspect of the theory of Copernicus was perhaps not his claim that the sun is at the center of planetary motions, but that this theory attempted to

of inquiry introduced by Bacon,[29] the rationalism of Descartes and, eventually, the comprehensive mechanical view of the universe developed by Newton.

The medieval synthesis, in which the place of God, the world and humanity were clearly indicated, and the sense of security provided by this cosmology, were gradually lost in this process.[30] Since the time of Newton's mechanical description of nature (and contrary to his own intentions), the physical world was increasingly rendered autonomous.

The famous *questions* raised by Luther (Where can I find a God of grace?), by the Heidelberg Catechism[31] (What is your only comfort in life and in death?[32]) and by Descartes[33] (Where can I find a point of departure which is beyond doubt?) all

---

describe reality itself. This constituted a move away from the Platonic conception of cosmology as the contemplation of the mind to a cosmology based on the senses. This new mode of observation and the search for empirical evidence featured increasingly in the work of Kepler and Galileo (see Wilkinson 1991:148-9).

28 See the detailed discussion of Wildiers (1973:160f) on the impact that these three astronomers had on the fragmentation of the medieval cosmology. Wildiers (1973:189) notes the remarkable fact that an astronomical paradigm shift eventually led to a complete revolution in Western culture. Ruether (1992:33) adds: "Not only did the heliocentric view shift the entire focus of reality from an earth-centered world to one where the earth was a minor planet circling around the sun, but it also destroyed a whole moral and spiritual system that had been built on this earth-centered view."

29 See the brief but telling assessment of Bacon by Swimme and Berry (1992:230): "Francis Bacon (1561-1626) ... established the basic pragmatic orientation that envisaged the scientific venture as serving human welfare, giving to science its commission to besiege the natural world until nature would give up its secrets in the service of the human."

30 See Oberman (1986:25-32) for more detail on this process.

31 See Kehm's comments (1992:199) on the anthropocentrism of the Heidelberg Catechism: "The Heidelberg Catechism has been praised for its pronounced personalizing of the meaning of the doctrines of the Christian faith. Beginning with the answer to the first question, the leitmotif of the catechism is that 'everything must fit his purpose for my salvation' ... Whatever 'pastoral' benefit may be provided by such teaching, an individualistic or, at best, tribal view of salvation and an anthropocentric view of the world are what it communicates."

32 The historical context in which the Heidelberg Catechism (1563) was written was one of great political, military, ecclesial and religious turmoil. It was the time of the Counter-Reformation, of protracted religious wars and of vehement theological controversies among Catholics, Lutherans, Calvinists and Anabaptists. The fragmentation of the *corpus Christianum* and the medieval theological cosmology understandably led to anxiety and insecurity. The questions raised by Luther and by the Heidelberg Catechism therefore did not merely reflect a need for a purely personal or quasi-existentialist sense of comfort.

33 See Toulmin (1990:56f) for an illuminating discussion of the trauma caused by the Thirty Years' War (1618-1648) as the background to Descartes' philosophy. Toulmin argues that the appeal of the "quest for certainty" in Descartes' rationalism should be understood as a desperate and somewhat reactionary attempt to cope with the anxiety, trauma and chaos of the early seventeenth century. By 1648, the collapse of the old

reflect to some extent this new cosmological insecurity.[34] In their different forms these questions relate to the problem as to where humanity may find a place, an anchor in an infinite cosmos that could no longer be based on a divinely guaranteed order. These questions reflect the insecurity of a world within which the system of harmonious relationships between God, the world and humanity has become obscure.

In an infinite universe there would seem to be no fixed theological, moral or epistemological center. Every position is a relative one.[35] Pascal was one of the first witnesses to express this feeling of being homeless in an endless universe: "The eternal silence of these infinite spaces frightens me."[36] Stephen Toulmin reads the poetry of John Donne (1611) as a lament for the disintegration of the medieval synthesis, introduced by the "new philosophers". In *An anatomie of the world* (1611) Donne observes that:

> 'Tis all in peeces, all cohaerance gone;
> All just supply, and all Relation;[37]

Or, in the words of Toulmin himself:

> Once the earth was displaced so that it became one of the minor planets of the sun, instead of occupying the center of the cosmos, albeit its corrupted center, people lost their former sense of "knowing where they were" in the overall scheme of things ...[38]

The anthropocentrism of the *answers* provided by subsequent generations of theo-

---

world order became evident. Descartes and Newton laid the foundations for a new cosmology based on mathematical certainty (Toulmin 1990:83).

34 It is unlikely that the cosmological fragmentation caused by the Copernican revolution had an impact as early as the sixteenth century. The Heidelberg Catechism followed just twenty years after the publication in 1543 of Copernicus' work, *De revolutionibus orbium coelestium* (published, interestingly enough by Osiander, the reformer at Nürnberg). Scholder (1990:46, 52-3) concludes: "... the consequences of the Copernican shift were not in fact obvious even to experts during the sixteenth century." However, it is perhaps equally valid to argue that, "Copernicus crowned an era hungry for reality, groping for answers, and seeking to initiate change" (Oberman 1986:201).

35 Moltmann (1985:142).

36 *Pensées* no. 206. Pascal here prefers to not even examine the opinion of Copernicus but to deal with the question whether the soul is mortal or immortal (*Pensées* no. 218). See Moltmann (1985:141f), Wildiers (1973:195f).

37 Toulmin (1990:v).

38 Toulmin (1982:221). See Toulmin (1982:219f, 1990:62f) for a discussion of this poem (1611). This poem follows a year after the publication of Galileo's *Sidereus nuncius* (1610) and reflects the same cosmological uncertainty in a world in which "all coherence is gone". The "new" astronomy was not only a new theory about the motion of the planets; it undermined the entire cosmopolis (Toulmin 1990:67). See Wildiers (1973:191) for a similar analysis of the poems of Shakespeare (1564-1616). The disorder in human society reflects the apparent cosmic disorder.

logians and philosophers (the *humanum* of humanism, the *cogito* of Descartes,[39] the "heart" of Pascal, the *ratio* of the Enlightenment, the empirical evidence of empiricism, the transcendental categories of consciousness of Kant, the "feeling of absolute dependence" of Schleiermacher, the quest for existential meaning in existential philosophy, etc.) could, in principle, not provide solutions to a problem which was not merely anthropological but cosmological in scope.

The fragmentation of the medieval cosmology also led to a detachment of scientific cosmologies from theological cosmologies.[40] This was, of course, prompted by the responses of the Roman Catholic Church to the emerging theories of Copernicus, Galileo and later Darwin. The church desperately tried to keep the legitimacy of the old cosmological myths intact. In 1633 this led to the infamous trial and condemnation of Galileo. The sciences hereafter gradually emancipated themselves from the medieval theological cosmology. Science and theology (until recently) increasingly drifted apart, even though some scientists (most notably Newton himself) believed that their work had a theological rationale and significance.

This process had a disastrous impact on Christian theology itself. Christian theology could no longer provide satisfactory answers to the problems energetically posed by new generations of philosophers, astronomers and scientists. In the emerging new world, it was simply impossible to fulfill the classic task of religious cosmologies: to provide a sense of the whole and of where we fit into it, a frame of reference with ultimate explanatory power, absolute legitimacy, moral cohesion and cosmic scope.[41] Theologians who were still clinging to discredited cosmological doctrines were fighting a losing battle. Those who were enthusiastically baptizing new scientific theories theologically found themselves stranded whenever these theories subsequently became outdated.[42] Indeed, a theology that marries the science of today may well be a widow tomorrow.[43]

Faced with this dilemma, Christian theology found an escape route in what

---

39 The dualism of Descartes, separating humanity from nature and mind from matter, led to a fragmentation of the single unified order evident in the Greek notion of cosmos. The worldview of Descartes and Newton therefore no longer represented a genuine *cosmos* (Toulmin 1982:224).

40 The new interest in astronomy was often born from and motivated by theological concerns. One may even argue that the astronomers pointed their telescopes to the sky in search of traces of God. For Galileo, Kepler and Newton, there was an intimate relation between theological and scientific understanding. Newton saw himself as a theologian as well as a scientist. He was describing the way in which the divine functions in the universe (Swimme & Berry 1992:227). However, the *results* of these investigations soon led to a tension between scientific and theological cosmologies.

41 Providing comprehensive views on the world, religions inevitably also give rise to cosmological reflection (see Boff 1995:62).

42 The order of the classic cosmology (and the harmony and "design" of the seventeenth-century worldview) was soon replaced by the more historic and uncertain notions of evolution and adaptation (Toulmin 1982:260).

43 Peacocke (1989:11).

Moltmann calls a "theological retreat from cosmology into personal faith."[44] In an attempt to protect itself from the scientific questioning of the status of the biblical creation narratives, Christian theology tried to demarcate its own field of specialization by detaching the doctrine of creation from cosmology.[45] Moltmann comments:

> So all that remained was the reduction of the doctrine of creation to the personal faith which says that human beings have to put their trust in God the Creator, not in his creatures. In order to protect itself from scientific attack, the Protestant theology of modern times liked to explain faith in creation as an expression of the feeling of absolute dependence. That is to say, it was interpreted as an existential truth.[46]

Moltmann continues:

> After its retreat from cosmology, theology concentrated on personal faith. "I believe that God created me ..." as Luther's Short Catechism says. Of course all belief in creation includes that personal conviction. But this personal confession of faith was now increasingly interpreted in an exclusive sense, although it was meant inclusively: for Luther goes on "together with all creatures."[47]

Due to the growing demarcation between science and theology, creation theology was gradually detached from (scientific) cosmologies. Expositions of the doctrine of creation no longer maintain a cosmological scope in their inquiries. In this theological climate, creation theology itself has often been marginalized. In Biblical theology, due to the influence of Gerhard von Rad and others, the belief in a creator God has often been regarded as a mere extrapolation of the belief in the Savior and Liberator.[48] In systematic theology, the almost exclusive focus on the

---

44 Moltmann (1985:34).

45 Moltmann (1985:34-5) explains the impact of this line of demarcation between science and theology in the following way:

> Johannes Kepler, like Galileo after him, maintained the view that God's intention in the Bible was not to correct erroneous opinions about the world, or to save people the effort of investigation. His sole purpose was to reveal to human beings everything that was necessary for their salvation. This Reformation tendency to interpret the biblical traditions in the light of the human – and indeed personal – questions of salvation was subsequently felt to be liberating, and is occasionally still seen as such today. ... But this concentration on the salvation of the individual person also cut theology off from human ways of knowing and mastering the world. Theology's domain became the soul's assurance of salvation in the inner citadel of the heart. The earthly, bodily and cosmic dimensions of the salvation of the whole world were overlooked.

46 Moltmann (1985:33).

47 Moltmann (1985:36).

48 Although the belief in God's salvation probably still has a noetic priority over a belief in God as creator, this noetic priority should not be allowed to become an ontic priority (see Durand 1982:84).

doctrine of redemption (or liberation[49]) has until recently not been paralleled by new explorations of the doctrine of creation.[50] There has indeed been an "eclipse of creation" in many twentieth century systematic theologies. Also in popular piety the diminished role of faith in creation was and often still is evident.[51]

As a result of these developments, Christian theology has focused increasingly on the problem of human (personal or societal) salvation or liberation. Preoccupied with the "inner agenda of guilt", theologians became unable to respond to the "outer agenda" of ecological despair.[52] Nature was only regarded as the "stage" (Calvin) for salvation history.[53] Human history alone has been seen as a sphere in which God can touch our reality, hence the natural world has more and more been considered irrelevant to theology.[54] At worst, redemption was portrayed as a future event whereby believers will be finally rescued *from* this world.[55] McDonagh comments on this escape route:

> Religious thinkers withdrew their attention from wider cosmic, earthly, and even cultural concerns and began to concentrate almost exclusively on the uniqueness of the Christian story. Consequently the theology of creation was generally ignored and almost all theological inquiry was confined to the process of redemption and salvation, the personality of Jesus, the interior spiritual disciplines needed to guide the individual soul along the path of salvation, and the internal constitution and juridical status of the ecclesial community.[56]

---

49 Liberation theologians (with notable exceptions such as Leonardo Boff) have until recently also limited their concern to *human* well-being (see McFague 1991:22, Landes 1984:140).

50 Tracy (1994:76).

51 Landes (1984:140).

52 Santmire (1989:267).

53 McDonagh (1986:62-3) asks instead: "(Is) the twenty billion years of God's creative love simply ... a stage on which the drama of human salvation is worked out?"

54 McFague (1991:22).

55 The hope for a cosmic redemption has biblical roots (Isa 11:6-9; 65:17, 25; Col 1:14-20; 1 Cor 15:28; Eph 1:10, Rom 8:19-22). In Western theology, expressions of this hope became relatively rare, but it was kept alive in Eastern Orthodoxy. Mainline Christianity saw the world as going downhill towards destruction (Ruether 1992:237). The ecological consciousness of the last few decades has led to a re-emergence of this hope for the redemption *of* the world as opposed to the redemption of believers *from* the world (see Nash 1991:125-132).

56 McDonagh (1986:62-3) argues that the problem could be traced back to the roots of the Western tradition in the theology of Augustine:

> Since the late Middle Ages and particularly since the Reformation, there has been an almost exclusive concentration in the western theological tradition on a Fall / Redemption theology, much of which can be traced back to Augustine. This theological tradition has no adequate theology of creation. The twenty billion years of God's creative love is simply seen either as the stage on which the drama of human

The retreat from cosmology and subsequently from creation theology eventually led to an impasse in soteriology itself. With the fragmentation of the medieval cosmology, the relationship between God, the world and humanity became obscure. Christian theology responded by desperately trying to heal the broken relationship between humanity and an increasingly transcendent God. The questions raised by Luther, the Heidelberg Catechism and others could (in principle) not be answered adequately because the insecurity that they wished to address was not only personal or societal, but also cosmic in scope. When the relationship between God and the world is obscured, it becomes virtually impossible to address the relationship between God and humanity adequately. The relationship between humanity and the cosmos therefore also remained obscure.[57]

This retreat from cosmology into personal faith had a similar impact on Christian eschatology. The hope for a new creation dissipated in modern eschatologies – which became focused more and more on history and, within the sphere of history, on individual human existence. The dominant question became: What hope is there for me? Any interest in the destiny of the universe was confined to scientific discourse only. Moltmann comments:

> In this process nothing split apart more widely than cosmology and eschatology. But without cosmology, eschatology must inevitably turn into a Gnostic myth of redemption, as modern existentialism shows.[58]

There is no redemption for human beings without the redemption of nature. There can be no eternal life for human beings without a change in the cosmic conditions of life. There can be no resurrection of the body without a resurrection of ecosystems. Although this hope is still expressed in eschatological visions of the resurrection of the dead and the coming of the new earth, the difficulties of actually conceiving this hope have become considerable as a result of the new cosmology.[59]

In this way, the retreat from cosmology led to a major impoverishment and distortion of Christian understandings of salvation, liberation and hope.[60]

---

salvation is worked out, or as something radically sinful in itself and needing transformation.

For a different appraisal of Augustine's ecological legacy, see Santmire (1985:55-74).

57 See McFague (1993:34): "We have lost the sense of belonging in our world and to the God who creates, nurtures, and redeems this world and all its creatures, and we have lost the sense that we are part of a living, changing, dynamic cosmos that has its being in and through God."

58 Moltmann (1996:260).

59 Moltmann (1996:260).

60 Tracy (1994:76). The line of demarcation between theology and science also did not guarantee that Christian theology would be left untouched by emerging scientific theories: "There can be little doubt that the events symbolized by the names Copernicus, Galileo, Newton, and Darwin changed forever the landscape of theological thought." (Tracy 1994:74).

7.3 The legacy of this retreat from cosmology

The theological retreat from cosmology did not affect Christian theology only. Let us look at three further dimensions of the legacy of this retreat from cosmology:

a) The legacy on the self-understanding of science and technology;
b) The legacy of the retreat from cosmology in South Africa;
c) The moral legacy: nihilism and a loss of a sense of identity.

a) The legacy on the self-understanding of science and technology

The segregation between theological and scientific cosmologies eventually had an ambiguous impact on (the self-understanding of) science and technology.

Despite the theological retreat from cosmology, the tension between theological views and emerging scientific theories continued to simmer for several centuries. This tension again flared up with the publication of Darwin's *On the origin of species* (1859).[61] The tension between theological views and scientific theories was eventually "resolved" by the tacit agreement to demarcate for each form of inquiry separate and non-overlapping spheres of authority. This separation of the spheres of science and religion followed the Kantian split between *reine Vernunft* and the *praktische Vernunft*, between facts and values, between that which can be empirically observed and scientifically verified and that which belongs to a realm beyond that: the ethical, the aesthetic and the spiritual.[62] Theology and science could therefore coexist by tacitly agreeing not to communicate with each other.

The detachment of the sciences from theological cosmologies was a necessary requirement for the emancipation of scientific inquiry from ecclesial and theological tutelage. The emergence of scientific cosmologies following the astronomical research of Copernicus, Kepler and Galileo indeed constituted the birth of modern science. Without this detachment from theological cosmologies, the spectacular achievements of science and technology would not have been possible.

However, as we have seen above, these achievements have now proved to be deeply ambiguous. Without sustained philosophical, religious and theological reflection on its basic assumptions and aims, science and technology seem to run into their own impasses. In fact, the former theological worldviews have simply been replaced by secular worldviews, whether mechanical, materialist, Newtonian, positivist, capitalist, industrialist, technocratic, or consumerist.[63] There is a clear

---

61 The theory of Darwin was indeed the second major blow (besides the one dealt by Copernicus) to the received Christian cosmology. See Ruether (1992:34).

62 Ruether (1992:35).

63 Despite the (legitimate) postmodern protests against closed systems, some form of comprehensive worldview or frame of reference seems to be unavoidable. "We are", argues Rasmussen (1994:178), "incorrigibly cosmic storytellers." The postmodern critique against "foundations", "objectivism" (Bernstein), "grand narratives" (Lyotard), or "large, overarching, communal vocabularies" (Rorty), appropriately undermines any notion that an existing underlying, unifying principle can be excavated or *identified*.

need for science and technology to reflect on its own basic assumptions and aims. The environmental crisis is functioning as a global antenna indicating that the strict demarcation between science and religion is defective.[64]

This demarcation between science and theology has also been undermined by recent developments within the philosophy of science. Although mechanistic, materialist and positivist notions of science are still alive in the popular imagination, these notions have been challenged by the changing paradigm in the philosophy of science (viz. the contributions of Barbour, Feyerabend, Hanson, Kuhn, Lakatos, Polanyi, Popper, Toulmin). It has also been undermined by developments in the sciences themselves (e.g. relativity theory, quantum and particle physics, evolutionary biology, DNA research, theories of chaos and complexity, etc.[65]). David Tracy insists that this shift in scientific self-understanding and the collapse of earlier mechanistic, materialist, and positivist models "... has freed science itself to a sense of the ultimate mystery of reality and to a chastened but real willingness to dialogue with any plausible philosophical and theological cosmological hypotheses."[66] The neat separation between religious and scientific cosmologies therefore seems to be clearly defunct.

b) The legacy of the retreat from cosmology in South Africa

There is no need here to document the roots and bitter fruits of the economic and social practices, political policy and theology of apartheid. The political policy of apartheid reinforced the divisions of class and race that had developed over centuries of colonial rule into a bitterly oppressive socioeconomic practice. The theology of apartheid provided a moral legitimation for these practices and policies.

It is, however, interesting to note that the theology of apartheid was, at its very roots, expressed as form of cosmology, one based on a particular brand of Kuyperianism and on the neo-Calvinist philosophies of Dooyeweerd and Stoker. The most prominent feature of this cosmology was its version of the doctrine of the "orders of creation".[67] God ordained (in creation) several distinct spheres of life (e.g. marriage, family, labor, arts, law, science, religion, ethnicity, nations, etc). To live

---

However, it is also possible to argue that social constructs such as "horizons" (Gadamer), "fiduciary frameworks" (Polanyi), "symbolic universes" (Berger), "language games" (Wittgenstein), "epistemes" (Foucault), paradoxical umbrellas (Wayne Booth) or "world-construction" (see Gordon Kaufman) do not *identify* but *create*, or attempt to create, a certain unity within a particular context. To prevent cognitive dissonance some form of *unifying* frame may therefore be necessary (*unificare* = not to *find* but to *create* a coherent whole).

64 Siegwalt (1975:225f).

65 See Russell's overview (1994) of factors in history, the philosophy of science, the sciences and in theology which questions the compartmentalizing of science and theology. See Chapter 14 for a more detailed discussion in this regard.

66 Tracy (1994:74).

67 See Peters (1989:102f) for a similar assessment of this notion of the orders of creation.

according to the orders of creation is to live according to God's will and to obtain God's blessing; whereas to attempt to live outside these orders is to court judgment and ruin. The way things are, is presumably the way things should remain.

Each of these spheres of life was said to be *sovereign within its own domain.*[68] This was translated into support for the idea that the variety of races, peoples and nations (with a reference to Babel) also had to retain their own sovereignty and therefore should remain "apart" from one another (hence apart-heid = "apartness").

Again, the details of this cosmology need not occupy us here. What is important, though, is to note that this theology could emerge because it filled the existing cosmological vacuum. This vacuum was precisely the result of the retreat from cosmology described above. The dominant theology amongst white Afrikaners was (before the advent of the theology of apartheid) a peculiar blend of the reformed theology of Kuyper and Bavinck, Scottish evangelicalism, and pietism.[69] However, a theology preoccupied with human (personal) salvation could not provide remedies to the urgent social, economic and political problems experienced in South Africa at that time. A theology was required that could provide a clear outline of the structure and basic aims of society. Lacking any articulated cosmology on which to establish such a social theology, a vacuum remained that was filled by the fatal ideological experiments of "apartheid", "separate development" and their theological rationalizations. However much one may despise the answers provided by apartheid theologians, one should recognize the pertinent questions which they raised and the cosmological scope of these questions. These questions seem to be far more adequate and penetrating than the limited concern with (individual) human salvation of many other reformed theologians of that time. The mistake of apartheid theology was not *that* it engaged in cosmological reflection, but the specific way in which this cosmology was developed to legitimize racist and classist practices.[70]

Ironically, while some were struggling to fill this cosmological vacuum, there were already forces at work that led to the increasing disintegration of the traditional worldviews (and the social fabric) of rural African communities. As in most traditional societies, these worldviews were essentially of a cosmological nature – telling stories of the origin of the universe and locating human societies within the cosmos. The plausibility of these cosmologies was gradually undermined by the impact of colonial rule and the processes of urbanization, industrialization, modernization, Christianization, etc.

The net result of these processes has been the disintegration of the fabric of society and its network of social relationships. Without the support of a broad cosmology, people are no longer sure where they fit into the world, how they should relate to other members of the family, clan and community, how they

---

68 This notion of sovereignty within the own domain soon turned into one of being totalitarian within the own domain (Durand 1985).

69 See Bosch (1984), Durand (1985), Kinghorn (1986:45f).

70 Kinghorn (1990:97).

should understand their own identity, how they should contribute to maintaining this social fabric, and so forth. In the words of Harvey Sindima: "Corrupt a people's thought systems and you have destroyed their value system; you have ruined the 'world' or cosmology which informs their way of life."[71] The disintegration of these traditional cosmologies (together with the increasing problem of the scarcity of resources) is perhaps evident in the present levels of crime, corruption, violence and a sense of rootlessness and moral bankruptcy in some spheres of the South African society.

Despite these processes, it is remarkable to note that the vision of many recent South African social theologies remains comprehensive (if not cosmological) in scope. This applies to the emerging theologies of African Instituted Churches and to theological reflections on the Reconstruction and Development Programme and the Truth and Reconciliation Commission.

c) The moral legacy: the loss of a sense of identity

Sean McDonagh comments that the malaise of modernity is in large measure due to a loss of a meaningful sense of identity.[72] Such a sense of identity is usually provided by comprehensive myths or stories that account for the emergence of the world and explain our place and role in the world. Without these comprehensive myths or stories people lose their sense of place. And if you no longer know where you fit in, everything becomes permissible. This concern for the loss of identity is echoed by Thomas Berry:

> It's all a question of story. We are in trouble just now because we do not have a good story. We are in between stories. The old story, the account of how the world came to be and how we fit into it, is no longer effective. We have not yet learned the new story. Our traditional story of the universe sustained us for a long period of time. It shaped our emotional attitudes, provided us with life purposes, and energized action. It consecrated suffering and integrated knowledge. We awoke in the morning and knew where we were. We could answer the questions of our children. We could identify crime, punish transgressors. Everything was taken care of because the story was there ...[73]

This loss of a sense of identity and place is not only unfortunate for humans; it has had devastating ecological consequences. We are, says Loren Eisly, the strange species which ...

> ... opened a vast hole in nature, sucked down the lightning, wrenched apart the atom, ripped open the seams of the earth, and drowned the ancient sounds of nature in a cacophony of wild and deadening noises that riddled the skies, shuddered the ground, and wilted the once proud grasses.[74]

---

71 Sindima (1989:541).

72 McDonagh (1986:61).

73 Berry (1988:123).

74 From *The immense journey*, quoted in Rasmussen (1991:357).

This loss of identity is most evident in nihilism, the classic expression of despair in the Western world. Körtner comments on the ecological significance of nihilism: "Nihilism involves thinking the ambiguous sentence 'Nothing matters,' which with diabolic relentlessness steers toward global annihilation through nuclear war or through exploitation of the earth's resources."[75]

In 1979 Arthur Peacocke observed that the comment of Proverbs 29:18, that people perish where there is no vision, applies more than ever to Western civilization. He says:

> In the Western industrialized world, the sensitive experience *Angst* and despair, and the insensitive indulge in a frenetic search for substitute ends – in domestic mechaniczation and other manifestations of private affluence, in elaborate holidays, in lethal speeds, in world-escaping religions of personal salvation, in cults of UFO's and space fiction and even in the occult. ... Those in control of the world's resources of power become more and more apprehensive of the future. We suspect that 'we've never had it so good' and we'll never have it again. There seems to be a widespread loss of faith in the ability of the future to bring something which is actually more fulfilling into men's lives.[76]

In South Africa this loss of identity has allowed the policies of colonialism, classism and racism to continue unbridled. And in the present dispensation it has led to the deterioration of the moral fabric of the South African society as a whole. The moral order of society seems to collapse whenever the sense of cosmic order becomes in disarray.[77]

7.4 A theological postscript on the retreat from cosmology

These legacies of the retreat from cosmology call for some further reflection to clarify its eschatological implications. Let us retrace the sequence of observations on the predicament of the limitations of human knowledge and power thus far.

In Chapter 2 we noted some of the ways which humans have followed through the ages to extend the limitations of their knowledge and power: philosophy, the sciences, technology, as well as social, economic, political and military organizational structures. In Chapter 3 we noted that Christian eschatology has, at times, been extrapolated to respond to the predicament of human limitedness in space. In the presence of an omnipotent and omniscient God our quest to extend our human knowledge and power will finally come to fruition.

In this chapter we noted the exponential growth in human knowledge and power, most notably in this century. The ambiguities of these achievements have also become clear. In the Western world, more importantly, the extension of human knowledge led to the dismantling of the Ptolemaic cosmology and its replacement by a succession of Newtonian, positivist, humanist and secular worldviews. Through these historical processes the dynamic and lively interaction

---

75 Körtner (1995:17).

76 Peacocke (1979:319-320).

77 Wildiers (1973:188).

between God and the world became obscured for many. Often medieval theism was replaced by deism, pantheism, atheism, nihilism or simply secularism. God became unemployed as the remaining gaps left to be filled by an increasingly transcendent God became fewer and fewer.

In the Western world the presumed absence of God still dominates the theological agenda. How can God's immanence in the world be clarified and how can God's transcendence be made intelligible in a post-Ptolemaic world? How exactly should one understand the possibility of God acting in the world? This is by no means an easy task. When our children ask us: "Where is God?" many pious people still point to the heavens somewhere above to provide a feeble Ptolemaic answer.

In the non-Western world (and often elsewhere) the theological agenda is also dominated by the absence of God, but in a different sense. This notion of the absence of God assumes the possibility of presence and is therefore quite different from deism or an atheistic denial of God's existence. The observation of God's absence is born from moral indignation. The apparent absence of God becomes the only feasible interpretation of experiences of evil, injustice and suffering.[78] Eschatology responds to this absence of God (the predicament of evil!) by reflecting on God's promise of salvation and the preliminary fulfillment of God's promises (e.g. in Jesus Christ).

How could or should Christian eschatology respond to the absence of God in the first sense? How should it respond to the predicament of human limitations in space – if at all? Should we not simply learn to accept the limitations of human knowledge and to acknowledge our limited control over the power that we do exercise? Is this acceptance of limitations not the prerequisite for an acknowledgement of God's transcendence? And is it not a prerequisite to confront the devastating (ecological) legacy of our relentless quest for knowledge and power? Can Christian eschatology therefore afford to offer the world the possibility of ultimately transcending human limitations?

In response to these questions, I argue that Christian eschatology should indeed focus on the predicament of evil and human sin. A preoccupation with the predicament of human limitations (in space) can all too easily degenerate into an intellectualist and rather abstract pursuit to find a place for God in the world of human knowledge and power (e.g. natural theology). Even the opposite (Barthian) strategy, that is, of finding a place for human knowledge and power in God's world, only becomes justifiable when its point of departure is the reality of sin (understood as misplacement?).

Does this imply that an extrapolation of Christian eschatology to respond to the predicament of human limitations in space Human knowledge and power) is invalid? In Chapter 18 I will argue that this pursuit remains important and to some extent inevitable. If Christian eschatology maintains that it is indeed God (and not human abilities) who will ultimately establish victory over evil and salvation from

---

78 See the perceptive distinction by Drees (1990:5f) between two types of theology (and of eschatology) based on a response to either the presence or the apparent absence of God.

sin, the immanence and transcendence of God needs to be sufficiently intelligible. The legacy of a retreat from cosmology into personal salvation provides a clear indication of the dangers of not taking this task seriously enough.

8. (South) African dimensions of despair

A few concluding notes

A sense of nihilism, doom and despair may be typical of only some sectors of the South African population. A remarkable spirit of hope still prevails in South Africa despite the daunting social and economic challenges facing the country and the sub-continent. Perhaps Klaus Nürnberger's comment is nevertheless valid for the South African context as well:

> Modern humanity is torn apart between the 'progressive' fervour of technological optimism and revolutionary enthusiasm, on the one hand, and fear of rapid deterioration and catastrophe on the other. Population growth, environmental pollution, breakdown of moral values and social cohesion, the growth of violence and brutality, the emergence of new diseases, the threat of nuclear holocaust these are the spectres of our time.[1]

Painting scenario's of the future in South African is the hobby of all South Africans and the task of analysts at every level of society. This chapter certainly cannot do justice to the complexities required for such a sophisticated analysis.[2] Yet, the challenges facing us seem clear:

- Meeting basic needs for nutrition, housing, water, electricity, health care, social welfare, etc;
- Developing human resources in terms of education, training, culture and recreation;
- Building the economy in terms of trade and commerce, finance, labor policies, development of each sector of the economy and above all finding opportunities for employment;
- Developing civil society through participation in decision making at all levels, encouraging tolerance and curbing crime and corruption;
- Building social cohesion through family life (both in nuclear families and traditional extended families) and community structures, retrieving a sense of cultural identity;
- Ensuring a clean and healthy environment.[3]

These political, economic and social challenges have to be understood within the context of global and regional forces. These forces have resulted in a widening gap

---

1 Nürnberger (1994:148).

2 For a highly interesting, sophisticated and sober analysis of possible, probable and preferred futures in a global and South African context, see the annual research report by the Institute for Futures Research, University of Stellenbosch (Roux 1997, restricted access).

3 For a similar list, see Govender (1995:137).

between the affluent and the poor in the last two decades, a centralization and safeguarding of economic power and the globalization of an overtly consumerist culture. Konrad Raiser's assessment of the impact of globalization is appropriate here:

> Increasing numbers of people are being excluded from the 'one world' of this integrated system, condemned to mere survival on its fringes. Globalization symbolizes a form of human power which can no longer be controlled. Because the global economic and financial system recognizes no limits ... it finally becomes self-destructive.[4]

Within the African context these forces have led to a pattern of decline, not growth. The plight of Africa is well-known. One is constantly reminded of problems like poverty, unemployment, hunger, debt, armed conflict, corruption, environmental degradation and HIV/AIDS. This constant flow of bad news has led to a numbing and self-fulfilling sense of despair, both abroad and perhaps even more in Africa itself.[5] These problems are manifestations of larger economic forces beneath the surface. Ndegwa and Green provide a helpful list of the tendencies that have led to a "pattern of decline" on the African continent in the last two decades:

1) A substantial decline in average per capita income and therefore living standards;
2) A rapidly deteriorating situation in the area of employment;
3) A steady decline in per capita food production on the continent;
4) A continuing loss of export market shares as well as import dependence;
5) Sharp and continuing declines in foreign direct investment;
6) Disintegration of basic physical, market and social infrastructure;
7) Rapid urbanization leading to the enlargement of slums and severe shortages of housing and social services;
8) A sharp and widespread decline in the rate of fall or in some cases a rise of infant mortality;
9) External debt has become an unmanageable problem for most African countries;
10) Wars have caused major social and economic disruptions in several countries and these will take many years to heal;
11) Environmental degradation, especially the loss of valuable soil, forests and vegetative cover has now reached alarming levels in many countries;
12) A marginalization of Africa in international politics, especially since the end of the Cold War.[6]

---

4 Raiser (1997:24).

5 Ndegwa & Green (1994:35).

6 Ndegwa & Green (1994:1-11). The analysis of these trends does not imply that there are neither present signs of hope, nor that these trends cannot be reversed (Ndegwa & Green 1994:24). Within the context of an analysis of dimensions of despair, it does highlight the very real and daunting challenges facing the African continent.

The quest for reconstruction and development in South Africa cannot be isolated from this plight of Africa. In an exceptionally chilling contribution on the challenges facing the new South African nation, Shun Govender (1995) argues that we are living "in between times" and that this has a special impact on our children. He comments:

> Our children live in a time when the past is uninspiring and the future holds no promise. If this is so we have placed an unbearable load upon the shoulders of our children; the unbearable load being that they live in a world of shattered utopias.[7]

Govender continues to concretize these shattered utopias and identifies the following aspects:

- The myth of an egalitarian, classless society of unlimited dreams has been shattered with the collapse of the Soviet empire.
- The collapse of socialism has given capitalism, with its globalization of market forces, unfettered reign, and has unleashed the utopian myth of the consumer society upon the world as never before.
- The end of the Cold War has reunited Germany and is turning Europe into a fortress, which is again becoming a breeding ground for racism, economic greed and ethnic rivalries.
- The period of decolonization in the Third World has brought the blessings of political liberation but the curse of economic enslavement. The poor of the Third World, especially the young people, perish in overpopulated cities, overcrowded slums and ghettoes, undernourished and hopeless.
- Young people in the wealthy West are becoming more and more conservative and uncaring of the world, while young people in the rest of the poor world are becoming rebels without a cause.[8]

Konrad Raiser also observes that there are no longer rival hopes competing with each other at the end of the twentieth century: "The dominant mood at the end of this century is shaped by the conviction, actively encouraged by the powerful, that there is no alternative to the system of the global market. Those excluded from the system are condemned to hopelessness. They are expendable."[9] Raiser adds that the discrediting of all critical alternatives has created a system that is almost obliged to reproduce itself. While the poor may hope against all reasonable hope others do not know what to hope for because they have everything.[10] The younger generation in Europe seems to have difficulty entertaining visions or dreaming dreams about a more just society: "Their energy for hoping seems to have been exhausted by the effort to preserve and defend the acquired way of living."[11]

---

7 Govender (1995:140).

8 Govender (1995:140).

9 Raiser (1997:80).

10 Raiser (1997:79).

11 Raiser (1997:78).

This, then, is the century that our children are inheriting from us, a century of shattered utopias, and insurmountable problems. Govender comments again:

> As our century draws to its close, our world stands accused by its children: the homeless children on the city streets of Brazil; the glue-sniffing children on the street corners of Cape Town; the starving children of famine-ravaged poor countries, the wounded children of war-torn countries; the battered children of broken homes, the countless children in overpopulated cities who look expectantly for a chance in life; the affluent children of the rich who have lost their reason to live. What shall we say to them?[12]

Indeed, where can we find hope for the children, for our country and for the earth? Any answer to these questions will have to face the cosmic depths of despair. As John Chrysostom already said: "What plunges us into disaster is not so much our sins as our despair."[13] Surely, we dare not try to sell cheap forms of hope.

In the light of the dimensions of despair which were discussed in this and the previous chapters, it seems clear that the world in which we live needs "a theological vision of the future that is larger and deeper than the hopelessness of our souls."[14] We need a vision of hope that includes hope for the earth. Where can such a vision be found? What *dare* we hope?[15]

---

12 Govender (1995:141-2).

13 Quoted in Moltmann (1997:39).

14 Santmire (1989:267).

15 See the title of Gerard Sauter's (1999) important recent study of eschatology.

Part C: The trajectories of Christian hope

In Part B we investigated the depths of ecological despair. Where can a vision of hope for the earth be found amidst such a widespread sense of despair? How can one avoid falling into the trap of offering cheap forms of hope?

An adequate answer to these questions requires a retrieval of the resources of Christian hope in the Biblical roots of Christianity and in the subsequent history of the Christian tradition. The task of Part C is to follow the trajectories of hope through the centuries until the dawn of the twentieth century. A few comments on this task are necessary:

- Biblical scholars have in recent years produced a wealth of literature on the eschatology of particular Biblical texts. These studies have indicated the radical plurality of perspectives on hope within the Bible. The socio-historical rootedness of various expressions of hope in the Bible has also become more and more apparent. To provide an overview of these contributions here would be impossible and presumptuous.
- The same rich if confusing plurality of eschatological perspectives has emerged from studies on the history of the Christian tradition. Again, it would not do justice to these studies to summarize their results in a few pages. It would also require far more erudition than what can be mustered here.
- The purpose of Part C therefore has to be modest. It serves merely as a reminder of the main trajectories in the history of Christian hope. It does not attempt to break new ground or to repeat results documented more adequately elsewhere. It simply reminds the reader of some of the important historical contributions to an expression of hope. This also explains the brevity of the various chapters in Part C. The discussion also relies heavily on several helpful summaries of the historical roots of Christian eschatology.[1]
- The eschatological "road map" suggested in Chapter 4 will again be used here. Some important shifts in the orientation of hope from one predicament to another will be indicated wherever appropriate.

A few further hermeneutical comments on the use of the notion of "trajectories" in Part C are important.

a) Walter Brueggemann's article on trajectories in the First Testament represent perhaps the most well-known use of this notion.[2] Brueggemann's analysis is rooted in the tradition history approach to Old Testament studies of Gerhard von Rad and others. Two features of this approach are important for present purposes: (i) The

---

1 See, especially Braaten (1985), Hayes (1989:15-67), McGrath (1994), McKim (1988), Nürnberger (1994).

2 Brueggemann (1993).

emphasis on a particular stable social location in which a trajectory evolves (e.g. a particular local shrine); and (ii) The emphasis on one particular symbol which becomes the root metaphor for theological reflection at that particular social location (e.g. the house of David, the law of Moses, the exodus, the temple). A trajectory is constituted when the same symbol is continuously being reinterpreted in the same social location in and for changing circumstances.

b) Brueggemann analyzes two dominant trajectories in the literature shaped and energized by the Mosaic and Davidic covenants: (i) The trajectory of "Mosaic liberation" that emerged in an early Israelite peasant revolt, in the Mushite priesthood of Shilo and Nob, in prophetic critiques, in the Deuteronomistic circle and in the displaced Levitical priesthood after the exile; and (ii) The "royal consolidation" trajectory surfaced in the Davidic-Solomonic state coup, in the Aaronid priesthood of Hebron and Jerusalem, the institutions of the monarchy and of the Priestly writings, and in the post-exilic Zadokite priesthood.[3]

c) In several recent articles Klaus Nürnberger followed a somewhat similar approach that also traces the development of certain "trajectories".[4] He focused on soteriological trajectories, that is, the memories of certain redemptive experiences that become a "soteriological paradigm" for a subsequently evolving tradition. Nürnberger cites various examples of such soteriological paradigms: the promise to the patriarchs, exodus and conquest, the divine order established by the rule of kings, covenant and law, creation and eschatological transformation, priesthood and sacrifice.

In an article on the "royal paradigm," Nürnberger traces, for example, different notions of political rule in the history of Israel, in the New Testament era and in the history of the Christian tradition. He shows how this trajectory has, at times, been influenced by new theological insights, but that these insights were distorted through ideological legitimation in subsequent times. Nürnberger then extrapolates this trajectory to reflect on the notion of democracy in the contemporary South African context.[5] In an essay on eschatology, he follows a similar approach.[6] He traces developments and distortions in the notion of hope throughout the history of the Jewish-Christian tradition and extrapolates these developments towards a contemporary Christian eschatology.

A few features of Nürnberger's approach are important. Although he does not use the notion of "trajectories" explicitly, there is a clear attempt to trace historical developments. He does not focus on a particular social location nor on a particular symbol but on a particular theme or problem to which people in different social locations, using different root metaphors, responded. He shows how aberrations of a trajectory occurred within the canonical texts but also how these aberrations were

---

3 Brueggemann (1993).

4 Nürnberger (1992, 1993, 1994, 1997).

5 Nürnberger (1992).

6 Nürnberger (1994).

often redirected in subsequent developments. The Biblical canon is regarded as a primal and prototypical period in the history of a larger tradition that includes further deliberations in the history of Christian doctrine.[7]

The extrapolation of these traditions is in both cases crucial. The task of contemporary interpretation is not to select texts that can be appropriated (directly?) within contemporary contexts. Instead, the task of interpretation involves an attempt to trace the history of a trajectory (in all its aberrations and innovations) carefully in order to identify the direction or underlying thrust of its developments, and, on that basis, to extrapolate this dynamic towards the future. Nürnberger comments:

> The hermeneutical cycle should not focus, therefore, on the translation of a particular text into a particular situation, but on extrapolating the dynamic and direction of the evolutionary process of a soteriological paradigm or tradition into present constellations of need.[8]

d) The value of the notion of hermeneutical trajectories is that it shows that the world of interpretive communities is dynamic and is continually being transformed through the process of ongoing interpretation. It has to be remembered, though, that the very identification of a trajectory remains a construction by contemporary scholars that can never do full justice to the plurality of voices in the Biblical canon. Although the task of selecting, prioritizing and organizing these voices (into a trajectory) is unavoidable and necessary, it remains open to ideological abuse and the danger of coercing marginalized voices.

e) What does an act of extrapolation actually entail? The notion of extrapolation suggests both an element of continuity and of critical innovation in a trajectory. Such extrapolation therefore requires something like an analogical imagination (David Tracy). Interpreters have to identify some aspects of the tradition that can be built upon to address the needs and questions of a present context. These analogies have to be expressed in a concrete material form that will be accessible within the particular context. There are no clear-cut rules for an act of extrapolation. It requires both an in-depth understanding of the tradition and the imagination to construct new, creative interpretations. It requires the prophetic ability to read the "signs of the time" and to have an appropriate word for a particular context. It requires a priestly consciousness to find an appropriate way of living in the presence of God in changing circumstances.

The extrapolation of trajectories is clearly a daunting task. It should be approached with the necessary caution. This will be the task of Part E.

---

7 See Nürnberger (1992:17): "The rationale of the closure of the canon was to demarcate a primal and prototypical period of evolutionary history, which could act as a criterion for the acceptability of subsequent developments."

8 Nürnberger (1992:17).

9. Hope in the First Testament[1]

9.1 Hope in the primal history

A historical reconstruction of Biblical trajectories on the theme of hope can only be done with a degree of confidence by commencing with the monarchical period in Israel. However, the Biblical narratives themselves seem undeterred by historiographical imponderables. The Deuteronomistic reconstruction of Israel's history stretches beyond the ancient patriarchal legends to the beginning of human history. It made use of the best available knowledge of its day to reconstruct the very origins of the cosmos itself.

A contemporary reconstruction of eschatological trajectories in the Biblical roots of Christianity perhaps needs to retain the cosmic scope of the Deuteronomistic vision. This would require the audacity to construct a theological vision on the origins of the cosmos, taking the best available (scientific) knowledge of our own period into account.

In Chapter 14 we will investigate various attempts within contemporary debates between theology and the sciences to engage in this constructive task. These contributions scrutinize the story of the universe, the "new creation story", for signs of hope. They seek to provide a theological vision on the origins, life and destiny of the cosmos.

The focus of this chapter has to remain reconstructive. The Biblical reconstructions of the divine origins of the cosmos are themselves, of course, less instructive about the origin of the universe itself. They reveal more about the cosmology of the much later periods in which these narrative reconstructions were transmitted. Nevertheless, one may, following the creation narratives in Genesis, retroject some features of hope to primal history.

a) The soteriological focus of the creation narratives was recognized and emphasized with considerable clarity by Gerhard von Rad. The expression of faith in God as Creator in the creation narratives responds primarily to the predicament of the evil manifestations of sin in the world. The question to which these narratives respond, is whether the forces of evil, destruction, and chaos will ultimately prevail. During the exilic period it seemed to many in Judah that the destructive forces of chaos will triumph. The message of the priestly authors of Genesis 1 is that God (not Marduk) is the creator of heaven and earth, that this God remains in control of history and that the destiny of Israel remains in God's hands. The retrojection of this trust in God to the most distant past therefore serves the purpose of a projection of hope in God into an unknown future. The "dangerous and encouraging recollection of God's original intentions for creation"[2] expresses the

---

1 For a more detailed discussion of eschatology in the First Testament see, for example, the helpful overviews by Von Rad (1965), Hubbard (1983) and Gowan (1986).

2 Duchrow & Liedke (1987:53).

hope that God will again establish victory over the evil forces of destruction, that God will liberate the people of Israel from the humiliation of the exile, that God will provide a new beginning (genesis) in which Israel's sinful inclination towards self-destruction will be healed at its very roots. In response, the priestly authors reminded Israel of the goodness of God's creation (Gen 1 & 2) before the appearance of sin in the world (Gen 3). This notion of creation therefore does not refer to an isolated event at the beginning of time but to an ongoing process leading towards redemption and consummation.[3]

b) The soteriological focus of the creation narratives indicates that cosmological speculation about the origins (and destiny) of the universe is not their primary concern. At the same time, the cosmic scope of Israel's hope in God needs to be affirmed. Only a God who transcends the whole cosmos can provide victory over the cosmic forces of chaos. Only a God who was there "in the beginning" and controls every day in the evolution of creation could continue to control the destiny of Israel beyond the present epoch of destruction. Only such a God could be worthy of trust and praise. Only then could the present generation express its hope for the future beyond the trauma of its own finite experience of history.[4]

c) In the vision of Genesis 1, the radical transcendence of the Creator is beyond doubt. However, this transcendence does not deter the possibility of knowledge of God. The presence of God permeates the whole creation and becomes manifested in the blessing of the Sabbath when the whole of creation celebrates the presence of God (Gen 2:1-4).

9.2 Hope in the patriarchal narratives

Any attempt to reconstruct the eschatology of the patriarchal narratives will be confronted by formidable historiographical obstacles. Anachronistic retrojections from the perspective of later trajectories cannot be avoided. A few comments on the *kerygma* of the patriarchal narratives will have to suffice here.

---

3 Macquarrie (1978:34).

4 In my view, this implies a dialectic between faith in Yahweh as Creator and Savior. Israel did not derive her knowledge of God from a general belief in creation (Yahweh as Creator). However, Israel did not have a developed doctrine of redemption (Yahweh as Savior) from its earliest period either. Paul Santmire (1985:193) observes a similar dialectic on the basis of an affirmation of Yahweh as "Lord" of heaven and earth and not only of (human) history:

> What captivated the minds of the people in the nation's earliest epoch was the experience of deliverance from bondage by Yahweh the Lord. Still, that very experience of lordship contained within it a vital faith in Yahweh's unsurpassable power in, with, and under the world of nature and a conviction that Yahweh knows how to exercise his power in order to achieve his gracious purposes. If Yahweh was not yet "the Creator," then he surely was the "Lord of heaven and earth."

a) A dominant motif in any reading of the patriarchal narratives is the promise of God to Abraham, Isaac and Jacob. This is indeed a narrative elicited and structured by a promise.[5] The soteriological thrust of this promise is crucial in a context where survival is dependent on production, reproduction and self-defense.[6] It touches on four aspects: 1) land for the landless *habiru*, 2) numerous descendents (providing labor and military protection), 3) a name that will be remembered by these descendents of the patriarchs, 4) a divine blessing for abundant livestock and protection in an often hostile desert environment.[7]

The subsequent narratives describe a history of the provisional fulfillment but also the frustration of these promises. At the roots of the hope of Israel lie memories and experiences of God's redemptive acts in history – in the liberation from slavery in Egypt, in God's guidance during the desert journey, in the occupation of the promised land, in the leadership of the judges in times of military threat and social and religious disintegration and in the provision of God's law for the sake of a just and stable social order.

These redemptive experiences always remained limited and provisional, never comprehensive and final. Each redemptive act by God constituted a new promise of something greater that is to come. The faith of Israel was therefore an expectant trust in God, oriented towards the future.[8]

b) Most commentators agree that there was little if any interest in life beyond death in the early history of Israel. Death that comes at the end of a long and full life is perfectly natural. In the imagery of Israel, the *nephesh* of the dead will linger behind in the shadowy world of *she'ol*. Finitude at a personal level posed a less serious predicament if one could enjoy a long life, if one could see one's own grandchildren, and if one's good name would be remembered by one's descendents. Life after death becomes possible through one's descendents. This is confirmed in the many genealogies found in Genesis.

c) The historical nature of Israel's faith has often been noted.[9] The focus of its sense of mystery and of the sacred was not so much the continuous cycles of nature, but the future fulfillment of God's promises within the context of history. God is the one who continuously holds out a fresh promise for the future, who calls

---

5 See Moltmann (1967).

6 See Van Zyl (1998) who argues that these threats to survival disappeared with the advent of the monarchy and that the patriarchal narratives were reconstructed during this time to lend ideological support for the monarchy as an institution.

7 See also Macquarrie (1978:51).

8 Nürnberger (1994:140).

9 See the classic assessment by Gerhard von Rad (1965:104): "Israel's belief that she was not bound primarily to the periodic cycle of nature but to definite historical events, was the expression of a faith that was probably at the time still completely unaware both of its absolute difference in kind from the Canaanite religion, and of its own vigour."

us to hope in a vision yet to be fulfilled.[10] Hans Küng observes that this, significantly, also implies a different notion of transcendence. He says:

> Transcendence ... is conceived no longer as in ancient physics and metaphysics, primarily spatially: God over or outside the world. Nor is it to be understood on the other hand as idealistically or existentially interiorized: God simply in us. No, in the light of the biblical message transcendence must be understood primarily in a temporal sense: God before us ... God is not to be understood simply as the timeless eternal behind the homogeneous flow of coming to be and perishing, of past, present and future, as he is known particularly from Greek philosophy; but it is precisely as the eternal that he is the future reality, the coming reality, the one who creates hope, as he can be known from the promises of the future of Israel and of Jesus himself: 'thy kingdom come.'[11]

The faith of Israel thus remained focused on history and not so much on the continuing cycles of nature.

9.3 The history of the monarchy and the divided kingdom

a) The memories and experiences of God's redemptive acts in history structured the subsequent history of Israel. The establishment of the kingdom, the stable Davidic dynasty, the city of Jerusalem and the building of the temple were again regarded as the fulfillment of God's promises. This stimulated the conviction that God was taking Israel towards a future in which God will establish a reign of peace from within Israel.[12] Yet, this reign of God remained highly provisional. The history of the monarchy and the divided kingdom was plagued by political division, foreign aggression and invasion, internal oppression by kings and the wealthy elite, economic misery, droughts, hunger, moral decadence, and religious apostasy. This history of failure culminated in the fall of Samaria in 722 BCE, the destruction of Jerusalem in 587 BCE and again in 70CE.

These events stimulated an orientation of Israel's faith towards the future. Whenever in trouble, Israel remembered what Yahweh had done in earlier times and expected Yahweh, "the hope of Israel" (Jer 14:8), to act again. The orientation of Israel's faith towards the future was exemplified in the prophetic vision. The prophets responded to times of crisis, or, in Nürnberger's terminology, to an "unacceptable present". The prophetic message was that God remains faithful to the promises but that these promises are not to be taken lightly. They combined judgment with promise, pointing to a new dispensation that God will bring about: a wise and righteous king, perhaps the coming of an anointed ruler (Messiah) from the house of David, the subjugation of Israel's enemies under a benevolent monarch, overall peace and prosperity, and a new moral and religious foundation for society.[13]

---

10 Haught (1993b:85).

11 Küng (1984:213-214).

12 Berkhof (1981:510).

13 Paraphrased and adapted from Nürnberger (1994:140).

The prophetic vision remained predominantly this-worldly; it expected the coming of the Day of Yahweh and, beyond that, a new dispensation here on earth. The message of judgment points to discontinuity with the existing order but also to the possibility of a radically different order that will emerge from Yahweh's faithfulness.[14] The prophetic vision of redemption included the earth. The earth is not merely a stage on which the drama of human salvation takes place. The earth is affected in numerous ways by the sins of humanity (Gen 6: 11-13; Is 24:1-6; Hos 4:1-3). As a result, God's judgment affects the whole earth and the earth shares in God's final redemption.[15]

This vision of cosmic redemption was depicted in graphic poetic imagery. The land will flow with milk and honey. Then God's dwelling place will be on the holy mountain of Zion. There will be a faithful and purified remnant in Israel. The whole society will live in righteousness. There will be peace amongst the nations. The desert will flourish. Even the wild animals will rest with the tame ones (Is 11:6-7). Although one may detect in such poetic language an idyllic longing for a "golden age" (Eden), the prophetic expectation remained thoroughly realistic, focused on justice, good government, freedom from oppression, a time of plenty, good crops, harmony and peace.[16]

These expectations were frustrated time and again. As a result, the prophetic vision became increasingly radical. The prophets gradually came to realize that the future will surpass even God's paradigmatic acts of salvation and liberation in the past.[17] Yet, the new would be effected in a way analogous to God's former saving work. Hosea speaks of a new entry into the land, Isaiah of a new David and a new Zion, Jeremiah of a new covenant, Deutero-Isaiah of a new Exodus, Ezekiel of a new temple, and Trito-Isaiah of a new creation.[18] Thus hope was no longer based on an affirmation of the golden past but was orientated towards a future that would surpass past and present in every way.[19] The imagery of hope also shifted from the vision of security provided by the temple and the Davidic dynasty, to the portrayal of an ideal king (Psalm 72), to the subversive projection of a future king (Is 11), to the cosmic vision of a new heaven and earth (Is 65). In this radically new dispensation everything is expected to be transformed: Israel, the nations, the social order, the human heart, the land itself (Ezek 36).

---

14 Moltmann (1967:129).

15 Gowan (1986:98f), also Hoekema (1978:11).

16 Macquarrie (1978:37).

17 Von Rad (1965:113).

18 Von Rad (1965:117).

19 Jonker (1998). Jonker neatly describes the impact on the hope of Israel of the theological tensions between the Mosaic and the Davidic covenants, between the rural population and the royal elite, between the Northerners and the Southerners and between the Levites and the Zadokites. Jonker argues that a shift took place from an affirmation of the present in the interest of security in the temple / Zion tradition to an expectation of a radically new future in some prophetic traditions.

9.4 The rise of apocalypticism

a) The radicalization of the prophetic eschatological vision flowered with the rise of apocalypticism. Contact with Persian religions during the time of exile helped Israel's visionaries to understand history as a movement through various stages. According to Persian religions, the last stage would culminate in a cataclysmic showdown between the forces of good (symbolized by Ahuramazda) and the forces of evil (symbolized by Angramainyu). The victory of good over evil would lead to ultimate salvation.[20]

On the basis of its faith in Yahweh as Creator of heaven and earth and Savior in history, Israel adopted the cosmic dimensions of this view of history as moving towards a universal culmination. This helped them to respond to subsequent times of severe crisis, now radicalized as the threat of the very *annihilation* of Israel (e.g. the persecution under Antioch, the destruction of Jerusalem). Apocalypticism anticipated a day of judgment, chaos, and destruction of cosmic proportions. The contrast between good and evil was drawn in absolute terms as a cosmic battle between darkness and light, demons and angels, God and the devil. The confrontation between good and evil requires a final judgment towards which the whole of history is moving.

The hope of Israel's faithful was equally radicalized to anticipate a new dispensation in which Yahweh will create a new earth, beyond the total destruction of the present dispensation. The conversion of human beings and of a whole nation in the prophetic message is thus radicalized towards the need for a conversion of the whole cosmos.[21] In some apocalyptic writings the historical and earthly aspect of the coming age is emphasized while others contemplate the transformation of the present word into a realm transcending the dimensions of space and time. In these writings there is a tendency to transform the this-worldly eschatological vision of the prophets into an otherworldly apocalyptic vision. The coming age would be discontinuous rather than continuous with present history.[22] These apocalyptic visionaries realized acutely that salvation can come from God alone and that God's salvation has to be universal in scope, including gentiles and the whole cosmos. In some cases, however, as Moltmann notes, "... the apocalyptic expectation is no longer directed towards a consummation of the creation through the overcoming of evil by good, but towards the separation of good and evil and hence the replacement of the 'world that lies under the power of evil' by the coming 'world of righteousness'."[23]

b) In apocalyptic literature, the hope of Israel retained its soteriological focus.[24] It

---

20 Paraphrased and adapted from Nürnberger (1994:140-141).

21 Moltmann (1967:137).

22 See the assessment of Macquarrie (1978:38).

23 Moltmann (1967:134).

24 In this sense, apocalyptic literature is not completely discontinuous with prophetic literature. See Braaten (1985:331).

anticipated a complete, comprehensive and universal redemption. Not even exile, death, destruction and annihilation would be able to thwart God's intention for the comprehensive well-being of the whole created order. If death may be understood in terms of the judgment of God, then the power of Yahweh extends also to death. Hence, on the periphery of the prophetic message, death appears as a suffering of divine judgment and salvation as a victory over death in which this judgment is annulled.[25]

In this way, the hope for salvation from sin, liberation from oppression, and victory over evil was extrapolated to include a response to the predicament of finitude – in its personal, historical and cosmic dimensions. Beyond the graphic portrayal of the "End of the world" in apocalyptic imagery, reality as a whole would be reconstructed. Evil in all its forms will be overcome. Even the faithful who died during persecutions will be able to participate in this new dispensation. They would be vindicated through the resurrection of the dead, a belief that also emerged during this period.[26]

It seems that three factors contributed to the emergence of this belief in the resurrection of the dead: 1) A growing sense of the significance and responsibility of the individual; 2) the conviction of the permanence of God's relationship with human beings; and 3) a trust that God will yet vindicate the faithful in the face of martyrdom and innocent suffering.[27]

It is within the context of the rise of apocalypticism that the message of the gospels was heard and interpreted. This introduces the theme of the next chapter.

---

25 Moltmann (1967:132).

26 For a more detailed discussion in this regard, see McDannell & Lang (1988:11f).

27 Hebblethwaite (1984:17).

10. Hope in the New Testament

10.1 Hope during the time of Jesus

There is little doubt that the coming kingdom of God was a central motif in the public proclamation of Jesus of Nazareth. He expected the imminent arrival of a new age, a new order. However, there is also little consensus among contemporary Biblical scholars on how to interpret Jesus' expectation of the reign of God.[1] To what extent did Jesus share an apocalyptic worldview?[2]

Both John the Baptist and Jesus of Nazareth proclaimed that the reign of God was imminent and that it was time to adapt to the coming reality. This required conversion to the values embedded in the reign of God. They warned that destruction loomed if the whole social order was not transformed to be in line with the coming reign of God. While John emphasized an imminent end, Jesus proclaimed a new beginning.[3]

The terminology about the kingdom of God in the gospels is related to Jewish teachings about the two ages – this age and the age to come. The present age is a time of sinfulness and rebellion against God. The coming age is the time when God's rule will be established and when sin and evil will be no more. Perhaps the basic thrust of the teaching of Jesus about the kingdom is that the reign of God will come fully in the future and that the new age has already dawned in the presence of Jesus himself.[4] Some sayings about the kingdom of God in the synoptic gospels therefore stress the imminence of the kingdom while others portray the delay and

---

1 See the helpful summary by Aune (1992) of the various scholarly positions in this regard. Aune distinguishes between those who support a consistent eschatology (Weiss, Schweitzer), a realized eschatology (Dodd), a proleptic eschatology (Cullmann, Jeremias, Kümmel) and those who de-emphasize eschatology (Glasson, Borg, Crossan).

2 For a discussion of these issues, see Arendse (1998) and Chilton (1984). The interpretation of Jesus' message about the coming kingdom of God is often clouded by confusion on the meaning of the concepts "eschatology" or "apocalypticism." This is especially evident in the unhelpful tendency among some Biblical scholars to reduce eschatology to a response to the historical dimensions of finitude (in which case the preaching of Jesus may or may not be "eschatological"). This also obscures the distinction between eschatology and apocalypticism (regarded as a response to the end of the world). Von Rad (1965:114) complains about a similar narrow definition of eschatology in Old Testament studies. In terms of the present analysis, the coming of God's kingdom is clearly also a response to the predicament of the evil manifestations of sin. Eschatology responds to all three predicaments. It is perhaps wise to refrain from an etymological definition of eschatology (the doctrine of the last things). Instead, this study uses the term in the widest possible sense as the discipline reflecting on the content and social impact of (Christian) hope.

3 The assessment of Berkhof (1981:124).

4 The assessment of McKim (1988:153).

the uncertain time of the coming kingdom.[5]

Jesus not only proclaimed the coming of God's reign, but also enacted its redemptive impetus. He healed the sick, fed the hungry, communicated with social outcasts, comforted the downtrodden, announced forgiveness for sinners. Jesus challenged the self-sufficient, the self-righteous, the rich and powerful.[6] Since the reign of God was made present in the ministry of Jesus, he could feast while John had to fast.[7] Israel expected a *future* act of God that would inaugurate God's reign. Jesus announced dramatically that the promises of the First Testament were presently being fulfilled in his own life and ministry.

The followers of Jesus expected him to establish, as the Messiah, a new political dispensation. This expectation was crushed when Jesus' entry into Jerusalem ended with capture, condemnation and execution as a heretic and revolutionary. The hope of the disciples was shattered. However, the witnesses to the empty tomb and to the appearances of the risen Christ gave them new hope. The resurrection of dead was no longer merely an idea, a hope. Resurrection has actually taken place in Jesus Christ. This unique claim lies at the very center of Christian hope.[8] The resurrection also convinced the early church that God's work in Jesus the Christ would continue.[9] The crucifixion was part of the redemptive purposes of God. Subsequently, the future had to be regarded as the unfolding of the impact of Christ's resurrection.[10] Christ would soon return to judge, to reconstruct the social order and to establish the reign of God.

10.2 Pauline eschatology

In his early letters (51-57 CE), Paul adopted the notion in Jewish apocalypticism of the two ages. He maintained the tension between "this age" and "the coming age". The whole of creation is still groaning (Rom 8) in anticipation of the new heavens and the new earth, a familiar theme in apocalyptic expectations.[11] The temporal tension (the age to come as a future dispensation) coincides for Paul with a spatial tension (the age to come as heavenly world prepared in eternity and waiting to descend from its eternal locus to the earth). Paul expected the imminent arrival of the age to come at the *parousia* of Christ. He certainly considered the possibility that this would take place within his own lifetime (Phil 1:23).[12]

Paul maintained that the age to come was already inaugurated through the

---

5 McKim (1988:154), also Lane (1996:85-87).

6 Paraphrased and adapted from Nürnberger (1994:142).

7 Nolan (1974).

8 Macquarrie (1978:69f).

9 Paraphrased and adapted from Nürnberger (1994:142).

10 Berkhof (1967:17).

11 See Santmire (1985:202) who thus highlights Romans 8 a key to understanding the whole of Paul's theology.

12 Aune (1992:602).

resurrection of Jesus. The lordship of Christ forms the integrating center of Paul's eschatology.[13] Christ, as the first born, is also the first to rise from the dead. His resurrection constituted the first stage of the future resurrection of the righteous who have died already (1 Cor 15:20-23). Christians may experience the future age in the present time (1 Cor 2:6, 7:29-31, 10:11).[14] Christian existence may thus be called a "new creation" (2 Cor 5:17). The full transformation will take place at the *parousia*. Then, at the sound of the last trumpet, the dead will be raised and will experience with the living a transformed existence in the presence of Christ. The hope for resurrection is thus focused on a life of sharing in the glory of Christ. The goal of God's salvific activity is the union of the believers with the risen Lord. In terms of the prophetic conception of the Day of the Lord, the impending judgment of the world will take place at the same time. This culminates in a universal vision of the unification of the whole creation under the cosmic lordship of Christ (Rom 11:36), of the ultimate realization of God's purpose in all things (*ta panta*). Then God will be all in all (1 Cor 12:6, Col 3:11).[15]

10.3 Hope in the deutero-Paulinic literature

The apocalyptic expectations of the early disciples were disappointed after several decades of waiting. The intense expectation of the future dawning of the last day, in all its radiant splendor, gave way to a more serene confession of the *present* rule of Christ.[16] Within the Biblical canon several attempts were made to explain the delayed *parousia* and to express the hope of the early church in new ways. Nürnberger provides an excellent summary of the theological shifts that followed subsequently. His description is worth quoting at some length:

> The apocalyptic expectation, too, was disappointed. After a few decades of waiting, disillusionment set in and new interpretations had to be found. Some saw the interim as a period of testing (1 Pet. 1:3-12). Some attributed the delayed return of Christ to God's patience with the wicked (2 Pet. 3:9). Some believed that all of humanity had to be reached by the gospel first, and that the missionary task had not been completed (cf. Matt. 14:14). Luke, the author of the book of Acts, concluded that Christ did not appear at the end of times, as had been believed till then, but in the middle of times. Between the time of Christ and the end there was the time of the church and its mission (Acts 1:6-8).
>
> But in the long run all these explanations proved unsatisfactory. As apocalyptic hope lost its plausibility, faith turned from a forward to an upward direction. Increasingly the theological expression of the discrepancy between what is and what ought to be was translated from the apocalyptic model of a conflict between this age and the 'age to

---

13 See Santmire (1985:202) who argues (with reference to the contributions of Christian Beker) that the prominent Pauline theme of justification by faith should be understood precisely within the context of the Lordship of Christ.

14 Aune (1992:602).

15 Aune (1992:602-603).

16 Santmire (1985:203).

come', to a Hellenistic model of a contrast between appearance and truth.[17]

Nürnberger claims that this change can best be observed in the evolution of the Pauline school. He formulates this shift in the following way:

> While Paul's early letters are steeped in the apocalyptic tradition (see 1 Thess. 4:13-5:11); 1 Cor. 15:20-28), the deutero-Pauline letters (Colossians and Ephesians) are no longer geared to the eschatological future. Instead they emphasise the validity of a truth claim. Instead of saying 'What ought to be, shall be!', they say 'What ought to be, is already here, though hidden.' God's intentions have been a mystery hidden from all generations in all ages but have now been revealed in Christ, mediated by the apostles and other teachers to his 'saints', so that the latter enlighten each and every human being (Col. 1:25-29; Eph. 3:2-10).[18]

From this thesis Nürnberger draws a number of consequences:

1) Hope is no longer directed towards a new earth in the eschatological future but towards God's glory in heaven (Col. 1:5).
2) Christ is not expected to subdue all his enemies when he comes, but is already enthroned above all the powers which determine the universe (Eph. 1:20-23); cf Col. 1:15-20). These powers only have to be informed by the church of God's intentions (Eph. 3:10), namely to reconcile the entire cosmos in Christ (Col. 1:19-20; Eph. 1:9-10).
3) While according to Paul we believe that we shall live with Christ (Rom. 6:8), the deutero-Paulines inform that we have already been raised and enthroned with Christ in heavenly glory (Eph. 2:6; Col. 2:13).
4) The new humanity has already been established in the church, which encompasses old enemies, namely Jews and Greeks (Eph. 2:11-22).
5) The true life of the members of the new community is already lived 'in heaven', though the fact still has to be made manifest (Col. 3:1-4). What matters now is that the community grows (Col. 2:19) or is built up, as Christ's 'Body', by gaining greater insight, living a new life (Eph. 4:1-16), and resisting and empowering the forces of darkness which are antagonistic to the rule of Christ (Eph. 6:10ff). While the effect on ethics seems to be the same, what ought to be has been transformed from the eschatological future to what already is 'in essence' but not yet fully revealed.[19]

Nürnberger's assessment of the realized eschatology and developed ecclesiology in the deutero-Paulinic literature represents a widely held position in New Testament scholarship.[20] Everything of importance has already happened; the only question is how we should realize the potential opened for us by God. Therefore "building up the body" (Eph 4) by means of institutional offices became important. As in the Pastoral Epistles, the focus shifted more and more to the authority of the church

---

17 Nürnberger (1994:142-3).

18 Nürnberger (1994:142-3).

19 Nürnberger (1994:142-3).

20 Wessels (1988).

and on appropriate behavior in the Christian community.

Although there are some allusions to a futurist eschatology in Colossians and Ephesians, there is indeed an undeniable emphasis on a realized eschatology in these letters. Wessels concludes that,

> This, however, is not because church triumphalism has taken the place of the expectation of Christ and his coming kingdom. Both letters respond to anticipate situations which asked for a clear statement about the consequences of Christ's death and resurrection here and now – hence the realized eschatology.[21]

It is significant to note that this shift towards a realized eschatology coincided with a response to the predicament of human limitations in space. The predominant perspective in the Hellenistic climate was spatial instead of the temporal schema of the prophetic and apocalyptic traditions. Reality was pictured as a hierarchy of overlapping dimensions extending from the earth upward through many layers towards the eternal heavens. The powers and limitations of human knowledge fostered an awareness of the gulf between the higher (heavenly) and the lower (earthly) realms. In response to this need for cosmic integration, a redeemer figure who descends to the earthly realm and then ascends to the eternal world above could be introduced readily. In the deutero-Paulinic letters, the crucified and exalted Christ is pictured not as the one who will help an elect few to transcend the lower regions of the universe, but as the Lord of all of finite reality.[22]

10.4 Hope in the Johannine literature

The Johannine literature provided its own distinct response to the incompleteness of the salvation over sin, liberation from oppression and victory over evil and over death that Jesus Christ inaugurated. In a time when early eschatological expectations were already fading, John focused on the confrontation of the believer with the *kerygma* of Jesus.

Although the gospel of John also contains eschatological statements that refer both to the present and to the future, an emphasis on "realized eschatology" is clearly dominant. In the gospel of John, eschatology is not so much portrayed as a future drama but as the confrontation with the incarnate Logos, redefined as God's personal self-disclosure in Jesus Christ. The fourth gospel describes the incarnation in the spatial imagery of descent (*katabasis*) and ascent (*anabasis*). Since Jesus comes from above (John 3:31), eternity may already be experienced in his presence. According to John, authentic, eternal life is possible already here and now through participation in Christ. The risen Christ is no longer portrayed as a mythological figure who will return at the end of time but as the exaltation of Christ, that is, as his present lordship in heaven and his present activity through the Spirit with

---

21 Wessels (1988:130).

22 Santmire (1985:204).

the disciples (John 14:17f).[23] The resurrection of Christ is thus no longer linked to the imminent resurrection of the dead and the cosmic renewal of all things (the historical and cosmic dimensions of the predicament of finitude in time).[24] Instead, the emphasis is on the protological vision of Christ as the incarnate Logos and on the present experience of eternal life, presenting perhaps the clearest example of "realized eschatology" in the Biblical canon.[25] The future becomes an unfolding and glorification of what has already happened in the Christ-event.[26] More specifically, the future is understood in terms of the metaphor of ascent. Christ does not descend to fill all things anew. Instead, Christ ascends to carry those whom he has called away from "this world" – which is described in predominantly negative terms in the Johannine literature.[27] Salvation is not understood as liberation from evil but as an escape from this world to the higher heavenly sphere of eternal life.

10.5 Eschatology in the letter to the Hebrews

Paul Santmire argues that an "ascending spiritual motif" has triumphed over an "ecological motif" in the eschatology of the letter to the Hebrews.[28] The letter integrates the eschatological expectation of Christ's return (on a horizontal, temporal axis) with the Hellenistic conception of a multi-layered world (on a vertical, spatial axis). Santmire's helpful summary of the eschatology of the letter to the Hebrews is worth quoting at length:

> For Hebrews, faith is the 'conviction of things not seen' (11:1-4). This faith envisions a high priest, Christ, in a heavenly sanctuary above, which has been built by God (8:1-2). The high priest, the letter informs us, came to earth in order to abolish the old sacrificial rites here on earth and to open the door to the sanctuary of God in heaven. This is where he went, then, as he 'passed through the heavens' (4:14).
>
> The famous narrative about the Old Testament saints in Hebrews 11 has the purpose accordingly of displaying the aforementioned heavenly tabernacle as the place of

---

23 Nürnberger (1994:145). An affirmation of this present salvation is only possible on the basis of an evading of the predicament of evil to respond primarily to the predicament of the limitations of human power and knowledge.

24 Santmire (1985:211).

25 Hayes (1989:60).

26 The gospel of John does not deny the expectation of a future coming of Christ. It simply allows this expectation to coexist next to its own emphasis on realized eschatology.

27 Santmire (1985:212).

28 Santmire (1985:215). See Santmire's well-known distinction between the metaphor of ascent (the spiritual motif) and the metaphors of fecundity and migration to a good land (the ecological motif). In the terms of the present analysis, the metaphor of ascent is clearly linked to a response to the predicament of the limitations of human knowledge and power (in space). By contrast, an ecological motif requires a retrieval of the soteriological core of eschatology, that is, a response to the impact of evil on the earth itself. This again indicates the danger of a noetic reduction of salvation and a conflation of the three predicaments.

> salvation. The Old Testament saints all were 'strangers and pilgrims on the earth' (11;13). They all looked forward, as Abraham did, 'to the city which has no foundations, whose builder and maker is God' (11:10; cf. 11;16; 13:14). The author uses the language of pilgrimage to a good land, but he leaves no doubt that he attaches a purely spiritual meaning to that image: those saints, he tells us, looked for 'a better country, that is a heavenly one' (11:16). Nor are we left in doubt about which metaphor is shaping his vision of salvation. It is the metaphor of ascent and as always it shapes a vision that ends with a purely spiritual world (12:22-23).[29]

Santmire observes that the Pauline vision of the whole creation waiting in travail is hereby eclipsed. Unlike the Johannine vision of the new Jerusalem coming down from heaven to be established on earth, the letter to the Hebrews portrays a vision of men and angels communing with God and Christ in ethereal regions above.[30] The city of the living God or the heavenly Jerusalem (Heb 12:22) does not descend to earth.

10.6 Conclusion

In the context of New Testament studies the delay of the *parousia* is often regarded as the single most important factor leading to the transformation of early Christian eschatology from an emphasis on the imminent expectation of the end to a vague expectation in the more distant future.[31] Since the imminent arrival of the end that was announced by Jesus in the gospels, and an early consummation which was expected by Paul did not occur, a theological readjustment became necessary. In this assessment of New Testament eschatology, the focus remains clearly on the historical dimensions of finitude. Unfortunately, the way in which the debate is formulated tends to obscure the soteriological focus of early Christian hope and expectation.

---

29 Santmire (1985:214-215).

30 Santmire (1985:215).

31 Aune (1992:606).

11. Hope in the history of Christianity

This chapter will continue the discussion in the previous two chapters. Its aim is to briefly sketch the eschatological trajectories in the subsequent history of Christianity until the advent of the Enlightenment. The following trajectories are usually recognized in this regard:[1]

11.1 Hope in the patristic period

The earliest Christians were convinced that the *parousia* of Christ was imminent, that Christ was coming soon, and that history was about to come to an end. The focus of this form of hope was not only on the historical dimensions of finitude, but also on the salvific impact of the coming reign of God (the predicament of evil). This integrated eschatology was gradually lost with the advent of the Constantinian period as a result of the disappointment of apocalyptic expectations and the trend towards ecclesiastical institutionalization in early Catholicism. Several eschatological tendencies resulted from this.

a) The focus of Christian hope shifted from the age to come to the present age, and to the fulfillment of God's promises in the church as an institution. As a result, the expectation of the coming end of the world (the predicament of historical finitude) could be postponed to the distant future. Braaten comments that, "The last day, the resurrection of the body, and the end of the world – events that were expected in the *near* future in the New Testament – were still affirmed but now removed to *distant* future."[2] Macquarrie also comments on the impact of this shift:

> The effect of such developments was to deprive the original eschatological expectations of most of their power. An event that had been relegated to a distant future and in any case made superfluous by what was to happen at death, could not create the sense of urgency and energy that the expectation of the end evoked in the first disciples, not (sic) could it be understood as a judgement on the prevailing order, for this was no longer understood as perishing but as likely to last for a long time.[3]

b) The doctrine of the last things (a response to the predicament of finitude) could remain immediately relevant only by focusing on the death of the individual, that is, the personal dimension of finitude. In this way, a confrontation with the nearness of the *parousia* in early Christian eschatology was transformed into the suddenness of death. The offices and sacraments of the church were legitimized as means to prepare the individual to face death. In this atmosphere, it was possible

---

1 For helpful overviews of eschatology in the history of Christianity, see Braaten (1985), Hebblethwaite (1984:43-92), McDannell & Lang (1988), McKim (1988:154-166).

2 Braaten (1985:334).

3 Macquarrie (1978:89).

for the organized church to require obedience to its authority as the absolute condition of salvation.[4]

c) In response to the predicament of personal finitude, patristic Christianity forged a synthesis between the Greek emphasis on the soul and the Hebraic appreciation of the bodily and earthly (in contrast to the Gnostic contempt for the body). This synthesis was possible on the basis of a separation between the resurrection of the mortal body and the affirmation of the immortality of the soul. With Plato, the patristic church affirmed life after death, and with Aristotle it held that the body and soul is united in the human person.[5]

d) In the Constantinian era the church became more and more at home in society so that any urgent sense of a revolutionary eschatology disappeared. Occasionally, a high-pitched awareness of the historic and cosmic dimensions of finitude would return, for example in Montanism and other millennialist movements. Millennialist expectations may be found in the writings of Papias (d. 130), the Epistle of Barnabas, Justin Martyr, Irenaeus, Tertullian and Hippolytus.[6] These movements were no longer dominant but they did function as protests against the secularization of the church and a call to purity of moral and spiritual life.[7]

e) Patristic Christianity nevertheless retained its focus on history and consummation. It did not simply follow the Hellenistic response to the predicament of finitude, namely that the cosmos was eternal and that everything that exists had to exist from eternity. It also did not simply emulate the Gnostic treatment of eschatology as symbolic, cryptic codes for present spiritual, inner knowledge without any reference to future consummation. The Christian doctrines of creation and eschatology ensured a more historical worldview that maintained that the world was created from nothing, remained under God's providence and is moving towards a consummation far surpassing the glory of the beginning. Braaten comments: "The Hellenistic axiom 'The end is always like the beginning' gave way to the dominical saying 'Behold, I make all things new.'"[8]

These tendencies are manifested in several of the leading theologians of the patristic period:

- The eschatology of Irenaeus (115-190) refutes the scheme of salvation of the Gnostics. They argued that the resurrection must be purely spiritual since matter is intrinsically degraded and that the flesh (and the earthly) cannot be

---

4 Braaten (1985:334).

5 Braaten (1985:335-336).

6 McKim (1988:155-157).

7 Braaten (1985:334).

8 Braaten (1995:335).

part of salvation. Irenaeus rejected these arguments by citing the resurrection of Christ, the indwelling of the Spirit in our bodies and in the Eucharist.[9] Likewise, Irenaeus expected Christ's reign as an earthly reality in which the Redeemer will gather together the whole of reality unto himself. The whole cosmos will be perfected in Christ.

- Tertullian (170-230) reaffirmed the early expectation of the return of Christ as an event that will still take place in history soon. In his great work *Against Marcion*, Tertullian insisted that the Biblical millennial prophecies will be fulfilled. He attacked those who questioned the coming reign of Christ and warned that a last day of judgment is coming for the affluent and the powerful. He found little hope in the present he knew and shifted his hope to a future dispensation that holds new promise.[10]
- In Origen's (185-254) eschatology, a tendency towards a figurative reading of the reign of God may be found. The promised kingdom will be a purely spiritual one because it is the soul and not the body that receives God's promises. He thus rejected a literal, spatio-temporal notion of resurrection. The kingdom of God is interpreted noetically as the apprehending of divine truth, as an intellectual contemplation of God, through the indwelling of the Logos in the believer.[11] Origen argued furthermore that since the divinity of Christ will become universally manifest, the final restoration and consummation of all things (*apokatastasis*) through union with God (in the *visio Dei*) may be envisaged.
- Augustine's (354-430) eschatology responded to the collapse of the Roman empire. A central theme in his work is the contrast between two cities – the "city of God" and the "city of the world".[12] These two cities may be understood as two great loyalties that are inextricably mixed in the world throughout history and that will be separated at the last judgment.[13] According to Augustine, Christians have to live in the intermediate period between the incarnation and the coming of Christ. During this period the reign of Christ and the saints have already begun in this world. In this sense, Augustine's is a realized eschatology.[14] In the church, Christ's rule is already prevalent. Yet, there is a strong eschatological tension between the present world in which the church exists as a community of sojourners and the future hope in which the church will be delivered from this good but transient world to share in God's abiding glory. Against the Donatist view of the church as a body of saints, Augustine main-

---

9 McKim (1988:156).

10 Stackhouse (1997:39).

11 McKim (1988:157).

12 Catherine Keller (1997:94) comments that Augustine thus "split the eschatological hope for a new age of justice and cosmic harmony within history into a 'City of God' transcending nature and history and a 'City of Man' within them and ending soon." This fostered the typical medieval dualism.

13 McKim (1988:158).

14 Bonner (1994:99f).

tains that the church, as a mixed body of the pure and the impure, saints and sinners, shares in the fallenness of this world but also belongs to the eternal city of God. We are saved in hope (*in spes*), not in reality (*in re*).[15] Salvation is inaugurated in the life of the believer and will find its completion at the end of history. Only on the last day will this tension be resolved.[16] "Eternal life is to be seen as the state in which our love for God, begun in this life, is finally brought to its completion and consummation, through union with the object of that love."[17] For Augustine, this temporal world may be appreciated as good, but it remains a passing good that should not distract the attention from what is immortal and abiding, that is, the city of God. The goodness of creation implies that creation will not be annihilated (against the Gnostics) but it will be transformed towards the abiding new heaven and earth. The world, like humanity will be transformed, not destroyed.[18]

11.2 Eschatology in the scholastic synthesis

Augustine's vision that the millennial rule of Christ was now taking place in the offices and sacraments of the church dominated the medieval period. Pope Gregory the Great (d. 604) could state that, "The present church is called the kingdom of heaven – for the congregation of the saints is said to be the kingdom of heaven."[19] To accomplish its work the church may need the help of the state. However, the city of God had absolute dominion over the city of the world - as Pope Gregory VII (1073-1085) maintained. McKim comments that "The kingdom that was eschatological and other-worldly also became highly political and this-worldly."[20]

Nevertheless, millennial hopes surfaced time and again in popular piety and reform movements such as the Albigensians, the Waldensians, the Joachemites, and the Anabaptists. In "heretical" and sectarian movements apocalyptic and revolutionary eschatological ideas also flourished. Vivid portrayals of heaven, hell, purgatory, the second coming of Christ, the end of the world and the final judgment featured as major themes of popular eschatology.[21] In this way, these movements "recovered the primitive apocalyptic view of the church as a transcendental

---

15 This implies an eschatological postponement of the concreteness of salvation from sin, liberation from oppression and victory over evil.

16 McGrath (1994:467).

17 McGrath (1994:467-468).

18 See Bonner (1994:92) with reference to *De civitate Dei* 20, 14. Bonner (1994:103) adds that "Augustine did not disparage this temporal world but his mind was fixed on things eternal, and he would have found much of our present concern with the environment excessive, and even dangerous as it distracts us from our final end." See the discussion in Chapter 19 on the ecological need to maintain the eschatological tension between an affirmation of this world and an anticipation of the next.

19 Quoted by McKim (1988:159).

20 McKim (1988:159).

21 Braaten (1985:336-337).

community that leaps ahead of the present world in anticipation of the future age."[22] In other movements, apocalyptic imagery evoked and sustained increasingly radical, revolutionary political hopes for the inauguration of a new age, a more immediate, earthly reign of peace that is to come. Whether the future dispensation was envisaged in purely religious or in political categories, eschatological images provided a powerful critique of a static worldly ecclesial order and corrupt feudal political structures.[23]

These tendencies were manifested in the work of several leading figures and theologians of this period:

- The eschatology of Joachim of Fiore (1135-1202) was particularly influential. He divided history into three ages: 1) The age of the Father corresponding to the First Testament dispensation and marked by law and fear; 2) The age of the Son corresponding to the New Testament dispensation as well as the history of the church, marked by grace and faith; and 3) The age of the Spirit that would witness the reform and renewal of the church and the final establishment of peace on earth. The center of gravity belonged to the third and final age that was still to come. The Spirit would create a truly spiritual community of believers in contrast to the depravity of the imperial church. What gave Joachim's scheme a sense of urgency is that he also attached particular dates to it. According to his calculations, the age of the Son would come to an end in 1260 (after 42 generations of 30 years each), to be followed by the radical new age of the Spirit.
- Dante Aligheri (1265-1321) gave a more poetic expression of Christian hope. The *Divine Comedy* represents the medieval worldview according to which the souls of the departed had to pass through a series of purifying and cleansing processes. Dante is led through various circles of hell, purgatory and heaven before obtaining the ultimate goal of the Christian life – the vision of God.

In scholastic theology, epitomized by the work of Thomas Aquinas (1225-1274), eschatology was treated as the doctrine of the four last things (*eschata*): death, judgment, heaven and hell. It schematized the events when the present world will come to an end in ever more detail. It elaborated on the place of death, the resurrection of the dead, the final judgment, the end of the world, the second coming, eternal damnation and eternal life in considerable detail. Other themes included purgatory, the notion of limbo, the Antichrist, etc. Hell implies eternal damnation and death; heaven implies eternal life as an everlasting reward for the saints. Perfect joy in the presence of God is possible forever on the basis of the perfection

---

22 Macquarrie (1978:). Migliore (1991:233) adds that the earthshaking hope of the New Testament was largely forgotten in mainstream, orthodox Christianity. It is not surprising then, that in the modern era hopes other than the biblical hope have dominated both secular and religious consciousness.

23 Hebblethwaite (1984:66f).

of the body and will culminate in the beatific vision.[24]

According to scholastic eschatology, the world will come to an end when the final judgment takes place. It will burn up in a ball of fire and come to naught. Braaten therefore observes a certain scholastic pessimism about this present world order. The world is not evolving towards glorious consummation; there is not gradual progress towards a new heaven and earth. Instead, the absolute annihilation of the present world is expected.[25]

11.3 Eschatology and the Protestant reformation

The leading reformers all attempted to recover the sense of urgency and immediacy of the New Testament hope. This hope was based on God's action and presence in Jesus Christ, of eternity breaking into the dimensions of space and time.

a) Martin Luther's (1483-1546) famous concept of the two kingdoms (the kingdom of Christ and the kingdom of the world) builds upon Augustine's notion of the two cities. He argued that the two kingdoms must be distinguished, though not ultimately separated. For Luther, the two kingdoms are two overlapping aspects of the one invisible reign of God. He provided a more positive view of God's reign in the secular world, the kingdom of God's left hand. Here God rules indirectly through father, mother, king, judge and hangman. In the kingdom of God's right hand, God is more immediately present through Christ. This distinction between the two kingdoms relates to Luther's other famous distinction between gospel and law. God rules the world through the gospel. God also rules through law in order to contain the evil consequences of sin in society. Since the Christian is both righteous and a sinner (*simul iustus et peccator*), the Christian needs both forms of rule.[26]

b) According to John Calvin (1509-1564), the church participates in the kingdom through the victory of Christ – although the church itself is not the kingdom. Christians need to be actively involved in society to extend the reign of God on earth. The kingdom was inaugurated with the coming of Christ. Through his death, resurrection and ascension, Christ has won the victory over sin, evil and death. However, this victory is not yet complete. The fullness of the reign is delayed until the final coming of Christ when God will be all in all. In the meanwhile, the church may participate in the victory through its union with Christ and through the Holy Spirit. The church needs to prepare the world for the final coming of Christ by establishing signs of God's coming kingdom on earth.

Calvin portrayed the time between the beginning of salvation and its completion in terms of two ages, the old world and the new world. Since these two ages overlap, the reign of God may already be a reality in Christ. It will last forever and

24 Braaten (1985:339).

25 Braaten (1985:338).

26 McKim (1988:160-161).

will bring with it the renovation of the world. Christians have to live "between the times" in a life of discipleship. In the meanwhile, the task of the church is to permeate all creation with the kingdom of Christ, thus realizing on earth more and more of the triumph that Christ has already won. Thus the pilgrim church may look to the future consummation of the new age with hope.[27]

c) The teachings of Joachim of Fiore were influential on the radical reformer Thomas Müntzer (1489-1525). He not only expected the imminent arrival of God's reign but also emphasized the need to prepare its way. He pictured the coming reign of God as an egalitarian community of the poor and tried to establish this by supporting the German peasants in their revolutionary struggle against the German aristocracy. This uprising provides another illustration of the way in which apocalyptic imagery may be used for a powerful, if devastating political critique. The Anabaptist uprising in Münster (1534/5) provided another extreme example of a political expression of millennialist expectations of the imminent arrival of God's reign.

d) John Wesley's well-known moral perfectionism represents a striking form of realized eschatology. The kingdom of heaven is already operative here on earth. This also implied the need for social transformation and the establishment of a Christianized world. However, everything done on earth remains penultimate and will be judged before God on the Last Day.[28]

e) The scholastic synthesis continued to dominate Roman Catholic eschatologies until and beyond the Enlightenment. Protestant orthodoxy followed a similar pattern. The sense of urgency and immediacy of the New Testament hope was lost in the attempt to clarify and formulate the exact content of the *eschata*. Eschatology again became the doctrine of the last things, thus responding to the personal and historical dimensions of finitude only. This reduction of the soteriological core of Christian hope[29] became an easy target for criticism in the era of modernity that was soon to follow.

---

[27] McKim (1988:162-163).

[28] Hebblethwaite (1984:105).

[29] Pannenberg (1998:588) nevertheless identifies an emphasis on eschatological transformation: "From the mid-18th century onward Protestant theology abandoned the older Lutheran doctrine of a destruction of the world by fire in favor of the even older idea of an eschatological transformation of the world." However, this sense of eschatological transformation remained embedded in a doctrine of the last things that always tended to become speculative, with little impact on the present era.

12. Manifestations of hope in modernity

The many manifestations of hope in modernity include a wide range of contributions from philosophers, psychologists, social scientists and novelists. Thinkers such as Bloch, Marcel, Marcuse, Fromm, Ricoeur, Maslow, and numerous others have made noteworthy contributions to the phenomenology of hope in human existence. The aim of this chapter cannot be to provide a survey of these contributions.[1] Instead, the focus will have to be restricted to the impact of modernity on Christian expressions of hope.

12.1 The impact of the Enlightenment

There is no need to discuss the worldview emerging from the European Enlightenment here. The contributions of Descartes, Newton, Kant, Rousseau, Adam Smith and numerous others are well-known. In the worldview of the Enlightenment the eternal laws that God inscribed into this world were elucidated. Underlying the apparent disharmony, chaos and misery there is a basically good natural order.[2] Accordingly, the task of humankind is to retrieve these natural laws (Newton), through the powers of human reason (Kant), in order to reestablish a natural social order (Rousseau) and the natural functioning of a market economy (Adam Smith).[3]

In terms of this worldview, the Christian doctrine of the last things (e.g. eternal life, heaven, and especially hell) was dismissed as superstition. As Ludwig Feuerbach (1804-1872) later argued, these symbols are simply projections of a human longing after immortality. Karl Marx sharpened Feuerbach's criticism by analyzing the social and economic basis of alienation. Marx argued that religion sought to comfort those who suffer by promising them joy in life after death. It is the opium of the people, precisely because it diverts attention from the changes that are necessary on earth by its illusory hope for a hereafter. This could only distract people from the task of transforming this world in order to eliminate present suffering.

The Enlightenment thus witnessed a movement away from the medieval preoccupation with the predicament of personal and historic finitude in order to return to the predicament of suffering and evil in the social order here on earth. Carl Braaten provides an excellent summary of the impact of the Enlightenment on Christian eschatology:

> The worldview of the Enlightenment, whether along the lines of Newton, Adam Smith,

---

1 See the work by Körtner (1995) for a survey of many of these contributions.

2 See Braaten (1985:339): "The thinkers of the Enlightenment believed that underlying the apparent disharmony, chaos and misery there is a basically good natural order founded on eternal laws that God himself built into the world. If something is wrong it is because human beings have not heeded the original laws written into the nature of things."

3 Braaten (1985:339-340).

> or Rousseau, collapsed the biblical God of history into the laws of nature and the eschatological vision of Christianity into a harmonious social order. The old image of the kingdom of God became a workable social model to be realized by the ability of human reason to conform itself to the order of nature. Throughout the Enlightenment the eschatological kingdom of God was brought down to the size of *this world*, as something to be realized by human beings in history. Its focus was on the *human*: human society, human welfare, human happiness. Religion was reduced to what is natural and reasonable, striving for the highest possible elevation of humanity and society.[4]

In the light of the Kantian distinction between facts and values, and the rise of modern biblical criticism, eschatological symbols could "clearly" not be regarded as propositional truths. The immortality of the soul could be maintained only as necessary moral condition to sustain the categorical imperative through a sense of punishment and reward. In response to Kant, the eschatology of liberal Protestantism opted to focus on the realm of moral values. The coming of God's reign was now understood as a gradual transition from ecclesiastical religion to a purely moral religion and an ethical state here on earth.[5] Braaten comments:

> Immanuel Kant ... proposed an ethical interpretation of the kingdom of God on earth, the realization of which depended on the sum total of morally responsible actions performed by human beings. The kingdom of God which Jesus announced became very much something of and for this world, dependent not on the will of God but solely on human achievement. The establishment of the kingdom on earth was tied to the forward motion of progress.[6]

12.2 Eschatology as progress in history

The Enlightenment stimulated a critical consciousness. Another feature of the rise of modernity was its historical consciousness. This also influenced Christian eschatology in many ways:

a) Hegel's (1770-1831) philosophy of universal history integrated the insights of the Enlightenment with the emerging historical consciousness. Hegel described the cumulative ways in which Absolute Spirit objectivized itself in the history of the world. In this way, he translated and validated the Christian doctrines of God's Spirit, creation, incarnation, redemption and consummation in the philosophical categories of German idealism. In expressing the inner teleology of history, Hegel's philosophy also provided a powerful impetus to the belief in historical progress that dominated the intellectual climate in the Europe of the nineteenth century.[7]

---

4 Braaten (1985:340).

5 Macquarrie (1978:94).

6 Braaten (1985:342).

7 See also Hebblethwaite (1984:109f).

b) Karl Marx (1818-1883) translated Hegel's idealist philosophy of history in materialist categories. According to his dialectical materialism, the revolutionary power of negation will lead to a new social order, i.e. that of a classless society. In this way, Marx secularized the response to the predicament of sin (alienation) in Christian eschatology. The notion of a classless utopia replaced the doctrine of heaven. This has to be achieved on earth, not in heaven one day. According to this form of secular eschatology, humanity itself will realize authentic existence. Braaten comments on this aspect of Marxian eschatology:

> Marx's vision of the end-state is of a classless society rising from the ashes of an apocalyptic-type struggle of good and evil forces. Here religious eschatology, mediated in its heretical chiliastic forms, becomes radically secularized. The transcendent becomes immanent, the theological becomes teleological, the hereafter nothing but the post-revolutionary future.[8]

John Macquarrie comments that Marx's vision ran into the same troubles as the expectations of the early Christians: things just did not turn out the way that had been predicted. He believed that the workers would become increasingly impoverished and wealth would be more and more concentrated in the hands of a few, until the crash came; and then the whole technological apparatus that had been built up would be available for a new utopian egalitarian society. But things turned out quite differently:[9]

> Thus, as in Christian history, Marxism begins with the announcement of the apocalyptic day of wrath and the speedy advent of the kingdom of God, but ends in the indefinite prolonging of the era of the Church, which can justify all persecution and suppression of liberty in the name of that final liberation which never comes but to which it is the exclusive gateway.[10]

c) The notion of historical progress gained special impetus through the publication of *The origin of species* by Charles Darwin (1809-1882). The Darwinian theory of natural selection, as expressed in popular versions of the theory of evolution, seemed to point to human history, like all other forms of life, moving upward toward higher and more sophisticated forms. The idea of a cataclysmic end to history was therefore set aside, in favor of the doctrine of hope that was grounded in the gradual evolution of humanity towards moral and societal perfection.

d) On the basis of the notion of progressive phases of history, August Comte (1798-1857) developed a notion of utopian socialism, understood as a society of equality and justice here on earth. Comte saw history as unfolding in three stages:

---

8 Braaten (1985:341).

9 Macquarrie (1978:6).

10 Rosemary Ruether as quoted in Macquarrie (1978:96-97). the original reference is to Ruether's work *The radical kingdom: The Western experience of messianic hope* (New York: Harper & Row, 1970).

the mythological stage of theology, the metaphysical stage of Western philosophy ad the final positivist stage based on scientific principles applied to human society. Again, the inherent potential of humanity will restrict the effects of evil in the world in order to establish a secularized version of God's reign on earth.

e) A common theme in these nineteenth century movements is that of dialectical and evolutionary progress in history. This fostered a spirit of optimism in all branches of knowledge. The march of progress will inevitably ensure a better future through continuous evolution. In the liberal Protestantism of nineteenth-century theology this myth of progress was expressed in the form of an ethical notion of the reign of God as a realm of moral values, a new social order that was steadily advancing as a result of human activity and moral progress in history. Nürnberger comments on this form of eschatology:

> During the time of the Enlightenment and Romanticism the kingdom was seen in terms of the religious, moral and cultural upliftment of the human race. Western imperialism was regarded as the instrument which carried progress, reason and morality to the ends of the earth. This cultural optimism reached its peak in Europe during the nineteenth century.[11]

This sense op evolutionary optimism is also evident amongst several nineteenth century theologians:

- For J.G Herder (1744-1803) the kingdom was the elevation of the whole race to its true humanity in accord with the law of nature, which is the power, goodness and wisdom of God.
- Friedrich Schleiermacher (1768-1834) attempted to secure Christianity from Enlightenment rationalism and Kantian moralism through the category of an immediate human awareness of absolute dependence. This implies an awareness both of our own finitude and of the infinite on which we depend. A God-consciousness that is aware of its own limitations, and beyond that, of its own imperfection, becomes a consciousness also of sin.[12] Sin and redemption may therefore be described in terms of a growth in God-consciousness. Schleiermacher saw the coming of God's reign accordingly as the highest form of God-consciousness. This is possible on the basis of the redeeming efficacy that rises from the redemption effected in Christ. The Christian consciousness of God is inextricably bound up and derived from Jesus Christ.
- Richard Rothe (1799-1867) envisioned the kingdom as the fellowship of redemption, initially established by the church leading to the fulfillment in the profane world and in the life of the state.

---

[11] Nürnberger (1994;144).

[12] Schleiermacher's notion of absolute dependence constitutes not only a response to societal sin but also to the predicament of human finitude. In this way Schleiermacher managed to avoid the Kantian dichotomy between facts and values.

- Albrecht Ritschl (1822-1889) saw the kingdom as coming through joint human activity where a fellowship of love works towards God's ultimate goal for humanity and the world.[13] The kingdom is a this-worldly moral ideal to be progressively realized through human efforts. Ritschl thus followed the Kantian emphasis on the ethical instead of the mystical significance of Christianity.
- Johann Wilhelm Hermann (1846-1922) adopted a similar ethical interpretation of the Christian gospel. In his eschatology, the reign of God is no longer seen as a future goal but as a present power of energetic action in the world. Eternal life is regarded as the power that God gives to Christians to bear their cross and to live freely, joyfully and hopefully for others.[14]
- A liberal interpretation of God's reign culminated in the work of Adolf von Harnack (1851-1930). For Von Harnack, the coming of God's reign, the fatherhood of God, the infinite value of each human being and love for God and the neighbor constitute the essence of Christianity. God's reign can only be understood from within this fellowship of love as the spiritual power to experience and realize this love. He avoided any emphasis on a transcendent or futurist aspect of Christian hope.

12.3 Contemporary manifestations of hope as progress

Since the Enlightenment, the Christian hope for an imminent coming of God's reign has often been trimmed to the culturally acceptable form of a liberal theory of progress.[15] Human history is regarded as a steadily upward-moving process. Despite the devastating effects in the twentieth century of two world wars, simmering ethnic and religious conflicts, increasing global poverty, looming ecological catastrophes, and Aids, this notion of progress continues to structure the expectations of many people for the twenty first century.

The lasting impact on eschatology of the pillars of modernity is evident from the following features:

a) There remains a persistent conviction that human reason as expressed in modern science and cultivated in systems of education will guarantee the progress of the human race. Also in South Africa, many previously disadvantaged learners still hope that a better education will ensure employment, social security and material prosperity for them and their children.

b) There remains a deeply ingrained faith in the ability of industry, through science and technology, to ensure material prosperity and to satisfy the insatiable wants of humanity. This belief lies at the roots of a consumption-orientated way of life in which nothing but the demands of humanity count.[16]

---

13 McKim (1988:163), paraphrased almost verbatim.

14 Hebblethwaite (1984:114-115).

15 Migliore (1991:233).

16 Olivier (1989:32).

c) The quests for a liberal market economy (Adam Smith) and a participatory democracy (Rousseau) continue to structure the global political economy in an era of increasing globalization. The sense of optimism that only capitalism and a liberal democracy can ensure prosperity in the new century was expressed in the famous article by Francis Fukuyama on "The end of history" (1989). All alternatives such as fascism, nationalism and socialism have now been exhausted. Or, as the *Herald Tribune* reported in 1990:

> After some millennia of trying out various systems we are now ending this millennium in the certainty that in a pluralist capitalist democracy we have found what we were looking for. There can still be endless improvements to the system and approaches to perfection in postmodernity, but there are no longer any alternatives to the fundamentals of the system.[17]

This reduction of hope to a belief in evolutionary progress has often been criticized. Thomas Berry, for example, speaks of the "myth of progress".[18] The notion of progress itself is also being undermined by its own fruits. As Jürgen Moltmann comments: "Progress is no longer an expression of hope, as it was in the nineteenth century. It is a fate to which people in the industrial countries feel themselves condemned."[19] Christian hope is clearly something different from optimism, from a belief in evolutionary progress. How, then, should the content and social impact of Christian hope be articulated?

---

[17] Quoted in Moltmann (1995:203).

[18] Berry (1992:204).

[19] Moltmann (1985:28).

Part D: Contemporary manifestations of Christian hope

In the previous main section of this study (Part C) we investigated the Biblical roots of Christian hope. We also followed the trajectories of Christian hope through the centuries and observed the plurality and ambiguity that characterize the various expressions of Christian hope.

The task of this part is to investigate various contemporary manifestations of Christian hope towards the end of the twentieth century. This has to prepare the way for the task of the next part namely to articulate a vision of hope for the earth at the dawn of a new century.

The three chapters that are included in Part D remain somewhat arbitrary. Nevertheless, each of these chapters has to make an important contribution towards the task of Part E.

- Chapter 13 investigates various aspects and dimensions of Christian hope as expressed in twentieth century (academic) theology. This will provide the necessary background for the systematic task of articulating a clear vision of Christian hope.
- Chapter 14 focuses on the relation between Christian eschatology and the picture of the universe emerging from contemporary science. This is important in order to address the cosmic dimensions of despair that were identified in Chapter 6 and to remind ourselves that an intelligible vision of Christian hope needs to engage in critical dialogue with modern cosmology.
- Chapter 15 investigates four contemporary manifestations of Christian hope in the South African context. This may help to ensure that local Christian communities can appropriate such a vision of hope for the earth towards an environmental spirituality and praxis in South Africa.

13. Hope in twentieth century Christian theology

13.1 Introduction: Typologies and criteria

The story of Christian hope throughout the centuries is one of numerous trajectories, characterized by distortions, retrievals and innovations. These trajectories are incredibly diverse, complex and often confusing. This is nowhere more evident than in the various schools of eschatological thought in the twentieth century.

The diffuse notions of Christian hope have induced almost every recent author on eschatology to search for a typology and criteria to guide oneself through the myriad of schools and approaches. In each typology, different criteria and line(s) of demarcation are identified to classify different eschatologies, for example:

- Eschatological / apocalyptic forms of hope;
- This-worldly (world-affirming) / other-worldly (world-denying) forms of hope;
- The continuity / discontinuity between earth and heaven, this life and the next;
- Realized / futurist eschatology;
- Evolutionary / revolutionary hope;
- Vertical / horizontal dimensions of hope;
- The doctrine of the "last things" / of Jesus as the Eschatos;
- Escapist / liberating forms of hope;
- Personal, historical and cosmic dimensions of hope;
- An emphasis on the things that are hoped for (physics) / on the phenomenon of hope itself (anthropology);
- An emphasis on the cross / on the resurrection of Christ.

In the light of this proliferation of typologies it may be worthwhile to list some attempts to provide such a typology. The difference between the lines of demarcation identified by each typology is of special importance here.

Numerous recent typologies simply trace, from one decade to the next, and amidst changing life perceptions,[1] the historical developments of eschatological reflection in the twentieth century.[2] They show how each new school of thought responded to the inadequacies of a previous one, but also how the line of demarcation between different eschatologies shifted. These historical overviews often leave one with the impression that eschatology is indeed a complex and confusing field of study.

---

1 See Berkhof (1967) who follows such changing perceptions of life in his overview of Protestant, European eschatologies in the first half of the twentieth century.

2 See for example the helpful overviews by Berkhof (1967:85f), Berkouwer (1972:24f), Braaten (1985), McGrath (1994), Runia (1997), Wainwright (1971, 1988).

Most of these historical overviews recognize and discuss the contributions of the following eschatological schools:

1) The "consistent" eschatology of Weiss and Schweitzer,
2) The "transcendental" eschatology of (the early) Barth, Brunner and Althaus,
3) The "existential" eschatology of Bultmann (and also of Tillich),
4) The salvation history approach of Cullmann (in debate with Dodd and Schweitzer),
5) The "futurist" eschatology of Moltmann, Sauter, Pannenberg,
6) The evolutionist eschatology of Teilhard and his followers,
7) The contributions of process theologians,
8) The prophetic approaches of political, liberation, black, feminist and ecological theologies,
9) The millennialist, dispensationalist and apocalyptic views of popular authors such as Hal Lindsay and numerous others.

Several other typologies try to identify certain tensions that dominate the debate or lines of demarcation that can clarify the debate. The following list of typologies (offered here simply in order of date of publication) is indicative of the disquieting complexity of this debate:

- In his illuminating typology, John Macquarrie (1978) identifies the following contrasts in Christian expectations: 1) A contrast between individual, social and cosmic forms of hope, 2) a contrast between this-worldly and other-worldly expectations, 3) a contrast between revolutionary and evolutionary understandings of Christian hope, 4) a contrast between realized, inaugurated and futurist eschatology. On the basis of this "system of coordinates" Macquarrie identifies the theoretic possibility of 16 basic types of eschatology and uses this typology to plot the history of eschatological reflection.[3]
- In a chapter on eschatological trends in *The future of creation* (1979), Moltmann first discusses the tension between presentative (Dodd and Bultmann) and futurist eschatology (Weiss, Schweitzer) and several attempts to formulate a balance between the "already" and the "not-yet" (Cullmann, Brunner, Kreck). He then argues that the basic methodological question in Christian eschatology should instead be formulated in terms of (Christological) continuity or discontinuity.[4] Should the future dispensation be understood as the prolongation or

---

3 Macquarrie (1978:87f).

4 Moltmann (1979:20) asks: "... should one start from 'the future of the present Christ' (or faith) or from 'the presence of the coming Christ'. Does the future determine the present, or does the present determine the future? Is the theme of Christian eschatology 'the future of what has already come' (Kreck) or 'the presence of what is still to come' (Iwand)?" A few pages later Moltmann repeats the same kind of question: "... is the incarnation the horizon of the eschaton, or is eschatology the horizon of the incarnation?" (1979:27).

"extrapolation" of experiences of God's presence (Berkhof) or should the present be understood as the anticipation of a radically new eschaton? A third debate centers around the question whether eschatology should be understood in terms of the tension between what is hidden and what is revealed (Barth). Will the future simply be the unfolding of what has already been revealed in Jesus Christ?[5] Moltmann proposes that a distinction between the future as *futurum* and as *adventus* may help to clarify these debates. For Moltmann, the future, Christologically understood as *adventus*, does not simply emerge from the present (through extrapolation); the present springs from a future which one must be expectant of.[6]

- In his work *What are they saying about the end of the world?* (1983), Zachary Hayes gives a brief overview of the recent history of eschatology and then indicates some shifts in the debate. He detects 1) a tendency to move from eschatology as the concern for personal meaning to eschatology as the question of the final destiny of the human race and the world;[7] 2) a shift from physics to anthropology (i.e. from a preview of the end of the world to a projection or extrapolation from the Christian experience of the present into the mode of future fulfillment); 3) a growing interest in the relation between hope as a human phenomenon and the specific content and dynamics of Christian hope; 4) a shift away from an exclusive concern for individual eschatology to a renewed sense of the collective; 5) a paradoxical pendulum swing from a focus on the immortality of the soul to the resurrection of the body to a less crudely materialist and somewhat spiritualized notion of resurrection.[8]
- In a somewhat different typology, Rosemary Ruether (1983) distinguishes between three patterns of hope, namely 1) nature religion (which regards the cycles of renewal in nature as the key to constant hope for renewed life, resurrected from drought and death), 2) historical religion (which locates the ultimate achievement of an ideal society in a final era of world history,[9] and 3) eschatological religion (which expects ultimate vindication in a historical millennium or beyond it in an eternal realm of heaven).[10] The line of demarcation in Ruether's typology seems to be the social impact of these forms of hope (constant renewal of community life, utopian thinking, or escapism beyond the confines of female bodiliness).
- In *Beyond the Big Bang* (1990), Willem Drees distinguishes between two basic types of theology and, correspondingly, eschatology. 1) Christian faith may

---

5 The tensions that Moltmann identifies here are, significantly, the same tensions which will be discussed below in relation to the three dimensions of the human predicament.

6 Moltmann (1979:29).

7 Hayes (1983:11).

8 Hayes (1983:12-28).

9 Ruether (1983:243) adds that this form of revolutionary hope has no immediate answer to the untimely sufferings and deaths of present and past generations.

10 Ruether (1983:237-245).

focus on God's hidden presence in the world. It investigates this hidden presence, extending the limitations of human knowledge and searching for ontological harmony (consonance) between theological thinking on the God-world relationship and scientific knowledge about the world. 2) Alternatively, Christian faith may focus on God's apparent absence from the world, illustrated by experiences of unjust suffering, evil, finitude and imperfection. This does not imply an atheist denial of God's existence but assumes the possibility of God's presence (an absence crying out for presence) and therefore confronts the tension between God and the world.[11] Likewise, Christian eschatology may focus on 1) the finiteness or creatureliness of existence or 2) on injustice, the brokenness of existence.[12]

- In *The Coming of God* (1996) Moltmann distinguishes between three forms of eschatology based on categories of 1) time, 2) eternity, or 3) his own proposal of the coming of God (time as *adventus*). The transposition of eschatology into time assumes a temporal tension between presentative and futurist eschatologies, between the already and the not-yet (debated by Schweitzer, Dodd, Cullmann).[13] In the transposition of eschatology into eternity (suggested by Barth, Althaus, Bultmann) eternity becomes simultaneous to all times and history is swallowed up by eschatology. By contrast, Moltmann suggests that eschatology should focus on the salvific and transformative coming (*adventus*) of God to creation.[14]
- In *The end of the world?* (1997) Reginald Stackhouse identifies three models of eschatology, namely 1) a *millennial* interpretation that believes in a better world still to come, 2) a *pastoral* interpretation holding that the church is already a manifestation of a kingdom which is beyond this world, and 3) a *social* interpretation assuming that a better world is possible in this dispensation.[15]
- In *What dare we hope?* (1999), Gerard Sauter distinguishes between three types of eschatology: 1) "consistent" eschatology: the notion that eschatology can only be understood as the expectation of imminent events in which the kingdom of God will break into our reality in order to transform it (Schweitzer); 2) eschatology as "a theology of history": a teleological view on the destiny of global history that integrates everything into a coherent whole and that sees it with the eyes of hope, if necessary contradicting particular historical conditions with the coming of God's reign (Pannenberg and Moltmann); and 3) "radical eschatology": an eschatology that focuses on God as the deepest reason and

---

11 Drees (1990:5-6).

12 Drees (1990:118f).

13 Moltmann (1996:6f) comments that this form of eschatology assumes a tension between what remains hidden (in my analysis a response to the predicament of limited human knowledge), but is not yet present (revealed?). The focus of hope is then that, that what is not yet, can after all still be. Moltmann criticizes this form of eschatology because it is undermined by transience (in my analysis the predicament of finitude).

14 Moltmann (1996:22-29).

15 Stackhouse (1997).

foundation of Christian hope, on what a radically transcendent God, the "wholly Other", alone can bring about beyond the confines of history (Barth).[16]

Several other scholars, instead of developing yet another typology, reflected on principles or criteria for eschatology. A few further examples may suffice:

- In an influential essay, Karl Rahner formulated a central Christological principle for Christian eschatology: "Eschatology is a forward look which is necessary to man (sic) for his spiritual decision in freedom, and it is made from the standpoint of his situation in saving history as this is determined by the Christ event."[17] Our present experience of God's grace in Christ is already eschatological but remains incomplete and hence contains in itself the dynamism of a projection of future completion and fulfillment. This also means that eschatological knowledge is not clear conceptual knowledge about future events or objects, but an obscure expectation of the possible fulfillment of the grace experienced already now.[18]
- Carl Braaten offers four criteria for making appropriate eschatological statements: it must be 1) existentially relevant, 2) controlled by the kerugma deriving from Scripture, 3) centered on Christ and 4) futuristic, that is, "concerned with the realm of hope which comes from God's victory in the resurrection of Christ".[19] Braaten also plots the various options for an understanding of God's reign on the basis of the tension between this-worldly and other-worldly eschatology and between the present and the future. Subsequently, Braaten asks: "Did Jesus think of the kingdom of God as something otherworldly and future (traditional orthodoxy)? Or as something otherworldly and present (Karl Barth and dialectical theology)? Or as something this-worldly and present (Rudolf Bultmann and existentialist theology)? Or as something this-worldly and future (Christian Marxism and liberation theology)?"[20]
- Geoffrey Wainwright simply identifies a series of eschatological categories, namely vertical and horizontal, present and future, time and eternity, earth and heaven, nature and super-nature, provisional and ultimate reality, hiddenness and disclosure, knowledge through faith and through sight, promise and fulfillment, purpose and destiny. He finds each of these polar categories valuable as a conceptual framework for eschatology.[21]

---

16 Sauter (1999). Sauter's distinction bears a resemblance to the three human predicaments analyzed in Part A of this work: "consistent eschatology" focuses on the predicament of historical finitude, the "theology of history" approach focuses on the salvation of world history (from sin), while "radical eschatology" focuses on the hope in what God alone can bring about beyond the limitations of human knowledge and power.

17 Rahner (1966:323).

18 Rahner (1966:323).

19 Hayes (1983:14).

20 Braaten (1985:332).

21 Wainwright (1971:1-17).

- In an overview of "new eschatologies", Rast identifies the following five major shifts: 1) A shift from eschatology as the final chapter of dogmatics to the eschatological positioning of theology as a whole; 2) A shift from an eschatology of the future to the eschatological significance of the present; 3) A shift from the content of hope ("essential" eschatology) to the existential significance of this hope; 4) A shift from an understanding of the *eschata* as things and events to a focus on Jesus Christ as the *Eschatos*; 5) A shift from individual to universal eschatology.[22]
- According to Ted Peters (with reference to the work of Moltmann and Pannenberg), the crucial line of demarcation between various eschatologies is a perception of the future as *futurum* or as *adventus*. In the one case the future is simply understood as the growth, development, maturation or fruition of forces or trends already at work in the present. An emphasis on the future as *adventus*, by contrast, allows for the appearance of something new. It is a future that can be anticipated or hoped for but its arrival is not dependent only upon present potentialities. In Christian eschatology the future arrives by the coming of God's kingdom.[23]
- In his work on *Jesus Christ, the Eschatos* (1989), König proposes a different kind of typology on the basis of the observation that the term Eschatos is often linked to the person of Jesus and that the whole history of Jesus Christ is described in eschatological terminology.[24] If eschatology is thus linked with Christology it is not primarily a historical or futuristic but a Christological category. König therefore proposes the following scheme: that Christ establishes the eschaton 1) *for* us (through his earthly ministry), 2) *in* us (through the continuing work of the Holy Spirit in the church) and 3) *with* us (by establishing the Kingdom of God through us in the whole world, culminating in the return of Christ).[25]
- In order to clarify the "often confusing and contradictory interpretations of Christian hope" Migliore (1991) identifies four conflicts in modern eschatology: 1) A conflict between futurist (Schweitzer) and realized eschatology (Dodd); 2) A conflict between existential eschatology (Bultmann) and corporate eschatology (Moltmann & liberation theology); 3) A conflict between historical eschatology (Western theology) and cosmic eschatology (Eastern theology, process theology); 4) A conflict in focusing on God's activity (neo-orthodoxy) or human activity (theologies of praxis).[26]

---

[22] Rast (1970). I am indebted to Thishiku (1983) for a helpful summary of Rast's argument.

[23] Peters (1978:20-21).

[24] König (1989:37f).

[25] König (1989).

[26] Migliore (1991:237). Migliore adds that these conflicts result from one-sided interpretations of eschatology. In his discussion, he therefore simply tries to balance these perspectives with one another.

The sheer variety of typologies, criteria and lines of demarcation in recent contributions to Christian eschatology does not seem to provide the clarity that one may have hoped for. To attempt yet another typology may be superfluous and may simply add to the confusion.[27] However, there may be good reasons why every scholar in eschatology seems to perceive the need for a typology: one simply has to gain some degree of clarity (if only for oneself) in an often obscure field of study.

The discussion in this chapter will follow and develop the analysis of the three human predicaments suggested in Chapter 2. It proposes that eschatological responses to these predicaments have led to various typical tensions in twentieth century eschatology. Since these are creative tensions (i.e. not dualistic tensions), an exclusive emphasis on one pole within this tension will lead to a distortion of Christian hope.

- Christian hope for salvation from sin, liberation from oppression and victory from evil maintains a tension between the "already" and the "not yet" of the fulfillment of God's promises.
- Christian hope for life beyond death maintains a tension between the continuity and discontinuity of this life and eternal life, this earth and the new earth, this dispensation and the next.
- Christian hope for being in the presence of God maintains a tension between the immanent and the transcendent, between the dimensions of space-time and eternity, between God and the world.

In Chapter 19 we will investigate similar tensions relating to the social impact of these dimensions of Christian hope.

13.2 An eschatological tension between the already and the not-yet

When eschatology is treated as the "perfectly harmless" last chapter of dogmatics it has little or no functional relation to soteriology. The shift of eschatology to the center of theological attention may be regarded as a reaction against this separation of eschatology and soteriology.[28]

The focus of Christian hope on salvation from sin, liberation from oppression and victory over evil accounts for the tension in many twentieth century eschatologies between promise and fulfillment, between the "already" and the "not yet" of experiences of salvation and liberation.[29] This is evident from the way in which the soteriological roots of eschatology is emphasized (or ignored) in numerous twentieth century eschatologies.

In the liberal optimism of the nineteenth century, the predicament of evil and

---

27 Moltmann (1996:6).

28 Braaten (1974:9).

29 These experiences may have personal, societal or cosmic dimensions. The tension between already and not yet is both present in the groaning of creation and in the individual pilgrimages of believers. See Berkouwer (1972:113).

sin was dangerously underestimated. Many believed that education, human reason, technology, biological evolution, an entrepreneurial spirit, a participatory democracy will be sufficient to ensure future progress in all spheres of society. Christian hope for an imminent eschaton was thus trimmed to the culturally acceptable form of the liberal theory of evolutionary progress.[30] Or, in the famous words of Richard Niebuhr: "A God without wrath brought men without sin into a kingdom without judgment through the ministrations of a Christ without a cross."[31]

This optimism, which still flares up with regular intervals, was shattered by the numerous crises that characterized the twentieth century (two world wars, the Holocaust, the development of nuclear weapons, ominous signs of ecological degradation, global poverty, ethnic and religious conflicts, etc).[32] This required a much deeper recognition of the pervasiveness of evil and sin. The locus of evil could no longer be restricted to the individual sphere. Sin emerged in countless new societal forms – as the evils of fascism, colonialism, racism, sexism, classism, elitism and anthropocentrism began to be named.

In eschatological reflection in the twentieth century, the predicament of sin was already prominent in the classic debate between "consistent", "realized" and "inaugurated" eschatology. The tension between promise and fulfillment, between the "already" and the "not yet" of salvation from sin became the focus of these debates.

The exegetical work of Albert Schweitzer and Johannes Weiss made it clear that the kingdom of God was more than an ethically ordered society, to be gradually realized on earth and toward which society was steadily advancing through a process of continuous evolution (Ritschl). The kingdom of God is not to be understood as the product of human accomplishments.

- Weiss's New Testament studies indicated that Jesus' understanding of the kingdom of God can not be separated from the apocalyptic expectations prevailing in his time. The kingdom of God is in Jesus' view in absolute contrast to this world. Weiss did not try to harmonize his modern Protestant worldviews with that of primitive Christianity but cheerfully accepted the difference. We neither believe that the world is passing away, nor (even less) do we pray for its passing. We may pass our lives in joyful confidence that this world will more and more become the showplace of the people of God.[33]

---

30 Migliore (1991:233).

31 Niebuhr (1937:193).

32 This shattered optimism was epitomized by the publication of Spengler's work, *The decline of the West* (1926) and by the sinking of the Titanic (1912) that became a symbol of impending catastrophe (see Körtner (1995). In Christian theology, Karl Barth expressed this shattered optimism with particular sharpness. Interestingly, his initial response was to emphasize the radical distance between God and humanity (related to the predicament of human limitedness) and not the contrast between sin and grace or fallen creation and new creation (related to the predicament of sin). See the discussion on Barth in Chapter 13.4 below.

33 Macquarrie (1978:98).

- Schweitzer built on the work of Weiss and argued that the whole of Jesus' teaching and ministry must be understood in a thoroughly eschatological way. Jesus expected the coming of the kingdom in the form of an apocalyptic event, something radically different, new, and diametrically opposed to the present world. The kingdom of God will intervene disruptively in the midst of human history through a surprising, transcendent act of God. Jesus was not to be seen as the moral educator of humanity, but as the one who proclaims the imminent coming of the eschatological kingdom of God. For Jesus, the preaching on the kingdom of God was not aimed at an amelioration of the world (Jesus as wisdom teacher), but was an announcement of its downfall and end (Jesus as apocalyptic preacher). Jesus is therefore a stranger and an enigma to the modern world. Schweitzer concluded that the whole momentum of the New Testament message and the New Testament faith lay in the hope of Jesus' return and the setting up of the kingdom of God on earth. The kingdom of God can only be understood as the expectation of an imminent catastrophe through which the kingdom of God will break into our reality in order to transform it. The reign of God does not "grow" out of history but rather breaks into history.[34] For Schweitzer this is a hope that had clearly not been fulfilled and was therefore erroneous.[35]
- In response, C.H. Dodd argued that salvation is not to be seen as something totally oriented toward the unknown future, but as something which had been realized in the coming of Jesus. It is already a present reality. "The inconceivable had happened: history had become the vehicle of the eternal; the absolute was clothed with flesh and blood ... The world has become the scene of a divine drama, in which the eternal issues are laid bare. It is the hour of decision. It is realized eschatology."[36] In Jesus Christ a new dispensation has arrived. In the presence of Christ, the Eschatos, in the body of Christ and through the Spirit living "in us", one can already experience eternal life, something of the comprehensive well-being, the eschatological *shalom*.[37] There will not be another coming of Christ in history, because he has already come once and for all. The coming of Christ is an event beyond history and not at the end of history. If the eschaton is not connected to one particular period in history, the salvation and judgment of Christ may be near to all ages.[38]

---

[34] See Sauter (1999:33).

[35] See, especially, Schweitzer's classic work, *The quest for the historical Jesus* (London, 1910). See also Moltmann's (1996:8) helpful discussion of these early twentieth century eschatologies.

[36] Dodd (1961:159).

[37] Dodd (1961). This emphasis on the eschatological dimension of "being in the presence of" the Father, Christ and the Spirit also responds to the predicament of human limitedness. In the presence of God the effects of sin are not only nullified, the limitations of human power and knowledge are also transcended.

[38] Schwarz (1984:521) notes that Dodd thus wanted to escape from an antiquated cosmology without falling into the trap of projecting an earthly utopia as the final goal

- In the salvation history approach of Cullmann, the "already" and the "not-yet" of salvation from sin are neatly balanced with one another in terms of a linear concept of time. In response to the problem of the delayed *parousia*, Cullmann argues that the kingdom of God was inaugurated by Christ. Through the resurrection of Christ the decisive battle against evil has been won. To explain this tension Cullmann uses the well-known image of D-day (the decisive battle), and V-day (the day of victory).[39] Since the ascension of Christ, the time of the Holy Spirit has begun. We therefore live "between the times", between the inauguration and the consummation of the kingdom. Salvation is at the same time a present reality and something that is yet to happen.[40]
- Kreck also argued that salvation from sin is simultaneously already present and not-yet fulfilled. This balance between the realized and futurist aspects of salvation is developed by him on the basis of the Lutheran axiom of *simul iustus et peccator*.[41] For Kreck, the reign of God is a present reality since the coming of Christ. However, it still remains hidden, and will yet be made manifest. The crucified will then be revealed as having been the Lord of history now. In the well-chosen title of his major study on eschatology, Kreck can therefore speak of "Die Zukunft das Gekommenen."[42] The tension between the already and the not-yet is therefore understood noetically as the future revelation of what is now still hidden, the future seeing of what is now only glimpsed.[43]

This tension between the already and the not-yet of salvation from sin was also the subject of debate between Walter Rauschenbusch and Reinhold Niebuhr:

- According to the "social gospel"-movement led in the USA by Rauschenbusch,

---

of history.

39 Cullman (1967:44).

40 See especially Cullmann's works *Christ and time* (1962) and *Salvation in history* (1967). See also McGrath's helpful summary of this debate (1994:340-1). It remains a question whether Cullmann really provides a satisfactory solution to the problem of the delayed *parousia*. See, for example, the comment by Hayes (1983:35):

> Christians claim that the eschatological event has been realized in the life, death, and resurrection of Jesus. But if the Christian claim is correct, why is it that history continues with no obvious difference in the face of this eschatological event?

See also Moltmann (1979:19, 1996:10-13) for a detailed critique of Cullmann's position. Moltmann argues that the inadequacies of Cullmann's eschatology are related to his linear concept of (calendar) time, reducing the eschaton to an event in history: "The reduction of eschatology to time in the framework of salvation history also really abolishes eschatology altogether, subjecting it to *chronos*, the power of transience. Is 'temporality' really 'the essence of eschatology'?" (1996:13).

41 Kreck (1961:14-76).

42 Kreck (1966).

43 Kreck (1961). See also Wainwright (1971:15), who comments with reference to Kreck that, beyond a fuller knowledge of what is already present, there needs to be room for God to also establish new things, a new heaven and a new earth.

the kingdom of God should not be understood in terms of the hereafter.[44] Heaven is a symbol of perfection that must be realized here on earth. For Rauschenbusch, this implied the need for social justice amidst the miseries of an industrializing society. The kingdom of God is equated with a just society. The progress and eventual triumph of the kingdom in this world was understood in an evolutionary way: each new social reform is a victory for the kingdom.[45]

- Niebuhr also emphasized the need to establish a new social order in this world – against the evils of capitalism and fascism. However, he did not share the evolutionary optimism of Rauschenbusch. He was far more under the impression of the enormity of sin and its influence on power relations in society. Society itself is under God's judgment. A new social order is only possible on the basis of repentance. Any structural social reforms towards justice would still be corrupted by sin because the hands building the new order remained sinning hands.[46] According to Niebuhr's "Christian realism", this may imply the use of coercion to reach the goal of justice at a societal level.[47] The kingdom of God remained ultimately beyond this world. History moves towards the realization of the Kingdom but the judgment of God is upon every new realization.[48] Christians therefore have to live in two worlds – called to live in this world but not to accept its fallen standards.

In the early "transcendental" eschatology of Barth, Brunner, Tillich, Bultmann and Althaus, the qualitative difference between God and the world was portrayed as a judgment of the world (i.e. with reference to the predicament of sin).[49] However, the focus of this form of eschatology was, somewhat surprisingly, not on salvation from sin but on the relationship between God and the world (a response to the predicament of human limitations in space).[50] The eschatological judgment of God

---

44 Rauschenbusch (1991:160) draws a sharp contrast between the hope for the kingdom of God and for eternal life in the early church. Nevertheless, a truly Christian hope should include both dimensions. He says of the earlier ascetic form of eschatology:

> But as eternal life came to the front in Christian hope, the kingdom of God receded to the background, and with it went much of the social potency of Christianity. The kingdom of God was a social and collective hope and it was for this earth. The eternal life was an individualistic hope, and it was not for this earth. The kingdom of God involved the social transformation of humanity. The hope for eternal life, as it was then held, was the desire to escape from this world and be done with it. The kingdom was a revolutionary idea; eternal life was an ascetic idea (1991:162).

45 Rauschenbusch (1991).

46 Niebuhr (1943:244f).

47 Niebuhr (1932:257-8).

48 Niebuhr (1943:286).

49 Barth (1933:500).

50 In his later work Barth did discuss the tension between the already and the not-yet of salvation from sin extensively. See Barth (*CD* 4.3.1, 1961:306f, 318f; *CD* 4.3.2, 1962:903f).

on the world is an expression of the current confrontation between this world and the eternity of God. The downplaying of and abstraction from temporal futurity was one of the conditions for making the biblical message relevant (in transcendental terms with Barth, in existential terms with Bultmann or in axiological terms with Althaus). Thus this form of eschatology lost a temporal structure and an emphasis on future consummation.[51] Eternity becomes simultaneous to all times and history is swallowed up by eschatology.[52] I will return to this shift in the discussion below (13.4).

This form of transcendental eschatology was severely criticized in the "futurist" approach of Jürgen Moltmann, Wolfhart Pannenberg, Johann-Baptist Metz and Gerhard Sauter. Eschatology is no longer understood as the entrance of eternity vertically into time, or as an event at the end of time (apocalyptic). Instead, the focus shifts to the impact of the envisioned future with God on each period in the course of history.[53] Each of these thinkers restored the emphasis on future consummation by retrieving the key function of the biblical notion of promise. The divine word of promise opened up the possibility of a new future, liberated from the suffering caused by present manifestations of evil. The suffering of the victims of the past thus becomes the very focus of Christian eschatology.

- In his *Theology of hope* (1967), Moltmann argues that Christian theology has been far too preoccupied with the problem of God's revelation and the true knowledge of God. Far too little attention has been given to the category of promise. God is not revealed in an "epiphany of eternal presence", but in the "apocalypse of the promised future"[54] and in the history that is marked by this promise.[55] Revelation is not a manifestation of what is hidden in Christ; it is a promise of what will be in the future.[56]

  Like Barth, Moltmann views the word of promise as a contradiction of the present reality.[57] But against Barth's claim that the eschatological future will

---

51 See Pannenberg's (1998:537, 594) assessment of Barth. See also Van Ruler (1972:102f) for a strong emphasis on the relationship between eschatology and history. The direction that history on earth is taking, remains important in order to emphasize that the earth itself must be cleansed from injustice and evil.

52 Moltmann (1996:13f). Moltmann observes that eschatology is thus transposed into eternity.

53 Gilkey (1976:228).

54 Moltmann (1967:57).

55 Moltmann (1967:42). This emphasis on revelation as promise has a curious side-effect if revelation is linked to salvation. Then salvation is always only promised, never experienced. Even the resurrection of Christ is interpreted as a promise of the eschaton. Moltmann is thus in danger of subsuming the tension between the already and the not-yet under a futurist notion of the not-yet.

56 Moltmann (1967:84f). See also Haught (1993b:89): "Promise is the form of revelation, and hope is the indispensable attitude for the reception of revelation."

57 See Pannenberg's (1998:538) assessment of Moltmann on this point: "In this respect

be an "unveiling" of that which was decisively accomplished by Christ in the cross and resurrection, Moltmann argues that Christian hope expects something new from him, something that has not yet happened before.[58] The future of the risen Lord involves not merely a noetic expectation of the unveiling of something that was hidden, but also the fulfilling of something that was promised and guaranteed by the resurrection event.[59] Moltmann speaks of the resurrection as a *creatio ex nihilo*. It is itself a promise, a foretaste of the coming kingdom. Moltmann therefore stresses the theme of openness to the future.

- A concern for the future is of special importance in the work of Pannenberg. In *Theology and the Kingdom of God* (1969), he introduces the notion of the "ontological priority of the future", which develops the relation between creation and God in terms of the present impact of the imminent future. God is the future of the world, pulling the universe from the future.[60] The present is an effect of the future; the future is not caused by the past or by the present.[61] The future has an imperative claim upon the present, alerting all people to the urgency and exclusiveness of seeking first the Kingdom of God. In this way one may get a glimpse of God's glory. This is understood *proleptically*: in Jesus Christ the future consummation of all things is already announced, provisionally actualized and thus anticipated. In the work of Jesus, and in the resurrection especially, the Kingdom is indeed already present.[62] The presence of Jesus Christ is the basis of the expectation of the Christian community for the consummation that is yet to come. The fulfilling of the promises of God in Christ provides a springboard to put these promises into force for us.[63] Salvation has not yet been definitively actualized merely by the mission of the Son. It will only be consummated by the work of the Spirit who bears witness to and

---

Moltmann was still close to the Word of God theology of Barth and Bultmann inasmuch as he refrained from trying to give validity to the word of promise in terms of the reality of human experience and viewed the promise essentially as a contradiction of the reality of the world as we now know it."

58 Moltmann (1967:228-9).

59 Moltmann (1967:88).

60 See also the admirably clear summary by Peters (1993:8) of Pannenberg's proleptic eschatology: "The anticipation of wholeness of meaning within common human experience is the key that makes Pannenberg's method work. We anticipate a wholeness of meaning that is not yet fully present, a wholeness that we hypothesize will come in the future as the gift of an eschatological act of the one God. The direct confirmation of this hypothesis is dependent on the actual coming of that eschatological wholeness. In the meantime, while we await the eschatological fulfillment, the faith hypothesis can gain indirect confirmation by the increased intelligibility it offers to our understanding of our experience of finite reality." See also Pannenberg (1969:53f).

61 Pannenberg (1969:54). See also the following formulation: "Thus does the future determine the present. If we, in our anxiety and hope, contemplate this power of the future, we recognize both its breathtaking excitement and its invitation to trust." (1969:59).

62 Pannenberg (1998:545).

63 Pannenberg (1998:545f).

completes the work of the Son.[64]

- Johann-Baptist Metz objected to the non-historical, metaphysical style of eschatology in Roman Catholic theology. For Metz, a Christian eschatology should provide a basis for the critique of ideologies and social structures that become absolutized and totalitarian. In the light of the "eschatological proviso" the status of every society in history is shown to be provisional.[65] The church itself, as an institution of social criticism, lives under this "eschatological proviso". The hope that it announces is hope, not so much for the church itself, but for the kingdom of God.[66]

  For Metz, Christian hope is orientated towards the future through the proclamation of God's words of promise that in this way initiates a new future.[67] This stimulates a creative and militant hope, a responsibility for the world and its future, a passionate and innovative initiative to change the world toward the coming reign of God.[68] For Metz, this hope is born from keeping alive[69] the challenging, dangerous and subversive memory of the suffering, death and resurrection of Jesus Christ. This memory becomes liberative, a dangerous emancipatory force, when it is not simply expressed in empty tautologies but when it shocks us out of ever becoming prematurely reconciled with absolutized power structures. In such contexts, the Christian *memoria passionis, mortis et resurrectionis Jesu Christi* recalls the God of the passion of Jesus Christ as the subject and meaning of history as a whole. The Christian remembrance of suffering thus becomes an anticipatory memory; it contains the anticipation of a future given through the resurrection of Christ to the suffering, the hopeless, the oppressed, the victims of this earth.[70] The suffering of past victims (especially the victims of the Holocaust) is thus not forgotten or ameliorated, but opens human history for its ultimate future with God.[71] Resurrection in the light of the memory of suffering means that the dead, those already vanquished and forgotten, have a meaning that is as yet unrealized.[72]

The emphasis in all these eschatologies is on future consummation. The future will

---

64 Pannenberg (1998:551).

65 Metz (1969:114, 1970:144, 1980:115f).

66 Metz (1969:94; 1970:146).

67 Metz (1969:85).

68 Metz (1969:91-97).

69 The need to keep the memory of suffering alive is born from the sublimation of such memories in totalitarian rule. Metz argues that every rebellion against suffering is fed by the subversive power of remembered suffering (Metz & Moltmann 1995:8). This need formulates precisely the urgency of the work of the Truth and Reconciliation in South Africa.

70 Metz (1995:15).

71 Metz (1972:124-131, 1980:88f, 109f, 1995:3-16).

72 Metz (1980:113).

bring something qualitatively new. In this way present experiences of sin, injustice and evil will not have the final word. A response to the predicament of evil is therefore prominent in these eschatologies. However, the focus often shifts to a metaphysical explanation of the very possibility of something new. This is often expressed in the form of a futurist ontology where the not-yet receives a certain priority over the present. Perhaps this indicates an awareness of the need for an integrated approach that also responds to the predicament of finitude in time and space. I will return to this feature in the discussion below (13.3 & 13.4).

The predicament of evil and sin became even more prominent in the eschatology of prophetic theologies (liberation theology, black theology, feminist theology, and some ecological theologies). In these theologies there is a very strong reaction against escapist, otherworldly forms of hope. The reign of God is not to be established in another world; it is coming into being within history, in this world, transformed and made new.[73] Local Christian communities have to function as a kind of socio-political avant-garde for the transformation of the whole society.[74] The focus of eschatological reflection therefore shifts to an analysis of the present context and a historical transformation of the conditions of life here and now. In line with the classic prophetic tradition, Christian hope becomes focused on the foreseeable future here on earth. The biblical vision of the eschatological reign of God is defined as a situation of freedom from political and economic oppression and social injustice. As a real utopia, the reign of God is always ahead of us in the form of a shifting horizon, and functions as a continuous challenge for us to transcend and overcome the oppressive structures of the present order.[75] It inspires people to commit themselves in solidarity with the oppressed and to work for justice, peace and environmental sustainability here on earth. This vision of the imminent future thus has a strong ethical impetus.

In these prophetic theologies the task of a contemporary Christian eschatology is to formulate a vision of a free, non-oppressive, non-sexist, non-racist, participatory, sustainable society. Examples of this form of eschatology can easily be multiplied. Since examples from South African liberation and black theology will be discussed in Chapter 15, a few classic examples from elsewhere in the world may be mentioned here:

- An eschatological vision of justice and peace is of special importance in the confrontation against racial injustice in the civil rights movement in the USA. The famous "I have a dream" speech (1963) of Martin Luther King (jr) articulated his eschatological vision of a society where the children of former slaves would sit down at the table with the children of former slave owners, where people will not be judged by the color of their skin but by the content of their character, where freedom will reign in every hamlet, village, city and state. The conviction that this dream will be realized in this world, "some day soon" was

73 Brown (1981:116).

74 Mudge (1998:152).

75 Nürnberger (1994:146).

expressed in the chorus, "We shall overcome ..."[76]

- In his seminal work, *A theology of human hope* (1969), Rubem Alves focuses on the need of the poor to be allowed to create their own history towards a humanization of the whole society ("political humanism"). This requires a human consciousness that is made free from the past and open to the future. Free human beings have to take power in their own hands in order to create their own future, a future which liberates them from the passivity under which the slave master keeps them. Human hope, and not technological or developmental panaceas, is the way in which a humanization of the world becomes possible.

  Christianity may offer a wider horizon for this shared hope and help to search for a language expressive of a commitment to the liberation of humanity. This happens when the community of faith discovers itself being ultimately concerned for the creation of a new tomorrow for humanity.[77] This also calls for a criticism of any form of other-worldly religion: "Religion, therefore is to be destroyed for the sake of the earth, for the sake of man's freedom to criticize his world in order to transform it."[78] For Alves, Christian language about God has to retell the story *of historical events* in order to make clear that the achievement of humanization is not only the result of human efficacy but also a gift (e.g. in Christ); that it comes through a power in history from beyond history that refuses to abandon history.[79] To speak about God is to speak about the historical events that make humanity free.[80] Messianic humanism is neither hope without history, nor history without hope; it expects that the messianic politics of God will bring to history and humanity a new future and a new hope.[81]
- In *A black theology of liberation* (1970, 1986), James Cone argues that the focus of eschatology should be shifted away from life after death. For blacks death is not really a future reality; it is part of their everyday existence.[82] Cone argues that hope must be related to the present. It must serve as a means of transforming an oppressed community into a liberated and liberating community. Black theology believes that when Christians affirm the resurrection of Christ they cannot be satisfied with the present world as it is.[83]
- In his classic work, *A theology of liberation* (1973), Gustavo Gutiérrez relates the Biblical eschatological vision with the harsh realities of poverty and oppression in Latin America. Moltmann's emphasis on God's revelatory promise is concretized as a promise for liberation, not only from sin, but also from poverty

---

76 Stackhouse (1997:107-9).

77 Alves (1969:73-74).

78 Alves (1969:33).

79 Alves (1969:87, 90f).

80 Alves (1969:99).

81 Alves (1969:100).

82 Cone (1986:136).

83 Cone (1986:140-141).

and oppression that orientates all history to the future. This promise unfolds (becomes richer and more definite) throughout history, culminating in Jesus Christ. Human history is the history of the slow, partial, uncertain and surprising fulfillment of this promise.[84] The promise is not exhausted by these fulfillments, but goes beyond them, giving them an ultimate meaning. Gutiérrez explains:

> The Promise is gradually revealed in all its universality and concrete expression: it is already fulfilled in historical events, but not yet completely; it incessantly projects itself into the future, creating a permanent historical mobility. The Promise is inexhaustible and dominates history, because it is the self-communication of God. With the incarnation of the Son and the sending of the Spirit of Promise, this self-communication has entered into its decisive stage.[85]

The prophetic vision of the reign of God, in contrast to present oppression, inspires a political praxis of liberation from the effects of sin within this world. This demands orthopraxis and not only orthodoxy. Through political action a new (although not final) embodiment of the kingdom on earth may be realized. Gutiérrez insists that a "historical, political, liberating event *is* the growth of the Kingdom and *is* a salvific event; but it is not *the* coming of the Kingdom, not all of salvation."[86]

- In *Doing theology in a revolutionary situation* (1975), José Míguez-Bonino insisted likewise, that the reign of God should not be individualized (in the dream of immortality) or spiritualized (e.g. by restricting what is eschatological to the ecclesial sphere). All the actions of women and men to achieve liberation point to the kingdom. They belong to a new eschatological order breaking into history.[87] God's reign is established in general history which is therefore not without eschatological significance.[88] The kingdom redeems, transforms and perfects history and the love that has operated in it.[89] Bonino adds (against a transcendental form of eschatology) that the problem of eschatology is not so much noetic (discerning the presence of the kingdom), but empirical. The kingdom is not a riddle to be solved, but a mission to be fulfilled in history.[90] The Christian faith provides a stimulus and a challenge for revolutionary action by encouraging us to work for historical realizations in the direction of the kingdom in terms of justice, solidarity and human community.[91]

---

84 See especially Gutiérrez (1973:160-168).

85 Gutiérrez (1973:161).

86 Gutiérrez (1973:177); the emphasis is in the original.

87 Bonino (1975:132-153).

88 Bonino (1975:137).

89 Bonino (1975:142).

90 Bonino (975:143).

91 Bonino (1975:152).

Amongst ecological theologians a similar approach to eschatology is, for example, evident in the work of ecofeminist scholars such as Sallie McFague and Rosemary Ruether (although is should be added that eschatology is not a dominant theme in ecofeminist writing):

- In *Sexism and God-talk* (1983), Ruether explicitly criticizes a preoccupation with immortality (the predicament of finitude) or with the otherworldly, transcendent realm of heaven (the predicament of spatial limitedness). Instead, the focus shifts to life on earth in all its fullness. The earth as a living organism is essentially good and trustworthy. To yearn for life beyond the cycle of life and death is pointless. Even to ask about human destiny is to risk being sidetracked from a proper concern for *this* time and *this* place. Our responsibility is to use our temporal life span to create a just and good community for our generation and for our children.[92] Ruether also criticizes the revolutionary dream of a final just society as being anti-ecological because it disregards finite limits and relationships between humanity and the non-human environment. It tends to absolutize a particular revolutionary construct. This dream also tends to idolize change and fails to respect the relational patterns of our bodiliness and embeddedness in nature's cycles.[93] By contrast, the vision articulated in Christian eschatology may help to relativize any particular struggle and thus to keep history open and able to constantly transcend itself. Ruether suggests that:

  > Instead of endless flight into an unrealized future, I suggest a model of hope based on conversion acknowledging the basic ingredients of a just and livable society. These ingredients have roots in nature and involve acceptance of finitude, human scale and balanced relationships between persons and between human and non-human beings.[94]

  A continuous conversion process may thus serve to respect the conditions for life to flourish. Ruether adds that this conversion process is not done once and for all. Each great social movement (e.g. the labor, women's and environmental movements) leaves undone some needed changes and generates other contradictions over time. This *metanoia* process takes place from within the context of base communities, local face-to-face groups within which one lives, works and prays. Here the necessary resources exists – in the form of healing therapies and liturgies, control over local institutions and organizational networks – to allow for an ecologically healthful life to emerge.[95]
- In a chapter on "A Theology of resistance and hope", Sharon Welch focuses on the need to celebrate the gift of life within the matrix of a beloved community.

---

92 Ruether (1983:258).

93 Ruether (1983:253-4).

94 Ruether (1983:254). Notice that Ruether refers to all three human predicaments but focuses on the predicament of sin only.

95 Ruether (1992:269).

She identifies two forms of finitude within the web of life. The "final limit," death, is not regarded as an enemy. Death is "part of the cycle of life, an event to be mourned but also an event that can be accepted as good in that it makes it possible for others to live."[96] However, finitude resulting from untimely death has to be resisted fiercely. For Welch, the beloved community, and not the kingdom of God, provides an appropriate eschatological symbol for the process of celebrating life, enduring limits and resisting injustice: "The kingdom of God implies conquest, control, and final victory over the elements of nature as well as over the structures of injustice. The 'beloved community' names the matrix within which life is celebrated, love is worshipped, and partial victories over injustice lay the groundwork for further acts of criticism and courageous defiance."[97] The deep and abiding joy in the wonder of life forms the basis for resistance against the forces that destroy this joy. From within the matrix of the beloved community there is a solid basis for social critique and self-criticism, the life-giving love constitutive of solidarity with the oppressed. Resistance against oppression is born from a healing, sacrificial love that transcends the limits of the self.[98]

- Sallie McFague's discussion of eschatology in *The body of God* (1993) contains sections on a vision for a sustainable society (here on earth), on the importance of ethics and on the church as a sign of the new creation.[99] In an "afterthought" (the title of her final section) she comments on the possibility of such hope discerning the immanence of God in creation. She gives attention to the predicament of ultimate finitude only in a few lines[100] and has very little to say about God's transcendence over and above the "common creation story."

Alongside these prophetic theologies, the prominence of a number of new (non-religious?) social movements may also be mentioned. These new social movements include labor, civil rights, welfare, peace, feminist, consumer protection, traditional health, organic agriculture, popular education, artistic, and environmental movements as well as psychological-therapeutic self-help groups.[101] They all focus on a well-defined social problem, perhaps a secular variant of the Christian identification of evil. Through a vision that healing is possible these movements present a powerful alternative to the dominant highly specialized and industrialized consumerist culture. Building a new civil society, they are all committed to the realization of simple and better life here on earth, soon.[102] In this way they provide concrete manifestations of the possibility of a realized eschatology.

---

96 Welch (1990:159).

97 Welch (1990:160-161).

98 Welch (1990:161).

99 McFague (1993:197f).

100 McFague (1993:201-2).

101 Richard (1994:98).

102 Küng (1984:187); Moltmann (1996:120).

13.3 An eschatological tension between continuity and discontinuity

In my assessment, the emphasis in prophetic theologies on the reality of evil and sin is crucial to retain the soteriological core of Christian eschatology. But is it sufficient? Should the promise of salvation from sin, liberation from oppression and victory over evil be extrapolated to address the predicaments of human limitations in space and time? Let us investigate the typical tensions emerging from an eschatological response to these predicaments.

a) The predicament of finitude: some recent approaches

i) "Realistic" eschatologies

In the popular imagination, Christian hope is still predominantly regarded as a hope for life beyond death. This is evident in grave inscriptions, in "in memoriam" notices, and in the popular interest in near-death experience. Heaven is often pictured as a beautiful holiday resort where we will meet our loved ones once again.[103]

Numerous orthodox and "evangelical" works on eschatology remain almost exclusively focused on the predicament of human finitude (and not on sin). In extreme cases, eschatology is virtually reduced to pastoral care for the dying. This tendency is somewhat curious since this focus tends to obscure the soteriological core of such evangelical eschatologies. These contributions often provide an exposition of eschatological symbols such as the return of Christ, the resurrection of the body, the final judgment, eternal life and the new earth. These symbols relate, at least at a surface level, to questions concerning the future of my personal existence after death, the ultimate fate of unbelievers and the future of the world as such (i.e. to the predicament of finitude).

According to many of these expositions, eschatological symbols can only provide comfort to believers if they are understood to refer to concrete or "real" future events (conceived in terms of linear time). The death of a loved one can only be alleviated if this person will be in some bodily form present with Christ, "if I will be able to recognize this person in heaven one day." Most of these expositions grapple with conceptual difficulties resulting from such "realistic" interpretations of the eschaton. How must one explain the delay of the *parousia*? What is the position of the dead between death and the *parousia*? How should the continuity and discontinuity between my body and a resurrected body be conceived?[104]

Some expositions focus on the sphere of personal life. They explore the mystery of death and investigate the Christian hope for life beyond death. Other contributions show an interest in the historical and cosmic dimensions of the future. Such expositions often engage in an analysis of the major stages of world

---

[103] McDannell & Lang (1988:311f).

[104] For one example of a discussion of these conceptual difficulties from an evangelical reformed position, see Berkouwer (1972:32f, 170f).

history[105] and discuss the graphic details of the historical events leading to the predicted end of the world (the signs of the time, the second coming of Christ, the millennium, etc.). The last things are thus understood as events in space and time, that is, as a continuation of the history of this world. The details of these events are debated with more or with less sophistication in millennialist,[106] Adventist, and dispensationalist[107] circles. These debates are often characterized by rampant speculation on what will happen at the "end of time".

- The well-known work by Hal Lindsey may serve as an example of this form of eschatology. According to Lindsey we are living in the endtime. Every one who reads the biblical prophecies "properly" (i.e. as literal predictions) and who scans the daily newspaper carefully will observe that the old prophecies are being fulfilled in our day (for the very first time). On this basis, Lindsey collects any available evidence in order to fit the pieces of the jigsaw puzzle together. Lindsey's work remains very popular despite the fact that his assertions did not take place as predicted.[108]

It is important to note that a response to the predicaments of sin and (cosmic) finitude are merged in these views. This form of apocalypticism is often duly criticized. Such apocalyptic predictions harbor the danger of rampant speculation on what will happen at the "end of time." They draw a caricature of the "last things" that has only "the furniture of heaven and the temperature of hell to offer"

---

[105] See Moltmann's (1996:141) discussion and critique of such attempts to identify stages in world history – which are predetermined by God and may therefore be predicted on the basis of divine revelations.

[106] Millennialist forms of hope have been prevalent in the Christian tradition at least since the days of Irenaeus. A distinction between pre-millennialism and post-millennialism is usually made. Some believe that after the first invisible return of Christ a millennium will follow after which a second visible return will take place (pre-millennialism). Others believe that the second coming of Christ will follow after the millennium, usually interpreted as the age of the church (post-millennialism). A-millennialism constitutes a denial of any future millennium.

[107] Dispensationalism in North America is often associated with the views of C.I. Scofield (1843-1921) whose *Scofield Reference Bible* (1909) became very popular. Two characteristic notions in dispensationalism are those of the "rapture" (the expectation on the basis of 1 Thess 4:15-7 that believers will be caught up in the clouds to meet Christ at the time of his return) and the "tribulation" (the belief, based on Dan 9:24-7, that the rapture will be preceded or followed by seven-year period of divine judgment upon the world). Dispensationalists remain divided on the question whether the rapture is to be understood as pre-tribulational (i.e. that believers will escape the pain of the tribulation) or post-tribulational (i.e that believers will have to endure the tribulation in assurance that they will be united with Christ). See McGrath's (1994:272-3) helpful summary of dispensationalism.

[108] Lindsey (1970). For a critique of Lindsey's approach, see Migliore (1991:235-6), Peters (1978:33-36).

(Reinhold Niebuhr).[109] They are seldom based on an adequate understanding of the literary genre of the Biblical texts. Despite these valid criticisms, it should be acknowledged that the popularity of this form of eschatology may be the result of the predicament of cosmic finitude being ignored in many other eschatologies.

ii) Metaphorical interpretations

In response to these crudely realistic views, several scholars have emphasized the metaphorical nature of classic Christian eschatological symbols.[110]

The language used in eschatological assertions should not be understood as detailed predictions of the future based on divine revelation. It is not possible for finite minds to comprehend that which transcends history infinitely.[111] We cannot *know* the future in the same way that we may remember the past and experience the present. Christians have no privileged access to revealed knowledge of the future. This calls for an acknowledgement of the poverty of our knowledge of the future.[112] We can only anticipate the future by relying on the images of memory and the powers of the imagination. In language about the future, the familiar logic of every-day language is stretched beyond its limits. Such language cannot be understood in terms of literal descriptions of the future.[113] Eschatological language expresses insight, not foresight.[114] It always remains analogical, involving both similarities and differences in its mode of description. Language about the future is therefore expressed in images, metaphors, symbols, or myths.[115]

The following quotations (all derived from well-known Catholic scholars) provide a clear indication of the rejection of crudely realistic interpretations of eschatological symbols:

---

[109] See Sauter (1999:4).

[110] Moltmann (1967:48) notes that the work of Kant forms the philosophical inspiration behind this shift. When he removed the *eschata* from the domain of theoretical reason and its knowledge of the world and relegated them to the domain of practical reason, Kant effectively reduced the cosmic *eschata* to transcendental conditions for the possibility of experiencing oneself in a practical way. The focus shifted from the eschaton to the possibilities and impact of human consciousness of the eschaton. See also Schuurman (1987:44).

[111] Niebuhr (1943:289).

[112] Metz (1969:97).

[113] Even an evangelical reformed scholar such as Berkouwer rejected what he called "reportorial eschatology", that is, an eschatology that attempts to calculate the future in the form of a detailed description of the endtime. He argues that the biblical witnesses have no intention of describing the actual phenomena of the *eschata* themselves. In his exposition of the signs of time, Berkouwer prefers an approach involving a continuous reinterpretation of the signs so that they are visible and can be recognized in all times, including one's own time. See Berkouwer (1972:246f).

[114] Robinson (1968:49).

[115] Hayes (1989:89f).

- Hans Küng: "... biblical eschatology is not a prognosis of end-events any more than the protology is a report of events at the beginning."[116]
- Edward Schillebeeckx: "The Bible gives no anticipating historical report over the eschaton. We know nothing about the transcendent ultimate things – judgment, Christ's return, heaven, hell, purgatory – except insofar as they are already indicated in the course of historical tenets expressing the actual relationship between the God of the covenant and mankind, particularly in Christ, 'the last Adam' – i.e. 'the man of the eschaton'."[117]
- Zachary Hayes: "Many theologians hold that – while the Christian faith believes the world has a future – faith offers no explicit knowledge of the final state of our planet just as it offers no specific knowledge of its first state."[118] ... "Hope expresses itself in pictures, dreams, and symbols which point to what lies beyond knowledge. ... What is the function of such language? It is certainly not to provide clear information about future world-events ..."[119]

According to "purely" metaphorical interpretations, eschatological symbols provide illuminating and inspiring visions for human self-actualization. Eschatological metaphors provide interpretations of experience that yield a particular depth and urgency to the meaning of present existence.[120] However, they are precisely *human* constructions and not descriptions of reality based on a privileged knowledge of the future. They remain purely intra-linguistic. In this "symbolic compromise"[121] eschatological visions do elicit hope but the source of this hope is based not in God, but in human capabilities (only). At the same time, there is a need to distinguish between signs and symbols. Whereas a sign bears no necessary relation to that which it signifies, a symbol participates in the reality for which it stands. This is also true of the Christ-event that participates in but also anticipates, proleptically, the fullness of the eschaton.[122]

Numerous examples of such a metaphorical eschatology may be mentioned. The contributions of Rudolph Bultmann and Paul Tillich remain classic:[123]

- Bultmann's program of demythologizing Biblical symbols is well-known. According to Bultmann, images of life beyond death as well as of the end of the world are "myths" which have to be interpreted existentially. The eschaton is

---

116 Küng (1984:252).

117 Schillebeeckx (1969:53).

118 Hayes (1983:44).

119 Hayes (1983:19).

120 Lane (1996:17).

121 McDannell & Lang (1988:326).

122 Schwarz (1984:556).

123 See further the contribution by John Robinson (1968:68-82) who also focuses on the significance of eschatological symbols for the present. Eschatology expresses the significance for the future of the present reality of the living God (1968:74).

constituted by the human response to the proclamation of the Word of God. This leads to an affirmation of this life, because "God is a God of the living, not the dead."

- In his *Systematic Theology*, Tillich acknowledges that there will be an end to human history, to life on earth, to the earth itself and to the whole cosmos.[124] However, eschatology is for Tillich predominantly related to the end of history in a second sense of the word, namely the aim or *telos* of history. This has to be understood in terms of that which transcends all moments of the temporal process and of time itself, that is, eternity. The eschaton is not indefinitely far in time and space, but becomes an expression of our standing in every moment in face of the eternal, although we do so by actually looking ahead toward the end of history.[125] Through eschatological symbols such as consummation, judgment and salvation, our closed existence is penetrated by an experience of transcendence in which we are called to fulfillment and existential decision.

These eschatological interpretations should be understood as protests against futuristic and realistic notions of the eschaton. The tendency to treat eschatology as the doctrine of the last things at the end of dogmatics is rejected. Instead there is a desire to explain the eschaton as an approaching reality and the message of the coming Lord as an imminent reality.[126] An exposition of the personal, historical and cosmic dimensions of finitude may and often is approached on this basis.

iii) Futurist eschatologies

An emphasis on the metaphorical nature of eschatological symbols may easily lead to a *de facto* avoidance of the theme of the future itself. Images of the future may be important only to inspire people in present predicaments, but the long-term future of the earth or the cosmos is of no direct theological concern. In this way one can escape from the embarrassment of crude apocalyptic or millennialist propositions.

A concern with the predicament of finitude returns in the "futurist" eschatologies of Moltmann, Pannenberg, Kreck, and Sauter.[127] This concern is already indicated in the title of Kreck's work *Die Zukunft des Gekommenen* (1961). This shift was born from the realization that the biblical categories of time, history and the end were neglected in a "transcendental" notion of the eschaton as a thunder

---

124 Tillich (1963:394).

125 Tillich (1963:395). See also Niebuhr's (1943:287) incisive comment (emphasizing the predicament of finitude) that, "The problem is that the end as finis is a threat to the end as telos."

126 Berkouwer (1972:24).

127 Berkhof (1967:93f) suggests that this eschatological shift is due to 1) Von Rad's emphasis on Israel's confessions of God's acts in history, 2) an awareness of social miseries (war, hunger, oppression, discrimination), and 3) a reaction against a purely existentialist approach.

flash of eternity requiring a decision in the here-and-now.[128] This can only lead to an eschatology in which history is swallowed up in the simultaneous presence of the eternal moment. The result is a gnostic, Platonizing form of eschatology that cannot address either the concrete, material world or the historical effects of evil on earth adequately. Eschatology without history is empty and history without eschatology loses any sense of purpose.[129] Christian theology must speak of a real future, not simply in terms of existential time, but in terms of real passage through chronological time from past to present to future.[130]

In response to this situation, the focus of "futurist" eschatology shifts to the problem of suffering and the pervasiveness of evil in society.

- Moltmann, especially, is not only concerned with the suffering that results from the effects of sin in the world. He acknowledges that suffering forms an integral part of God's good creation. This is the result of the temporal finitude of creation that necessarily implies suffering and death. Moltmann therefore develops a notion of the eschaton that can address the effects of evil and temporal finitude at the same time. The eschaton has to be new (thus his overwhelming emphasis on the category of the *novum*) both in relation to a history of sin and to the created order itself.
- Pannenberg's eschatology (at least as I read him) is born from the same realization as Moltmann's, namely the need to overcome both the effects of sin and of temporal finitude. In addition, Pannenberg also emphasizes the need to address the end of history itself. The goal of history may be located beyond the end of time itself. However, the eschatological future is more than a symbol. The end also includes a sense of completion. In this sense the historical future and the course of history remains of eschatological significance.[131]

  For Pannenberg, God is revealed not only in the history of salvation but also in universal history. Although God was revealed in history, particularly in Jesus Christ, this revelation remains provisional. Only on the Last Day, God will be revealed as the Lord of all history. On this day, God's judgment on society, which is already revealed proleptically in Jesus Christ, will become fully evident and validated. The impact of an event today will only be fully revealed then. Pannenberg argues that Bultmann and Dodd correctly emphasized the *present* impact of the imminent future in the preaching of Jesus. However, they exaggerated the distinction. The presence of God's Kingdom has to be understood as the presence of God's *coming* Kingdom.[132]

---

128 Hayes (1983:37f).

129 Van Ruler (1972:106-7).

130 Moltmann (1996:13f).

131 Pannenberg (1998:586f).

132 Pannenberg (1969:53-4).

iv) Finitude and the cosmic dimensions of the future

The predicament of finitude, especially cosmic finitude, is not only a feature, but the very focus of attention in three other recent approaches to eschatology, namely those of 1) Teilhard de Chardin and his followers, 2) process theology, and 3) the new interest in dialogue between theology and the sciences.[133]

In all three these (often related but also diverse) approaches there is a new interest in the reality of an end to human life, all living species, the earth and the universe itself – in other words in the eschaton as End. There is nevertheless a clear rejection of any crudely realistic interpretation of eschatological symbols. The plausibility of such eschatological assertions is undermined by the scenarios for the long-term future of the earth and the universe emerging from the astrophysical sciences. There is a new awareness that Christian eschatology cannot simply postulate visions of the future without taking the insights emerging from the disciplines of futurology[134] and cosmology into account. At the same time, there is an urgency in these three schools of thought to address the problem of

---

[133] For a discussion of a similar list of eschatological contributions that are "seriously concerned with the future", see Peacocke (1979:334f).

[134] For a discussion of the relationship between futurology and Christian eschatology, see Berkhof (1967:79f), Olivier (1989), Peters (1978). A clear distinction between these two disciplines is not only appropriate, but is also urgent in the light of Christian attempts to regard Biblical evidence as apocalyptic predictions for the long term future of the planet. Futurology is concerned with the future on the basis of the growth, development, maturation or fruition of forces or trends already at work in the present. It sees the future in terms of what is already there. The scope of futurological inquiry may relate to the future of specific human societies (e.g. futurology from an economic perspective) or to the future of the universe itself (e.g. from the perspective of the astrophysical sciences). Christian eschatology is concerned with the very same future that is discussed in futurology and cosmology. However, Christian eschatology puts the future of the cosmos into an even more comprehensive perspective, namely in terms of what may transcend the whole cosmic history. It reflects on the future of the cosmos on the basis of God's future presence in the world (also cf. Berkhof 1967:79f).

The necessity of a distinction between futurology and Christian eschatology should not, however, lead to a complete separation of these two disciplines. There is a temptation in Christian theology to elaborate on the content of Christian hope and its vision of the future without any cognizance of the reflections on the future within the discipline of futurology. Olivier (1989:25) insists that: "Both eschatology and futurology address the same future. No reflection from a Christian perspective on the future of our world in the grip of the ecological crisis can afford not to take futurology seriously." This separation between eschatology and futurology can only lead to an undermining of the plausibility of Christian hope. Christian eschatology will only be plausible if it can show that the envisaged eschaton (whether as *venturum* or *adventus*) of Christian hope and the future of the world (*futurum*) refers to one and the same future. The cosmic scope of Christian eschatology therefore requires a plausible understanding of the origins, history and destiny of the universe. If God is indeed the world's future (the title of the work by Peters, 1992), it remains important to show how this relates to the present world and especially to the earth itself.

(cosmic) finitude directly. This urgency is born from the need to reflect on the relation between Christian eschatology and the very graphic scenarios emerging from the sciences. Indeed, how should Christian eschatology conceive the end of history itself?[135]

- Teilhard's attempt to relate the biblical message to the theory of evolution is well-known. Teilhard describes a process of "cosmogenesis" in which new and higher forms of life emerge through a process of differentiation and complexification, reaching consciousness in the human species (*noogenesis*).[136] Teilhard identifies the cosmosphere (the inanimate world), the biosphere (the animate world), the noosphere (the human world) and the christosphere (the realm of Christ) as the main stages of the universal evolutionary process. God is the "Prime Mover Ahead", the one who forwards the evolutionary process, the ultimate point upon which all realities converge.[137] Through christification the evolutionary process will come to its fulfillment where everything will enter into the realm of Christ. The creativity of the divine Spirit guides the entire process toward its consummation, that is, the "Omega point", at the end of the world.[138] Behind this whole process Teilhard sees the principle of incarnation, that is, the idea that a hyperpersonal world will emerge out of this human world which will reach a climax in a spiritual fellowship with the glorified Christ as the center. In this optimistic and teleological response to the meaning of history amidst the finitude of species, the problem of evil is marginalized.[139]
- A concern for the future is integral to process thinking. Humans are co-creators with God, who with them is evolving towards new possibilities in the future. Each moment is a new creation and is pregnant with possibilities as human beings progress together with God into a more unified and harmonious coming day. The kingdom and the church are both in the process of evolving. At the same time, process theologians resist any notion of an ultimate end of history or a final consummation of the evolutionary process. There is no End at which history as process will come to rest. If being lies in becoming, the end of becoming would signify the annihilation of all things, including God. We may have hope in God, but it is equally true that God has hope in all the creatures, trusting us to accomplish God's purposes by actualizing the lures God provides.[140] The future therefore remains open. There is no assurance that the human species will not decay or destroy itself.[141]

---

[135] This question implies, in terms of the well-known typology of Lindbeck's (1984), a renewed interest in the propositional content of Christian eschatology.

[136] See, especially Teilhard (1959).

[137] Teilhard (1960:114).

[138] Teilhard (1959:257f, 268f).

[139] Braaten (1974:22). See Teilhard's brief comments (1959:311-3, 1960:83f) on the place of evil in a world in evolution though.

[140] Ford (1972:136).

[141] Cobb & Griffin (1976:117).

- The theme of eschatology has received significant attention in the re-emergence of the debate between theology and the sciences. The focus of the debate is the relationship between the cosmic dimensions of Christian hope and the long-term future of the universe as discussed in the astrophysical sciences (i.e. the possibilities of an "open", "closed" or "flat" universe – see Chapter 6). The cosmic dimension of the predicament of finitude is the almost exclusive focus of these eschatologies. I will return to this debate in Chapter 14 in more detail.

b) Creation and eschaton: continuity and discontinuity

This discussion shows how the scope of the Christian hope can and has been broadened to anticipate a future dispensation that would bring salvation from sin (the eradication of evil) and life after death (the predicament of finitude) simultaneously. This response to the predicament of finitude accounts for the tension in many eschatologies between the continuity and discontinuity of our present bodiliness and the resurrection of the dead, this life and eternal life, this earth and the new earth, *Urzeit* und *Endzeit*, this dispensation and the next.[142]

Any eschatological response to the predicament of (human) finitude needs to address the continuity and the discontinuity between the present and a future dispensation. The aspect of continuity is vital in order to ensure that the content of hope is indeed applicable to the one who hopes. At the same time, the aspect of discontinuity is crucial to ensure that what is hoped for will indeed be new and not merely a continuation of the present.

This tension between continuity and discontinuity is exceptionally difficult to maintain. There are long-standing debates on the question as to how the relation between creation and eschaton should be formulated. It is even more difficult, especially in the light of the earth's own finitude, not only to postulate, but also to imagine what this continuity and discontinuity entails. In what does the continuity between this earth and the new earth lie? And how should the very possibility of a *novum* be conceived? Let us look at this debate in more detail.

i) An emphasis on continuity

The continuity between creation and eschaton was emphasized with considerable determination by Arnold van Ruler.

In numerous articles on eschatology Van Ruler emphasized that salvation cannot imply salvation *from* the earth, but should always be a salvation *of* the earth itself. The world is God's own creation and will not be abandoned by God.[143] It is in this visible and touchable world that the reign of God is to be established.

---

[142] This tension is also sometimes, somewhat vaguely, referred to in terms of the difference between eschatology (a reflection on hope) and apocalyptic ("a way of speaking about future events which portend disaster"). See Bridger's (1990:292) similar description of the notion of apocalypticism in popular discourse.

[143] Van Ruler (1969:223).

Eternal life is no other life than the life that we now live in space and time, this life redeemed from the power of sin and death.[144] The continuity between creation and eschaton is based on the faithfulness of God to creation and is manifested therein that creation itself is taken up in the eschaton. The discontinuity between creation and eschaton is primarily the result of sin. Sin has interrupted God's nurturing care for creation and required a soteriological "emergency measure". The work of Christ and the Spirit is a necessary "intermezzo" to ensure that God's reign in this world will indeed come. Both the epoch of the Messiah and of the Spirit will pass by in the coming reign of God on earth.[145] The continuity between creation and eschaton is guaranteed only through this soteriological intermezzo.[146]

Van Ruler strongly recommends the use of the term *recreatio* instead of *nova creatio* to formulate the relationship between creation and eschaton.[147] The latter term cannot do justice to the concern that it is this earth, this life, this body that will be saved. The new earth is not a different earth, but this, the old earth, radically renewed, no longer broken through sin.[148] Without this assurance, any promise of salvation will remain empty. A completely new creation is regarded by Van Ruler as an anabaptist denial of the earthly. By contrast, the term *recreatio* suggests continuity and discontinuity as long as the "re" and the "creatio" are equally emphasized.[149] In fact, Van Ruler speaks not merely about a continuity, but also

---

[144] Van Ruler (1947:56).

[145] For a defense of Van Ruler notion of these two intermezzo's against his critics see Lombard (1982).

[146] Lombard (1982:79).

[147] Van Ruler (1969:168, 1971:222).

[148] Van Ruler (1969:225, 1971:223, 1972:29). For an even stronger emphasis on the new earth as a transformation of *this* earth, see the following words by Edward Thurneysen: "The world in which we shall enter in the Parousia of Jesus Christ is therefore not another world; it is this world, this heaven, this earth; both, however, passed away and renewed. It is these forests, these fields, these cities these streets, these people, that will be the scene of redemption. At present they are battlefields, full of strife and sorrow of the not-yet accomplished consummation; then they will be fields of victory, fields of harvest, where out of the seed that was sown with tears the everlasting sheaves will be reaped and brought home" (quoted in Hoekema 1978:281). With his sensitivity for cosmological reflection, Emil Brunner (1954:202), by contrast, insist that, "Transience is the very mark of the structure of this world, which is destined to pass away."

[149] See also Theron (1978:8f) who concurs with Van Ruler's rejection of a *nova creatio*. The continuity suggested in the notion of *recreatio* refers to the continuation of a relationship with God. Salvation in Christ implies a reparation of a relationship devastated through sin. The eschaton implies a continuation of this relationship even beyond death. Death as the final judgment of God on sin is itself understood relationally. However, the reality of death requires an equal emphasis on an eschatological discontinuity. Recreation is recreation out of death (not out of nothing). This ensures that the continuity is not limited to the idea of relationship (*relatio*), but also applies to the related elements (*relata*). Theron concludes in a concise formulation that recreation passes through *death* (thus discontinuity) but at the same times *passes* through death (thus continuity).

about the *identity* of this world and the eschaton. Salvation does not imply a substantial adaptation of this good creation, only its liberation from the effects of sin.[150]

This does not mean that the eschaton will bring a return to some "original" creation. There is indeed an element of consummation. The notion of eschatological consummation also surpasses the notion of fulfillment. In history the fulfillment of God's promises remains hidden, provisional, temporal. In the consummation this hiddenness will be removed. The consummation will thus exceed everything that we now see. However, the consummation in the eschaton will not lead to a cancellation of the proton.[151] The proton is incorporated in the eschaton, but without the contamination of sin. Van Ruler maintains that the eschaton will be "fire-proof" against sin and will thus exhibit a certain "plus" in relationship with the proton.[152] There is therefore no dualism between creation and salvation; the whole creation is taken up in the eschaton.

Noticeably, it is this earth that needs to be cleansed from its contamination. God's judgment therefore remains crucial. In order to establish God's reign on this earth, the earth itself must be cleansed from injustice, violence and, one may surely add, environmental degradation.[153]

Hendrikus Berkhof also emphasizes the continuity between cosmos and eschaton. Eschatology is a projection of Israel's confession of God's faithfulness onto the screen of the future.[154]

Berkhof uses the notion of "extrapolation" to indicate that the Christian hope for the future implies a continuation and consummation and glorification of earlier experiences of God's faithfulness to God's promises.[155] It is indeed this earthly existence that is transformed in the eschaton. This life therefore has eternal significance. Salvation does not imply an escape from this world but an eschatological

---

[150] Van Ruler (1954:54, 57).

[151] Van Ruler (1969:169).

[152] Van Ruler (1969:171).

[153] Van Ruler (1972:107).

[154] Berkhof (1967:16-17). See Berkhof (1981:37-48) for a careful exegetical and theological discussion on the relationship between *Urzeit* and *Endzeit*. He says: "De schepping is basis, patroon, analogie en profetie van de herschepping die in Christ aanvangt" ("Creation provides the basis, pattern and prophecy of the recreation that commenced in Jesus Christ") – (1981:43). Berkouwer (1972:13) also emphasizes that the promise of the future is inextricably connected with events of the past. "It is not the unknown of the future but the known in the future that is decisive for eschatological reflection."

[155] Berkhof (1967:37). He understands the notion of extrapolation as "het doortrekken van ontdekte wetmatigheden naar nog niet of onvoldoende bekende terreinen." This means that the resurrection and glorification of Christ and the work of the Holy Spirit in the lives of believers is projected onto the hitherto empty screen of the eternal consummation. This notion of extrapolation is epitomized in the *parousia* of Christ which refers to the final coming (not a return) of Christ in glory (1985:512f).

renewal of this world.[156] To describe this event, Berkhof prefers the concept *transformatio* instead of either *nova creatio* or *recreatio*. Berkhof adds that this continuity ensures the possibility of expressing the eschaton in metaphors and images while a sense of discontinuity ensures that eschatological language remain nothing more than suggestive images.[157]

Karl Rahner introduced the similar notion of "transposition" to explain the continuity between salvation and eschaton.

Rahner argues that knowledge of the eschaton is not a supplementary (and thus potentially discontinuous) piece of information added to our present knowledge of salvation in Christ. Knowledge of the eschaton is confined to what may be derived from present eschatological experiences. The source of eschatological assertions is present experiences of God's salvation in Christ. Christian eschatology thus ultimately remains Christology; it describes the beginning, continuation and completed end of the work of Christ. The eschaton is the transposition of these experiences into the guise of fulfillment towards the end of time. Rahner regards eschatology as an extrapolation from the present into the future, while he denounces apocalyptic as an interpolation of the future into the present.[158]

These notions of extrapolation (Van Ruler, Berkhof) and transposition (Rahner) are explicitly criticized by Moltmann. He argues that the notion of extrapolation fails to account for the newness of the eschaton compared to creation.[159] Such extrapolations do not anticipate a new future, but only extend the old present into the future. This results in a conservative or even reactionary imposition of present conditions onto the future.[160] We will return to Moltmann's argument in the discussion below.

Berkhof responded to this criticism by acknowledging the importance of a sense of discontinuity. However, he indicates the danger of an eschatology that does not argue from the center (Christ) to the future but simply postulates a utopian future. The already of God's salvation is emptied of its soteriological content when interpreted merely as a signifying promise.[161] Berkhof concludes that the future becomes in this utopian form of eschatology a mere formal principle.[162]

Pannenberg's assessment of the continuity between cosmos and eschaton provides a creative and perhaps more balanced approach. He rejects a view of the future standing in utter contradiction to past and present. He argues that it is through the events of the past that we are able to anticipate the future at all. However, in terms of Pannenberg's notion of the ontological priority of the future, the past itself has been brought about by the generic power of the future. He maintains

---

156 Berkhof (1967:38).

157 Berkhof (1967:31-32).

158 Rahner (1966).

159 Moltmann (1979:41f).

160 Moltmann (1972:91).

161 Moltmann (1967).

162 Berkhof (1985:512).

somewhat cryptically that: "The genuine and radical newness of the future is not weakened by the idea that the power of the future embraces to itself the past and present of which it is both the source and destiny."[163] This is especially evident in those events that have a highly "proleptic" character, that is, events that signal further realizations of the future from which they are derived. Especially in Jesus, creation itself is set in the light of the eschatological future and becomes a parable of the divine rule.[164] With this emphasis on the ontological priority of the future, Pannenberg thus steers between both an idealist (Hegel) and a materialist (Teilhard) eschatology. Creation and eschatology belong together because it is only in the eschatological consummation that the destiny of creation, especially the human creature will come to fulfillment.[165]

Any emphasis on continuity has to account for the nature and possibility of this continuity. Despite an earlier enthusiasm for the hope in the resurrection of the body (instead of a dualist notion of the immortality of the soul) and the new earth (instead of a hope to be in heaven, one day), there seems to be a new hesitation to explain this continuity in any crudely materialistic way (i.e. in terms of earthliness or bodiliness). This hesitation is the result of a realization that, due to the earth's own finitude, the eschaton simply cannot imply an infinite continuation of life on earth. The new earth cannot simply be a renewal of this earth (contra Van Ruler). How, then, should this sense of continuity be understood?

- Berkhof argues that, at the level of personal eschatology, it will be "I" who will continue to exist beyond death. He refuses to speculate on the nature of this personal existence since this is influenced by philosophical notions of personhood. But he adds that the resurrected Christ provides a guarantee for this continued personal identity.[166]
- Berkouwer discusses the question whether the eschaton will imply a total annihilation of the created world, therefore allowing no continuity in terms of substance (Althaus).[167] He argues that the discontinuity should be understood in terms of God's judgment over the fallen world and that some form of continuity will be retained. However, the nature of this continuity is not clarified in the Bible. Berkouwer concludes that: "The Bible can be understood only on the presupposition of continuity. This continuity lies in the hand of God, it is true, but in that hand it will become reality."[168] On this basis, Berkouwer can also emphasize that it is this earthly existence that is redeemed in the eschaton. Life on earth is not devaluated in the eschaton but called for. The new earth is never a strange and futuristic fantasy but a mystery that penetrates into this

---

[163] Pannenberg (1969:22).
[164] Pannenberg (1994:145).
[165] Pannenberg (1994:139).
[166] Berkhof (1967:31-38).
[167] Berkouwer (1972:219f).
[168] Berkouwer (1956:331).

existence.[169]

- Doug Schuurman maintains that the continuity between creation and eschaton should be understood in terms of three central relationships: 1) fellowship and obedience to God, 2) complimentary partnerships among human beings, 3) stewardly care for nature. He allows for relative discontinuity in terms of salvation from the fallen creation and for consummation in terms of fulfillment of the good creation's potential.[170] Schuurman feels that it is best to regard discontinuity in terms of the insufficiency of God's otherwise good creation to overcome sin. Suffering is a new experience that presumably would not have occurred, at least not with the same quality and depth, had there been no sin.[171]
- König argues that the continuity should not be located in "something" in creation. It should be based primarily on the faithfulness of God. König nevertheless rejects the notion in Lutheran orthodoxy of an eschatological *creatio ex nihilo* in which this earth will be totally destroyed in God's judgment. There will (somehow!) also be continuity between the new earth and this earth.[172]

The pathos of this emphasis on continuity is immediately evident. However, such continuity cannot simply be postulated. An all too easy sense of material continuity often results from a failure to take the predicament of planetary and cosmic finitude seriously. How must relationships between human beings and nature (see Schuurman's suggestion) be conceived if the history of the whole cosmos will come to an end? The eschaton cannot simply be a continuation of this body, this earth, this universe.

This question has led several other theologians to put the emphasis on the discontinuity between creation and eschaton. Whatever continuity there may be, is interpreted Christologically or theo-logically. Any continuity between creation and eschaton ultimately rests *only* in God, in God's existence beyond space or time and in God's faithfulness to God's promises in history. [173] This is exemplified in the Christological continuity between the cross of Jesus and the resurrected Christ, sitting "at the right hand of the Father."[174] This emphasis allows for a far more

---

[169] Berkouwer (1972:234). For a similar argument against the annihilation of the present cosmos, see Hoekema (1978:280-1).

[170] Schuurman (1995:156) explains: "The Bible encourages us to see the eschaton as the fulfillment of creational potential, the manifestation of what is hidden and foggy, the fullness of what is partial, the more of what is now less, the reward following present trials, the harvest of the first fruits."

[171] Schuurman (1995:156).

[172] König 1989:235).

[173] Sauter (199:18-19) criticizes Moltmann's "theology of history" approach to eschatology. Sauter argues that this approach is too preoccupied with world salvation, thus trying to find some continuity in and beyond world history. Instead, Sauter wishes to focus on what God alone can bring about, namely a new creation that cannot be deduced from the world or from history.

[174] Moltmann (1967:200) argues that the locus of continuity here also resides in God's

radical sense of discontinuity but does not seem to provide the same degree of consolation in the face of imminent death. Let us investigate such an emphasis on an eschatological discontinuity in more detail.

ii) An emphasis on discontinuity

An emphasis on the discontinuity between creation and eschaton is often born from an acknowledgement that suffering and death in the world is not merely the result of sin. The predicament of finitude – which implies immense suffering and death – forms part and parcel of God's good creation. Creation always had a "shadow side" (Barth). Nature was never really a paradise but only the promise thereof (Haught).[175] The eschaton therefore cannot be merely a restoration of the original good creation. The predicament of finitude calls for a more radical discontinuity between creation and eschaton. Let us investigate this position and the criticisms it has elicited in more detail:

Karl Barth sharply opposes the idea of an extension of human life after death. There is no continuation, no further happening after the "sounding of the last trumpet." Barth rejects any notion of immortality as an anthropological given and warns against "pagan dreams of glory in a time after human death."[176] The time will come when the whole created reality will cease to exist, when time as a form of existence will no longer be, when there will be a present without an afterward.[177] However, not the extension or "continuation" of our finite existence in an unending future, but the "eternalizing" of our ending life is the content of Christian hope. This life that has been, life in all its limitation and finiteness, finds room in communion with God. *This* is the resurrection of the dead. This ending and dying life will be glorified in God's presence.[178] Whatever continuity there is between the finite life and God's presence in eternity is not based on any aspect of human existence that will endure, but on God's mercy that endures forever (Psalm 136). Barth's notion of continuity thus has a theocentric and Christological and not an anthropological or a creaturely basis.[179]

Barth's emphasis on the discontinuity between creation and eschaton has been

---

faithfulness and not in the person of Christ: "In the act of raising by God, Jesus is identified as the crucified one who is raised. In that case the point of identification lies not in the person of Jesus, but *extra se* in the God who creates life and new being out of nothing." Schuurman (1981:99) objects that this contrast between the faithfulness of God and that to which God is faithful can only court confusion.

175 See Haught (1993:112f). Haught's work will be discussed in more detail in Chapter 14.

176 Berkouwer (1956:330).

177 See Barth's lengthy discussion on allotted (and therefore limited) time (*CD* 3.2, 1960:437-633).

178 Berkouwer (1956:158). Barth's position is the result of a distinction between the dimensions of eternity and an endless continuation of time. See the discussion of the eschatological tension between time and eternity below (13.4).

179 Barth (*CD* 3.2, 1960:587f).

questioned, notably by Berkouwer. Berkouwer focuses his criticism, significantly, on the relationship between the predicaments of sin and finitude. He is clearly hesitant to allow for suffering in God's good creation. He asks:

> Can death be regarded as belonging to human nature as it came from the hand of God, or is death an alien, destructive power which has penetrated the good creation and is contrary to human nature? ... Is death, although standing under the power of God, anything else than evil *only*?[180]

Berkouwer strongly criticizes Barth for allowing, despite his own intentions, a particular anthropology, a "phenomenological idea of limitation" to obscure his Biblical exegesis.[181] Berkouwer prefers to stay within the boundaries of Biblical proclamation. He refuses to allow any distinction between natural death and death as judgment. Death is simply the wage of sin.[182] Salvation from sin therefore implies simultaneously victory over death.

Oepke Noordmans, in his own distinct way, also emphasized the radicalness of God's recreation. For Noordmans, the eschaton is in no way merely a continuation of the worldly. In fact, creation itself can only be understood in the light of eschaton. More importantly, both creation and eschaton has to be understood within the context of the central soteriological thrust of the Bible.

The position of Noordmans has to be understood in the context of his sustained rejection of any form of natural theology – even in the disguise of a Biblical theology of creation. The millions of years of the cosmos is the domain of astronomy and biology and not of theology. It cannot yield any knowledge of God, only heathendom.[183] Knowledge of God the Creator cannot be derived from the world itself, but only from Christ. The Creator can only be recognized retrospectively as the father of Jesus Christ. Moreover, to understand creation one must understand the cross. Noordmans cryptically describes creation as "a place of light close around the cross".[184] What does this mean?

Noordmans describes creation as a "critical" category. A Christian doctrine of creation, he argues, should not be focused on the formation of matter. Creation should be understood soteriologically: it implies separation (of good and evil), not

---

[180] Berkouwer (1956:154). Berkouwer concludes (in his assessment on the basis of Biblical evidence *only*?) "... that it is quite impossible to speak of death as belonging in any sense to human nature which came forth *good* from the hand of God" (1956:155).

[181] Berkouwer (1956:337,340).

[182] Berkouwer (1956:343). Berkouwer is perhaps correct to insist that in this empirical death human finitude and judgment over sin *coincide*. To raise questions about the death and suffering in a world without sin will remain an abstraction, removed from Biblical proclamation. Nevertheless, an eschatological response to the predicament of finitude cannot be avoided – as Barth, Moltmann, Pannenberg, Van de Beek and numerous others clearly realize.

[183] Noordmans (1979:246).

[184] Noordmans (1979:245).

formation.[185] The Bible knows very little, if anything, about creation in the beginning and thus outside the contamination of sin (except that creation must have been good).[186] Creation can only be understood from a position after the fall. Sin has indeed contaminated creation in every possible way. Humanity has pulled the whole cosmos with it in the fall. Sin goes as far as creation itself – without destroying it completely.[187] Furthermore, the depths of sin cannot be discovered through everyday experience but only in the light of the cross where sin is revealed for what it really is. In this sense creation is for Noordmans a "spot of light close to the cross". The fallen creation can thus only be understood soteriologically and Christologically.

This exclusive soteriological focus is balanced by Noordmans with an equally strong emphasis on salvation as recreation. Salvation is not merely a matter of the reparation of the original creation. It is recreation. Retrospectively, in the light of the cross, creation in the beginning also has to be understood eschatologically as re-creation (out of sin).[188]

Jürgen Moltmann, especially in his earlier work,[189] also stresses the sharp discontinuity between creation and eschaton. Moltmann's theology of hope may be understood as a response to the problem of suffering. However, Moltmann makes it quite clear that the causes of suffering cannot be restricted to the predicament of evil and sin. Suffering and death also forms an integral part of God's good creation. Moltmann says: "We cannot say 'if there were no sin, there would be no suffering.' Experience of suffering goes far beyond the experience of guilt and the experience of grace. It has roots in the limitations of created reality itself."[190] An eschatological response to suffering therefore has to reflect on the predicament of finitude and not only on that of sin. The problem of death, that is a characteristic of the frail, temporal creation, has to be overcome through the new creation of all

---

185 Noordmans (1979:251, 255).

186 Noordmans (1979:247).

187 Noordmans (1979:255).

188 See Van Ruler's criticism that this position of Noordmans leads to a certain dualism where creation is actually replaced by the reign of God. This is the result of an eagerness to emphasize the qualitative newness of the eschaton so much that no trait of the eschaton can be detected in history, not even in the history of salvation (except within a narrow Christological focus). Against the intentions of Noordmans, this may easily lead to a form of eschatological docetism. See Berkouwer & Van der Woude (1969:18) in conversation with Van Ruler.

189 See Schuurman (1991:103f) for a detailed analysis of Moltmann's earlier emphasis on the discontinuity between creation and eschaton. Schuurman (1995) and Volf (1995) recognize that Moltmann does acknowledge a sense of continuity as well.

190 Moltmann (1981:50-51). Note the language of "limitation" used here. Schuurman regards the denial that there ever was a pristine state of creation as "... a collapsing of the traditional distinction between creation and fall" leading to "a very negative assessment of the limitations of that creation which, as Augustine so often said, God called very good" (1987:61).

things for eternal life.[191] Moltmann's repeated emphasis that the eschaton implies *consummation* and not merely *reparation* must be understood in this light.

Moltmann stresses that the "new" in the new creation is not only new as compared to sin, but also as compared to creation.[192] God cannot be content only to overcome sin but also to overcome the conditions that make sin possible. The radically new and different eschaton breaks the paramount power of this closed future and crushes disabling despair by opening new possibilities.[193]

In *The future of creation* (1979), Moltmann even suggests, with reference to the resurrection of Christ, that the eschaton, like the original creation, will be a *creatio ex nihilo*, a radically new thing.[194] The most fundamental structures of creation will be annihilated: "The new creation does not emerge out of the restoration of the old creation; it follows from creation's end. Out of 'the negation of the negative' a Being arises that has overcome the conflict between being and non-being and is hence absolutely new."[195] However Moltmann does not propose an apocalyptic *annihilatio mundi*. He prefers the notion of *transformatio mundi*: the world will be "transfigured" in the eschaton.[196]

In *The coming of God* Moltmann insists that he wishes to affirm both a sense of continuity and discontinuity. He again uses the term *nova creatio* to characterize the newness of the eschaton: "What is new announces itself in the judgment of what is old. It does not emerge from the old; it makes the old obsolete. It is not simply the old in a new form. It is also a new creation."[197] The new is surprising, it could never have been expected. It evokes astonishment and transforms everything that it touches. However, Moltmann adds, the eschaton is not without analogy: "What is eschatologically new, *itself creates its own continuity*, since it does not annihilate the old but gathers it up and creates it anew. It is not that another creation takes the place of this one: 'this perishable nature must put on the imperishable, and this mortal nature must put on immortality' (1 Cor 15:53)."[198] The

---

[191] Moltmann (1996:78).

[192] For Moltmann, the goal of creation is not a return to the primordial condition of paradise, but rather the revelation of the glory of God (1985:207). The eschaton is the opening up of systems that are closed in themselves. We can therefore call salvation in history the divine opening of closed systems (1979:122).

[193] Moltmann characterizes sin as closing off possibilities and grace as opening them up. Schuurman (1991:106) provides a helpful explanation of Moltmann's dual and somewhat confusing emphasis on both continuity and discontinuity. He argues that creation and eschaton are continuous in that both states are marked by openness to new possibilities and the conditions necessary for this openness. They are discontinuous in that some of the features of creation which limit possibilities are removed in the eschaton.

[194] Moltmann (1979:161-163).

[195] Moltmann (1979:48).

[196] Moltmann (1979:164).

[197] Moltmann (1996:27).

[198] Moltmann (1996:29) (emphasis - EMC). See also Moltmann (1993:88): "The eschatological new creation of this creation must surely presuppose the whole creation. For

coming God is not a new God, but the God who is faithful to his creation.

Moltmann's intentions are clear: he wishes to ensure the newness of the eschaton. He maintains that the eschaton is not merely a continuation or extrapolation[199] of the present world. It constitutes the possibility of something completely new. The eschaton has to overcome suffering – both suffering caused by sin and suffering resulting from the predicament of finitude. The eschaton not only contradicts suffering, evil and death, but also the conditions for the possibility of sin and death. This is evident from the resurrection of Christ that Moltmann also interprets as an absolutely unique event. To recognize this victory over death is to expect a similar future for the world from this risen and exalted Lord.[200]

Moltmann has been sharply criticized for his emphasis on the discontinuity between creation and eschaton:

- In response to Moltmann's eschatology, Van Ruler objects that the eschaton is no *creatio ex nihilo*.[201] The radical newness of the eschaton must be connected with God's equally radical faithfulness to creation, to everything God ever said or did.[202] The eschaton should be understood not as *nova creatio*[203] but as *recreatio* in the sense that there is movement, progression, and consummation in God's creation towards the eschaton.
- Berkhof argues that Moltmann's eschatology becomes utopian. Instead of an extrapolation from the Christological present (Barth), Moltmann regards the Christological center (even the resurrection itself) merely as a promise of a radically new future.[204] The future is thus narrowed to a formal principle.
- Rubem Alves argues that Moltmann's understanding of the dialectic between future and present becomes docetist because the future is no longer mediated by the present.[205] If there are no present traces of the future that has to eliminate suffering, this future soon becomes implausible. Alves says:

> The pure futuricity of God is a new form of Docetism in which God loses the present dimension and therefore becomes ahistorical. ... A God who is always future

---

something new will not take the place of the old; it is this same 'old' itself which is going to be created anew."

199 See Moltmann's (1979:27f) criticism of Berkhof's notion of "extrapolation." Moltmann prefers a notion of eschatological anticipation, thus stressing the possibility of a radically surprising *novum*.

200 Moltmann (1967:194).

201 Van Ruler (1972:102-118).

202 Van Ruler (1972:113).

203 See Moltmann (1967:179, 1993:286, 1996:27) where Moltmann uses the term *nova creatio* to refer to the resurrection of Christ. See also Moltmann (1967:215,222) where the cosmic dimensions of the eschaton / the kingdom of God are described as the expectation of a *nova creatio*.

204 Berkhof (1985:512).

205 Alves (1969:94-97, 152).

> is a God who does not become historical in terms of power but who remains ahead, attracting history to himself by means of eros. The biblical communities, however, had a hope for the future because God was present, and in his present, through the exercise of power, which was historical through and through, he negated historically and presently the power of 'what was,' thereby making man and history open for a new tomorrow.[206]

- Langdon Gilkey also criticizes Moltmann for positing such a sharp discontinuity between creation and eschaton. If God is merely coming and not here in any sense, then the biblical language of eschatological hope is meaningless. Hope is related to the faithfulness of God to God's own promises. If God is to be faithful to these promises in future, the same God must then also prove to have been faithful in the present as well. Eschatology presupposes a God who acts within time but who also transcends the passage of time, a God who is, was and is to come.[207]
- Doug Schuurman argues that Moltmann makes contradictory remarks: On the one hand Moltmann maintains that the eschaton is the fulfillment or telos of creational life; on the other hand he says that the eschaton is the annihilation or *finis* of creational reality. Any hope for some sort of continuity between creation and re-creation is effectively smashed.[208] If all creation is to be annihilated, how can there be hope for the future of creation? Annihilation may be dreaded but surely it cannot be hoped for.[209] Schuurman only sees the need for an eschatological annihilation of sin and a transformation of the good creation that God in his providence continues to uphold. The eschatological future contradicts the present only insofar as it is subject to sin.[210] Accordingly, the Christian hope is for the renewal of this ravaged, sin-torn world, and not for a

---

[206] Alves (1969:94). Alves perhaps provides a more balanced approach. For him, God is neither the 'eternal present' nor the 'absolute future'. The community of faith came to see, through its historical experience, that what God's action does, is to create an explosiveness that is both present and negates the present. The present is thus the presence of the past. At the same time, the presence of the Spirit in the present becomes a pregnancy in which a new future already determines the present toward a historical tomorrow. We are infected by the presence of a new future. Alves concludes that,

> The future is therefore being engendered now, amid the history where man is living, compelling him to respond to the vectors of the events that are bearers of freedom. Hope is possible and real because now, in the center of history, new historical liberating events are being created ... The language of messianic humanism about God is therefore a language about an ongoing activity in which the present is broken open - really open - toward the new (Alves 1969:96-98).

[207] Gilkey (1968:41,57; 1970:97).

[208] Schuurman (1987:50, 1991:93). In a subsequent article Schuurman (1995:148-9) acknowledges that Moltmann allows for continuity (through the importance Moltmann attaches to the category of creation) more than he (Schuurman) earlier appreciated.

[209] Schuurman (1991:103).

[210] Schuurman (1987:52).

second world created *ex nihilo*.[211]

- Steven Bouma-Prediger also finds Moltmann's radical discontinuity between creation and eschaton problematic. He concludes: "The old creation will be caught up and absorbed (*wird aufgehoben*), when the kingdom is fully consummated, creation will be discarded (*abgetan*). In short, the new creation is not the renewal but the annihilation of creation."[212] Bouma-Prediger argues that Moltmann is driven to this problem due to his conflation of creation and fall. Creation is necessarily faulted due to the bondage to transience (*Knechtschaft unter die Vergänglichkeit*)[213] since death and transience is ontologically constitutive of creation itself (Rom 8:19f). Moltmann does indeed integrate (for Bouma-Prediger *conflate*) the predicaments of sin and finitude. Moltmann regards sin as the "self-closing of open systems" and salvation as the "divine opening of closed systems."[214] The effect of both sin and nature's "bondage to transience" is therefore a (premature) closure. If creation is essentially faulted, Bouma-Prediger argues, then only a radically new creation can provide an adequate solution to such faultedness.[215] To posit the necessity for a new creation in this way undercuts the goodness of creation. Moltmann is therefore unable to ultimately affirm creation.[216] His overwhelming emphasis on the new future leads to a devaluation of present creation.[217]

To summarize: according to these criticisms, Moltmann fails to distinguish adequately between (in the terms of my analysis) the predicaments of sin and finitude, between the fall and the goodness of the created order.[218] The created order itself is faulted. The eschaton therefore requires an annihilation of the created order.[219] This results in an inability to appreciate the continuity between God's good creation and the eschaton.

The line of demarcation between Barth, Moltmann and their critics therefore

---

[211] Schuurman (1987:67).

[212] Bouma-Prediger (1997:89). The reference here is to Moltmann (1985:63).

[213] The reference here is to Moltmann (1985:69).

[214] Moltmann (1979:122).

[215] Bouma-Prediger (1997:89).

[216] Bouma-Prediger (1995:238; 1997:89). See Walsh (1987:57) for a similar criticism of Moltmann: "If the new is totally new and even a *novum ex nihilo* or a *creatio nova*, then how can it take up and preserve the old within itself?"

[217] Bouma-Prediger (1995:247).

[218] Schuurman (1987:66).

[219] Schuurman comments: "Humanity stands in need of redemption from sin and its effects, not from creation itself" (1987:62). Volf (1995:136) defends Moltmann against such criticisms by pointing to Moltmann's insistence, especially in his later work, that the eschaton does not imply an annihilation of creation. Although Moltmann tries to (and has to) defend both a sense of continuity and of discontinuity, his emphasis is clearly on the newness of the eschaton.

seems to be whether it is accepted that mortality was part of the original creation.[220] One may, at a purely conceptual level, propose notions like transformation but how, one has to ask, must such a transformation of this creation be conceived of, given the predicament of not merely personal but indeed cosmic finitude? How, then, is it possible to maintain a balance between radical continuity and radical discontinuity, between restoration and annihilation?

In the discussion of the possibility of continuity between creation and eschaton the question was raised whether this continuity is only based on God's faithfulness and continuing love? Or is there a sense in which creation itself will be continued in the eschaton? A similar question applies to the aspect of discontinuity. Any emphasis on the discontinuity between cosmos and eschaton has to account for the possibility of a *novum*. Is the possibility of a *novum* only related to God's transcendence? Or is reality itself structured in such a way as to allow new things to emerge?

On the one hand, the possibility of a *novum* may be defended on the basis of materialistic categories. The dialectic materialism of Marx and the materialist ontology of not-yet being of Ernst Bloch could provide a point of departure is this regard. Alternatively, the evolutionary biology of Darwin may also provide the stimulus in this regard. In the work of Teilhard de Chardin this is built into a comprehensive worldview where God's presence becomes evident exactly in an evolutionary history that continuously produces novelties.

On the other hand, the possibility of a *novum* may also be related to God who "calls into being the things that are not" (Rom 4:17). This calls for further reflection on who this God is, how God's transcendence should be understood and how a transcendent God acts in this world (or only beyond?) to introduce a *novum*. The eschatological significance of God's transcendence is the topic of the next section.

13.4 The eschatological tension between transcendence and immanence

In the history of the Christian tradition, the scope of eschatology has often been broadened to address the predicament of limitations in space, with specific reference to the limits of human power and knowledge. This hope is expressed as the desire for true knowledge of God, to be in the presence of an omnipotent and omniscient God. This hope accounts for the typical eschatological tension between what is revealed and what is hidden, between the immanent and the transcendent, between God and the world, between the dimensions of space-time and of eternity.

a) Transcendence

The more evolutionist, this-worldly view of the kingdom of God which character-

---

[220] Schuurman (1991:161), for example, does not seem to regard finitude as a predicament and resists any notion that death and suffering belongs to the good creation. In fact, he sees this as a "trenchant obstacle to repentance" and "a rage against God which alleges that God is the author of the misery of the world and which blinds humanity to the goodness of God mirrored in the world."

ized the nineteenth century (in Europe) was put into question by the catastrophic events of the early twentieth century. Instead, the kingdom was portrayed as a more transcendent, triumphant interruption of history. In this it could build on Kierkegaard's notion of the "infinite qualitative difference" between God and humanity, between the finite and the infinite, between eternity and time. The heart of Christianity lies in the recognition of God's revelation in Jesus Christ as the "absolute paradox" in which time and eternity intersects.[221] Eternity is not regarded as something that comes "after" time, nor is it a force that provides an impetus (from the beginning) or a lure (from the end) to time. Instead, eternity is diametrically opposed to time and history. This leads to an incomparably intensive awareness of the present moment as it is encountered by eternity, of human limitations in the light of God's transcendence.[222] In this way, dialectical theology tried to cut Christian eschatology loose from the faith in historical progress.[223]

The dialectic approach to eschatology of the early Barth brought this dimension of Christian hope to prominence in the twentieth century.

Barth interpreted the radically new and imminent kingdom described by Schweitzer not so much as something new and imminent but as something radically *different* from human expectations. Responding to the far-reaching shift from theology to religious anthropology in modern liberal theology, Barth emphasized the qualitative difference between human beings and God. For Barth, the eschaton is constituted by the transcendent judgment of God on any human morale, culture, or religion. This shift required a notion of the eschaton that was no longer based on temporal categories (the end of history) but on God's existence in the realm of eternity. Braaten comments: "In Barth's 'theology of crisis,' eschatology became a doctrine revealing the unbridgeable gap between human history here and now and the totally other world of God in heaven and eternity."[224] Macquarrie summarizes the eschatology of dialectic theology neatly:

> Whereas the liberal theologians, including Weiss and Schweitzer, had been uncomfortable with the strangeness of the New Testament eschatology, it was precisely the strangeness and otherness of the biblical revelation that Barth emphasized. Since the Enlightenment, liberal theologians had been trying to show the continuity of Christian faith and modern culture. Barth accused them of having domesticated Christianity, thereby depriving it of its offence and its power. To him the Word of God was discontinuous with every human word and achievement. It was a word of crisis or judgment, breaking into the human situation in sheer otherness.[225]

However, for the early Barth, the eschaton is not distant, or temporally remote, but extremely close to us. It brings us, from moment to moment, on the edge of eterni-

---

[221] Heron (1980:48).

[222] Sauter (1999:19).

[223] Moltmann (1996:17).

[224] Braaten (1985:343).

[225] Macquarrie (1978:99).

ty and thus imposes a limit experience on us.[226] Jesus Christ is in this sense the bare mathematical point where time and eternity meet.[227] The eschaton is the unveiling of what God from all eternity has decided to do in Christ. Traditional eschatological symbols have, also for Barth, nothing to do with real events that Christians may expect to happen in future.[228] The *parousia* does not take place in any specific time because it forms the eternal basis of all times.[229] Eschatological symbols are therefore "... dimensions of a transcendental eschatological Word that descends vertically from the alpine heights of eternity, never taking shape incarnationally in the horizontal categories of history, past, present and future."[230]

It must be noted that Barth did not regard Christian hope as the yearning to overcome the limitations of human knowledge and power. However, he was indeed responsible for a shift in the connotations of the eschaton that was now understood as the immanence of a radically transcendent God.[231] The categories of time, eternity and the eschaton were subsequently understood noetically as the revelation of this transcendent God in history. The focus of eschatological reflection therefore became the contrast between God's glory in eternity and the finite dimensions of space and time.

This emphasis on the distinction between God and the world, between time and eternity, between what is hidden and what is revealed, also characterized the earlier work of scholars like Brunner, Althaus and Bultmann. In each case, the eschaton is understood as the transcendental presence of eternity in time.

- Brunner's eschatology counters the distortion of the idea of progress that ignored the destructive and demonic tendencies in history. In response, Brunner follows Barth's emphasis on the qualitative distinction between eternity and

---

[226] Barth (1933:314).

[227] Braaten (1985:343).

[228] See Barth (1933:500): "The End of which the New Testament speaks is no temporal event, no legendary 'destruction' of the world; it has nothing to do with any historical, or 'telluric,' or cosmic catastrophe." In the *Church Dogmatics* Barth again stressed that the New Testament expectation is not for an amelioration of present conditions or for a better future, but for the coming of the Lord which would constitute a wholly new order. This will set a term to the whole time process and in its perfection will include and surpass the time process. Christian hope for God's judgment and consummation is therefore not a distant prospect but a sure and immediate hope (*CD* 3.2, 1960:486f).

[229] Barth (1933:402)

[230] Braaten (1985:343).

[231] Sauter (1999:98) notes that the word "transcendence" is probably far too pale a description of God's inaccessibility: "The word gives the impression that the boundaries of human capabilities are crossed and that God is to be met on the other side, but that the ideas still remain in the realm of human thought." Instead, the eschaton indicates the boundary of all human discourse about God. God is wholly and completely Other, impossible to depict, intangible and incomprehensible.

time. God alone has eternity. To speak about eternity is to speak about God.[232] This transcends any cyclical or linear notion of time. For Brunner, the decisive aspect of a Christian view of time is that, "in the midst of time eternity has revealed itself, that He who is above and beyond all time – Christ, the same yesterday, to-day, and for ever – has entered into time, has become clothed with temporality, in an event which differs from all other events by the fact that it is unconditionally once-for-all."[233] In Jesus Christ, the corruption through sin and guilt of the past, the anxious expectation of the future, and the present communion of believers with Christ become orientated towards eternal life in the communion of God and creature.[234] Moreover, in Jesus Christ the meaning of the history of humanity is revealed and integrated with the history of the whole cosmos.[235]

- In the first edition of his *Die letzten Dinge* (1922), Paul Althaus constructed a vertical or "axiological" eschatology. The eschaton is understood as the experience, in the midst of life, of absolute norms and values (*axia*). In the eschaton humanity is being confronted with the "transcendent Holy". The eschaton is not primarily related to the future or to the final epoch of history but to each moment of time.[236] Every wave of the sea of time breaks, as it were, on the beach of eternity. For Althaus, the eschaton thus relates primarily to eternity. Every time is the last time. All the dimensions of time, not just the last time is perpetually gathered up by eternity.[237]
- Bultmann agreed with Barth that the New Testament is essentially "eschatological". He also rejected (with the early Barth) any form of futurist eschatology, any expectation of something that is still to take place. We can no longer hope for the return of the Son of Man on the clouds of heaven. Instead, the experience of the eschaton is one where human beings are confronted with the radically Other Word of God. The eschatological moment becomes present through life changing decisions in the face of this challenging Word. Thus the existential meaning of the myth of the end of history relates to the fact that human beings must face the reality of their own deaths. Likewise, divine judg-

---

[232] Brunner (1954:54).

[233] Brunner (1954:47-48).

[234] Brunner (1954:53) specifically adds that this communion includes not only humanity but the whole cosmos.

[235] See Brunner's (1954:186f) discussion of the theanthropocentrism revealed in the God-human, Jesus Christ, as a theological vision transcending an idealist focus on the history of humanity or a materialist focus on the history of the cosmos.

[236] Althaus explains: "We arrive at the completion not by traversing the longitudinal lines of history to their end, but by erecting everywhere is history the perpendicular line. That is to say, just as every time is equally close to the primordial state and the Fall, so every time is also equally immediate to the completion. In this sense every time is the last" (quoted in Moltmann 1996:16).

[237] I am indebted to Moltmann (1996:16-19) for his helpful discussion of the work of Althaus.

ment will not take place at some future event, at "the end of the world", but through the present act of our own judgment of ourselves, based upon our knowledge of what God has done in Christ.[238] Through faith, the old world has reached its end; the believer is a new creature in Christ.[239]

In this way, eschatology becomes an event not at the end of time or beyond death, but an event repeatedly taking place in contemporary Christian proclamation of the transcendent Word of God. Jesus Christ is an eschatological event, not as an established fact of the past, but as taking place repeatedly through preaching in the present.[240] Eschatology is interested in the "final things" only in an "ultimate" and not in a temporal sense; it refers to nothing more than the moment in which humans find meaning to their existence in history, the eschatological moment of ultimate decision before God.[241] All is focused on the eschatological "now". Now is the time of salvation (2 Cor 6:2). Bultmann concludes eloquently that, "In every moment slumbers the possibility of being the eschatological moment. You must awaken it."[242] In this way what is temporal, and especially the future itself, soon disappears behind the eschatological horizon.[243] What remains is merely a new human self-understanding, a change in human consciousness.[244]

Several representatives of dialectical theology shifted their focus in later years from this emphasis on the vertical dimension of eschatology.

- In his later work Barth admitted that his earlier notion of eschatology was framed too much in terms of an abstract notion of time and eternity (referring to "limits" in a time of crisis instead of to God). This had prevented him from fully honoring the horizontal line of continuity from present to future in God's redemptive action.[245] Eternity was too much conceived as supra-temporal with insufficient attention to the actual End. Barth acknowledged that, "… although I was confident to treat the far-sidedness of the coming kingdom of God with absolute seriousness, I had no confidence in relation to its coming as such."[246]

  In the *Church Dogmatics*, Barth builds on the insight of Boethius – that

---

238 I am indebted to McGrath's (1994:471) clear discussion of Bultmann's eschatology.

239 Bultmann (1957:151).

240 Bultmann (1957:151-2).

241 See Van de Beek (1996:197f). Macquarrie (1978) labels Bultmann's eschatology therefore as an extreme form of realized eschatology and adds that Bultmann managed in this way to deal with Schweitzer's demonstration of the thoroughgoing eschatological conditioning of the New Testament.

242 Bultmann (1957:155).

243 Runia (1997:111).

244 See Sauter (1999:89).

245 Barth (*CD* 2.1, 1957:635).

246 Barth (*CD* 2.1, 1957:635).

eternity has the authentic duration that existence in time lacks – to develop a notion of eternity.[247] Eternity, for Barth, is not an endless continuation, an infinite extension of time both backwards and forwards. Eternity is not within time. Rather, it breaks into time. It is also not timelessness, but includes time. Eternity is the source, epitome, and basis of time. God's existence in eternity surrounds time on all sides and therefore includes all its dimensions. God precedes the beginning of time, accompanies its duration, and exists after its end. Time is like an island amidst the ocean of eternity.[248] God is therefore sovereign over every moment in time.

Barth's discussion of time and eternity also maintains his typical trinitarian and Christological focus. God's eternity is not outside time. The triune God creates time (and history) by calling the world into existence. God acts in time to save and perfect what God wills. In the incarnation, more specifically, eternity enters into time. In Christ, God embraces time and submits to time. It is only in Christ that we can discover what eternity means.[249] Furthermore, in Jesus Christ it becomes clear that God has time for us. God therefore grants us the most precious gift imaginable. "When I really give anyone my time, I thereby give him the last and most personal thing that I have to give at all, namely myself."[250] This soteriological dimension of time is understood noetically as the unveiling of the new time that has dawned in Christ. The focus of this revelation of a new time is not the category of time itself, but God as the subject of time; therefore: "God's time for us." The divine self-revelation in Jesus Christ will stand revealed for all eyes at the end of history. Jesus as the Lord of time, is the one in whom we may discover the full significance of existence in time.[251] The eschaton is the revelation (unveiling) of what God from eternity decided to do in Jesus Christ.[252]

- Although Althaus allowed in his earlier work for a teleological dimension besides an axiological dimension to eschatology, an orientation towards the

---

[247] See Barth's discussion of time and eternity in *CD* 1.2 (1956:45f), *CD* 2.1 (1957:608f) and *CD* 3.2 (1960:511f). The way in which Barth's discussion of time is structured in *Church Dogmatics* 3.2 is significant. He starts with a discussion of Jesus Christ as the Lord of time. He then moves to the notion of allotted time (in which he stresses that time is a gracious gift from God and that human beings live within certain temporal limitations). It is only on this basis that he subsequently discusses time as beginning and as end.

[248] Barth (*CD* 2.1, 1957:617-9). It must be added that, for Barth, eternity may not be understood as "a gray monotonous sea" but in terms of the glory of God. We do not believe in eternity but in the God of Jesus Christ.

[249] Barth (*CD* 2.1, 1957:616)

[250] Barth (*CD* 1.2, 1956:55).

[251] Barth (*CD* 3.2, 1960:437f).

[252] Runia (1997:107). Moltmann (1967:57) is not entirely impressed with Barth's self-correction for in the *Church Dogmatics* too, Jesus' cross and resurrection are at the very center of all history and the future is nothing more than the unveiling of this center.

future became more prominent in the fourth edition of *Die letzten Dingen* (1933) through the category of promise. Here he argued that the hidden presence of divine revelation and salvation in Jesus Christ involves the promise of coming disclosure. The eschaton was now understood as the goal towards which human life is orientated. This notion allowed for the meaning of time and the future while maintaining the seriousness of the actual moment in which one is confronted with the eschaton.[253]

- This shift from a purely vertical eschatology to allow for the historical dimension of eschatology is also evident in the work of Paul Tillich. For the early Tillich, the eschaton is the moment of intersection between eternity and time. The eschaton comes into contact with time in the experience of a *kairos*, the moment in which the Absolute is glimpsed in time. The *kairos* is the moment in which history comes into being.[254] In volume three of his *Systematic Theology*, Tillich identified two sides to the symbol of the kingdom of God: an inner-historical side and a trans-historical side. The kingdom of God provides direction to the quest for meaning in history itself. The transcendent dimension of the kingdom presents a challenge to any absolute claims for historical and concrete manifestations of the kingdom.[255] For Tillich, an emphasis on the inner-historical features of the kingdom does not exclude an equal emphasis on its transcendent dimension. The fulfillment of history lies in its end (telos) which is continuously present throughout history. This end is the transcendent side of the kingdom of God: the participation, elevation and purification of history into eternal life.[256] Eternity is the inner aim, the telos of finite creation, permanently elevating the finite into itself.[257]

At face value, this emphasis on the vertical dimension of eschatology (at least in the earlier phase of dialectic theology), seems to give little attention to the theme of the future.[258] Barth's eschatology is therefore often criticized for being strangely a-historical. All is focused on the eschatological "now"; the dimension of the future is amputated,[259] it disappears behind the horizon.[260] The presence of the Absolute

---

[253] Also cf. Berkouwer's (1972:30) helpful discussion of Althaus's eschatology.

[254] Tillich (1936:278-282).

[255] Tillich (1963:356-361).

[256] Tillich (1963:397-8).

[257] Tillich (1963:399). See also Pannenberg's (1998:602-3) criticism that Tillich's notion of essence obscures the way in which this transition from time into eternity takes place (i.e. inside or outside time itself). Duration in time is only possible due to its proleptic participation in eternity.

[258] Runia (1997:114), Moltmann (1979:39).

[259] Brunner (1954:119).

[260] Runia (1997:109). See also Berkouwer (1972:83): "(In the Bible) ... there is no trace of a vertically suspended eternity-concept that absorbs the eschaton in permanent, timeless relation and leaves no room or meaning for the continuity of history as such."

in Christ and through his spirit renders any temporal tension in eschatology superfluous because everything is already there.[261] The future has only a noetic significance.[262] It will bring fuller knowledge of what has already been revealed in Jesus Christ.[263] It is not so much concerned with a call for new things to happen (e.g. salvation from sin, liberation from oppression or victory over evil). It only yearns for a final unveiling of what is now still hidden.[264] The horizon of the future is swallowed up by the eternal blitzing from above. Eschatology is trapped in an eternalized present experience. The emphasis thus shifts to the authority of the Word of God in contrast to humanity and to the demand of faith in that authority.[265] Moltmann argues that the logos of eschato*logy* is thus based on the Greek logos of the epiphany of the eternal present of being instead of the Christian category of promise.[266] He says:

> The dynamic metaphor which Paul uses in Rom 13.11f about the night being far gone and the day at hand is pressed by both Barth and Althaus into the statics of the time-eternity dialectic. ... It confuses God's kairological Today for gospel and faith with the eschatological 'moment' of the raising of the dead (1 Cor. 15.52) when Barth talks about the eternal moment which every moment of time can become. Even his own metaphors betray this: the image of the overhanging rock-face which he uses for eternity points to the limit and end of the way, and if 'every wave of time breaks on the shore of eternity', we no longer have to do with a river, not even with a 'river of time'. We are then dealing with the eternal return of the same thing, in the tides, with their ebb and flow. Here time is understood neither eschatologically nor historically, but naturalistically, as transience. To the eternal One, all times are simultaneous and of equal validity. This view is in line with the blithe resignation of Ecclesiastes, but not with the messianic

---

261 Pannenberg (1970:27f).

262 Moltmann (1979:23) criticized Barth's eschatology on this way: "The future of Christ contains no new event in the creative sense, but - being the 'revelation' of what 'has already been completed' – is now merely a noetic event."

263 König (1989:209) notes that, if eschatology is indeed closely linked to Christology (as König argues), then this motif of revealing what remains hidden is legitimate. However, König also defends a promise-fulfillment structure in eschatology on the basis of the future work of Christ to establish the eschaton "with" us. In this way, König allows for both "revealing" (e.g. the Lordship of Christ, the children of God and the judgment of God will become apparent although it can already be discerned) and "fulfillment" (e.g. the resurrection of the body, the new earth).

264 Braaten (1985:343), see also Berkouwer (1972:147f). Berkouwer (1972:153f) argues that the element of unveiling in the eschaton refers to an unveiling of God's judgment over the world and humanity. In this judgment all ambiguity will indeed be removed. However, the notion of unveiling is an all too noetic way to construe the relationship between God's presence and absence. Van Ruler (1972:111) agrees that the eschaton thus simply become the unveiling of what remains hidden.

265 Pannenberg (1970:31) concludes that the removal of the time element in this form of eschatology results in an authoritarian supernaturalism.

266 Moltmann (1967:40).

passion of Isaiah.[267]

In response to this one-sided form of eschatology, theologians like Moltmann, and Pannenberg shifted their attention in the 1960's to the eschatological significance of the future. We have already noted that this shift coincided with a response to the reality of suffering. Moltmann's theology of hope emphasizes the possibility of a *novum*, while Pannenberg defends the ontological priority of the future. In both cases the not-yet receives a certain priority over the present to show that suffering does not have the final word.

The need to defend the possibility of a *novum* in the face of suffering (both as a result of sin and of temporal finitude) leads Moltmann and Pannenberg to an exploration of the *future*, instead of the eternal *presence*, as a new paradigm of transcendence.[268] Transcendence is thus understood with the help of especially two categories: openness and attraction. The present is open to the future. The future may contain new possibilities, not yet recognized in present experiences. In this way the future "transcends" the present. Furthermore, the new possibilities that the future may yield also exert a certain attraction on the present. We are pulled towards the future, not only pushed from the past. In *The experiment hope* (1975), Moltmann formulated God's future mode of existence in the following way:

> If we follow the biblical discourse about the "God of hope," we will have to give prominence to the future as the mode of God's existence with us. God is not present in the same way that the things of the world are at hand. God, like the kingdom, is coming and only as the coming one, as future, is he already present. He is already present in the way in which his future in promise and hope empowers the present. He is, however, not yet present in the manner of his eternal presence. Understood as the coming one and as the power of the future, God is experienced as the ground of liberation ...[269]

Several theologians have adopted this transcendence of the future over the present as a paradigm to understand God's transcendence. God's transcendence is conceived as the absolute power of the future. The following examples of such phrases may be noted: The future is the mode of God's being or "coming" (*Kommen*).[270] God comes to us not 'from above' but 'from ahead' (Moltmann). God is the power of the future impinging on the presence.[271] God comes to us from his future.[272]

---

267 Moltmann (1996:19).

268 See especially Moltmann (1979:1-17).

269 Moltmann (1975:50-51).

270 Moltmann (1970:9f; 1975:53). In this early essay Moltmann already adopted the notion of God's "coming" (*Kommen*). He says: "God being is coming, that is, God is already present in the way in which his future masters the present because his future decides what becomes of the present" (1970:10).

271 Pannenberg (1969:61).

272 Pannenberg (1991b:49) says: "Every single event as well as the sequence of such events springs contingently from the future of God ... because it is through the future that eternity enters into time."

Out of the future God pushes forward into the present. God is the power coming to us from the future unifying the world and bringing a future for humanity (the early Pannenberg).[273] God as the "wholly new One" is "the future of man". God is the "One who is to come" in the very history that God nonetheless transcends (Schillebeeckx).[274] God is the world's future. God's creative activity is not so much a push from the past; God is pulling the world towards the future (Ted Peters).[275] God is the absolute power of the future, impinging on the present, pressing for a radical conversion of the present.[276] Eschatology reflects on the future of God itself (Carl Braaten).[277] God's being is still in the process of coming to be (process theology). An evolutionary cosmology requires not a "metaphysics of being," but "a vision of all reality being drawn through a process of cosmogenesis – without being dissolved – into union with God" (Teilhard).[278] God as our future is a magnet drawing us from the stability of the present into an unknown future that ultimately is God himself (Zachary Hayes).[279] Evolution demands that we think of God not as "up above", but "up ahead", as the "transcendent future horizon that brings an entire universe to the fulfillment anticipated by Christian hope. God is less Alpha than Omega" (John Haught).[280] Haught concludes that a new "metaphysics of the future" is therefore required:

> A metaphysics of the future is quite simply the philosophical expression of the religious intuition that the present and the past in some sense receive their being from out of the future. From this perspective, the past and the present are in some sense only deficiently real. ... But, the "future" is always faithfully arriving at the green edge of each moment, holding at least the potential for new being. A religion of hope and promise will interpret ultimate reality - or God - as coming toward the present, and as creating the world from the sphere of the future "not-yet."[281]

The use of temporal instead of spatial categories to understand God's transcendence is clearly attractive. Its appeal is related to its dynamic thrust; it cannot acquiesce in the status quo or in an idealized past epoch.[282] However, the use of

---

[273] Pannenberg (1969:61, 1973:209).

[274] Schillebeeckx (1969b:181-3).

[275] Peters (1978:153).

[276] Braaten (1969:68-69).

[277] See the title of Braaten (1969): *The future of God.*

[278] Haught (1998a:2), Teilhard (1960:114).

[279] Hayes (1983:26).

[280] Haught (1998:2). Haught adds that according to a metaphysics of the "eternal present," the natural world is always the deficient reflection of a Perfection that exists beyond time: "In accordance with this metaphysics of the eternal present, the inevitable 'becoming' that occurs in evolution can only be interpreted as an inherently meaningless straying from the timeless perfection of being" (1998a:2).

[281] Haught (1998a:3).

[282] Haught (1998a:4).

temporal categories remains insufficient to fathom God's transcendence. It often results in an all too restricted notion of eternity as the locus of God's presence. Clayton observes that to prioritize the future in any consistent manner, "... is to give up viewing God as 'a being' – indeed even as 'being' at all! On this view, God must be sheer becoming, essential openness, the indeterminate lure to creativity.[283] In addition, the present becomes devoid of any salvific meaning or experience of divine presence. If God is solely future, and not also the God of the present, the possible impact that God's future may have on current social realities become obscure.[284] The trust that God will remain faithful to God's promises in future is undermined unless this faithfulness can be recognized from previous encounters with God.

An aside on such futuristic notions of God's transcendence is important here. Any strong emphasis on the ontological priority of the future is bound to be foreign to traditionalist societies, for example in Africa.[285] It also harbors the perennial danger of an abstraction from a Western ideology of progress instead of a prophetic notion of kairotic time. Furthermore, if God is pushed to a distant past or future then God may become irrelevant. Such options are in danger of ending up with a God who is no-where instead of now-here. Willem Drees therefore emphasizes the present as God's primary locus: God symbolizes the notion of "otherness" with respect to each state of affairs.[286] The question here remains whether this Barthian emphasis on otherness can escape the criticism of an eternalizing of the present.[287]

In the mature work of Moltmann and Pannenberg, the pendulum has swung again away from a one-sided emphasis on the transcendence of the future. A new interest in the relationship between space-time and eternity as the appropriate locus for a discussion of God's transcendence becomes evident. In their notions of eternity, the earlier criticism against a Barthian eternal presence is maintained. The eschaton is not equated with an eternal presence that can only stand in contrast to time and leads to an annihilation of time. History is not swallowed up completely in the eschaton. Instead, history itself – and therefore also the future – finds room within God's eternal existence as a dimension of eternity. God's being in eternity encompasses all times (past, present and future). Let us investigate the positions of

---

283 Clayton (1998:16).

284 Gilkey (1976:234).

285 By contrast, Haught argues that a strong emphasis on the future is precisely crucial in a culture of poverty. He says: "To the poor, however, the present and the past are always inadequate to sustain them. They can only live off the future. Thus, it is those most oppressed by present circumstances who usually awaken the rest of us to revelation's promise. Not those who hold the power, but the weak and the dispossessed, bring us the promise, often clothed in the imagery of a seemingly inaccessible future. It is especially those compelled to wait for this future who open our present existence to the Good News of history's promise" (Haught 1993b:177). Whether this future consciousness provides an adequate account of a life lived in poverty and misery remains debatable.

286 Drees (1990:199).

287 Moltmann (1979:18f, 1996:13f).

Moltmann and Pannenberg in more detail.

Moltmann's earlier work has often been criticized for presenting a thoroughly horizontal eschatology.[288] According to this criticism, Moltmann regards Christian hope as an altogether human phenomenon. This hope awaits the fulfillment of God's promises in this world (viz. the influence on Moltmann of Ernst Bloch). This accounts for the revolutionary impact of Christian hope and the influence of Moltmann on liberation theology. In the light of the unfolding of Moltmann's oeuvre this criticism cannot be sustained. Let us track some of the crucial texts in which the notion of transcendence is discussed in relation to God and creation.[289]

The theme of transcendence is discussed in *The Future of Creation* in an important essay on "The future as a new paradigm of transcendence."[290] Moltmann discusses various models of transcendence, e.g. in terms of physics and metaphysics, and being and human existence. He suggests the transcendence of a qualitatively new (eschatological) future (i.e. not simply the future as such) impinging on and transforming present history. Transcendence is not understood in terms of spatial metaphors (as a noun) but in historical categories (as a verb).[291] The future is the realm from which the transcendent God comes to us *in* history. God's immanence is therefore understood in historical terms. Moltmann concludes that, "the vision of a qualitatively new future of history can become a transcendent horizon which opens up and stimulates the process of transcending towards a new historical future."[292]

In *The Trinity and the Kingdom*, Moltmann develops the notion of God's presence in creation in terms of the notion of God's indwelling (*Shekinah*) through the Spirit. Through the Holy Spirit, "the world will be transfigured, transformed in to God's world, which means into God's own home."[293] This hope is expressed in a vision of the perichoretic indwelling of God (*Einwohnung Gottes*) in this new world.[294] In the eschaton the whole world will become God's home so that God will be "all in all" (1 Cor 15:28); God will be in the world and the world in God.

In *God in creation,* Moltmann develops an ecological doctrine of creation in which he again stresses the immanence of God "in creation" (compare the immanence in history above). He rejects a deist notion of God in which the transcendence of God is overemphasized. He says: "In the Western tradition, God kept moving increasingly into the sphere of transcendence, and the world came to be understood in purely immanent and this-worldly terms."[295] And further: "Through

[288] See, e.g. Schwarz (1984:525f).

[289] See Bouma-Prediger's (1997:76-84) helpful discussion of the dual emphasis on God's transcendence and immanence in Moltmann's thinking (prior to *The coming of God).*

[290] Moltmann (1979:1-17).

[291] Moltmann (1979:11).

[292] Moltmann (1979:15).

[293] Moltmann (1981:104).

[294] Moltmann (1981:104).

[295] Moltmann (1989:54).

the monotheism of the absolute subject, God was increasingly stripped of his connection with the world, and the world was increasingly secularized."[296] Instead, Moltmann proposes a trinitarian and specifically pneumatological[297] understanding of the *immanence* of God in creation. God is present in the world, but the world is also present in God.[298] This formula indicates Moltmann's relative sympathy for a form of panentheism, although he does not adopt the term explicitly.[299] Moltmann is nevertheless clear in his determination to preserve God's transcendence and the fundamental distinction between creator and creation.[300] He therefore rejects the process view of a dipolar relationship between God and creation which leads to a fusion of God and nature and a divinization of nature, which subsequently becomes co-eternal with God.[301] He also rejects a "pantheistic dissolution

---

[296] Moltmann (1985:1).

[297] See Moltmann (1985:9f, 98f) for an emphasis on "Creation in the Spirit". Creation comes into being through the Spirit (Gen 1:2), exists in the Spirit and is renewed through the Spirit. He adds: "When we say that the creation's Creator Spirit indwells both every individual creature and the community of creation, we mean that the presence of the infinite in the finite imbues every finite thing, and the community of all finite beings, with self-transcendence." (1985:101).

[298] Moltmann (1985:13, 17; 1989:15).

[299] Moltmann's position has subsequently been referred to as panentheist, for example by Bouma-Prediger (1995, 1997) and Torrance (1997). This calls for further investigation in terms of Moltmann's own discussion of the term. He clearly treats the theme of panentheism with sympathy (see, e.g. 1981:19, 110, 1985:98). He says, for example, that:

> The one-sided stress on God's transcendence in relation to the world led to deism, as with Newton. The one-sided stress on God's immanence in the world led to pantheism, as with Spinoza. The trinitarian concept of creation integrates the elements of truth in monotheism and pantheism. In the panentheist view, God, having created the world, also dwells in it, and conversely the world which he created exists in him (1985:98).

However, Moltmann seems to think that the strengths of a panentheist position can be accommodated through a trinitarian theology in which the immanence of God's Spirit is emphasized. This is evident from the following two important formulations: "In the panentheistic view, God, having created the world, also dwells in it, and conversely the world which he has created exists in him. *This is a concept which can really only be thought and described in trinitarian terms*" (emphasis - EMC). And even more explicitly: "But differentiated panentheism is not capable of linking God's immanence in the world with his transcendence in relation to it. This is the benefit of the trinitarian doctrine of creation in the Spirit and of the Creator Spirit who indwells creation. This doctrine views creation as a dynamic web of interconnected processes. The Spirit differentiates and binds together ..." (1985:103). The notion of *zimsum* (see the discussion below) also stresses the distinctness of the creation from the Creator – even though Moltmann adds that creation still takes place "in God."

[300] Moltmann (1985:79).

[301] Moltmann (1985:78). Moltmann concludes that process theology does not have a doctrine of creation; it can only account for the continuing preservation of the world. Pannenberg (1991b:29) comes to the same conclusion.

of creation in God."[302] The world is not in itself divine, nor an emanation from God's eternal being.[303] Also in the eschaton, the distinction between Creator and creature will be maintained.[304]

The key to an understanding of Moltmann's position is in his use of the kabbalistic notion of *zimsum*.[305] This notion suggests the primordial self-restriction (*zimsum*) of God to create room for the emergence of creation.[306] In this kenotic protology,[307] God withdraws God's presence to make room for creation. From God's self-restriction emerges a *nihil*, a nothingness that is a partial negation of divine Being, but not the negation of creaturely being.[308] Within this nihil God allows a

---

302 Moltmann (1985:89).

303 Moltmann (1985:72).

304 Moltmann (1985:64). See also Bouma-Prediger (1995:116).

305 Moltmann's discussion of the notion of *zimsum* is derived from the kabbalistic tradition, retrieved by Isaac Luria, who argues that God's indwelling in the temple (Shekinah) is only possible if the infinite God contracts the divine presence. See already Moltmann (1981:108f) and in more detail (1985:86-93). He again builds on this notion in *The coming of God* (1996:281,296f).

306 This does not mean that creation takes place "out of God" (which would suggest a monistic form of emanation for which Moltmann criticizes Tillich). The world was created neither out of pre-existent matter, nor out of the divine Being itself. It was called out of being by the free resolve of God, and, more specifically, out of the ecstatic love of God. See Moltmann (1985:75f).

307 See Moltmann (1985:88) for a kenotic understanding of God in terms of self-restricting, self-emptying love as the motive behind his emphasis on the notion of *zimsum*. The term "kenotic protology" is also used by Torrance (1997:90). For a similar emphasis on the notion of *zimsum* as kenosis, see Haught (1998a:234f). See Johnson (1992:234, 302) on the need for a feminist revision of *zimsum* as *kenosis*, given the problem of women's internalization of the role of victim. Haught also refers to the following lucid formulation by Michael Wyschogrod: "A world in which the divine light penetrates and filled all is a world in which there is nothing but God. In such a world no finitude and therefore no human existence is possible. ... The creation of man involves the necessity for God's protection of man from God's being. This protection involves a certain divine withdrawal, the tsimtsum of the kabbalists, who were also puzzled by how things other than God could exist in the light of the absolute being of God. To answer this question they invoked the notion of tsimtsum, by which they meant that the absolute God, whose being fills all being, withdraws from a certain region, which is thus left with the divine being thinned out in it, and in this thinned out region man exists." (The anthropocentric and androcentric terminology used by Wyschogrod is corrected by Haught to include the whole cosmos).

308 Moltmann (1985:87) describes this *nihil* as God-forsaken space, even as hell and absolute death. This creates the possibility (but not the actuality) of the demonic. This seems to assume that evil is a necessary product of creation and that the Creator is therefore the author of evil. This emphasis on a primordial *nihil* remains, in my view, quite problematic.

Moltmann's use of the notion of *zimsum* has subsequently been severely criticized, especially by Bouma-Prediger (1995:254f; 1997), Torrance (1997) and Walsh (1987).

world to come into being that is different from Godself (*extra Deum*), a world that exist before, with and in Godself.[309] God created the world in Godself, giving it time in God's eternity, finitude within God's infinity, space within God's omnipresence, freedom within God's love.[310] At the same time, if creation is relatively distinct from God, then God can also dwell in creation. The eschaton may therefore be understood as God's indwelling (*Shekinah*) in creation,[311] which is already anticipated in the celebration of the Sabbath.[312] Moltmann adds that even in the kingdom of glory the world remains God's creation and will not become Godself.[313] In this way Moltmann tries to balance the transcendence and immanence of God. He concludes that:

Torrance (1997:90) observes that the notion of *zimsum* (which is a response to God's omnipresence) assumes spatial categories. It suggests that "a kind of primal mystical space" (1981:110) is created, or, more precisely, *vacated* temporally prior to the creation event. This tends to encourage a container or receptacle model of space and a linear notion of time (where creatio *ex nihilo* is prior to the *creatio originalis* and *creatio continua*). Bouma-Prediger (1997) comments that, for Moltmann, the self-limitation of God assumes a primordial *nihil* as a necessary condition of the world to exist. The eschaton constitutes a refilling of this *nihil*. In that case, a distinction between God and creation becomes difficult to maintain in the eschaton. The eschaton requires a redeeming *annihilatio nihili* in which God gathers the nothingness into God's own being (Moltmann 1985:90-3). Walsh (1987:75) comes to a similar conclusion:

> Redemption, then is not primarily a restoration of a covenantal relationship with God broken in history, but a 're-filling' of that space, an overcoming of God's self-limitation by means of an *annihilatio nihili*. But if this *nihil* was for some reason necessary for the *creatio originalis* then how can the God/creation distinction still be maintained when this *nihil* is vanquished and God is all in all? Is the distinction between pantheism and panentheism only semantic?

It should be noted that these criticisms are based on Moltmann's work prior to *The coming of God* where he still uses the notion of *zimsum*, but balances this with the notion of "aeonic" or relative eternity (see the discussion below).

309 See also Moltmann (1996:306):

> Through the space conceded by God, creation is given detachment from God and freedom of movement over against him. If God were omnipresent in the absolute sense, and manifested in his glory, there would be no earthly creation. In order to make himself endurable for his earthly creatures, God has to veil his glory, 'since he who looks upon God must die'. Remoteness from God and spatial distance from God result from the withdrawal of God's omnipresence and the 'veiling of his face'. They are part of the grace of creation, because they are the conditions for the liberty of created beings.

310 Moltmann (1981:109).

311 This implies that God will dwell in the whole creation (Rev 21:3) and the whole creation will be "the manifestation and mirror of his glory" (Moltmann 1985:288).

312 Moltmann (1985:5) explains: "If the creative God himself dwells in his creation, then he is making it his own home, "on earth as it is in heaven". All created beings then find in nearness to him the inexhaustible wellspring of their life, and for their part find home and rest in God."

313 Moltmann (1985:184).

> It is therefore impossible to think of this world-transcendence of God unless we think simultaneously of his world-immanence; and it is equally impossible to conceive of God's evolutive immanence in the world, without his world-transcendence. The two are mutually related.[314]

In *The coming of God,* Moltmann again makes use of the notion of divine self-restriction (*zimsum*). However, this is now embedded in more sophisticated understanding of the relationship between time and eternity. Here he develops the patristic notion of the *aeon* or *aevum* to distinguish between God's absolute eternity and the relative eternity of the new creation beyond space and time.[315] With Augustine, Moltmann wants to maintain that the world was created with time not in time. There was no time before creation. However, God's eternity does not imply a negation of temporality; it is not timelessness. On the contrary, eternity as the fullness of creative life includes an opening for time "in" eternity.[316] Here Moltmann again follows Augustine's distinction between the primordial beginning in which God created heaven and earth (Gen 1:1) and the historical beginning of earthly time (Gen 1:5).[317]

It is within this context that Moltmann speaks in *The coming of God* about God's creative resolve to create a world different from Godself which subsequently requires a primordial self-restriction of God's omnipresence (*zimsum*).[318] Out of this self-restriction of God's eternity there emerges a time for creation, the primordial aeon, an opening for time within eternity.[319] Furthermore, the space created by God's self-withdrawal is not an empty vacuum of nothingness (unlike in *God in creation*), but is living space in God. God becomes hospitable, a God who can be inhabited.[320] This also constitutes an ecological (*oikos*) doctrine of God.

---

314 Moltmann (1985:206).

315 Moltmann (1996:282), also earlier in Moltmann (1990:158).

316 Moltmann (1996:281).

317 Moltmann (1996:282).

318 Moltmann (1996:281-2). Moltmann (1996:298) adds that God does not leave a vacuum as the kabbalistic doctrine of *zimsum* suggests (and for which Moltmann is criticized by Torrance – see the note above). God allows a world that is distinct from Godself to exist before God and in Godself. The primordial nothingness which Moltmann seems to defend in *God in creation*, is not mentioned in *The coming of God.* God makes living space in Godself.

319 Moltmann (1996:282).

320 Moltmann (1985:88, 1996:299) acknowledges that God as the living space of the world is a motherly metaphor, but does not develop the obvious suggestion of creation taking place within a divine womb. Johnson (1992:234) criticizes Moltmann's exclusive use of male metaphors as a "blatant anomaly". In *The coming of God* (1996:300-301) Moltmann does mention the experience of space by a fetus in the uterus. This is an ecological experience of *Geborgenheit.* The fetus (that is not the mother) grows for nine months "in" the mother. When the mother gives birth to the child she allows the child a certain independence. Moltmann concludes that human beings are both inhabitants and inhabited. This provides an analogy for the Christian affirmation that Christ is "in" us but that

This protological distinction has an eschatological parallel. Creation will not be taken up into God's absolute eternity. Instead, there will be an eschatological transition of the temporal creation into aeonic time and space (i.e. where the transitoriness of time will be transcended towards the "fullness of time").[321] The consummation implies that everything that had ever been before is gathered up and brought back in the eschaton.[322] On this basis Moltmann finds room to maintain both God's immanence and God's transcendence. He develops this in terms of the notion of God's *Shekinah*, God's indwelling in the new creation, the coming of God to creation (*adventus*), instead of creation simply being taken up into God's presence.[323] He suggests that a mutual indwelling of the world in God and of God in the world will come into being in the eschaton. This implies a reciprocal *perichoresis* where God's salvific presence infuses the world and where the world is taken up and transformed in God's presence.[324] This mutuality and reciprocity characterizes God's loving relationship with the world. It is an expression of a more fundamental perichoresis within the triune God (Moltmann's preferred way of expressing the unity within the Trinity).[325] This is exemplified in the mutual *Shekinah* of God and humanity in Christ. "In Christ" there is a double indwelling: the indwelling of God and of believers.[326]

In the mature work of Pannenberg a similar interest in a notion of eternity is evident. He argues that the category of promise cannot by itself provide a basis for hope. The openness of the future has to be related to an understanding of eternity and its relation to time.[327] Let us follow the developments in his thinking on this specific aspect:

In many of his works Pannenberg argues that the category of "the whole" provides a necessary framework within which meaning could be ascertained. We interpret experiences within larger wholes.[328] However, due to the temporality of an ever-changing world, this whole does not yet exist as a totality. If there is a whole it must be future (at least for us). The whole can therefore only be anticipated. We can only anticipate a wholeness of meaning that is as yet incomplete.[329]

---

we are also "in" Christ. See Elizabeth Johnson (1992:233f) for one example of such a quintessentially female perspective on the notion of *zimsum*.

321 Moltmann (1996:279f).

322 Moltmann (1996:265). He adds: "In the eschatological Shekinah, the new creation takes the whole of the first creation into itself, as its own harbinger and prelude, and completes it." (1996:266).

323 See also Moltmann (1985:149f).

324 See already Moltmann (1981:157, also 1985:16f, 150f; 1996:307).

325 Moltmann (1981:150f). See also Bouma-Prediger (1995:119-126).

326 Moltmann (1996:306). See also Johnson (1992:235) on a feminist retrieval of the power of friendship as a suitable metaphor for mutual indwelling.

327 Pannenberg (1998:595).

328 Pannenberg (1990:23).

329 See also Pannenberg (1998:590).

"Hence, in the march of time," Pannenberg concludes, "we can only seek and hope for a totality of life from a future that will integrate the many moments of life into a unity."[330]

In *Theology and the kingdom of God* Pannenberg argued on this basis that Christians think of this coming whole as the kingdom of God. The coming of the kingdom can only be confirmed eschatologically by an act of God. In the meanwhile we can gain indirect confirmations through our experiences of finite reality in history, most notably in the history of Jesus Christ.

In a few cryptic comments Pannenberg then (in)famously adds that "In a restricted but important sense, God does not yet fully exist"[331] (i.e. as a whole). "God's being is still in the process of coming to be."[332] "The eschaton is eternity in the fullest sense, and this is the mode of God's being in the coming of his Kingdom."[333] "The reality of God, then, is the creative arrival of this powerful future in the event of love. ... God is not an existing entity but is the future of his coming Kingdom."[334] For Pannenberg, this does not imply a development in God (as in Whitehead's process metaphysics), but it does imply that the dimension of time is incorporated into the idea of God. God's presence in eternity is not understood in terms of the Greek idea of eternity as timelessness or an everlasting present without change.[335] Pannenberg's view (which is modified in his mature work) remains somewhat obscure. He clearly wishes to maintain that eternity is not the antithesis of time or change, but that it includes time. Still, the difference between present, past and future is overcome in the eschaton. What turns out to be true in the future will then be evident as having been true all along.[336]

In *Metaphysics and the idea of God*, Pannenberg develops a metaphysical notion of eternity, based on the position of Plotinus that eternity is the source of time. Eternity is for Plotinus, unlike for Augustine, not understood in terms of timelessness but as inclusive of time, it is the presence of the totality of life as a whole. Eternity is a presupposition for understanding time. Temporal moments relate to eternity as parts relate to the whole. In Pannenberg's reading of Plotinus, eternity thus hovers over time as the future whole.[337] Human existence in time participates in eternity through an anticipation of the future whole. The future is the source of the wholeness of finite being.[338] Pannenberg concludes that, "...

---

330 Pannenberg (1998:601).

331 Pannenberg (1969:56).

332 Pannenberg (1969:56).

333 Pannenberg (1969:64).

334 Pannenberg (1969:70-71).

335 Pannenberg (1969:62-63).

336 Pannenberg (1969:62-64).

337 Pannenberg (1990:77) quotes Plotinus in this regard: "Instead of the completed infinite and whole, [there is only] the moment after moment into the infinite; instead of the unitary whole, [only] the partial and always merely future whole."

338 Pannenberg (1990:88).

when the theory of time is oriented toward the eternal totality, the consequence is a primacy of the future for an understanding of time."[339] Plotinus therefore not only regarded eternity as inclusive of time; he also defended the primacy of the future wholeness.[340]

In his *Systematic Theology*, Pannenberg builds on this analysis for a more sophisticated notion of God's being in eternity. He argues that God's transcendence may be understood as infinity.[341] Infinity is not simply the antithesis or negation of the finite but transcends its own antithesis to the finite by incorporating it, that is, by giving existence to the finite, by invading what is finite and by giving it a share in God's own life.

Pannenberg then defines eternity as a manifestation of the infinite in relation to time.[342] He distinguishes between the eternality in which God resides and the flow of time in which humans exist. He argues that eternity encompasses time in every sequence of events (past, present and future). Time proceeds from eternity and is constantly encompassed by it.[343] Eternity does not imply timelessness or the antithesis of change but includes all the dimensions of time.[344] Eternity means "the whole of time in the form of one undivided presence."[345] God's eternity can therefore be regarded as constitutive of time and space. More precisely, it is through the future that eternity enters time. This allows God to come to us, so to speak, from the future, while at the same time conceiving God as complete and "already"

---

339 Pannenberg (1990:77).

340 Pannenberg argues that Augustine did not follow Plotinus in this insight, despite its obvious resonance with a prophetic eschatology. Augustine focused, instead, on the time-bridging present within the life of the soul. This led to a very limited notion of eternity as simultaneity (and not also as an anticipation of completed wholeness – see Chapter 18). The primacy of the future whole emerges again in the philosophy of Heidegger (and behind him Kant and Hegel). However, this is no longer discussed within the context of a metaphysics of eternity, but is reduced to an analysis of human subjectivity (Kant) and the finitude of the *Dasein* (Heidegger). Pannenberg (1991:407) concludes that Plotinus' notion of eternity has not been superseded by any subsequent or modern discussions. See Peters (1996:280) for a less sympathetic reading of Plotinus on this point.

341 Pannenberg (1991:397) acknowledges that infinity is not a biblical term for God, but argues that this is a philosophical expression of God's holiness.

342 Pannenberg (1991:397).

343 Pannenberg (1994:92). This emphasis is also present in *Theology and the kingdom of God* where Pannenberg says: "The God of the coming Kingdom must be called eternal because he is not only the future of our present but has been also the future of every past age" (1969:62). He adds: "Only in the future of his Kingdom come will the statement 'God exists' prove to be definitely true. But then it will be clear that the statement was always true."

344 See already Pannenberg (1969:62, also 1993:25). This inclusion of time within eternity is for Pannenberg the value of the process metaphysics of Whitehead and Hartshorne – although he does not share with them the notion that there is also development or process within God. God's being in eternity includes, but also transcends all times.

345 Pannenberg (1991b:48).

existing.[346] Although God's eternity is complete, it is still future for us. Eternity as the complete totality of life is thus seen from our standpoint in time only in terms of a fullness that is sought in the future.[347]

Pannenberg argues that the inclusion of time in eternity can be understood in trinitarian language. This allows for the difference of the eternal Creator from the temporality of creatures, the presence of eternity in time (in Christ)[348] and the incorporation of creatures into God's eternal present through the Spirit.[349] Pannenberg concludes: "The thought of eternity that is not simply opposed to time but positively related to it, embracing it in its totality, offers a paradigmatic illustration and actualization of the structure of the true Infinite which is not just opposed to the finite but also embraces the antithesis."[350]

It is on the basis of this analysis of eternity as a function of God's infinity in relation to time, that Pannenberg finally discusses the relationship between God's transcendence and immanence. He regards this tension as a function of God's omnipresence (infinity in space).[351] His argument is structurally similar to the one on eternity and time. God's transcendence is described in the spatial Biblical imagery of heaven. This allows a distinction between God and creatures "on earth". God grants creatures an independent existence in their own space where they have room to live their own lives alongside God.[352] At the same time, God is also present in creation through the creative presence of the Spirit, and more specifically through the incarnation of the Son. Pannenberg concludes:

> Only the doctrine of the Trinity could basically clarify the question of union and tension between transcendence and immanence. ... The doctrine of the Trinity made it possible to link the transcendence of the Father in heaven with his presence in believers through the Son and Spirit. ... Thus the trinitarian life of God in his economy of salvation proves to be the true infinity of his omnipresence.[353]

This analysis of God's infinity in relation to time (eternity) and space (omnipre-

---

346 See Pannenberg (1991:408f), Clayton (1998:16). Clayton observes that Pannenberg's earlier view that, "In a restricted but important sense, God does not yet fully exist." (1969:54), is modified by this sense in which God "already" exists."

347 Pannenberg (1991:408).

348 Pannenberg (1998:604) says: "Only in the history of Jesus of Nazareth did the eschatological future, and with it the eternity of God, really enter the historical present."

349 See Pannenberg (1991:407-8). Pannenberg notes that Plotinus could not account for the emergence of time from the realm of eternity other than in negative terms as the "fall" of the soul from original unity.

350 Pannenberg (1991:408).

351 See Pannenberg (1994:85): "The idea of God's transcendence also demands space if it is not to be reduced to the logical distinction of the Infinite from everything finite."

352 Pannenberg (1991:412).

353 Pannenberg (1991:415).

sence) allows Pannenberg to develop a trinitarian[354] protology and eschatology. In creating, God allows finite creatures space alongside God and over against God.[355] God also grants creation a sequence of time which is necessary for a finite being, distinct from God, to act and manifest itself as the center of its own activity. To achieve its own individuality a being therefore requires the conditions of becoming and perishing in time (thus the predicament of finitude).[356]

If the origin of creation is in eternity outside itself, the destiny of creation is also beyond itself. God, and not nothing, is the end of time.[357] Throughout its existence in time, creation exists in anticipation of the future totality.[358] In the eschaton time itself will end (Rev 10:6f). The end of time marks the transition to eternity. Finite beings may then be preserved and renewed as it participates in the eternity of God. When creation participates in the eternity of God, the disintegration of human life and the separation of the past from the present and the future (that is a feature of cosmic time) will be overcome.[359] Then these moments will be integrated into a unity and totality: "... In the future of the divine rule the life of creation will be renewed for participation in the eternity of God. In it eternity comes together with time. It is the place of eternity itself in time ...[360] ... "Only participation in the eternity of God can overcome the disintegration of human life into moments that are sundered by the march of time and integrate such moments into unity and totality."[361]

In their later work Moltmann and Pannenberg therefore do not move away from dialectical theology entirely. On the contrary, it assumes and builds upon the insight of dialectic eschatology that the eschaton cannot be understood in terms of purely temporal categories. The eschaton has to be understood in terms of the

---

[354] Pannenberg (1991b:45) also deliberately disassociates himself from pantheism and panentheism and argues that a trinitarian model provides an alternative approach.

[355] Pannenberg (1994:86). Pannenberg discusses two influential concepts of space, namely as the relatedness of bodies or spaces (viz. the space of the creaturely world) and that which is prior to every relation (the immensity of God that constitutes this space). He agrees with Moltmann that the space of the created world should be distinguished from God's presence. However, he criticizes Moltmann's adoption of the notion of God's self-restriction (*zimsum*). He argues that the notion of space that precedes creation constitutes an empty space next to the absolute space of God's presence and the concrete space linked to the existence of finite creatures. It also assumes a receptacle notion of space that has become outdated as a result of relativity theory. Instead, Pannenberg argues that God is omnipresent also within the space of creatures. Creatures in space cannot exist in isolation from the presence of the Creator who is constitutive for their existence. See Pannenberg (1994:89, note 229)

[356] Pannenberg (1994:95-6).

[357] Pannenberg (1998:594).

[358] Pannenberg (1994:96).

[359] Pannenberg (1994:95; 1998:601).

[360] Pannenberg (1991:408-9).

[361] Pannenberg (1998:601).

qualitative difference between time and eternity. However, the present no longer provides the dominant locus for understanding the relationship between time and eternity. Past, present and future is incorporated in the eschaton in such a way that the future receives a certain priority.

b) Immanence

At the other side of the spectrum, a number of eschatologies, in which the immanence of God is emphasized almost exclusively, have recently become more prominent. These eschatologies look for a more promising future within the material history of the cosmos itself. In these radically immanent, panentheist or even pantheist eschatologies, the source of hope is not primarily linked to God's transcendence, but to the transformative potential within the material evolution of creation.

An emphasis on God's immanence is of special importance in the work of Teilhard de Chardin and his followers as well as in process theology (and often in combination) and many expressions of ecofeminism. Process theology radically shifts the locus for our hope; the ultimate meaning of the world is not to be found in its future, but in its ongoing contribution to the life of God. The ultimate horizon of hope is situated not at the end of history but in the present experience of God.[362]

- John Cobb bases the possibility of real novelty and radical change on the material aspects of nature. He says: "Also, progress is possible. Over hundreds of millions of years and culminating in man, despite temporary reversals, there was fundamental progress on this planet in the realization of greater values. Within human history, too, threads of progress can be discerned. God's activity in the world makes for progress, as well as mere change."[363]
- John Haught also relates the source of hope to the material aspects of creation. This is indicated in the title of his work, *The promise of nature* (1993). Haught argues that nature and reality itself has its own inherent teleology; it is "seeded" and "saturated" with promise. We may look at the cosmos itself as the embodiment of God's promises – instead of looking vertically above to a completely different, transcendent world for the fulfillment of God's promises. The cosmos seems to share in the hopes of humanity: "Billions of years before our own appearance in evolution it was already seeded with promise. Our own religious longing for future fulfillment, therefore, is not a violation but a blossoming of this promise."[364] For Haught, Christian eschatology "resonates" with this "promise of nature" and provides a clue to the ultimate meaning of this cosmic story. The authentic life of Christian faith and hope is one of looking to the fulfillment of God's promise, based on the experience and trust in God as a promise keeper (e.g. the fulfillment of God's promises in Jesus

---

[362] Ford (1972:136).
[363] Cobb (1972:5).
[364] Haught (1993:109).

Christ).[365] I will return to Haught's argument in Chapter 14 in more detail.

- Arthur Peacocke also emphasizes God's immanence in the created world. For Peacocke, the creator God is continuously active, creating in and through the open-ended processes of the natural order.[366] The starting point for hope must therefore be found within the present reality. We look toward a God who is present in the world as the source of hope. All that we can perceive at the moment is how God works out God's purposes in space and time. It is up to us as human beings to listen, discern and respond to this meaning. Peacocke adds in language typical of the predicament of finite human knowledge: "Yet, however carefully we try to perceive God's meaning, to hear the leitmotifs he is developing in creation, clearly, it comes through to us muffled and distorted by our own ignorance and waywardness, obscured by our intellectual inertia and blurred by our sufferings. We need a more ample and clearer communication of his meaning ..."[367]

  Although Peacocke alludes here to God's presence in Jesus Christ, the primary source of hope is not so much based on Christ, but on the trustworthiness and viability of the created order, as is manifested in its regularity and ability to be subsumed under scientific laws and interpretative concepts. The experience of this trustworthiness and viability of the created order is an unveiling of God's meaning and purpose for the world. In experiencing the world as trustworthy and as viable we are encountering God as generator and basis for hope.[368] Furthermore, God as creator is operating in us and through us like a composer who structures a musical performance, but also allows for rich improvisations.[369] Creating is the act of God the composer at work.[370] Peacocke repeatedly states that we live and move and have our being in One who is not far from us (Acts 17:28). God is uniquely present to the world as a whole and to each of its individual component.[371] God could not be closer than that – and therein lies our hope.[372] The metaphor of the God as composer also accounts for the transcendence of the composer in relation to the music she creates. At the same time, the presence of the composer is experienced precisely *in* the music and not as some kind of additional factor added to the experience.
- Teilhard introduces the notion of the "divine milieu" to illuminate the presence of God in the world and the world in God. He says: "In the divine milieu all the elements of the universe touch each other by that which is most inward and

---

365 Haught (1993:102).

366 Peacocke (1993:105).

367 Peacocke (1979:353).

368 Peacocke (1979:350-1).

369 Peacocke (1993:171-178).

370 Peacocke (1989:13)

371 Peacocke (1993:159)

372 Peacocke (1979:352, 358, 1993:158f).

ultimate in them."[373] The manifestation of the divine presence does not necessarily modify the apparent order of things. God's transcendence becomes evident through the "incandescence of the inward layers of being."[374] Transcendence is thus understood in terms of *transparence*, that is, the presence of transcendence in immanence. Especially in the incarnation of Christ, a powerful radiance is evident. Reality becomes translucent with divine presence. For Teilhard the great mystery of the incarnation is not the appearance, but the transparence, of God in the universe.[375]

- In the context of dialogues with Marxism, Alves also maintains that transcendence should not be understood in terms of what is beyond the earthly, but, instead, as the deepest dimension of the world of visible things in which we live. The sensorial is the only place in which we as human beings can experience transcendence. The language of faith therefore does not speak about a meta-historical, meta-worldly realm in which hopes are fulfilled and suffering is brought to an end. Faith remains historical through and through. It is within this historical and earthly context that the reality and possibility of human liberation has to be addressed.[376]

Many ecofeminist theologies argue vehemently against triumphalist and monarchical images of God, ruling from a distance and controlling the world through domination and benevolence. The isolation of the world from God in much of classic theism is rejected. Instead, the immanence of God in creation is usually emphasized. A feminist concern for mutuality and reciprocity in relationships calls for a presence of God in the world that fosters and nurtures such relationships.[377]

- In her well-known work, *The body of God*, Sallie McFague uses the body-spirit analogy to clarify and radicalize both God's immanence and transcendence. Human existence is necessarily an embodied existence. Yet, human consciousness cannot be reduced to bodily functions. Likewise, if the world may be regarded as God's body, God's transcendence may be acknowledged without falling into the trap of a mind-matter dualism.[378] God's transcendence is an embodied transcendence; we only have access to God through God's embodiment in and through all bodies – the sun and moon, trees and rivers, animals, people and in Jesus Christ as the paradigm and culmination of divine embodiment.[379] McFague considers God metaphorically as the Spirit that breathes life

---

373 Teilhard (1960:114).

374 Teilhard (1960:131).

375 Teilhard (1960:130-131). See also Boff's (1997:153) use of the notion of transparence as the presence of transcendence in immanence.

376 Alves (1969:150).

377 Johnson (1992:229-231).

378 McFague (1993:252-3).

379 McFague (1993:133).

into the universe. The breath of God enlivens each and every entity in the body. She suggests that "God is not primarily the orderer and controller of the universe but its source and empowerment, the breath that enlivens and energizes it."[380] The Spirit is the source of life and of the renewal of life.

- In a brief article on "Ecology, feminism and African and Asian spirituality" Chung Hyun Kyung also explores the immanence of God in the interwoven web of life on earth. If nature is a God-infused, God-breathed place, it is also sacred. Using eloquent feminine images to illustrate God's immanence in the earth cycles, she adds:

  > The earth becomes sacred. The rhythmic ebb and flow of the rivers and seas becomes God's dance. The life-giving fecundity of the land with the water is the source of food coming from God's bosom. The wind and air become God's life-giving breath. Then we cannot destroy earth since God is there. God is the life-giving power. The cosmos is God's womb. ... God energizes the cosmos, and the cosmos in return moves with the creator in a cosmic dance of exquisite balance and beauty.[381]

- In *A feminist ethic of risk*, Sharon Welch proposes a communicative ethics in which the "beloved community" becomes the locus of belonging to the web of life, the matrix within which the gift of life is celebrated. For Welch, the divine is the immanent power that sustains and transforms this web of life. It is "neither necessary nor liberating to posit a substance or ground that exists outside of relational power."[382] Divinity is not that which is other than the finite. Grace does not come from the outside to transform the conditions of life; "Divinity, or grace, is the resilient, fragile, healing power of finitude itself."[383] Welch concludes: "We who are feminist theologians find much that is divine – work for justice, love, creativity itself, the web of life, joy, and beauty. Innumerable states and qualities of acting are divine. By naming joy as divine, we affirm that these aspects of human existence are worthy of worship. Attentiveness to the web of life, to the exuberance of children, to the beauty of nature, provides a sense of peace, of belonging, of exultation, of ecstasy."[384]
- Elizabeth Johnson, by contrast, maintains an equally strong emphasis on God's transcendence.[385] This transcendence is understood noetically in terms of mystery and divine incomprehensibility. Elsewhere she describes divine transcendence in sacramental and incarnational categories as "a wholeness that

---

380 McFague (1993:145).

381 Kyung (1994:177).

382 Welch (1990:173).

383 Welch (1990:178).

384 Welch (1990:178-9). Welch acknowledges divine transcendence but defines it in radically immanent terms as the complexity, wonder and beauty, resistance against oppression, and social transformation within the web of life itself.

385 Johnson (1992:104f).

includes all parts, embracing the world rather than excluding it".[386] This allows for a panentheist vision in which the (noetic) mystery of the infinite transcends but also includes the finite. Johnson formulates this vision as one of "mutual coinherence in which Holy Wisdom is present throughout the universe while everything is embraced in her inclusive freedom and compassionate love."[387] She rejects both the tendency towards isolation in classical theism and the pantheist tendency toward absorption and criticizes the "culturally induced tendency for women to submerge themselves in the 'all' of a man or family or institution to the detriment of their own genuine personhood."[388] Instead, she opts for a model of free, reciprocal relations between God and the world in which both remains radically distinct. Johnson uses the spatial image that God is like the boundless sea encompassing a tiny island. She concludes:

> Rather, the universe, both matter and spirit, is encompassed by the matrix of the living God in an encircling which generates uniqueness, futurity, and self-transcendence in the context of the interconnected whole. Holy Wisdom transcendingly embraces all of finite existence in an inclusive relation that sets it free and calls it to communal, personal and cosmic shalom.[389]

This emphasis on God's immanence therefore does not necessarily imply a denial of God's transcendence[390] (which would constitute a form of pantheism[391]). However, the source of hope is often not primarily located in the transcendence of God. To argue that there is indeed hope for the future, this hope must be rooted in the material aspects of creation that exists in a bipolar relationship with God.

One crucial problem with this notion of transcendence in terms of immanence (e.g. as "transparence") is that it cannot account for hope in the face of the radical finitude of the universe. If and when this world itself comes to end (the predicament of finitude) the only source of hope that remains is to be "taken up" in the eternality of God. This emphasizes once again the importance of maintaining some notion of God's transcendence.[392]

Conclusion

An emphasis on God's transcendence remains, in my view, vital for any Christian

---

386 Johnson (1992:231).

387 Johnson (1992:232).

388 Johnson (1992:231).

389 Johnson (1992:232).

390 See Cobb & Griffin (1976:120): It is because God exercises power upon us, persuasive power, that a space is opened up for us within which we are free. If there were no God, there would be no freedom. The future is open and we are free because of God.

391 Peacocke (1993:168) correctly observes that, if the world is identified too closely with God (e.g. as God's body), then evil becomes a part of God's own being.

392 Worthing (1996:198).

eschatology. If hope for deliverance from evil is hope in God and not simply in either the evolutionary potential of the material cosmos or in the power of positive thinking, ideas and imaginary visions, then it remains important to understand how history can be influenced by a God who is more than merely a pantheist synonym for the world. If there is hope beyond the ends of human persons, the human species, life on earth, the planet itself and the universe, then this hope can only lie in being taken "up" into God's eternal presence. But then, again, it remains crucial to explain how God transcends the cosmic dimensions of space and time.

A further question is how this hope in God can be understood in such a way that it provides inspiration in a context of unmitigated despair? How can a vision of hope for the earth inspire an environmental praxis and spirituality in the South African context? These questions need to be addressed in any constructive vision of hope for the earth (see Chapter 16-18).

14. The cosmic dimensions of hope

14.1. Introduction

In Chapter 6 we investigated the evidence for what was described as the "cosmic depths of despair". Can Christian hope offer consolation in the face of such despair? Or is the destiny of the universe finally devoid of any meaning? Will the history of the universe ultimately culminate in a lifeless "heat" death or "cold" death? Do the gloom associated with the laws of thermodynamics and what Haught calls "cosmic pessimism" have the final word on the story of the cosmos?

If the universe itself shows no apparent promise, does this not undermine the plausibility of any all too easy Christian assurance of hope? A lofty, but intrinsically hollow vision of hope will only lead to fatigue. A mere metaphorical wealth of eschatological images will not be sufficient to sustain an environmental praxis in the face of ecological despair. Christian eschatology dare not offer cheap forms of hope. This observation seems to warrant some further investigation of the evidence for hope and despair in the cosmos itself.[1]

In the last decade several participants in the contemporary dialogue between science and religion have responded to the need to reflect on the relationship between cosmology and Christian eschatology.[2] These contributions are, not sur-

---

1 Such an investigation raises important theological questions concerning the place of scientific insights and debates in theological inquiry. Can scientific data provide either a foundation or perhaps supporting evidence for theological truth claims? The question of the relationship between science and theology is the subject of several proposed typologies in recent literature. See the suggestions of "hypothetical consonance" (Peters 1989), "constructive consonance" (Drees 1990). Polkinghorne (1998:86) identifies a spectrum of possibilities ranging from assimilation to consonance. Also compare the four models (conflict, independence, dialogue, integration) identified by Barbour (1997:77f) and adapted by Haught (1995) (conflation / conflict, contrast, contact, confirmation).

This chapter will follow the classic Anselmian approach of *fides quaerens intellectum* in this regard. The task of theology is to articulate, clarify, explain, defend, reformulate and reconstruct a position of faith that one *already* holds. It shows a willingness to "give an account of the hope that is within us" and to do this in conversation with other discourses. This does not imply that the language of Christian faith should be "translated" into the categories of a different discourse. The danger, as identified by Lindbeck (1984) and Comstock (1987), is that such a "translation" of Christian truth claims into the categories of another discourse will turn it into something that it is not. But it does call on us to become sufficiently "bilingual" (Bellah 1989:89) in order to be able to communicate with other discourses (e.g. that of science). For Christian theology, the hope of a dialogue with the sciences is that this may help one clarify one's own theological position.

2 I have been able to collect contributions from Barbour (1997), Caldecott (1988), Drees (1990), Haught (1993b, 1995, 1998), Klink (1994), Lane (1996:174-193), Murphy & Ellis (1996), Peacocke (1979), Peters (1989), Polkinghorne (1994), Russell (1986, 1994, 1997), Truesdale (1994), and Worthing (1996). Theologians such as Körtner (1995),

prisingly, dominated by responses to the predicament of cosmic finitude.

Several theologians have noted the tension between the Christian hope for the coming of a new earth and the "cosmic depths of despair"[3] suggested by the scientific discussions of the long-term future of the earth and the universe itself. Indeed, what hope is there for the earth itself, if any intelligible ground for hope is undermined by scientific prospects[4] and if the alternatives of an interventionist and an other-worldly eschatology[5] are to be avoided?

In the quest for a more hopeful response to the cosmic dimensions of finitude, either evolutionary biology or physical cosmology may be used as a point of departure for further theological reflection.[6] The next two sections (14.2–14.3) will look at the option of evolutionary biology, while section 14.4 will return to the second option, namely astrophysical cosmology.

14.2 Cosmic pessimism and evolutionary biology

John Haught's notion of the "promise of nature" may be used as a point of departure to investigate the relationship between eschatology and evolutionary biology. Haught's work in *The promise of nature* (1993), *Mystery and promise* (1993) and *Science and religion* (1995) provides one important recent response to the predicament of finitude on the basis of Teilhard's notion of an evolutionary cosmology and with the help of process categories. Moreover, his work shows an explicit ecological consciousness. Let us therefore investigate his argument in more detail.

Haught maintains that a sense of "cosmic pessimism" is undermined by recent developments in the sciences. He identifies several features in the picture of the universe emerging from contemporary science that allows for a less pessimistic assessment of the material base of reality. Haught argues that nature itself shows an inherent promise. Christian eschatology "resonates" with this promise of nature. He cites the following evidence in this regard:

a) Openness instead of predictability

From recent developments in the sciences (notably quantum and relativity physics,

---

Küng (1984), Lodahl (1992), McFague (1993), Moltmann (1996), Pannenberg (1998), Peters (1992, 1995), Ruether (1993), Van de Beek (1996) and Ward (1998) have also shown an awareness of modern cosmological parameters in their contributions towards Christian eschatology.

3 See my contribution under this title (Conradie 1998).

4 See Peacocke (1979:329).

5 See Russell (1997:213). Russell describes an "interventionist" eschatology as "an irreversible disruption and termination of the process of nature by a supernatural divinity occurring within an intracosmic scenario" while an "otherworldly eschatology" suggests "a completion of human (and perhaps natural) history in an entirely supernatural realm disjunct from the universe at present." On the notion of an "interventionist" eschatology, see also Worthing (1996:193f).

6 See Barbour (1997:216f), Drees (1990:122f), Russell (1994), Worthing (1996).

DNA research, evolutionary biology, chaos theory) it has become abundantly clear that the material base of nature is much less predictable and quantifiable than earlier scientists have assumed.[7] This is not only the result of human ignorance or limitations but of the inherent structure of nature itself. We have to abandon the belief that science can in principle explain everything. Each new scientific breakthrough leads us still deeper into unfamiliar territory.[8] We still know the story of the universe only in fragments.[9] Indeed, "The greatest of all the accomplishments of twentieth-century science has been the discovery of human ignorance."[10] Haught concludes that this elusiveness calls for an openness and appreciation for the mystery of nature instead of the modern obsession with clear and exhaustive explanation. A sense of mystery is not restricted to the sphere of existential subjectivity but extends to the world of nature as well.[11] To encounter mystery in nature is to realize that the voyage of human discovery is open to the future.[12] I will return to this aspect of the argument in section 14.4 below.

b) The universe as a narrative

A new awareness of the dynamic, ever-changing history of the universe is also emerging from contemporary science.[13] This has been illustrated dramatically in the biological sciences (since the days of Darwin) and in the discovery of an expanding universe in astrophysics in this century. This awareness that nature (and not only humanity) is inherently historical constitutes one of the most significant discoveries of modern science.[14] In fact, as Brian Swimme argues,

> The laws that govern the physical universe today, and that were thought to be immutable are themselves the result of developments over time. We had assumed that the laws were fixed, absolute, eternal. Now we discover that even the laws tell their own story of the universe. That is, the Cosmic Story, rather than being simply governed by fixed underlying laws, draws these laws into its drama.[15]

---

7 Curiously enough, the scientific awareness of our ignorance has grown in parallel with, indeed faster, than the growth in our knowledge (Peacocke 1993:31).

8 Haught (1993b:120).

9 Swimme & Berry (1992:237).

10 Quoted in Templeton (1994:10).

11 Haught (1990:163).

12 Haught (1993b:121).

13 Von Weizsäcker calls the realization that nature is inherently historical the most significant discovery of modern science. See Haught (1996:57).

14 Haught (1996:57). Thomas Berry (1991:54) argues that the recent reconstruction of the story of the cosmos constitutes a new revelatory event (analogous to the incarnation of Jesus Christ) which will challenge our Ptolemaic understanding of the cosmos and the place of humanity in the cosmos. It will awaken in us a new ecological sense of community with all living things. It also illustrates the cosmic scope of revelation. In fact, for Berry (1988:195), the universe itself is the primary revelation.

15 Swimme (1988:50). Haught (1993b:63-4) quotes and develops Swimme's metaphor of

Swimme therefore states that the universe, at its most basic level, is not so much matter or energy but *story*. Nature has the character of a narrative and scientists have become storytellers. Picking up Swimme's argument on the narrative character of the universe, Haught comments that:

> Science has increasingly and almost in spite of itself taken on the lineaments of a story of the cosmos. The cosmos itself increasingly becomes a narrative, a great adventure ... The most expressive metaphor for what science finds in nature is no longer *law*, but *story*.[16]

And further:

> ... as a result of developments in physics and astronomy, we discern the inherently narrative character of all physical reality. Scientists, in spite of much initial resistance to their new task, have now become story-tellers. The cosmos they describe is no longer just a set of laws, but a narrative the quest for whose outcome is perhaps the major intellectual and spiritual inquiry of our time.[17]

The reconstruction of this story into an integrated whole is a relatively recent scientific achievement in which the insights emerging from astrophysical, geological and biological sciences have been weaved together with those of the social sciences and history. This story has also been popularized, for example in *The universe story*, the well-known contribution by Thomas Berry and Brian Swimme. Several authors in ecological theology, including Leonardo Boff, James Conlon, Jay McDaniel, Sean McDonagh, Sallie McFague, Larry Rasmussen, and Rosemary Ruether, have drawn insights from this reconstructed story of the universe, often detecting an ecological "moral" to the story.[18] For present purposes, Haught's brief version of the story may suffice:

> For nearly uncountable millennia our universe labored before it was in a condition of readiness to bring forth life. The heavy chemical elements required for life (carbon, oxygen, nitrogen, phosphorous, and so forth) took several billion years of cooking time at the heart of stars before supernovas eventually dispersed them throughout space. Countless more epoches elapsed before these elements began to cluster into planetary bodies like our earth. The chemicals that make up our terrestrial home, having finished their previous careers in some now dead star, finally coalesced five billion years ago

---

the cosmic story by the notion of a "cosmic adventure".

16 Haught (1990:173, also 1993b:62f), Rolston (1987:119).

17 Haught (1993b:122).

18 The "moral of this story" is eloquently expressed by Sallie McFague (1993:104):

> On the universe's clock, human existence appears a few seconds before midnight. This suggests, surely, that the whole show could scarcely have been put on for our benefit; our natural anthropocentrism is sobered, to put it mildly. Nevertheless, since it took fifteen billion years to evolve creatures as complex as human beings, the question arises as to our peculiar role in this story, especially in relation to our planet.

into our own planet. Then a billion or so later, after the earth's surface had cooled sufficiently to sustain primitive organisms, life began to appear. And following endless more spans of patient waiting and experimentation, it bursts forth into the extravagant arrays of higher organisms such as reptiles, birds and mammals. Finally, perhaps two million years ago, our immediate prehuman ancestors began to appear in abundance and spread out over the face of the earth. That is not very long ago in terms of evolutionary time, and we can safely surmise that much more of the cosmic journey, perhaps the bulk of it, still lies ahead of us.[19]

c) A narrative of increasing complexity

The plot of the cosmic narrative is not one of linear progression. For vast periods of time little happened. There are numerous quiescent interludes, blind alleys and periods of regression. However, the plot does show a tendency towards increasingly complex forms of order. Says Haught: "Without too much difficulty we can make out a kind of story-line along which nature has traveled from trivial to more intricate and eventually sentient, conscious and self-conscious states of being."[20]

The history of humanity is merely a brief episode in this cosmic story. In the vast dimensions of space and time, the human story pales into insignificance. Human beings came into being a mere million or so years ago. We have been created on the late afternoon (after God's siesta?) of the sixth day – after the other animals![21] However, as Teilhard maintained, significance should not be measured by size and duration but by criteria such as complexity and consciousness.[22] The story of the universe has indeed been characterized by increasing complexity, advancing toward more sentient, conscious, and eventually self-conscious forms, culminating temporarily in the emergence of the human species.

Moreover, this "predisposition" of nature towards complexity was prevalent from the very beginning. Billions of years before the arrival of life, physical reality already had a puzzling propensity towards becoming alive and conscious.[23] Recent contributions to astrophysics indicate how hospitable the material universe has always been to our eventual arrival here.[24] From the very beginning, the physical conditions in the universe were extremely delicately configured in such a way as to make the eventual emergence of life and consciousness a possible and even probable development.[25]

---

19 Haught (1990:176-177).

20 Haught (1998a:239).

21 Van de Beek (1987:46).

22 Teilhard (1959:226-228). Barbour (1997:214-5) cites the human brain as a striking example of such complexity. There are a hundred trillion synapses in a human brain. The number of possible ways of connecting them is greater than the number of atoms in the universe!

23 Haught (1995:65).

24 See Haught (1995:51).

25 Haught (1993a:154). The relevance of the ongoing debate on the so called "anthropic

In the relatively recent history of the cosmos, this increasing complexification has become manifested in human culture and religion. The emergence of religion may thus be situated in this more encompassing cosmic narrative. The story of religion (including Christianity) forms part of the story of the universe.[26]

d) A sense of cosmic adventure

Haught suggests that the story of the universe may further be characterized by the notion of a "cosmic adventure", filled with restlessness, suspense and mystery. The restlessness that impelled matter toward complexity, beginning with the big bang, has not yet been stilled.[27] The story's plot is full of dramatic and surprising developments. Anyone who might have witnessed the Primordial Flaring Forth (to use Berry's poetic name for the "Big Bang") or the formation of the earth would never have anticipated the arrival of life or the emergence of self-consciousness billions of years later.[28]

The story of the universe is also a lengthy "saga" with vast epochs of redundancy and mere repetition but, with great patience, also of continual experimentation with novel forms of order. Nature itself is inherently restless refusing to acquiesce in trivial forms of (sacramental) harmony.[29]

It is an ongoing adventure story that is still unfolding before our eyes, still keeping us in suspense about its final outcome. As new scientific discoveries unfold, one cannot suppress the question that readers of any great story would ask: how is the story going to end? For Haught, the direction that the story is taking towards increasing consciousness (Teilhard) and an intensification of beauty (Whitehead) can only be interpreted through the eyes of faith as an enormous promise.[30]

e) The promise of nature

If the history of the cosmos resembles an adventure story more than a set of eternal laws, Haught feels justified in speaking of the "promise of nature" itself. Nature and reality itself has its own inherent teleology; it is "seeded", "pregnant" and

---

principle" (in both its weak and strong versions) is simply noted but not discussed on this point. According to the Strong Anthropic Principle (SAP) the constants established at the big bang were fine-tuned in such a way that the human species would *inevitably* be forthcoming. In a theological context this has led to new interest in the question whether a divine design or purpose could be detected in nature. See the numerous contributions of Barbour, Drees, Ellis, Murphy, Peacocke, Polkinghorne, Russell and others for helpful discussions of these issues.

26 Haught (1990:175-6).

27 Haught (1993a:151).

28 Haught (1993b:124).

29 Haught (1998:8).

30 Haught (1993b:122).

"saturated" with promise.[31] The present stage of the cosmic story is pregnant with potential for blossoming into still more abundant new creation.[32] In this way the cosmos seems to share in the hopes of humanity: "Billions of years before our own appearance in evolution it was already seeded with promise. Our own religious longing for future fulfillment, therefore, is not a violation but a blossoming of this promise."[33] The story of the universe reconstructed by science therefore "... corresponds with the basic religious sense of reality as rooted in a promise that invites from us the response of hope."[34]

Haught argues that Christian eschatology "resonates" with this promise of nature and provides a clue to the ultimate meaning of this cosmic story. The authentic life of Christian hope is one of looking for promises at the heart of all realities and events. It anticipates the fulfillment of God's promises, based on the experience and trust in God as a promise keeper (e.g. the fulfillment of God's promises in Jesus Christ).[35] Haught explains:

> To have "faith", at least in the biblical sense of the term, is to become skilled in the habit of looking for promises at the heart of all realities and events, even when they are apparently dead ends. This attitude, passed on through creed, worship and the example of others, and brought to expression in the best of our theologies, goes back to the trust attributed to Abraham and his followers, to Moses and the prophets, to Jesus and to his friends who, in spite of his execution by crucifixion, were brought to new hope at the very moment when all was lost.[36]

Christian faith and hope, Haught argues, need to scan not only human history but the whole cosmic horizon for signs of the fulfillment of God's promises.[37] Through the eyes of Christian faith, nature's own adventure towards heightened consciousness and beauty can only be interpreted as an enormous promise.[38] It nourishes a trust that reality is ultimately pregnant with promise, that the past is not

---

31 Haught (1993b:102).

32 Haught (1998:9).

33 Haught (1993b:109). Also Russell (1989:201-205).

34 Haught (1995:176).

35 Haught (1993b:102).

36 Haught (1993b:118).

37 It is certainly not customary to extend signs of the fulfillment of God's promises to the world of nature. All too often the scope of God's ongoing creative love is confined to the sphere of human history only. Human culture and religion forms an integral part of the story of the cosmos. As Thomas Berry (1988, 1991) has often repeated, human activity is not only something done by our species on earth, but also something the earth does through us. In his typically evocative language, Berry (1988:198) says: "The human (is) that being in whom this grand diversity of the universe celebrates itself in conscious self-awareness." Every historical event is also an occurrence within nature, not outside it. The same applies to the history of the Christian tradition that has to be rooted within the larger story of the earth and the cosmos.

38 Haught (1993b:122).

necessarily determinative of the future, that the present is always open to unexpected and surprising forms of fulfillment and that the future may be expected to be new and fulfilling.[39] By dwelling within the stories of the Christian faith, we are enabled by grace to discern a pattern of promise in the evolving universe – a pattern that science by itself may not be able to detect.[40] It is only in retrospect that we may conclude that the same Word of promise "... that planted hope in the hearts of our ancestors in faith had earlier aroused the cosmos into being and continually stirred it toward further evolution."[41]

f) An ecological ethos

What is the moral of this story of the universe? For Haught, an environmental ethos may be based on a Christian sensitivity for the promise of nature itself. Nature deserves the kind of care appropriate to the treasuring of a promise.[42] To destroy nature is to turn away from a promise.[43] Haught explains:

> By killing off the ecological richness of nature, which it has taken so many millions of years to attain, we prohibit fresh creation, and in doing so we violate the mysterious future which faith knows by the name God ... We save nature because of the incalculable promise it holds.[44]

If nature itself is promise, this also implies that nature should neither be neglected nor worshiped. It does not provide us with a direct inscription or revelation of God's will. It only contains a promise of future fulfillment. The drama and beauty of nature are occasions for present enjoyment. But through them we gain a glimpse of a future beauty that is still to manifest itself.[45] To demand complete fulfillment of nature's promise now, is a mark of an impatience that is hostile to hope.[46]

This view of nature as promise also enables Haught to acknowledge the ambiguity of nature, the "shadow side", the pain, suffering and catastrophes, the *finitude* that are part of nature. Nature has not yet arrived at the final peace of God's kingdom. It is therefore, contrary to the impression fostered by an ecological theology based on a sacramental vision, not necessarily sacred. Understanding the cosmos as a promise invites us to cherish it without denying its ambiguity.[47]

---

39 Haught (1995:176).

40 Haught (1993a:155).

41 Haught (1993a:156).

42 Haught (1993b:104).

43 Haught (1993b:110). For his own constructive views on Christian eschatology, see the discussion in Chapter 5 of *The promise of nature* (1993b:113-142).

44 Haught (1993b:124).

45 Haught (1993b:114).

46 Haught (1993b:110).

47 Haught (1993b:111).

Nature is indeed not paradise but only the promise thereof.[48] The story of the universe clearly indicates that there never was, literally or historically speaking, a primordial cosmic state of perfection. According to the priestly authors of Genesis 1, creation was said to be good, not perfect. In a post-evolutionary world, a Christian environmental ethos need not be dominated by a nostalgia for what has been lost, but can be structured primarily by an anticipation of what might still be.[49] Instead of longing in vain to restore what has been lost, it may become a creative force in the birth of something truly new. Perfection lies in the eschatological future and not in the temporal past or the eternal present.[50] The present experience of beauty is thus not a disheartening reminder of what could have been, but a joyful harbinger of new and unprecedented epochs of creation.[51] The whole cosmic process is a purposeful struggle to realize an unprecedented promise of new being.

14.3 Other scientific evidence for the "promise of nature"

a) Introduction: the positivist roots of cosmic pessimism

Haught's thesis on the "promise of nature" may serve here as a hypothesis for further investigation. What scientific evidence can be gathered to support the thesis that the story of the cosmos itself is "seeded with promise"? Can such evidence endure sufficient critical testing to counter a sense of cosmic pessimism? And how should such scientific evidence be integrated theologically within Christian eschatology, if at all? Let us consider these questions in more detail.

Haught describes cosmic pessimism as "the conviction that the world has no transcendent origin and no divinely shaped destiny."[52] The universe as a whole has no inherent purpose; it is heading for eventual doom. The universe is "composed of mindless chunks of matter with no intelligible explanation, originating by chance, moving in no particular direction, and fulfilling no inherent purpose."[53] Cosmic pessimism denounces imaginative religious projections of a hopeful future as illusory. It is content to rely on a common sense derived from empirical reason and logic to live this life in all its brevity without any dreams of future fulfillment. This view is expressed pertinently in the comment by Stephen Weinberg that the more the universe seems comprehensible, the more it also seems pointless.[54]

---

48 Haught (1993b:111).

49 Haught (1997:9).

50 Haught (1997:9).

51 Haught (1997:9).

52 Haught (1993b:14-17). "It sees no promise in cosmic events, but instead reads natural history as a vacuous process leading only to eventual doom." (1993a:152).

53 Haught (1995:152).

54 See Haught (1995:168). The reference is to Weinberg's book *The first three minutes* (1977:144). Barbour (1997:218) notes that Weinberg later corrected himself: "I did not mean that science teaches us that the universe is pointless, but only that the universe

Haught argues that cosmic pessimism is the logical consequence of the (positivist) assumptions of scientism, materialism, determinism, and reductionism. Let us therefore investigate these assumptions briefly.

According to materialist assumptions, everything in the universe, including the emergence of life and of human consciousness, can be explained in terms of material processes. All phenomena can, in principle, be causally explained in terms of the behavior of their material components. Restrictions in our current understanding are merely the result of the complexity and computability of some problems.[55] This also applies to classic thermodynamics where the behavior of gases had, for the sake of convenience, to be described statistically in terms of probability because the motions of gas particles proved too complicated to calculate. If the position and velocity of every particle in the universe could be determined, the future can, in principle, be predicted for the rest of time – as Pierre Simon Laplace once boasted.[56]

Reductionism claims that the laws and theories of all the sciences are in principle reducible to the laws of physics and chemistry. Human culture can ultimately be reduced to biology and biology itself can be reduced to chemistry and physics.[57] Likewise, it is possible to account for (human) consciousness by using the same physical laws and raw materials that suffice to explain radioactivity, photosynthesis, reproduction, nutrition and growth.[58]

The growth of scientific knowledge in this century illustrated that nature is infinitely more complex than what Laplace imagined. Each new scientific breakthrough leads us still deeper into unfamiliar territory yet to be explored. Despite the vast extension of human knowledge through computer technology, we now have to acknowledge its inherent limitations. Nevertheless, the aim of predictability remains the basis of current scientific investigations. The aim of the sciences is still to analyze, stipulate and measure various forces influencing a particular system, to formulate the laws of nature pertaining to such a system, to detect cause and effect in specified natural processes and on that basis to predict, calculate and control such natural processes.

Scientific materialism and determinism have indeed shown a remarkable tenacity in scientific practice itself. This is the result of the undeniable and overwhelming success of the reductionistic research program.[59] The spectacular technological

---

itself suggests no point."

55 Barbour (1997:78), also Peacocke (1993:39f).

56 Russell, Murphy & Peacocke (1995:36).

57 Haught (1995:33f, 77f). Haught refers to a comment by Francis Crick that "the ultimate aim of the modern movement in biology is to explain all of life in terms of chemistry and biology."

58 This view is expressed by the philosopher Daniel Dennett. Quoted in Barbour (1997:81).

59 See the more sober assessment of Polkinghorne (1995:150): "It is clearly worthwhile to pursue the program of reductionistic explanation as far as it can legitimately be pursued, but that is a methodological strategy for investigation, not a metaphysical strategy determining the total nature of reality."

applications of scientific predictions bear witness to the feasibility of causal explanation and the amazing applicability of sophisticated mathematical models to describe and predict natural processes.[60] Indeed, as expressed in Einstein's famous comment, "The eternal mystery of the world is its comprehensibility."

Spurred on by the success of science and technology, scientific materialism and determinism assume that the task of causal explanation and prediction remains *in principle* possible. Only the limitations of human knowledge prevent us *in practice* from (ever) being able to fully explain highly complex processes in nature.

These assumptions, of course, leave little room for human freedom, for divine action in the world[61] or for anything qualitatively new occurring in the history of the cosmos. Every moment in history, including the final destiny of the universe, is determined by material processes following the laws of nature. This clearly paves the way for a sense of cosmic pessimism. This is exemplified by the apparent implications of the second law of thermodynamics. The second law indicates that all creative processes in the universe will eventually dissolve into a state of entropy (the measure of disorder in a system). There seems to be an inevitable and inescapable linear process from creative order to lifeless disorder.

Positivism has been widely discredited in twentieth century philosophy of science. The contributions of Ian Barbour, Paul Feyerabend, Norman Hanson, Thomas Kuhn, Imre Lakatos, Michael Polanyi, Stephen Toulmin, and numerous others have shown that scientific data are influenced by theoretical assumptions, "fiduciary frameworks", scientific paradigms, linguistic and cultural presuppositions, interpretive models, metaphors and even myths. All data are indeed theory-laden (Hanson). This assessment is echoed by the historical, hermeneutical, linguistic, and postmodern "turns" in twentieth century philosophy and social theory. We have also become much more sensitive to the influence of gender, culture, race and class on our basic presuppositions, including scientific assumptions.

Several participants in recent science and religion dialogues maintain that scientific materialism and determinism have also been undermined by recent developments in science itself.[62] Barbour, for example, identifies three assumptions of Newtonian physics (i.e. realism, determinism and reductionism), that have been called into question by developments in quantum theory, relativity theory, theories of chaos and complexity, evolutionary biology and DNA research.[63] For Haught, this assessment has important implications for a sense of cosmic pessimism. He refers specifically to current scientific investigations on chaos and complexity to

---

60 This fruitfulness of science is the stimulus behind the notion of "critical realism" that remains popular amongst scientists (most scientists are "incurably realist") and amongst the classic exponents of science and religion dialogue. See Barbour (1997:117f), Peacocke (1993:11f), Polkinghorne (1998:101-124).

61 See the detailed discussions on the possibility of divine action in the world by Barbour (1997:295f), Clayton (1997), Murphy & Ellis (1996:213f), Peacocke (1993), Polkinghorne (1998:48-75), Russell, Murphy & Peacocke (1995), Russell (1997).

62 Barbour (1997), Polkinghorne (1998:50f).

63 Barbour (1997:106f, 165f).

illustrate this.[64] Let us investigate the argument in more detail.

b) Chaos and complexity

Theories of chaos and complexity build largely on the pioneering work of Ilya Prigogine and his associates on non-equilibrium thermodynamics.[65]

Prigogine illustrated that, when a system is far from equilibrium, a new complex form of order sometimes emerges and achieves a stable form. In such cases small fluctuations in the behavior of particles in the system is amplified (thus "order through fluctuation"). This leads to a new and more complex form of order that resists further fluctuations and maintains itself with a throughput of energy from the environment. These ordered configurations are called dissipative structures because they are created and maintained precisely through the entropy-producing dissipation of energy in open systems. "Order out of chaos" is therefore indeed possible. They can emerge when a system is a) open to the flux of energy, b) not at equilibrium (preferably far from equilibrium), and c) non-linear in that there is a strong interaction between the processes in the system.[66]

Prigogine's work indicated that the structures of these complex forms of order are governed by a new and different set of laws. In some cases the new order can be predicted by considering the average statistical behavior of the myriad of components. But in other cases there are many possible outcomes and no predictions can be made. Multiple divergent solutions can be offered to describe the behavior of these non-linear systems.

Chaotic systems, like the thermodynamic systems studied by Prigogine, initially seem to be governed by simple, non-linear, deterministic equations. Thus their future states can in principle be predicted if an exact set of initial conditions and the forces influencing them are given. However, in many cases the behavior of chaotic systems appears to be random. Chaos theory seeks to account for this behavior – either by focusing on the initial conditions or on the influence of what is called "strange attractors."

Firstly, research indicates that infinitesimally small uncertainties concerning initial conditions may lead to enormous uncertainties in predicting subsequent behavior. Weather patterns provide a classic example. Mathematical models used to illustrate such chaotic systems show that outcomes may diverge exponentially due to small fluctuations in the initial conditions. This is sometimes referred to as

---

64 It should be noted that Haught could perhaps have strengthened his arguments on the basis of the indeterminacies indicated by quantum theory. Certain weaknesses in his argument based on chaos theory (see the discussion below) may have been avoided in this way.

65 Since research on chaos and complexity does not form part of my scholarly competence, I rely in the discussion below heavily and gratefully on the discussion of Barbour (1997:180f). See also the reflections on chaos and complexity from the point of view of the dialogue between religion and the sciences by Haught (1995:142-161), Peacocke (1993), Russell, Murphy & Peacocke (1995).

66 See Peacocke (1995:137).

the "butterfly effect" (Edward Lorenz), since a butterfly flapping its wings in Brazil may, in terms of mathematical calculations, influence the weather a month later in China. Likewise, the movement of an electron in a distant galaxy may be amplified over a long period of time to influence events on earth.

Secondly, research by Edward Lorenz on meteorological orbits indicates that the random behavior of chaotic systems is not only influenced by initial conditions but also by what is called strange or chaotic attractors. Well-known predictable attractors such as friction and viscosity attract a system (e.g. a pendulum) to settle down in state of equilibrium. The attractors studied by Lorenz relate to the complex shape of orbits. These orbits seem to be "folded", revealing (as fractals) more detail each time when they are magnified. This is caused by the "mixing" of orbits in chaotic systems. The effect of these uneven orbits is that small-scale uncertainties are amplified and widely separated trajectories are brought together. In this way any exact measurement and prediction soon become impossible.[67]

The implication of this research is that the traditional scientific method of verifying a theory by making predictions and testing them against experimental data is no longer viable. Barbour comments that, "Deterministic laws are strictly applicable only to closed systems; they are an approximation to reality because actual systems that are extremely sensitive to initial conditions can never be isolated from outside influences."[68] Thus it challenges the reductionist view that a system can be understood by analyzing it and studying the behavior of individual components.

Other studies have focused on the phenomenon of self-organization in complex systems. In the research of Stuart Kaufman, common patterns are identified in the behavior of a variety of systems, such as molecules, cells, neural networks, ecosystems, and economic systems. Most physical systems will return to the most probable, disordered state of equilibrium if disturbed from it.[69] However, Kaufman's research indicates that intricate and complex patterns (i.e. complexity) may emerge unexpectedly and "spontaneously" out of a state of thermodynamic turbulence (i.e. a system at a state far from equilibrium, on the border of chaos). This emergent form of order cannot be explained in terms of the influence of the constituent parts of the system but seems to be an effect of the system itself and is therefore referred to as "self-organization".[70]

c) Some implications of chaos and complexity theory

Two features of this research on chaos and complexity are important for Haught's argument on the promise of nature, namely a) the unpredictability and *apparent* indeterminacy of chaotic systems, and b) the possibility of downward causation.

---

67 I am indebted to the very helpful discussion by Crutchfield et al (1995) on strange attractors.

68 Barbour (1997:183).

69 See Barbour (1997:183-4).

70 Templeton & Herrmann (1989:121): "There is a whole world of forms still to be explored and harmonies still to be discovered."

a) The unpredictability of the emerging forms of order in a chaotic system is of special importance. This unpredictability may be the result of the slightest disturbances, deviations and uncertainties in the initial conditions of a system.

This feature of complex systems may still be interpreted as being the result of imprecise initial calculations (and therefore due to human limitations).[71] Indeed, the initial conditions of many natural processes cannot be specified with the degree of exactness that could make predictions sufficiently accurate. Even if they could, the information necessary to specify the initial conditions is so vast that calculations to predict behavior in complex systems over a long period of time would require more information than could be stored on all the electrons of our galaxy! However, chaos theorists maintain that chaotic systems are *in principle* not predictable. Moreover, chaotic systems would amplify the quantum indeterminacies that set limits to the accurate specification of initial conditions both in theory and in practice.[72]

Haught argues that this inherent unpredictability has important implications for the self-understanding of science.[73] According to chaos theory, natural processes simply cannot always be calculated in linear terms. This is only possible when relatively simple processes are investigated. By contrast, developments in complex systems (e.g. weather patterns) are much too complex to map and predict processes beyond their first few stages. Mathematical precision in scientific calculations can only be obtained through abstraction, namely in closed systems under specific conditions and by discounting the features of complexity. The world of nature is much more intricate and subtle than what such mathematical abstractions can account for. Causally determined processes with complete predictability occur rather seldom in nature.[74] While this unpredictability of chaotic systems is often viewed by the scientific community in terms of the limitations it implies, nature may employ chaos constructively:

> Through amplification of small fluctuations it can provide natural systems with access to novelty. A prey escaping a predator's attack could use chaotic flight control as an element of surprise to evade capture. Biological evolution demands genetic variability; chaos provides a means of structuring random changes, thereby providing the possibility of putting variability under evolutionary control.[75]

b) Complex systems are not only unpredictable as a result of the fluctuations in their initial conditions. The research on complexity describes the emergence of higher levels of systemic order from lower-level disorder. It indicates that in many natural systems, especially living organisms including cells, minds and civilizations, some form of order may "emerge" unpredictably and stabilize for varying

---

71 Stephen Kellert as quoted in Barbour 1997:183).

72 Barbour (1997:183).

73 Haught (1995:143f).

74 Haught (1995:143).

75 Crutchfield et al (1995:47).

periods of time at states far from equilibrium (living systems are typical examples).[76] It is also this feature that makes full predictability impossible. Haught argues that the order previously detected by science may be "a thin mathematical facade masking an inexhaustibly rich tapestry."[77] By contrast, the kind of order investigated in theories of chaos and complexity is that of intricate, spontaneously emerging, self-organizing and self-adaptive patterns.[78] Since classical science was overly analytical and atomistic, it failed to discern clearly the remarkable fact that the universe unfolds in the shape of self-organizing systems striving to adapt themselves to the universe.[79]

This feature of "emergence" or self-organization in complex systems furthermore indicates the possibility of "top-down" causation and not merely "bottom-up" causation.[80] There are, in other words, physical laws pertaining to systems that cannot be derived from the laws of the components. In classical physics, the behavior of the larger whole is deduced from predictive causal laws governing the interactions of its constituent parts.[81] However, theories of complexity maintain that there are new variables emerging at the level of a system that cannot be accounted for by the behavior of components of the system.[82] It claims that, once a material system reaches a certain level of complexity, manifested in a high degree of relatedness of its components, then genuinely novel properties and processes may emerge, which cannot be explained by the material properties of the components themselves. Nature is composed of intricate adaptive systems that cannot be adequately understood simply by dissecting them into their constituent law-bound particulars.[83] This implies the possibility of "downward causation" expressed in the theses that a) The whole is more than the sum of the parts (emergence), and b) The whole determines the behavior of its parts (downward causation).[84] James

---

76 Haught (1995:148).

77 Haught (1995:144).

78 See the helpful distinction by Cilliers (1998) between complex and complicated systems. In complicated systems (e.g. a game of chess, computers) a complete description of the system can be given in terms of individual constituents. In complex systems (the human brain, language, social systems), by contrast, the system as a whole cannot be fully understood simply by analyzing its components. Cilliers also argues that chaos theory is less helpful to understand complexity because it tends to describe deterministic, if highly complicated systems (e.g. fractals).

79 Haught (1995:146).

80 Murphy & Ellis (1996:16) states that: "It is now becoming widely recognized that in addition to reductionistic or 'bottom-up' accounts of causation, it is also necessary to countenance 'top-down' causation."

81 Barbour (1997:182).

82 See Murphy & Ellis (1996:16, 24f) for a detailed defense of top-down causation. Also Barbour (1997:175).

83 Haught (1998a:238).

84 Küppers (1995:94).

Gliek explains this holistic and anti-reductionist[85] aspect of chaos theory neatly:

> Chaos is anti-reductionist. This new science makes a strong claim about the world: namely, that when it comes to the most interesting questions, questions about order and disorder, decay and creativity, pattern formation and life itself, the whole cannot be explained in terms of the parts. There are fundamental laws about complex systems, but they are new kinds of law. They are laws of structure and organization and scale, and they simply vanish when you focus on the individual constituents of a complex system - just as the psychology of a lynch mob vanishes when you interview individual participants.[86]

The emergence of novel forms of complexity from the edge of chaos implies that the laws of thermodynamics are less linear than what was earlier assumed. Within the broader parameters of an overall increase of entropy in a system (which remain valid!), it is now necessary to allow for the emergence of new ordered patterns. Matter itself has the potential for self-organization. Novelty and order is not the product of somewhat esoteric (even divine) interventions or of conjectural forces but can be described on the basis of known material forces.[87] Crutchfield and his colleagues explain: "a system can have complicated behavior that emerges as a consequence of simple, nonlinear interaction of only a few components ... Through amplification of small fluctuations it (nature) can provide natural systems access to novelty."[88]

For Haught, this has important implications for the cosmic pessimism often associated with the second law of thermodynamics. He states:

> For a century or more the second law of thermodynamics has dominated both physics and intellectual culture - leading usually to cosmic pessimism. The universe seemed to be heading down the slope of entropy toward an abyss. But there is nothing in the notion of entropy that helps us to understand why the cosmos, from its very beginning, has also moved toward increasingly various and more complex forms of order ... Neither physics nor the evolutionary principle of natural selection can tell us exactly why the cosmos is put together in such a way that it keeps "breaking symmetry" and reaching toward richer modes of ordered novelty.[89]

Haught argues further that entropy is not necessarily the dead end of disorder but a

---

85 Barbour (1997) uses examples from quantum theory for a similar critique of reductionism. He refers to the Pauli Exclusion Principle describing the way in which the attributes and behavior of electrons are influenced by their situatedness in the larger whole of an atom. Barbour comments: "In quantum reasoning any attempt to describe the behavior of the constituent electrons is simply abandoned; the properties of the atom as a whole are analyzed by new laws unrelated to those governing its separate 'parts', which have now lost their identity."

86 Quoted in Barbour (1997:183).

87 Peacocke (1993:53).

88 Quoted in Peacocke (1993:53).

89 Haught (1995:148).

breeding ground for new creativity. Rigid orderliness has to give way as nature veers entropically toward the edge of chaos. Too much order makes change impossible; too much chaos makes continuity impossible.[90] Atomic, molecular and organic structures first have to "loosen up" if they are to make way for more intricate configurations.[91] Without a degree of entropy there would be no room for emergent complexity, since the cosmos would have permanently solidified into triviality.[92] Entropy "guarantees that the cosmic story will avoid repeating forever the same old refrains, and permits it to wend its way toward an always open and often surprising experimentation with novelty."[93] Entropy is, Haught wagers, not necessarily signaling the heat death of the universe but must now be understood as an essential condition for matter to realize new possibilities.

For Haught, this counts as evidence for the promise of nature – at least from the perspective of a faith that educates people to look for signs of new life in all things. Indeed, the interplay between chaos and ordered complexity illustrates both the reliability and the openness to surprise inherent in nature. This resonates with the Christian understanding of God:

Nature's reliability points us toward the theme of God's fidelity; and its openness to novelty seems to augur the surprise we anticipate from our trust in a God of promise.[94]

Haught concludes that nature is perpetually open to indeterminate outcomes. Nature is and has always been pregnant with promise. Cosmic pessimism is thwarted because it is based on scientistic, materialistic and reductionistic assumptions following the non-narrative, abstract over-simplifications of a purely linear science.[95] This "made the cosmos appear absolutely determined by the dead necessity of the past, utterly closed off to unpredictable modes of new patterning."[96] Haught adds that "... the intellectual appeal of cosmic pessimism is supported not so much by nature itself as by abstract mathematical representations that inevitably

---

90 Barbour (1997:184). For a similar emphasis, see Van Ruler's article on "God and chaos" (1972:32-45). Van Ruler argues that order is not necessarily preferable to chaos. God created the chaos in the beginning and still disturbs rigid forms of order through creating some chaos. God created the chaos to play with it, like with the Leviathan, and to harness its energies (Ps 104).

91 See Haught (1995:154f). Haught also detects significance in this process for a doctrine of God's providence: Chaos is the consequence of a divine discontent with the status quo. The God "who makes all things new" is hovering very close to chaos. Chaos and complexity are marks of an unfinished world in which God is continuously creating anew. Haught concludes: "Theologically speaking, then, chaos and complexity follow from a divine longing that the world becomes ever richer, more diverse, and more beautiful" (1995:155).

92 Haught (1995:178).

93 Haught (1995:178).

94 Haught (1995:158).

95 Haught (1995:170, 177).

96 Haught (1995:177).

overlook the elusive complexity and indeterminacy that open the cosmos to a genuinely novel future."[97] Therefore, "All the morose modern ruminations about the remorselessness of the second law of thermodynamics and final cosmic doom were plausible only so long as science had fixated on emaciated mathematical abstractions that ignored the contingent openness of nature's *de facto* historicity."[98]

d) A word of caution

From the point of view of Christian hope such conclusions are certainly attractive and evocative. However, a word of caution is called for on both these features of unpredictability and emerging order on which Haught bases his argument.

i) The unpredictability of chaotic systems would probably be acknowledged by most scientists – *in practice* (due to the limitations of human knowledge and power / computer technology) and maybe also *in theory* (due to quantum indeterminacies or on the basis of mathematical models). This acknowledgement of unpredictability does not, however, necessarily invalidate the scientific materialism and determinism rejected by Haught. The behavior of chaotic systems may still be determined by material processes – even though the result may not be predictable. In other words: Though the future is determined by the past, small uncertainties are amplified exponentially by chaotic systems so that, in practice, their behavior rapidly becomes unpredictable. From this point of view, limited predictability is simply a function of the exponential amplification of small perturbations (as Henri Poincaré already suggested in 1903).[99]

Furthermore, as Wesley Wildman and Robert John Russell argue in an essay in an important volume on *Chaos and complexity*, chaotic systems are indeed predictable in principle in terms of their governing equations. They *become* eventually unpredictable in practice, yet are even then temporarily predictable since one can predict the amount of time which will elapse before mathematical calculations will cease to match the state of the system. Chaotic systems thus embody elements of determinism, predictability *and* unpredictability.[100]

Wildman & Russell add that many of the central themes in chaos theory can also be regarded as supporting evidence for metaphysical determinism – although there are new limits on how well determinacy can be established.[101] Chaos in nature gives no evidence of any metaphysical openness in nature. The fact that a natural dynamical system is open to its environment does not entail metaphysical openness, for the entire environment may still be causally determined. Also, the "butterfly effect" testifies to the high degree of causal connectedness in certain

---

97 Haught (1998:7).

98 Haught (1995:177).

99 Russell (1995:14).

100 Russell (1995:14-16).

101 Russell (1995:17).

natural systems, and so is most naturally exploited in support of the thesis of metaphysical determinism.[102] They conclude that the hypothesis of metaphysical determinism is actually strengthened by chaos theory because it enables the apparent randomness of even simple natural dynamical systems potentially to be brought under the umbrella of determinism. They add a strong warning against a misplaced enthusiasm for the theological implications that chaos theory may have:

> While chaos theory offers not a shred of evidence against metaphysical determinism, it does introduce an imposing limit on how well the deterministic hypothesis can be supported. It must be said, therefore, that the hypothesis of metaphysical determinism has never been as well attested as it is after chaos theory, and that it cannot be made stronger than chaos theory makes it. ... There can be no doubt that chaos theory adds its considerable weight to the side of determinism. ... Laplace would have been delighted with chaos theory.[103]

In his contribution to the volume on *Chaos and complexity*, Thomas Tracy also argues that unpredictability does not necessarily imply indeterminism.[104] In the same volume Willem Drees agrees with Russell and Wildman that a naturalistic explanation may be available even in the absence of predictability. He argues that predictability is not a necessary condition for explainability.[105]

It should be noted that an argument against metaphysical determinism may also use quantum indeterminacies (instead of chaos theory) as a point of departure. This may well prove to be a more fruitful approach.

ii) A second word of caution concerning the emergence of novel forms of order in self-organizing systems and therefore of downward causation is also appropriate. John Polkinghorne admits that: "There may be much more potentiality for complex structure built into the very fabric of the universe than we have yet fully realized."[106] But he cautions that chaos theory and complexity theory are still in their infancy and that their metaphysical message is ambiguous. Barbour agrees that much of the work on complexity remains exploratory and speculative.[107]

In another contribution to the volume on *Chaos and Complexity*, Küppers acknowledge the appeal of the notions of emergence and downward causation but cautions that these concepts remain rather vague and mysterious for scientists working on the borderline of physics and biology.[108] Drees adds that although the possibility of downward causality may be accepted, it is not unproblematic and its plausibility depends upon exhibiting intrinsic gaps in the bottom-up description in

---

[102] Wildman & Russell (1995:82).

[103] Wildman & Russell (1995:83).

[104] Tracy (1995:313).

[105] Drees (1995:223f).

[106] Polkinghorne (1998:96).

[107] Barbour (1997:184).

[108] Küppers (1995:94).

order to afford it room to maneuver.[109]

It should be noted that scientific materialism is not necessarily denied by the notion of self-organization. One may argue that self-organization is a property of matter itself. Matter is simply more complex and subtle than what crude mechanical models previously assumed. It is in the material world that chaos spontaneously gives rise to order. Nature blindly selects those systems that are most adaptive.[110]

What theories on complexity have indeed questioned, is scientific reductionism, not so much materialism or determinism. It has indicated at least the possibility of downward causation. Sociology therefore cannot be simply reduced to biology. Likewise, biology cannot be reduced to chemistry, or chemistry to physics. However, physics, chemistry and biology *do* describe the material constraints to what is possible on a "higher" level of organization. This also implies, for example, that the scenarios for the long-term future developed in astrophysics apply despite any (necessarily temporary) form of higher organization.[111] Any "self-organization" that an individual may muster (e.g. achievements in culture, sport, politics, economics and education) cannot undo the inevitability of human finitude and death.

On the basis of these comments some caution is therefore appropriate. Russell reminds us that the possibility should not be excluded that the theories of chaos and complexity may be replaced by a better model and that theological implications should not be drawn too hastily from scientific work in progress.[112] And, as Arthur Peacocke warns: "All kinds of metaphysics and theology have grown like weeds in the garden of thermodynamics."[113]

Haught himself acknowledges that a different reading of the available scientific evidence may indeed be possible.[114] The data may still be interpreted in terms of the assumptions of metaphysical determinism instead of openness. However, he maintains that the available evidence is not conclusive in any direction. There is no reason to assume a priori that a posture of pessimism, cynicism or neutrality provides a better reading of the data.[115] In the picture of the universe emerging from contemporary science there it at least room (once again) for surprise, promise and hope: "There is at least the possibility that the nature of things, in the final analysis, runs more closely along the lines of hope than of tragedy."[116] Haught even specu-

---

109 Drees (1995).

110 See Haught's (1995:149) own exposition of the "conflict" position on complexity in nature.

111 I am grateful to a conversation with Professor Robert John Russell for a clarification of this important reminder.

112 Russell (1995:17).

113 Peacocke (1995:128).

114 Haught (1993b:119).

115 Haught (1993b:119).

116 Haught (1995:179).

lates that entropy may not have the final word:[117] "For lurking beneath what physics takes to be a cosmic trend toward maximum thermodynamic disorder, there may be nothing less momentous than the surprise of a final patterning whose beauty we are not yet able to fathom, but for which we have every reason to hope."[118]

The inconclusiveness of the evidence has another important implication. Haught insists that both science and religion should resist an inclination toward omniscience. We are simply not able to articulate the ultimate outcome of the universe with any clarity. There is a need to acknowledge that the outcome of the story of the universe cannot be grasped from within. This calls for some humility and perhaps silence in this regard – as is recognized in the apophatic traditions of Christianity.[119]

14.4 Cosmology and the cosmic dimensions of finitude

The impact of cosmic pessimism on Christian eschatology may also be discussed from the point of view of astrophysical cosmology. Russell suggests that the mood of theology and science discussions on eschatology often switches from optimism (e.g. Teilhard) to pessimism (e.g. Weinberg) whenever the focus shifts from biology to cosmology.[120] Indeed, the emergence of evolutionary novelties is only possible within the physical constraints described by the laws of physics. Although physical explanations are not exhaustive (leaving room for higher levels of order to emerge) they do put some restraints on what is physically possible. The astrophysical scenarios for the long-term future of the universe (see Chapter 6) therefore cannot be nullified at the level of evolutionary biology.

Discussions on the relationship between Christian eschatology and astrophysical cosmology have been dominated by the contributions of Freeman Dyson and Frank Tipler, both eminent physicists. Dyson's work is based on the scenario of an open universe while Tipler's is based on the alternative scenario of a closed universe. Both present their work as a form of "physical eschatology" in which the feasibility of a continuation of human consciousness (understood in a minimalist sense) in the distant future of the universe is considered. Both are optimistic that some form of "human" consciousness may indeed survive a cosmic catastrophe.

---

[117] See also Teilhard (1959:271-2).

[118] Haught (1995:159). Moltmann (1995:209) sees a similar possibility: "As we now know, chaotic, complex and evolutionary systems of matter and life are built up in such a way so as to display a growing openness to time and to an abundance of possibilities. These possibilities increase as their complexity increases, thus expanding the scope of their open, indeterministic behavior. ... the future of the world can only be imagined as the openness of all finite life systems to the abundance of eternal life. In this way they can participate in the inexhaustible sources of life and in the divine creative ground of being."

[119] Haught (1995:181).

[120] Russell (1997:196).

- In an essay on "Time without end: Physics and biology in an open universe" (1979), Dyson argues that biological life may be able to adapt to an expanding universe. It has usually been assumed that this would lead to a "cold death" for all life as temperatures approach absolute zero amidst the decay of galaxies, stars, planets and fundamental particles. Dyson disagrees. He defines "life" in a minimalist way as the organization of matter instead of sentient and animate forms of living. Life resides in organization rather than in substance. Non-biologically based forms of information storage may continue into the infinite future. He bases his arguments on the possibilities of genetic engineering to redesign organisms for extreme conditions. New forms of consciousness may be able to survive at very low temperatures if the human brain's information can be transferred to other mediums. The energy requirements of such systems will be relatively low since this is proportional to the temperature of its environment. Dyson concludes that life and intelligence are potentially immortal:[121] "I have found a universe growing without limit in richness and complexity, a universe of life surviving forever and making itself known to its neighbours across unimaginable gulfs of space and time."[122]
- In his work, *The physics of immortality*, Tipler investigates the same problem, but on the basis of the cosmological model of a closed universe (both finite in size and with a finite future). Tipler also bases his argument on the information processing capacity of the human brain (from the viewpoint of physics). He argues that information and communication networks may spread throughout the universe through the colonization of space. The information processing rate and memory storage could be increased virtually without limit. Such information systems may be programmed to replicate themselves, culminating in what Tipler calls the Omega Point where all knowledge will be drawn into a singe mathematical point in which the universe (along with all that is, was and will be in it) becomes god.[123] Everything will be simultaneously present in the Omega Point. Life will encompass the universe and will thus be omnipresent. It

---

[121] Tipler explains the possibility of immortality in the following way:

> All timelike and lightlike curves converge upon the Omega Point. In particular, all the light rays from those people who died a thousand years ago, from the people now living, and from all the people who will be living a thousand years from now, will intersect here. The light rays from those people who died a thousand years ago are not lost forever; rather, these rays will be intercepted by the Omega Point ... All the information which can be extracted from these rays will be extracted at the instant of the Omega Point, who will therefore experience the whole of time simultaneously, just as we experience simultaneously the Andromeda Galaxy and a person in the room with us. Quoted in Worthing (1996:173).

[122] Dyson (1979:459). I am indebted to Ian Barbour (1997:219) for his brief and clear summary of Dyson's work.

[123] This notion of an evolving God amounts to a form of eschatological pantheism. See Drees (1990:128f), Polkinghorne (1994:166), Worthing (1996:172), Clayton (1997: 134). Tipler himself suggests that his position is panentheist because God is immanent on the one hand and transcendent, omnipotent and omniscient on the other.

> will regulate all matter and manipulate the evolution of the universe as a whole (omnipotent). It will also be able to know everything knowable (omniscient). For Tipler, this constitutes a form of this-worldly immortality.[124] Within this Omega, a continuity of identity (understood as information) may be maintained for the cosmos, the earth and individual human beings. Tipler's model allows for life beyond death and also for the possibility of perfection (a reductionist notion of salvation) in the eschaton (e.g. with reference to bodily defects).[125]

The scientific merits of both these contributions to "eschatology" remain controversial. Several critics point out that their accounts (on the future of humanoid forms of life) are highly speculative and overly optimistic.[126] Indeed, Russell wonders whether these scenarios may not be "little more than whistling in the dark".[127] Polkinghorne finds Tipler's scenario "desperately implausible"[128] while Ellis and Murphy reckons that it "pushes science to the borders of absurdity."[129] In my assessment, the speculative character of these attempts provides a sobering indication that science cannot *qua* science address the predicament of finitude. The origins and destiny of time and space indicate "singularities" at which physical equations and mathematical models loose their explanatory power. The predicament of (human and cosmic) finitude (in time) presents an ultimate question that lies, precisely as *finis* (boundary), at the edge of scientific competence.

For theological reflection it is perhaps more important to note that there remains a clear difference between the hope for an infinite continuation of information processing and storage, offered by the models of Dyson and Tipler, and the hope for personal resurrection and eternal life with God, expressed in Christian faith.[130] However, these contributions have at least stimulated Christian theologians to reflect on the intelligibility and plausibility of the Christian hope for the resurrection of the dead, a new earth and eternal life.[131] It has also clarified the need to reincorporate an account of the "End" in theological reflections on the *eschata* (even where this is no longer the primary focus of eschatology). Indeed, how should a transition to a new era ushered by God beyond this "End" be conceived?[132] "Is the Christian affirmation of an imminent end of this world," Pannenberg asks in his now famous 'questions to scientists', "reconcilable with scientific explorations of the continuing existence of the universe for billions of

---

[124] Tipler (1988, 1994, 1997).

[125] Tipler (1994:227f), Peters (1995:12).

[126] Barbour (1997:219).

[127] Russell (1994:571).

[128] Polkinghorne (1998:21).

[129] Ellis & Murphy (1996:62).

[130] Worthing (1996:197).

[131] Russell (1997:206) suggests that the contributions of Dyson and Tipler have reestablished the possibility of addressing the cosmic scope of the biblical eschatological horizon.

[132] Worthing (1996:175).

years ahead?"[133] Several theologians have subsequently explored these questions:

- Karl Peters argues that the eschatological vision portrayed in the Bible simply cannot be made intelligible in the context of modern cosmology. The cosmology in which Christian eschatology is embedded has been superseded by contemporary cosmology. He says:

  > A universe in which the overcoming of evil by good, in which justice is finally served, is vastly different from the current scientific picture of an expanding universe with billions of galaxies with billions of stars. It is so different that it is difficult to see how the details of biblical eschatology can be translated into the current scientific world view as a future, universal eschatology. This applies ... even to the notion of the creation of a new heaven and a new earth.[134]

  Peters suggests a reduced form of "interpersonal" or "local" eschatology where small communities realize the overcoming of evil among themselves and thus serve as a catalyst for the future in order to reduce evil, to eliminate hatred and to conquer hunger and disease.[135]
- Pannenberg agrees that scientific theories about the remote future of the universe are incompatible with the Biblical expectation of an imminent end to the world. He concludes that, "We cannot readily argue, then, that they relate to the same event."[136] The earth and its human inhabitants remain the primary focus of the apocalyptic events described in the Bible. The *parousia* of Christ and the new earth cannot be equated with the end of the entire universe in the remote future as predicted by physicists.[137]

  Pannenberg nevertheless notes a "remarkable convergence of Tipler's Omega point theory with Christian eschatology. He mentions Tipler's support for the existence of a Supreme being, the notion that God will become "all in all" (1 Cor 15:28), the possibility of an eschatological resurrection together with the rest of creation, etc.[138] This enables Christian theology to take the cosmic scope of eschatological affirmations seriously once more – while earlier eschatologies stood in sharp contrast to our knowledge of the destiny of the universe.[139] Significantly, Pannenberg also lists several aspects of Christian

---

133 Pannenberg (1993:14).

134 Quoted in Worthing (1996:176). Worthing comments that Peters allows science to write the eschatological script and then attempts to redefine the term eschatology in a way that would not bring it in conflict with modern cosmology.

135 Worthing (1996:176-7).

136 Pannenberg (1994:159, 1998:589).

137 See also Worthing (1996:178-9). Even if this may be true, a reduction of the cosmic scope of eschatology can scarcely be maintained in the light of the Christian affirmation that God transcends the whole cosmos.

138 Pannenberg (1997:436f).

139 Pannenberg (1997:437).

eschatology which remain unaccounted for in Tipler's work – notably the reality of sin and evil in world history, the possibility of salvation, the role of Christ in the eschaton, etc.[140]

- Robert John Russell, in an article on "Cosmology from Alpha to Omega", insists that the cosmic and not merely human or planetary scope of the Christian vision of an ultimate fulfillment for all of creation has to be maintained.[141] This is, for him, precisely the value of the contributions of Dyson and Tipler: "Tipler proposes the first truly global eschatological scenario, in which the activity of life within the universe as it meets the boundary conditions becomes part of the global transfiguration of the universe contained in the Omega point."[142] Like Pannenberg, Russell also notes that the problem of evil and redemption receives too little attention in Tipler's work. He maintains that, in contrast to the scenarios of Dyson and Tipler, the vision of Christian hope is not for unending life but for eternal life, not timelessness but being in the presence of an eternal God.[143]
- In an excellent discussion of the debate, Mark Worthing concludes that Christian theology has at least the responsibility to demonstrate to what extent and in what ways Christian faith may be compatible with cosmologies that may later prove to be an accurate description of the universe. It must do more than simply to hope that a seemingly theology-friendly cosmology will win the day.[144]

Other contributions to this debate are hesitant to locate the Christian hope for a new earth in terms of the long-term future of the universe and within the dimensions of space and time. Instead, they focus on notions of eternity and explore God's transcendence as a basis of hope:

- In a section on cosmic eschatology in *The coming of God*, Moltmann notes that the task of cosmic eschatology is not to affirm or confute scientific theories of the end of the world. He adds that notions of the infinity of the universe are as far removed from Christian eschatology as are modern ideas about the end of the universe. Christian hope has its foundation in Christ's death and resurrection. On this basis Christians may expect an eschatological new creation of all things. Moltmann acknowledges that since the rise of modern cosmology it has become increasingly difficult to not only express this hope but also to imagine it (leading to a split between eschatology and cosmology). He responds to this task by reflecting on a Christian concept of space and time in order to provide "points of access" for the dialogue with scientific theories.[145] Moltmann subse-

[140] Pannenberg (1997:438f).

[141] Russell (1994:572).

[142] Russell (1997:202-3).

[143] Russell (1994:572).

[144] Worthing (1996:195).

[145] Moltmann (1996:259-261).

quently develops the patristic notion of the *aeon*, of relative eternity (which he distinguishes from God's absolute eternity) to account for the transition from temporal to eternal creation.[146]

- In a brief comment, Ted Peters insists that, "Whether frozen or fried, the picture of nature's future painted by science is not consonant with the Christian picture of new creation."[147] Christian hope is based on God's promise for an utterly transformed creation. This is not possible simply by projecting the continuance of natural processes, but only through a powerful act of an omnipotent God.
- Worthing also suggests that apocalyptic expectations in the Bible need not be equated with the more radical end of the entire universe in the remote future as predicted by science. While the scope of apocalyptic expectations may be only planetary, Christian hope may retain a cosmic scope if the end of the universe is instead related to a Christian notion of eternity.[148]
- Barbour asks whether it would contradict biblical assumptions if a heat death or a freezing death ultimately cannot be avoided.[149] Would such a future imply that the universe is meaningless? Barbour suggests that eschatology provides an ultimate framework for history and does not describe events in history. Instead, they are symbolic expressions of trust in God applicable to all times.[150]
- Polkinghorne expresses several objections against Tipler's Omega point theory and concludes that it merely presents a form of evolutionary optimism.[151] He rejects Tipler's "pantheism" and concludes that we are driven back to God as the ultimate basis for the Christian hope of redemption in a new creation.[152] He refrains from speculation as to the nature of the continuity between this creation and the new creation that will emerge out of the old one (*ex vetere*) – except to indicate that, in terms of the space-time continuum, this problem has to be addressed in terms of the relation between time and eternity.[153]
- Willem Drees maintains that it is not realistic to relate eschatology to the future on a cosmological scale, counted at least in billions of years. This has very little significance within a human life span. In response to the legacy of injustice, Drees prefers to relate eschatology to values and subsequently develops an axiological eschatology that he bases on a notion of God's eternal presence.[154]

---

[146] Moltmann (1996:279f). See the discussion in Chapter 13.3 for more detail on Moltmann's position.

[147] Peters (1998:25).

[148] Worthing (1996:178).

[149] Barbour (1997:219-220).

[150] Barbour (1997:220).

[151] Polkinghorne (1994:165).

[152] Polkinghorne (1994:166).

[153] Polkinghorne (1994:170).

[154] Drees (1990:117).

14.5 Concluding reflections

What, then, does this story of the universe as reconstructed by the sciences contribute towards a vision of hope for the earth in Christian theology? What hope is there for us, the earth and for the universe? Does cosmic pessimism have the final word?

It is perhaps wise to conclude that science cannot *qua* science provide a decisive answer to these questions.[155] The scientific evidence remains inconclusive. A few further comments on this debate in terms of the eschatological "road map" that was suggested in earlier chapters may suffice here.

a) The cosmic dimensions of finitude

Haught's argument on the "promise of nature" relates primarily to the future of evolutionary history in the cosmos. This "promise of nature" is no guarantee against the transience of life, the earth and the universe itself though. A blossoming youth provides no guarantee against old age. All events, all forms of life, even the cosmos as a whole remain ultimately finite.[156]

The possibility of emergence and self-organization also does not invalidate the well established parameters of the second law of thermodynamics. Haught acknowledges that the totality of the cosmos may still be headed toward a death (by entropy?) analogous to our own individual deaths.[157] However, he insists that the totality of nature is precisely a promise rather than paradise. This should temper our expectations of what nature can provide and reconcile us to its inherent limitations and finitude.

However, on the basis of the promise of nature, Haught suggests that the final destiny of the cosmos is not nothingness, but that it will be taken up into God's own life. God will keep the entire history of the cosmos in faithful remembrance.[158] Haught concludes: "A sincere hope for eventual cosmic fulfillment liberates us from an immature clinging to the natural world as though it were by itself capable of satisfying our deepest longings."[159]

A few tentative comments on these investigations of the predicament of finitude may be noted:

- Eschatology, as the Christian doctrine of the future of God, is not so much concerned with the last things that will occur at the end of history, billions of

[155] See Murphy & Ellis (1996) who maintain a clear distinction between science and theology and acknowledge the limits of both. Science cannot by itself provide satisfactory answers to the ultimate origin and future of the universe. Whenever science engage in such questions it becomes highly speculative and looses its distinctness as science.

[156] Haught (1993b:115).

[157] Haught (1993b:115).

[158] Haught (1993b:125).

[159] Haught (1995:197).

years from now. A preoccupation with the last things would void eschatology of its existential significance in the present, that is, as the power of God coming to us from the future and impacting on the present.[160]

- Christian eschatology is distinct from the science of futurology[161] and runs counter to both pessimistic and optimistic views of the future.[162] It cannot and does not provide any guarantee that some form of global or cosmic catastrophe will be averted.
- The cosmic scope of Christian eschatology nevertheless necessitates an inclusion of the last things in an eschatological vision. A Christian response to the predicament of finitude need not be based on an endless continuation of the history of the cosmos. An evolutionary optimism that finds fulfillment within the confines of the unfolding of physical processes is ultimately unhelpful to address the reality of cosmic finitude.[163] The finitude of the universe itself (whether everything will become fried or frozen) should pose no threat to cosmic eschatology. Christian hope is ultimately based in God's faithfulness. It simply expresses the trust that my life and the future of the universe will somehow, beyond death and destruction, be taken up into God's nurturing, creative and corrective love – which became evident in the resurrection of Jesus, the Christ. This theme will be developed in Chapter 17 in more detail.

b) The limitations of human knowledge and power

The broader context of the science and religion dialogue within which these contributions on cosmic finitude is situated, remains dominated not so much by the predicament of finitude but by the limitations of human knowledge. This is hardly surprising given the spectacular if relentless quest in science and technology to extend the frontiers of our knowledge and power. This agenda is largely shared by participants in science and theology dialogues – who usually focus on a clarification of the cognitive content of theological truth claims. This agenda responds to the intellectual challenges posed by modernity in the context of academia. It participates in the quest for knowledge by reflecting on the possibilities of reliable knowledge of God – whether through natural theology or not. Although this quest for knowledge is seldom framed in eschatological terminology, it shares the pathos of a longing for a beatific vision, to "understand the mind of God" (Hawking), to know "how the Old One thinks" (Einstein).

There is no need to deny the importance of a theological clarification of the cognitive status of its truth claims. This remains of crucial importance at the dawn of a new century. The contributions emerging from current science and theology dialogues certainly indicate the kind of sophistication and commitment that is necessary for this task.

---

160 Braaten (1974:66).

161 Berkhof (1967:79f).

162 Berkhof (1967:83).

163 See Polkinghorne (1994:162) for a similar criticism of Teilhard.

The deliberations in this chapter also provide an illustration of this tendency to focus on the predicament of human limitations. In Haught's argument, the motifs of the mystery, complexity and narrative character indicate the success but also the limitations of the sciences to reconstruct the story of the universe. Likewise, the discussion of chaos and complexity is dominated by the issues of predictability and the limited value of a reductionistic logic in the sciences (i.e. in the light of self-organizing forms of complexity). That scientific evidence on the destiny of the universe remains inconclusive also illustrates the ultimate limitations of human knowledge.

Two somewhat general observations regarding an exclusive theological focus on the cognitive content of theological truth claims may be offered in terms of the eschatological grid proposed in Chapter 4.

i) The limitations of human knowledge can and should only be addressed together with the limitations of human power. The science and theology dialogue cannot afford to marginalize ethical reflection on the use and abuse of power. The whole scientific enterprise is itself inextricably linked (if only financially) to the quest for more sophisticated forms of technology (the enhancement of human power). Science cannot teach us what it is that we most need to know and to do.[164] This calls for a reintegration of the dialogue between theology, physics and biology within the long-standing debates between theology, philosophy, ethics, all the social sciences, as well as the creative arts – since artists are the antennae of society (Ezra Pound).[165]

ii) An eschatology that focuses only on the predicament of the limitations of human knowledge and power will soon become abstract and intellectualist. The language of the sciences and the favored categories of process metaphysics remain foreign and not immediately recognizable compared to the language in which the Christian faith is expressed traditionally. There is also an urgent need to situate the science and theology dialogue within the broader concerns of civil society. It has to show its relevance to the global issues of poverty, ethnic and religious conflict, patriarchy, HIV/AIDS, and environmental degradation.[166] Tracy warns that the suspicion of some liberation theologians towards the new interest in cosmology may be entirely appropriate:

> The suspicion that "cosmological" interests in theology *can* function as a distraction from these historical responsibilities or even as ideology for intellectual elites ... seems,

---

[164] Rolston (1997:77).

[165] See Rolston (1987) for one such approach which also allows him to treat the problem of evil in social systems more extensively.

[166] This requires an interaction between those involved in the social agenda of the ecumenical movement and those involved in science and theology dialogues. See the volume edited by Mangum (1989), especially the essays by Liedke, Russell, and Westhelle, for an important contribution in this direction, indicating an awareness of global economic context within which the science and theology dialogue has to be situated.

> admittedly, in order. The importance of these suspicions should not be domesticated. Indeed, any pure models of "progress" unable and unwilling to face the tragedy and suffering in human existence, fully deserve Christian theological suspicion, indeed contempt.[167]

Christian eschatology should, in my view, remain rooted in Christian soteriology. The proclamation of the gospel has to remain focused on the Christian vision of hope for salvation from sin, liberation from injustice and victory over evil. It is precisely within this context that the need to reflect on the cognitive content of this message emerges. The contribution of the dialogue between Christian theology and the sciences may be to clarify the meaning of the Christian claim that this salvation, liberation and victory ultimately comes from God. To express this in different terms: there is a need to relate prophetic resistance against evil to mysticism (a reflection on the knowledge of God).[168] Resistance is empowered by the critique of absolutes in mystic experiences. At the same time, true mysticism leads to prophetic resistance. Science and theology together may and should help us to protect the provocative mystery of God's presence in the world.

c) The predicament of sin, injustice and evil

The science and theology dialogue is clearly dominated by a renewed interest in the doctrine of creation. This shift was important to counter the preoccupation with the motifs of redemption and liberation and the marginalization of creation theology in the prevailing climate of twentieth century theology. However, the pitfalls of natural theology[169] can only be averted through a thorough reintegration of the motifs of redemption and creation. But in the new focus on creation theology, relatively little attention is given to the motifs of salvation from sin.

The theme of evil is, although not dominant, certainly not completely absent from major contributions to the science and theology dialogue. It often emerges in the form of a discussion of the theodicy problem and within the context of the ambiguity of nature. It thus relates to the suffering induced by nature itself (especially death) instead of by human sin. It is therefore perhaps more appropriately linked with the predicament of finitude.

- In *Theology for a scientific age*, Peacocke treats the problem of natural evil (earthquakes, floods, accidents)[170] in a few pages and mentions the theme of

---

[167] Tracy (1994:76).

[168] See Tracy (1990) on the relationship between the mystic and the prophetic.

[169] See Barbour (1997:98-103) for a careful distinction between natural theology and a theology of nature. Polkinghorne (1998:13) also comments on this important shift: "We are not now looking to the physical world for hints of God's existence but to God's existence as an aid for understanding why things have developed in the physical world in the manner that they have."

[170] Peacocke (1993:125-6).

sin – which he relates to a sense of human incompleteness, perhaps alienation – only briefly.[171]

- In *On the moral nature of the universe*, Ellis & Murphy discusses the predicament of sin in the context of the theodicy problem in depth and reject the inadequacies of the Augustinian emphasis of human responsibility for sin and evil in the world.[172]
- In *Science and Christian belief*, Polkinghorne acknowledges with Niebuhr that human sin may be the only empirically verifiable Christian doctrine.[173] Following the themes of the Nicene creed, he also addresses the theme of atonement for sin in some detail.[174] The problem of evil (natural and social) is discussed twice in the context of the theodicy problem.[175]
- In *God, creation, and contemporary physics*, Worthing engages in a detailed discussion of the theodicy problem and investigates the correspondence between theological models of natural evil and scientific models of entropy. Significantly, he mentions, but does not discuss evil within social systems.[176]
- Haught's view of nature as promise enables him to acknowledge the ambiguity of nature, the "shadow side", the pain, suffering and catastrophes, the *finitude* that are part of nature (see the discussion in Chapter 14.2 above).

The treatment of the predicament of sin and evil under the rubric of the theodicy problem (only?) does not solve but in fact heightens the issue at stake here. The focus is on the clearly important question how evil could have emerged in the created order that God announced to be good. However, evil remains in this way linked with a theology of creation. It is no longer addressed within a soteriological context.[177] Departing from the heritage of the Hebrew prophets, Paul, Augustine, Calvin and Barth, the emphasis is no longer on the radical contamination of sin, human responsibility for such sin and the equally radical message of God's grace. The presence of evil and suffering is addressed and balanced through the theological short-cut of a kenotic understanding of God who suffers in, with and under the creative processes in the world.[178] This kenotic doctrine of God thus tends to become a cosmic principle.[179]

Although the shadow-side of nature is acknowledged, a certain optimism, based on evolutionary biology (Haught) or on information technology (Dyson and

---

171 Peacocke (1993:125, 250).

172 Ellis & Murphy (1996:243f).

173 Polkinghorne (1994:15).

174 Polkinghorne (1994:136-9).

175 Polkinghorne (1994:82f, 169f).

176 Worthing (1996:146f).

177 See also Farrow (1998:442).

178 Peacocke (1993:126).

179 See especially Ellis & Murphy (1996), Peacocke (1993:123f), also Haught (1993b, 1998a).

Tipler), and which remains undisturbed by the radicalness of human evil, is often retained. The Omega point may be reached on the basis of sufficient information only. The predicament of sin is solved by addressing the problem of ignorance or by emphasizing the continuation of life amidst the death (finitude) of individual living specimens. Sufficient knowledge will guarantee the goodness of the human will.

This assessment does not provide a full picture though. There are several contributions (from the same and other authors) in which the importance for eschatology of the predicament of sin, injustice and evil is beginning to be recognized in the context of science and theology dialogues. This emphasis often provides the room for these authors to address the stark realities of environmental degradation directly.

- Barbour devotes 4 pages of *Religion and Science* to the problem of evil and suffering and focuses on the issue of theodicy.[180] He does acknowledge the fallenness of human nature elsewhere and calls for a more sober assessment in the light of the manifestations of evil in the twentieth century (e.g. nuclear annihilation).[181] In response, Barbour refers to the prophetic eschatological vision of encompassing shalom which calls for justice, democratic participation and environmental integrity.[182]
- In *Science and Religion*, Holmes Rolston III incorporates contributions from the psychological and social in his overview of the field. This enables him to acknowledge the pervasiveness of evil in society and history.[183] In this and other works Rolston continues to emphasize the role of appropriate social values to ensure a sustainable environment.
- In a contribution to the volume *Cosmos as creation* (1989), Paul Santmire questions a preoccupation with the "inner agenda" of personal guilt, and its correlate, the forgiveness of sin, while the "outer agenda" of despair (in all its ecological and cosmic dimensions) is being neglected.[184] Santmire suggests that although sin is radical and has thwarted God's creative intent, there is no cosmic fall. The drama of human salvation, of God "walking the extra mile" with us, forms a smaller part of the larger history of the consummation of creation.[185] Santmire unfortunately does not relate this eschatological vision to the horizons of cosmic finitude.
- Russell also makes a helpful distinction between local and universal eschatology. The focus of a local eschatology should indeed be humanity within its terrestrial environment. This more local drama of judgment and redemption

---

[180] Barbour (1997:300-304).

[181] Barbour (1997:270).

[182] Barbour (1997:279-280).

[183] Rolston (1987).

[184] Santmire (1989:267).

[185] Santmire (1989:276).

> takes place within a cosmic context that requires a universal eschatological panorama.[186] The universal horizon of eschatology that is, for example, emphasized by Tipler, does not (yet) account for the theological problems of evil, redemption and universal resurrection.[187] Russell suggests the need for an eschatological vision in which "the groaning of all of nature will be taken up in and healed by the transfiguration of the universe which has already begun with the resurrection of Christ."[188]

Indeed, creation and redemption belongs together. We need a vision in which the soteriological focus of God's acts of creation is recognized and where the cosmic scope of God's acts of salvation is at the same time emphasized.[189] Perhaps we need to learn to speak of the history of 15 billion years of God's creative, nurturing and corrective love. The story of human sin and salvation is one brief episode within this larger history of God's love for the cosmos. This notion of love includes the aspects of creativity, nurturing and salvation.

This vision has important implications for eschatology. Eschatology has to retain its soteriological roots. An independent curiosity in the predicaments of human finitude and limitedness (both aspects of createdness) has to be avoided by addressing these predicaments within the context of the effects of sin. However, eschatology cannot be reduced to soteriology. It is only within the eschatological vision of a new creation that a theology of redemption and creation can be adequately integrated.

---

186 Russell (1997:202-3).

187 Russell (1997:211).

188 Russell (1994:572).

189 See also Moltmann (1981:99-100).

15. South African manifestations of hope

15.1 Introduction

Where on earth can one find a living and lived form of hope that encompasses hope for the earth? How can a Christian vision of hope inspire an environmental praxis within the South African context? And how can such a vision of hope be rooted within the spirituality of present Christian communities in South Africa? In order to address these questions, this chapter will investigate three South African manifestations of Christian hope with a view to retrieve elements of such a sense of hope, namely:

a) The theme of hope in literature from the "struggle" period in South Africa (1960-1994);
b) The theme of hope in secondary literature on the African Initiated Churches in South Africa;
c) The theme of hope in recent popular Christian literature in Afrikaans.

A full study of eschatology in the South African context cannot be attempted here. This would require a detailed investigation of the eschatology of Afrikaner Calvinism and nationalism, English liberalism[1], evangelicalism[2], liberation theology, black theology, and African Pentecostalism, amongst others.[3] It will also be helpful to study the emergence of apocalypticism in secular and religious literature in South Africa. Any such investigations will certainly prove to be richly rewarding, but will require a full-length study in its own right.

15.2 Hope in the "struggle" period (1960-1994)

a) The theme of hope in some ecclesial documents

The theme of hope is certainly a prominent feature of Christian literature from the struggle period in South Africa. The struggle itself was characterized by a vibrant, indomitable sense of hope – often in the midst of circumstances where no deliverance seemed possible.

This sense of hope is not primarily found in the numerous theological publica-

---

1 See the comment by De Gruchy (1979:205) that this kind of liberalism believes that the kingdom will come through education and social programs.

2 The Student Christian Association, an evangelical student movement in South Africa has as its motto, "Make Jesus king". Although this is often interpreted in a personalistic way, this has helped many prominent South African figures to also work for the lordship of Christ in the South African society.

3 One helpful overview of such eschatologies may be found in the various articles of Volume 15 of *Missionalia*.

tions from this period. There are, in fact, very few detailed and systematic discussions on the content and social impact of Christian hope in the struggle.[4] Although an emphasis on hope recurs throughout this literature, it is often mentioned almost occasionally in the context of vivid prophetic descriptions and sharp criticisms of despairing circumstances. Hope is thus defined negatively as resistance against the present. There seems to be a hesitation to dream about the future, to focus on what lies beyond, on what remains distant. Instead the focus of attention is on the reality of continuing suffering. In this context the hope is expressed that this suffering will not endure forever.

Furthermore, references to the theme of hope are often found, not in the context of academic theology, but in the context of people embodying such a vibrant sense of hope. Hope is a desirable virtue, not so much a belief. The word hope features, not surprisingly, in the titles of several publications by prominent figures in the struggle. *Resistance and hope* (1985) is the fitting title of a *Festschrift* for Beyers Naude. An interview with Beyers Naude and Dorothee Sölle is called *Hope for faith*. A selection of sermons by Desmond Tutu is entitled *Hope and suffering*. *Fighting for hope* is the title of Carl Niehaus' biography. After the Boipatong massacre and the failure of preliminary negotiations in 1992, David Philip published *A book of hope*, with 30 essays and poems by leading South African thinkers, including several theologians. Finally, a collection of 21 conversations by Villa-Vicencio with eminent South African political figures and church leaders (who are "bearers of a message of hope") has the appropriate title of *The spirit of hope*. In most of these publications there is no specific discussion on the content or nature of Christian hope. It is primarily regarded as an exemplary virtue that these "heroes" of the struggle embody. It is a spirit of hope, often against all expectations, that enables people to continue struggling against the forces of evil.[5]

A comprehensive study of the eschatology of the "struggle" period will therefore have to investigate the liberating praxis, the pre-reflective experiences, the forms of resistance, the spiritualities, the prominent personalities of this period.

Within the limitations of this study a different route had to be followed. I therefore restricted the investigation to references to hope in some of the major ecclesial documents of this period and on literature from this period in which the theme of Christian hope is discussed explicitly. The dates of publications that were taken into consideration are demarcated, somewhat arbitrarily, by the events of Sharpeville and Cottesloe (1960) and the first democratic elections (1994).

The message to the people of South Africa (1968) provides one the most important earlier critiques of apartheid. This document states that the gospel of salvation in Jesus Christ offers hope and security for humanity. This salvation is to be understood in a cosmic and universal sense as the salvation of the world and of

---

4 Most of these more systematical reflections on hope were done by white, male English speaking theologians who tried to articulate some of the trends in the struggle of the period. See especially De Gruchy (1979, 1986); Nolan (1987) and Cochrane, De Gruchy & Petersen (1991).

5 See also Ndungane (1998).

human existence in its entirety. It declares that we live in the expectation of a new heaven and a new earth in which righteousness dwells and that the kingdom of God is already present in Christ and through the Spirit.

On this basis it launches a powerful critique on the inadequacies of apartheid and the doctrine of separation which has become a false gospel offering happiness and peace to the peoples of South Africa through separation (only). Apartheid theology is based on the presumed orders of creation. This does not take the new eschatological community of diverse people who are reconciled with one another in Christ as a point of departure. This reconciliation is already a reality in Christ here and now.

The eschatology of the *Confession of Belhar* (1982, 1986) remains implicit. A particular eschatology nevertheless structures the statements on the unity of the church, the ministry of reconciliation and the need for social justice. 1) The church is the work of God who called a new community together from the whole human race. The unity of this new community is built on the reconciliation in Jesus Christ. This eschatological reality should be expressed concretely and visibly in and for the world to see and to believe. 2) The church is called to the ministry of reconciliation as witnesses of the new heaven and the new earth where justice will prevail. Through this ministry of reconciliation, the power of evil, hatred and enmity can be conquered by the life giving Word and Spirit. 3) Since God is in a special way the God of those who suffer, the church is also called to stand for justice and with the oppressed so that "justice will flow like a river and righteousness like a stream".

The *Kairos Document* (1985) exemplifies the prophetic genre of numerous publications from the struggle period. It provides a vivid description of the injustices, oppression and tyranny of apartheid and confronts the inadequacies of what it called "state theology" and "church theology".

In the true prophetic tradition and style, it denounces sin and announces salvation. Yahweh liberated the slaves from Egypt; Jesus Christ took up the cause of the poor and the Spirit of God will act again to liberate the people of South Africa from oppression. This expectation empowers a prophetic call for repentance and conversion – leading to action, discipleship, solidarity, participation in the political struggle, civil disobedience, special campaigns, etc.

It is within this prophetic mould that the Kairos Document includes two sections on "Liberation & hope in the Bible" (4.5) and "A message of hope" (4.6). In terms of the analysis of the three human predicaments to which Christian eschatology responds (sin, finitude and limited human power and knowledge), the emphasis of the *Kairos Document* is clearly on the evil effects of sin.[6] Christian hope is understood as hope for a victory over the forces of evil, injustice, oppression, and tyranny. Hope thus remains thoroughly this-worldly. Any reference to

---

6 See also Moila (1990:18) who uses the term "human predicament" explicitly. He opts for an understanding of the human predicament in terms of oppression, inequality and bondage (Sobrino, Fiorenza, Ruether, Metz) and contrasts this analysis with those of the human predicament as unbelief (Barth, Thielicke), hopelessness (Pannenberg), alienation and estrangement (Tillich and Gilkey), chaos, disorder and distress (Cobb, Knitter and Wingren) and isolation (Schillebeeckx).

Christian hope for life beyond death or for "going to heaven one day" is carefully avoided. Salvation can only be understood as a concrete, historical reality. There are indeed explicit references to eschatological symbols such as the resurrection, the lamb lying down with the lion (Is 11:6), and the tears which will be wiped away (Rev 7:17).[7] But these categories are interpreted as evocative symbols of the coming of God's kingdom in our world. They are specifically related to the predicament of evil and not that of finitude.[8]

One may ask what consolation this form of hope provides for the victims of the struggle (those who died without seeing the "promised land"). The *Kairos Document* does not deviate from its primary focus on the need for liberation from tyranny to address this question. Likewise, in the countless funerals for the slain victims of the struggle, the primary message reverberated time and again: *aluta continua* (the struggle continues). The only consolation that this could provide to the victims and their relatives is the firm conviction that liberation is ultimately assured. Justice will triumph in the end. This conviction was also reflected in the battle cry of numerous demonstrations against apartheid institutions: "We shall overcome."[9]

In the *Kairos Document* this assurance of liberation is motivated on the basis of God's presence. God is at work in our world, turning hopeless and evil situations to good so that God's kingdom may come and God's will may be done on earth as it is in heaven. Goodness and justice will therefore triumph in the end and tyranny and oppression cannot last forever (section 4.5). The churches must therefore become God's partners to secure, with God's help, this future in South Africa (section 4.6).

Significantly, the *Kairos Document* is, precisely in its eschatology, primarily concerned with the present, the moment of truth, the *kairos* and therefore with resistance against tyranny. This does not imply that reflection on a vision for the future is of no concern. Throughout the struggle period, dreams for the future were expressed in committee meetings, in speeches, in pamphlets and in manifestos, perhaps most notably in the ANC's *Freedom Charter*. These reflections yearn for a kind of society that would be different from the present one. This vision is often described in purely secular terms as a democratic society – which is further negatively defined with attributes such as "non-racist", "non-sexist", "undivided" (not balkanized through ethnic "homelands") and "inclusive". This vision is sometimes virtually equated in religious terminology with the actual coming of God's

---

7 See section 4.5 of the *Kairos Document*.

8 See Nolan's (1987) reflection on the eschatology of the Kairos Document. Nolan argues that the eschaton should be understood as a radically new event in the near future in which God is going to put right all that is presently wrong. This act of God determines the quality, the mood and the seriousness of our present time; it turns the present moment into a particular kind of kairos. This notion of the *eschaton* is therefore closely related to the notion of *kairos*. It seems to imply little more than the presence of God in a *kairos*, leading to both salvation and punishment.

9 See Worsnip & Van der Water, D (1991) who use this slogan as a title for an investigation of the spirituality of the struggle for liberation.

kingdom.[10]

The *Evangelical Witness in South Africa* (1986) provides a similar critique of evangelical theology and practice, amidst the South African realities of the mid-1980's, by a group of "concerned evangelicals". The basic thrust of the document is to expose an evangelical conservatism that served to legitimize apartheid, the political status quo, naked capitalism, oppressive ecclesial structures and practices. Instead, the radical demands of the gospel are emphasized. An evangelical concern with sin should not be selective, but should address all the personal, collective and structural dimensions of sin. Such sins need to be exposed and condemned. The gospel thus requires a radical form of repentance and conversion. In its prophetic critique, the document does not address the issue of hope directly or the need to challenge an escapist form of eschatology in evangelicalism.

The *Road to Damascus* (1989) clearly draws its vision of hope from the coming reign of God. It emphasizes that this reign of God is not simply a way of speaking about the next world. The reign of God is for this world which should be completely transformed in accordance with God's plan (par 38). God is on the side of the poor, the oppressed, and the persecuted. When this message is resisted by the rich and powerful and when God hears the cries of despair this may lead to a moment of truth, a time for decision, a time of grace, a God-given opportunity for conversion and hope (par 43). The Damascus document also resists the idolatry of consumerist materialism because it is a denial of all hope for the future. Such consumerism resists and fears change because it finds security in the status quo.

Somewhat unlike the *Kairos Document*, the *Road to Damascus* adds that the reign of God begin in this life, but stretches beyond this life. It is transcendent and eschatological without being unconcerned about the problems and suffering of the poor in this life (par 38). The meaning of this formula is not spelled out in any more detail. Instead, it again focuses on the need of prophetically challenging the status quo by preaching the coming of the reign of God.

In its conclusion the Damascus document also refers to the theme of hope. The aim of its critique of the idolatry of consumerist materialism is to give an account of the hope that is in us. This is the bold hope, built on faith in Jesus, for something that fulfills and transcends all human expectations, namely the Reign of God (p. 21). This will not come without much suffering, pain and the bearing of one's cross. As disciples of Christ, we have to travel on this road, knowing that the way of the cross is the only way to freedom and salvation. But this pain registers at the same time the birth pangs of a new creation (p. 21).

At the threshold of the democratic era in South Africa, the *Rustenburg declaration* (1991) speaks about its vision of a new society (1.1-2). It expresses the hope for a democratic, peaceful and just dispensation (1.1), but immediately adds a reference to the continuing suffering of many. It states that this hope of a new society will elude us unless we can break completely with the past (1.3). The Rustenburg declaration therefore continues to deal extensively with the apartheid past.[11]

---

10 See Nolan (1988).

11 See the similar comment from Cochrane & West (1993:33): "There is no hope where the

b) Some features of hope in the struggle literature

On the basis of this investigation of some of the major ecclesial documents from the struggle period, a number of features of this form of hope may be noted. These features also recur in a number of other theological texts that are drawn into the discussion here. The observations below assume the eschatological road map suggested earlier.

a) In the struggle literature, Christian hope responds almost exclusively to the predicament of human sin. Sin is predominantly understood in terms of the sins of the powerful and as the power of evil manifested in social structures: oppression, injustice, and tyranny. Sin is a deeply rooted reality in human existence. The removal of sin requires more than the conversion of people's lives; it also demands a radical liberation and transformation of society and humanity itself.[12]

b) The predicament of finitude (understood as individual death) receives attention only in the context of the numerous funerals of the slain victims of the struggle which were often (especially in the 1980's) used as a political platform for a continuation of the struggle. In this context the primary problem is not that of finitude, but of untimely death. Finitude is therefore understood in terms of the predicament of sin. The same applies to the predicament of limited human power and knowledge. The power of the poor and the oppressed is limited concretely by the powerful – the government, its military wings, the social impact of the apartheid system, and the economic power of those who control the means of production. Little attention is given to human limitations in any ontological sense of the word.

c) In response to these predicaments, Christian hope focuses almost exclusively on the theme of liberation from oppression. The anticipated liberation is understood in thoroughly this-worldly terms and will be manifested in concrete, earthly changes. The event of liberation is closely and specifically linked with the downfall of the apartheid regime.

Salvation from sin therefore does not imply an escape from this miserable world but calls for a transforming of social structures. Only in this way can the message of salvation bring good news for the poor, the outcasts, the hungry, and the alienated.[13] The theme of hope as life beyond death seems to be avoided in the literature from the struggle period. Christian hope neither promises a pie in the sky when you die, nor does it imply a flight from this world of tears to be with God in a distant heaven. Hope does not operate as a tranquilizing instrument.[14]

This liberation is sometimes virtually equated with the coming of the kingdom of God. Shun Govender says, for example, "The biblical teaching of the Kingdom

---

memory of suffering is silenced."

12 Maimela (1986:109).

13 Maimela (1986:107).

14 Maimela (1986:107).

of God is the story of how God assists people in their earthly struggle for liberation and all the fruits of a life of peace and justice."[15] By contrast, De Gruchy argues that: "The gospel contains much more than the promise of earthly shalom. The message of the Kingdom is concerned with victory over demons, with eternal life, with a new world."[16] De Gruchy adds that the message of the kingdom is not just about the ultimate arrival of shalom but also about the penultimate signs of the coming of the kingdom. In Jesus Christ we may experience a foretaste of this shalom. This eschatological Christian hope may therefore stimulate and intensify our historical hopes. Simon Maimela adds: "To be sure, God's coming Kingdom will include far more than these limited historical victories which God's saints and their Creator gradually win, but God's coming Kingdom is not entirely divorced from their present struggles in which the Saviour and his disciples are engaged ..."[17]

d) How is this liberation from slavery and oppression possible? The dominant rhetoric of the struggle period was activist. Liberation is only possible through a concerted effort of the people of South Africa, aided by the pressure of the international community. However, in some of the struggle literature it is acknowledged that this is only possible through the grace of God. According to Maimela, black liberation theologians ground this defiant hope of a radical liberation in the gift that Christ offers to the world.[18] Maimela adds: "Liberation theologians ... understands life in terms of the human response to the hope of divine promises which liberate mankind from the limits imposed by existing structures of this world and enable humanity to think and behave according to the possibilities which God's future holds out to them."[19]

e) What is the social impact of this form of hope? The eschatology of the struggle literature is dominated by the critical relationship between the eschaton (of liberation, the coming of God's reign on earth) and the present (the context of oppression, suffering, tyranny). Hope is therefore often negatively defined as a rejection of the present reality. The social impact of this hope is especially one of *resistance*. A hope that is born in the struggle for justice empowers people to resist evil and to oppose those who maintain their positions of power. This resistance often leads to further suffering and even martyrdom, but this suffering often serves as a new source of inspiration for those who remain committed to the struggle for justice.[20]

This hope is manifested precisely in despairing situations. Albert Nolan observes that the system of apartheid destroyed any optimism, any illusionary hopes and expectations (e.g. that change may come from the top, that the white electorate

---

15 See Govender (1987:9).

16 De Gruchy (1979:228). De Gruchy quotes Verkuyl here with approval.

17 Maimela (1986:112).

18 Maimela (1986:109).

19 Maimela (1986:111).

20 See Tutu (1983:66f); Cochrane, de Gruchy & Petersen (1991:82).

may actually change their hearts, that the regime may be toppled simply through the pressure of boycotts, strikes and stay-aways). Hope emerges only when it is stripped of all illusions.[21] Indeed, one of the remarkable characteristics of those who were involved in the struggle against apartheid is that, despite so much despair and frustration, despite the long and weary battle fought over many decades, there remained an underlying conviction that a new day will finally dawn.[22] Despite so much evidence to the contrary, De Gruchy argues, the Christian refuses to surrender hope and become cynical about the future of the world, because it is God's world.[23]

Christian spirituality is understood as keeping this "hope against all hope" alive. This spirituality of hope recognizes that while the coming of the kingdom is ultimately in God's hands, the Christian community is called to live and to act as the agents and instruments of its coming here and now.[24] The Christian ethic is an ethic of hope. The struggle against oppression coexists with the anticipation of victory as an event already realized.[25] The Christian therefore cannot escape in a spiritual or ecclesiastical ghetto, but has the task of inspiring hope amongst those who are toiling in suffering.[26]

At the same time, the expected day of liberation will not only bring salvation for those who are being wronged, but also punishment for those who are doing wrong. The proclamation of the coming of this day of liberation therefore also functions as a call to repentance and conversion.[27]

c) Concluding comments

The strength of the eschatology of the struggle period is certainly its return to the prophetic roots of Christian hope. It does not engage in abstract speculation about life beyond death or heaven one day. It simply addresses a specific context of oppression and announces liberation for the poor and the oppressed. This illustrates the importance of understanding the predicaments of finitude and human limitations in the context of the predicament of evil.

The liberation that is announced in the struggle literature is concretely and vividly linked with the eventual downfall of the apartheid regime. In hindsight, this vibrant sense of hope seemed justified. Political liberation was indeed achieved through the democratic elections of 1994. However, the realities of post-apartheid South Africa prompts one to raise the question whether the same sense of hope would also be applicable for the new struggles towards (global) economic justice

---

21 Nolan (1988:139-140).

22 Cochrane, de Gruchy & Petersen (1991:82).

23 De Gruchy (1986:154).

24 Cochrane, de Gruchy & Petersen (1991:83).

25 Manas Buthelezi, quoted in De Gruchy (1986:157).

26 Manas Buthelezi, quoted in De Gruchy (1986:157).

27 Nolan (1987:66).

and a sustainable environment. Is victory really assured in all these struggles? What about the many histories of failure to fight against colonialism and its new manifestations in the form of globalization? Can this form of eschatology provide reassurance that all is not lost at the point when the revolutionary struggle collapses? Does it take seriously enough that unjust social structures are not simply the product of history, but are the result of human sin and that no revolution can thus ensure the birth of a political utopia?[28]

What about the victims of these struggles who never experienced liberation? Can their deaths really be ameliorated by a final, somewhat distant event of liberation – which, as history often shows, remains all too provisional, all too incomplete. The more metaphysical question posed by finitude and death (in its various dimensions) therefore remains: What is, after all, the meaning of our personal histories, of the histories of nations and indeed of the earth itself? The literature of the struggle period, perhaps understandably in the "heat of the struggle", refrains to address these questions.

One may also question the limited scope of the liberation that is announced. It seems to be reduced primarily to liberation for people[29] (for both the oppressed and for the oppressors). Little attention is given to the theme of liberation for the land and for the whole of creation.[30]

One may also express reservations about the clarity of a distinction between political liberation in South Africa and the coming of God's kingdom. To link political liberation with God's kingdom is certainly appropriate. However, they should not be equated with one another. The kingdom ultimately remains God's, not ours. Likewise, the coming of the kingdom is an act of God's grace, not merely the product of human struggles. Hope for the earth remains in God's hands, not in ours. This calls for attention to the involvement in the world of a God who is also beyond human limitations in space and time.

15.2 Eschatology in African Indigenous Churches[31]

a) Introduction and some important disclaimers

There has often been a preoccupation with life after death (the predicament of

---

28 De Gruchy (1979:205).

29 Maimela (1986:109) does speak of a "cosmic, all embracing salvation" but this seems to be used simply as a metaphor to explain that salvation includes the transformation of the entire human existence and the social relationships in which people live - and not just of pious individuals.

30 Daneel (1991) emphasizes a broadening of the scope of liberation to include liberation for the whole of creation.

31 The acronym "AIC" remains controversial. It can be used for "African Independent Churches", "African Instituted Churches", "African Indigenous Churches", "African Initiated Churches", etc. I follow Makhubu's (1988:13) suggestion that the notion of "African Indigenous Churches" demonstrate that these churches originate from the people themselves and not from Europeans.

finitude) in the eschatology of the Christian tradition. The discussion of hope in the struggle literature represents a powerful return to the predicament of sin. Hope is explained in terms of a resistance against evil and the anticipation of the fulfillment of God's promises of shalom. The hypothesis that guided the present investigation of the eschatology of African Indigenous Churches (AIC's) is that amongst these churches a return to what Nürnberger called the rudimentary logic of eschatology, namely the experience of an unacceptable present may be found.[32]

To recall the earlier discussion (Chapter 2.1), Nürnberger argues that the orientation of faith towards the future is instigated by an unacceptable present. The rudimentary desire of most people is indeed not aimed at lofty ideals of shalom or the quest for immortality but simply for a prolongation of their current situation – *without* some of the problems that they experience at the moment, for example illness, misery, death, the threat of witchcraft. The indomitable human predisposition of hope maintains, even against all odds and expectations, the possibility that the future may bring some improvement of current difficulties.[33]

Any adequate investigation of this hypothesis would require a detailed empirical study of the eschatology of specific AIC's. Such an empirical study would extend well beyond the scope of the present analysis. I therefore had to rely on the emerging wealth of secondary material on AIC's in the Southern African context. In following this strategy it is vital to keep several shortcomings and some severe difficulties in mind:

- In a publication entitled *Speaking for ourselves*,[34] some representatives of the AIC's complain that secondary material often describes AIC's in language and categories that they find difficult to recognize themselves in. They find such secondary literature seriously misleading, generalizing, judgmental, often far from the truth, and full of misunderstandings, misconceptions and falsehood.[35] They feel that AIC's have become a fertile field for outsiders to do research that would be "interesting" to their own interlocutors (i.e. other academics, often abroad).
- Since the publication of John Mbiti's controversial thesis on Biblical eschatology and an African notion of time, the very existence of an indigenous African eschatology has been contested. Mbiti argued (with reference to the Akamba of Kenya) that traditional African cosmology has "virtually no concept of the future" (beyond a few years at most).[36] It has a two-dimensional concept of

---

32 Nürnberger (1994:139, 140).

33 Nürnberger (1994).

34 *Speaking for ourselves* (1986).

35 *Speaking for ourselves* (1986:5).

36 Mbiti (1969:17). He adds: "There is virtually no future dimension of time, beyond a few years at most. What is certain to occur in the future must either take place shortly, or be embedded in the rhythm of natural phenomena like birth, procreation and death, or day, night and seasons." (1971:30).

time, an indefinite past and an intensely active present.[37] The center of temporal gravity lies in the past. There is virtually no future dimension or general notion of the end of the world. Whatever orientation towards the future have emerged is the result of Christian teaching but remains focused on the short term and this has little impact on people's lives.[38] The generalizations in Mbiti's thesis have often been criticized.[39] However, even if Mbiti's thesis about traditional African culture is accepted, this does not imply that no orientation toward the future, no place for a Biblical concept of hope which runs contrary to human expectations and secular optimism[40], can be identified amongst AIC's – if only because of the influence of Christian symbolism.

- It remains striking that relatively little attention is given to the theme of eschatology in secondary literature on the AIC's.[41] This is even true of some of the standard works on AIC's.[42] This relative lack of secondary material on eschatology also limits the validity of the present investigation.
- Any preliminary investigation of the AIC's should call blanket generalizations on the "eschatology of AIC's" into question. This is also obvious from the controversies surrounding an adequate taxonomy of AIC's (e.g. based on Bengt Sundkler's classic taxonomy of Ethiopian, Zionist and Messianic groups).[43] The emergence of thousands of new (often Pentecostal) churches, each with its own distinct history, varied practices, beliefs and leadership intrigues, simply precludes any such generalizations.
- This disclaimer certainly also applies to the eschatologies of AIC's. The full range of traditional Christian eschatological images and projections – as well as some novel manifestations of Christian hope – may be found in particular groups. This plurality is already reflected in the names and adjectives used to describe individual churches, e.g. "Zionist", "Messianic", "Adventist" etc. To

---

37 Mbiti (1971:24f).

38 Mbiti (1971:31).

39 See, i.a. Gillies (1980), Kato (1975), Ray (1972).

40 See Oosthuizen's (1968:104) assessment of the eschatology of AIC's.

41 See Pretorius (1987) for a brief but very helpful overview of the most important literature on the eschatology of AIC's. Pretorius discusses the contributions of Hans Margull, Bengt Sundkler, Marie-Louise Martin, GC Oosthuizen, John Mbiti and Inus Daneel.

42 Daneel (1987:264-269), Martin (1964:157f), Oosthuizen (1976:130-156) devotes significant portions of their works to eschatology. In Sundkler's (1961) and Makhubu's (1988) discussions of a theology of AIC's, little if any attention is given to eschatology.

43 Sundkler (1961) identified two basic types of AICs that he labels as Ethiopian and Zionist. Ethiopian churches were classically independent in that they broke away from mission churches but retained much of the liturgical, theological and organizational structures. Zionist churches represent a combination of Pentecostalism, and African traditional religion, some of which center around a holy shrine (Zion). Daneel (1989) argues that such "Zionist" movements should be referred to as "spirit type churches", while Anderson (1992) suggest the term African-Pentecostal churches. See also Turner (1967), Daneel (1987:36f) for a discussion of such typologies.

avoid the danger of reductionism, it is furthermore vital for a proper appreciation of any eschatology to understand it within the context of a group's whole belief system. Again, this task is well beyond the possible scope of the present study.

- Any comparisons between AIC's and mainline forms of Christianity remain problematic. Such comparisons are all too often based on facile distinctions, for example that between a presumed Western linear, chronological notion of time and an African cyclical notion of time.[44] Such comparisons also tend to ignore differences between mainline churches and often assume a particular (Western) theological system as normative.
- A comparison between the AIC's and prophetic theology in the South African context is also subject to controversy. In his illuminating study of *Kairos* theology, Petersen shows that prophetic theologies usually affirm the existence and indigenous nature of AIC's, but fail to appreciate their seemingly non-political stance and lack of participation in the struggle.[45]

---

44 Gillies (1980) argued that the relationship between objective time and time consciousness, between the chronological future and the imagined future is not unique to Africa or the West. Mbiti assumes that Christian eschatology requires a linear concept of the future while many Western theologians understand the eschaton as a category far transcending the chronological future. Gillies (1980:20) concludes: "Perhaps if Mbiti had considered the concept of the 'future' within eschatology as neither linear nor ontological, but as the reality which penetrates and influences every present, he would have interpreted his research finding very differently." Gillies argues that there is in fact a strong affirmation of the future in African communities and quotes Mbiti's own words to substantiate this: "People expect the years to come and go in an endless rhythm, like that of day and night. ... They expect the events of the rain season, planting, harvesting ... dry season, raining season again, planting and so on, to continue forever." This clearly constitutes an awareness of the future, based on the biological necessity of providing for the future (even though, as Mbiti correctly argues, the time span of such planning may not exceed two years) (Gillies 1980:22). Gillies concludes: "To deny the imagined future is to deny the basis of hope" (Gillies 1980:24).

Perhaps an awareness of the future in traditional African culture (and often elsewhere) should be understood in terms of a notion of narrative time. In narrative time the emphasis is clearly on the past (telling the story of what happened). The aim of telling a story (a fable, myth or one's life story) is to explain, illuminate, justify and to challenge the present situation and to indicate an appropriate ethos for the audience in the immediate present. Narrative time assumes that the story will continue but, since the future is open-ended, it obviously cannot narrate what will happen in future. Instead, the narrative keeps one in suspense for what is about to happen. Such a notion of narrative time is certainly conducive to a sense of hope. I am grateful to Professor Ted Peters (PLTS, Berkeley) who helped me to reach clarity on this notion of narrative time.

45 In his study, Petersen (1995) suggests that AIC's are evaluated in "Kairos theology" (literature from the struggle period) by two different norms. According to a socio-cultural norm AIC's are praised, according to ethico-political norm they are often questioned for a lack of overt and public involvement in the struggle for liberation. Goba (1988:55, 54) comments, for example, that "the black Independent Church movement has become apolitical, under unreliable leadership, and unable to offer any significant

- In this study, secondary literature on AIC's in the whole Southern African region is taken into consideration – also because this provides access to more material.

b) Some observations

After all these disclaimers one would hesitate to make any observations on the eschatology of AIC's in general. It may be more appropriate to simply test the validity and fruitfulness of the eschatological grid developed in the earlier chapters in conversation with the secondary literature on the eschatology of specific groups. This grid may also illuminate aspects of a notion of hope that is not always recognized by researchers as such.

i) There is some consensus that the hopes and expectations of members of AIC's focus on concrete predicaments in the lives of many poor people: sicknesses, a lack of money, employment, housing, threats to social security, the threat of demons and evil spirits, etc. One of the main reasons why many AIC's thrive is that they respond to these basic predicaments. They promise (and often deliver!) immediate salvation, healing and delivery from evil spirits through ritual forms of worship, music and dance, often interwoven with themes from traditional African culture.

Even if this salvation is not immediately forthcoming, the AIC's provide to their members a sense of belonging, a social place where one may feel secure in.[46] This is crucial in helping the poorest of the poor to survive in an otherwise hostile (urban) environment.

These observations seem to validate the hypothesis which was stated above, namely that the hope expressed in the AIC's indicates a return to the rudimentary orientation towards the future of most people: We basically hope to live and enjoy this life without some of the problems that we are experiencing at the moment.

The emphasis on immediate salvation and healing has prompted some observers to describe the eschatology of AIC's as "realized."[47] Through missionary teaching many have discovered a future which, they expect, will suddenly bring

---

political contribution. Petersen suggests that the use of analytical categories like "coded resistance" (James Scott) may lead to a different assessment. He concludes that "it is possible to demonstrate that it is precisely in the specificity and dense symbolic ritual forms of the AIC that a profound logic of resistance and reconstruction is at work. A form of resistance which, while not undermining the importance of the forms of overt struggle valorized in Prophetic theology, demonstrates that, far from being an apolitical and irrelevant practice of piety, these rituals, symbols and rites are to be located within the logic of everyday forms of life that seek to provide space for those who have no place, that seek to contest the forms of nonagentive domination that structure the lives of the marginalized poor, and that do so in a manner that is oftentimes far more 'radical' and far-reaching than many forms of overt protest and resistance" (1995:131).

46 This is reflected in the title of Inus Daneel's important and sympathetic study on AIC's, *Quest for belonging* (1983).

47 See, for example, Martin (1964).

them to a land of bliss, comfort and long life. However, this future seems to retreat faster than their hopes and expectations can follow it.[48] They feel frustrated and long for the full manifestation of a visible kingdom, here and now, in order to alleviate physical and social suffering and satisfy people's yearning.[49] In the Messianic churches a new city of Zion, Moriah, Eden,[50] or Jerusalem is established which implies the realization of liberation and salvation in the present existence.[51] The vision of John with regard to the new Jerusalem has been realized (e.g. in Zululand).[52] In some movements, the kingdom of God has already been established, with the Messiah in their midst (e.g. Isaiah Shembe of the Nazarites).

This form of realized eschatology is often criticized in secondary material. According to such criticisms, Christian salvation is whittled down to healing, success, security and prosperity in the present existence. The profoundly felt need for liberation from bodily and social suffering and tension results in the message of future salvation becoming a stumbling block. Full salvation must be already available.[53] Because there is a "snatching of the future", taking it by force, there is a loss of true hope; the perspective of eternal life and Christ's second advent are lost (Oosthuizen[54]). Martin asks: "Is it the kingdom that has come in Christ once and for all and that will come as the revelation of Christ's victory and reign? Or is it a psuedo-eschatology, based on biblical terms, inspired by American sects or by "culture-Protestantism" and secularism and their ideas of progress that influences African thinking?"[55]

---

48 Mbiti (1971:57-60).

49 Pretorius (1987:35).

50 "When I come near to the garden of Eden I will rejoice completely because I am now going to Ekuphakameni." (Oosthuizen 1976:141).

51 Daneel 91983:8).

52 Oosthuizen (1976:136).

53 See Daneel's paraphrase of this line of argumentation. (1983:8).

54 Oosthuizen (1968:97f).

55 Martin (1964:157). She defines "African eschatology" as an eschatology of "a kingdom of this world, of black messiahs who already reveal the glory of the coming kingdom or of a kingdom of bliss and prosperity that still lies in the future and has to be taken by force (a holy war!) or that will appear on the return of the black messiahs who were imprisoned or killed by colonial governments." She suggests that the kingdom is understood as increased power and links this to the deep longing among Africans for speedy deliverance from suffering and tension.

On the basis of this assessment Martin asks: "Is the future conceived of as a real future, as the coming of God to man, or is the future misunderstood as the realization of secular desires ..." (1964:158). She then comments that: "Whenever man [sic] takes it upon himself to stretch out his hand to seize the future (i.e. the kingdom) and to take it by force, he has no real hope. What he has seized upon is always a hope of his own making, a messiah who is a false Christ, and sooner or later disappointment follows" (1964:160). Martin concludes that this results in an inadequate eschatology on the basis of an inadequate Christology (a messiah without a cross) and an inadequate pneuma-

This would indicate that the eschatological tension between the already and the not-yet (in response to the predicament of evil) is resolved in such a way that the future holds little promise. Beyerhaus puts the question quite bluntly: Are the emergence of messianic movements not the result of an awareness of the benefits that may be obtained from Western civilization, coinciding with a gospel message of God's imminent kingdom of peace, resulting in a discharge of the eschatological tension between the 'already' and the 'not-yet' of God's kingdom by means of a secularist short circuit?[56]

Other observers have rejected the one-sidedness of such generalizations. Daneel points to the fervent eschatological expectations of some messianic and Zionist groups as counter examples. He argues that, "It would be erroneous to judge that, because of this heavy emphasis on God's kingdom here and now, the future perspective had been lost, and that no hope of a coming salvation and return of Christ remained, implying the complete twisting of eschatology into a materialistic, secularistic dimension."[57] Oosthuizen suggests that one should differentiate between various types of movements, for example, futuristic (Simon Kimbangu), millenarian and apocalyptic (Enoch Mgijima), or messianic (Shembe and Lekganyane). Pretorius concludes that: "AIC's perspectives on eschatology reputedly vary from a futuristic (Zion lies far away and high above, in heaven) to a one-sided realized eschatology (the full manifestation of the kingdom here and now)."[58]

In addition, the implied notions of time in these reflections on the 'already' and the 'not yet' of Christian salvation should be carefully analyzed. Some critics assume that a linear (or at least non-cyclical) notion of time is also Christian. A Christian view of time is therefore often associated and confused with the Western ideal of progress – which indeed assumes a linear notion of time, with devastating ecological consequences. Daneel refers in this regard to Camps, a Dutch missiologist, who maintained that the black man's cyclical concept of time – his orientation to the past and constant preoccupation with the ancestors – impedes the West-

---

tology (a *theologia gloriae* instead of a *theologia crucis*).

56 Beyerhaus (1967:516).

57 Daneel (1983:60). Daneel thus questions Martin's (1964) charge of a materialistic and secularistic distortion of eschatology amongst AIC's. Daneel (1987:265) maintains that "In a realized kingdom which is not merely in but also of the world, Christian salvation and redemption are narrowed down to healing, success, security and prosperity in this life. The deeply felt need for deliverance from physical and social suffering and stress has meant that the message of future salvation has become a stumbling block. Full salvation must be available now. Consequently the quest is for healing instead of salvation" (1987:266)

58 Pretorius (1987:38). He adds that the blessings that Zionists experience and expect (such spiritual blessings as the ability to see evil, to drive demons or bad spirits away, being prayed for, the forgiveness of sins and everyday matters such as good crops, health, protection against witchcraft, having children) cannot be reduced to a realized or a futurist form of eschatology. Those who value present blessings simultaneously and explicitly look forward to eternal future blessings: for example, peace among people, eternal sunshine, the absence of sickness and hunger, demons, death, fighting, crime and hail.

ern idea of progress: "What we need is a new theology of time and of the ancestors so that they can wholeheartedly and from within accept progress [sic!]."[59]

ii) How do AIC's respond to the predicament of (human) finitude? There is obviously a wealth of literature and controversy surrounding life in the hereafter and a respect for one's ancestors in traditional African cultures and in AIC's.

Most AIC's would probably share, with the early Hebrew imagination, a rather limited interest in a personalized existence after one's death. Almost all over Africa, traditional myths assume that human beings were originally intended to inherit immortality. Death came only afterwards, caused, it is most commonly held, by human disobedience, or by the maltreatment or failure of the messenger of immortality. Physical death is accepted as both inevitable and unnatural. After death one's continued earthly presence may linger on as long as one is remembered by the living. As long as a person is remembered by name, she or he is not really dead, but are amongst the living-dead. A respect for the graves of the ancestors, one's bodily remains, and perhaps a shadowy world of spiritual presence allowing one to communicate with the living is usually affirmed. After four or five generations, the living dead are finally forgotten as individuals because those who knew them while they were alive will by then have died as well. Their spirits are consequently lost to human memory but enter into the collective immortality, of the group. Beyond these observations, ideas about the after life usually become vague.[60]

The notion of a continuation of existence after death is sometimes extended with the help of the notion of resurrection. According to the Church of the Nazarites resurrection has already taken place. All people become 'shades' or rather saints; "... all are active and all are deeply and intimately associated with what is happening at Ekuphakameni."[61] This constitutes a realized eschatology where the communion of saints, koinonia or fellowship with Shembe is already possible.

The theme of historical finitude is also not entirely absent in the beliefs and practices of AIC's. Perhaps under the influence of Pentecostalism, evangelicalism and Adventism, some AIC's maintain a vibrant expectation of the end of the world and the return of Jesus Christ. The emphasis if often on the Day of Judgment, where the "sheep will be separated from the goats", thus articulating the need for a suitable moral preparation in this life. Sundkler comments on the future vision of many of the Zionist churches: "To the great majority of these churches, Zion is an object of longing, a projection of hope. Zion is not in Johannesburg, nor in Zululand. It lies far away and high above, in heaven. Theirs is a futuristic eschatology."[62]

---

59 Daneel (1987:269). The original reference is to the following text: Camps, A 1971. Religion and change: some missiological implications. *Bulletin Secretariatus pro non-Christianis* 16, 7.

60 Mbiti (1975:121). See also Peters (1995).

61 Oosthuizen (1976:134).

62 Sundkler (1976:197). Also quoted in Pretorius (1987:35).

These dimensions of personal and historical finitude are usually not extended towards a notion of cosmic finitude. Mbiti argues that: "Both linguistically and mythologically there is no notion in traditional African thoughts that the world will ever come to an end. The rhythm of nature ensures an endless continuity of human life and the world. What comes to an end is really what is eventually removed from the present (*mituki*) period of time to the past (*tene*)."

iii) How should one come to terms with the limitations of human power and knowledge? How can one obtain reliable knowledge of God? And how would such knowledge of God help the illiterate and the powerless in their daily struggles to survive? Any answer to these questions would require a detailed investigation of God's transcendence and immanence in the world in the view of specific AIC's. Again, this would prove beyond the possible scope of this study.

Many observers have identified a lack of public activism amongst AIC's. There seems to be a spirit of quietism in which church members are not encouraged to challenge the power of the powerful. Instead, the emphasis is on a personal struggle for survival.

A few other factors may influence such an acceptance of human limitations amongst AIC's. An emphasis on God's somewhat remote transcendence in traditional African cultures is well documented. According to a traditional African worldview, human beings are subjected to an interplay of powers beyond one's control. This often leads to fear and anxiety – unless the evil powers could be confronted by "the Spirit of God who is more powerful than any other spirit."[63] Security is therefore not found in human power but in God's own power. This emphasis clearly reflects the experiences of the powerless who have become disillusioned and skeptic about those who wield worldly power.

15.4 Hope in popular Christian literature in Afrikaans

a) Introduction

A third manifestation of hope in the South African context, that may be worth investigating, is that of white, Afrikaans speaking Christians within the reformed tradition.

The tragic history of apartheid in South Africa and the theological justification of apartheid by the leadership of the Dutch Reformed Church (DRC) are well-documented and need not be discussed here. Instead, the present focus is on the effects of the transition to democracy in 1994 on reformed Afrikaans speaking Christians in general and the members of the DRC specifically. What vision of hope for the future in South Africa, if any, may be found within such a context?

The urgency of this question has to be understood within the context of the role that those who lost political power could or should play in the formation of civil society in a new South Africa. A few observations and generalizations may be

---

63 *Speaking for ourselves* (1986:27).

needed here to understand the impetus of this question. The transition to democracy implied a loss of political power for whites in general and a loss of influence for the DRC in particular. For some this loss of power was traumatic, creating an environment of uncertainty. However, this was alleviated by the fact that those who had voting rights in the past retained much of their economic power. The policy of apartheid was to a considerable extent devised to uplift the predicament of "poor whites" in the first few decades of this century. In this respect the economic climate created by apartheid was indeed successful: most white families moved to urban areas where they eventually managed to become relatively affluent. Although economic privileges and job security are no longer assured, educational and financial conditions remain favorable for whites to prosper.

The social environment is much more complex. Apartheid implied social isolation in schools, neighborhoods and churches. This cultural isolation was amplified by the ideological support of Afrikaans language media. While this isolation is slowly disintegrating in many social institutions (schools, hospitals, neighborhoods), most local congregations of the DRC find it difficult to move beyond the old barriers. To make matters worse, affirmative action policies and public perceptions on the level of crime have created a climate where the affluent experience themselves as being threatened from all sides and therefore prefer to retreat into enclosures of safety behind high walls, barbed wire, and alarm systems. Many feel no longer inclined to dedicate their lives to social upliftment for all South Africans. They prefer to be left alone, to mind their own business, to make money, to gather for themselves whatever they can and to enjoy hedonistic, consumerist lifestyles. This continued isolation may perhaps explain the lukewarm attitudes (at best) of most members of the DRC towards the Reconstruction and Development Programme (RDP) of the ANC government. The activities of the Truth and Reconciliation Commission (TRC) met with open animosity from the Afrikaans press, while the DRC officially decided not to make a submission to the TRC. This indicates an unwillingness to come to terms with the past – even though many Afrikaans speaking people now distance themselves from apartheid (it is indeed hard to find anyone who ever supported apartheid!).

What is the vision of the future expressed by Afrikaans speaking Christians within this context? A sophisticated answer to this question will require a detailed sociological investigation – which is beyond the scope of this study. A different strategy had to be followed. A number of publications by Lux Verbi, one of the leading South African publishers of popular Christian literature in Afrikaans were therefore investigated. Only publications since 1994 and only those that touched somewhere in the text on the theme of hope were considered.

A few further comments are important in this regard. Although Lux Verbi has formal historical links with the DRC, its (intended) readers include not only DRC members, but also Christians from other denominations as well as Afrikaans speaking Christians from the so-called colored community. An increasing number of popular English texts are also published by Lux Verbi.

Given the geographical limitations of Afrikaans as a language, the authors of Lux Verbi naturally have to keep the specific expectations of their readers into account. This does not necessarily imply that the views of the authors would simply mirror the hopes and fears of their readers. Some of the authors are or were pastors or lay leaders in DRC congregations and retain a strong pastoral emphasis in their work. Their style is perhaps less academic, less challenging, trying to meet their people where they are. Many of these publications appear in the form of diaries or shorter tracts. On the other hand, a number of authors[64] have a stronger academic background; many have completed doctorates, some are teaching theology at some or other university or college. Their texts are not overtly academic since Lux Verbi focuses on the market of popular literature. Such publications are therefore popularized and are often the result of a series of sermons or talks in a congregation. All authors tend to assume that an evangelical piety is (or was) prevalent amongst their implied readers.

It is also important to note that some authors (from both the above mentioned categories) are (as individuals) deliberately making an attempt to challenge the socio-political isolation of the DRC, while the work of other authors may simply reflect this isolation. Such authors often prefer to focus on the spiritual life of believers at a purely personal level.

These observations make any generalizations difficult, if not impossible. The eschatological road map that was developed and used in earlier chapters may nevertheless be helpful to plot the different notions of Christian hope reflected in these popular Christian publications in Afrikaans.

b) Christian hope for salvation from sin and victory over evil

What vision of hope for salvation from sin and victory over evil is expressed in the Lux Verbi literature?

One may expect a tendency in some publications to spiritualize the predicament of sin. Accordingly, sin is understood as separation from God. Salvation implies a restoration of one's personal relationship with God. This takes place through the forgiveness of sin. It implies a pardoning of any guilt as well as freedom from any feelings of guilt (also for reaping the benefits of apartheid?). Salvation is in this mold a present reality, providing assurance for believers in a threatening environment. This tendency is unmistakable in some of the literature:

- Ozrovech urges his readers to move beyond the struggle against sin and to accept that Christ has already achieved the victory over sin and to rejoice in this assurance.[65]
- In his diary, Johann Cilliers often covers the theme of hope and emphasizes that victory over sin and death has already been achieved through Christ's resurrection. The tone of his meditations is one of triumph over sin. Christian hope can

---

64 This category would include myself (EMC) who have published two manuscripts through Lux Verbi (*Rus vir die hele aarde* and *Die Bybel in fokus*). I therefore have to accept ownership and responsibility for any (hidden) criticisms that may be expressed in the text below on Lux Verbi's authors.

65 Ozrovech (1998:29).

therefore be characterized as joyful, friendly, untroubled and peaceful. This leads to the imperative to proclaim and practise the victory in the world. Cilliers does concretize this imperative, for example also by stating that the earth must be cleaned and cleansed from garbage.[66] Curiously, Cilliers, who often quotes Dutch and German case studies, seldom relates his message to the South African realities.[67] Even the issue of guilt and forgiveness is discussed in the relatively abstract religious terminology of forgiveness of sins before God and with no reference to the TRC.

This emphasis on the eschatological "already" is often coupled with an equally strong emphasis on the not-yet of a victory over evil. Indeed, the world in which we live is described as threatening, uncertain, full of violence and corruption. Believers can only trust in God that these evils will not become completely beyond anyone's control. This attitude clearly reflects the experience of those who have lost political power and distrust the ability of the current political establishment to address these evils. Victory over these forms of evil remains in God's hands only and will ultimately take place in a different dispensation, probably only in heaven one day.

- Nina Smit writes to women who feel threatened and are worried about theft, strikes, rape, violence, murders on elderly people, unrest in the country, economic uncertainty and inflation. Her implied readers experience a loss of social security in the transition to a new South Africa. The source of such evil is clearly located outside the white community, threatening those within. Her readers have become negative and pessimistic, with no vision for the future. She therefore calls on wives to create a haven of love within their own families and to reach out in love to those who hate. The challenge that she identifies is reconciliation and peace, not so much justice. Even though the future is uncertain, Christians can approach it with confidence because the future remains in God's hands. Smit thus urges her readers to try and maintain a positive attitude towards change in South Africa.[68]

Those authors who wish to challenge the socio-political isolation of (some of) the Lux Verbi readers are forced to follow a different strategy. They emphasize the need to establish signs of victory over poverty, suffering, deprivation and degradation in society. The heuristic key that is used to express this is the familiar one of signs of the coming kingdom, here on earth as it is in heaven.

- Bobby Loubser urges his Dutch Reformed audience in Empangeni, KwaZulu-

---

[66] Cilliers (1997), meditation for 16 December.

[67] The meditations for 28 & 29 December are possible exceptions although he does not refer to apartheid or the Truth & Reconciliation Commission at all and remain somewhat neutral in his examples.

[68] Smit (1994).

Natal, to approach the future during a time of transition with confidence because "a more beautiful future awaits us."[69] He challenges and urges them to cross the boundaries of social isolation and narrow-mindedness and to embrace the values of freedom, democracy, human dignity, human rights and tolerance in the new dispensation.

- Annes Nel and four colleagues make a similar appeal to Dutch Reformed Church members in Namibia. Their intended readers have lost a sense of social security, their traditional enemies (Swapo) are now in government; the policy of affirmative action inhibits employment prospects for white males, Christian education in schools is abolished. In their diary a whole section is devoted to the need for Christians to maintain a hopeful vision for the future – despite apparently difficult circumstances.[70]
- Hennie Pieterse discusses the theme of hope for the future during a time of transition in South Africa quite explicitly. He argues that whites have lived in isolation and affluence during the years of apartheid. The demise of apartheid has brought poverty, crime, violence and unemployment on the doorstep of his readers, resulting in a widespread sense of uncertainty and insecurity. He urges his Afrikaans readers to identify positive signs in these changes, referring to the Afrikaner's history of adapting to new circumstances, positive changes in Eastern Europe, the emerging vision of Justice, Peace and the Integrity of Creation, and God's salvific, if hidden involvement in history. Indeed, at the dawn of a new century, Christians should learn to discern these signs of hope. In this way Christian faith may kindle light amidst the darkness that surrounds us.[71]
- Several other authors also try to picture a vision of hope in a time of transition, Coenie Burger, for example, tells the story of Abraham and Sarah as a story of hope for a time of transition.[72] Van Niekerk reflects on the depths of despair and the Christian hope in a time of uncertainty.[73] Naude recalls a number of stories embodying the virtue of hope for a time of despair.[74]
- Deist writes to readers who realize that they are loosing their political power and that their social security and affluence can no longer be taken for granted. Deist argues that prosperity leads to a false understanding of the gospel and urges his readers to accept a form of spirituality that acknowledges life as a gift from God, that is based on discipleship and that does not worship God for the sake of the possible benefits that may ensue from this.[75]
- Several authors also emphasize the importance of notions of resistance and waiting for a spirituality of hope. We need to wait upon God in time of need,

69 Loubser (1996). The Afrikaans title of his meditations is, *'n Mooier toekoms wag*.

70 Nel (1995).

71 Pieterse (1994).

72 Burger (1994).

73 Van Niekerk (1994).

74 Naude (1997).

75 Deist (1994).

illness and suffering.[76]

c) Hope in the context of human finitude

In the theological roots of the Dutch Reformed Church a strong affinity to Scottish evangelicalism, reformed pietism and missionary zeal may be detected.[77] On the basis of this form of piety, one may expect a strong otherworldly eschatology where believers are promised an award in heaven one day.

The traditional evangelical beliefs in eternal life in the hereafter, the return of Christ, divine judgment and the resurrection of the body certainly remains an unquestioned assumption in the Lux Verbi publications on Christian hope. Insofar as these symbols are discussed, there is a clear preference for individualized forms of eschatology (instead of historical or cosmic dimensions of finitude), that is, the promise of life after death for the individual believer.[78]

- After a serious heart attack, JJ de Klerk assures his readers that death holds no threat for people who may die "in the Lord." Throughout the text he quotes the life stories of pious Afrikaner people, amongst them Totius, the famous church leader, poet and Afrikaner nationalist. The pilgrim may cross the boundary between time and eternity with the knowledge that God will carry us through this lonely hour. He rejects unbiblical fantasies about heaven but assures his readers that it is a place within the universe (!) where pain, sorrow, tears, handicaps and brokenness will be no more.[79] For believers heaven is not a "pie in the sky" but a present spiritual reality. We need to live in the present moment with vistas of eternity, patiently awaiting the full glory of heaven and the return of Christ.
- After the death of a son, Nico Louw, a DRC pastor, also finds comfort in the knowledge that his son is not really dead, but enjoys eternal life, in heaven, together with Jesus. Indeed, for him there must be a heaven, because it would otherwise be impossible to explain where his son has gone to.[80] The prospect of meeting his son in heaven is what gives him comfort, not the vain hope to receive his son back on earth. This also relativizes the importance of earthly matters like wealth, ambition, or time. The hope for eternal life and the imminent coming of Christ now replaces a preoccupation with this life.[81]

---

76 See, for example, De Klerk (1994:25).

77 Bosch (1984). The a-political expression of this evangelical piety together with a fundamentalist hermeneutical vacuum left room for a highly political justification of apartheid through a peculiar version of neo-Calvinist cosmology. This strong sense of personal piety, and an underlying sense of selective justice, explains why most members of the DRC could never understand why anyone in the struggle against apartheid would accuse them of idolatry or heresy.

78 Ozrovech (1998:8).

79 De Klerk (1994:52).

80 Louw (1996:38).

81 Louw (1996:50f).

- Ozrovech discusses death a surprising number of times in his diaries. He often links death with fear – for old age, for social insecurity (in the new South Africa?), for death, for being separated from God. In response, Ozrovech regards death as the final chapter in the salvation of human beings. Death for the caterpillar does not spell the end but a transition to the new life of a butterfly. Death is a new beginning, illustrating that this life is not what is ultimately important. Christ has promised us eternal life after death. The world is not our real home, but only a temporary canvas.[82] For Ozrovech and his readers the realism of a classic array of comforting symbols – eternal life, heaven and a reunion with loved ones beyond the grave – is beyond dispute and a source of comfort in the face of death. Death is not to be feared, in fact it is a friend, the entrance hall to eternity, an opportunity to meet God.
- In two books on aging, Anthonissen also addresses the fear of approaching death. Unlike Ozrovech, he argues that death is not simply to be welcomed by believers. It remains an imminent threat and it brings the pain of irreversible parting. With this realization, Anthonissen remains slow in offering easy comfort of a heavenly hereafter to the aging.[83]
- Botha investigates the theme of life beyond death, affirms the reality of the resurrection of Jesus and provides his readers detailed and graphic answers to questions about what life after death would be like.[84]

Two comments on these examples are important. Firstly, they are all related to personal dimensions of finitude. There seems to be a hesitation to even consider historical and cosmic dimensions of finitude. Unfortunately, the comfort that is offered on a personal level is undermined by the experience of historical insecurity (in the social context of white South Africans) and cosmic insecurity (where it becomes increasingly difficult to imagine heaven in the post-Ptolemaic world that many secularized, urbanized DRC members share).

Secondly, despite the deliberate attention given to the predicament of personal finitude and despite the consolation that these authors offer, it has to be noted that Christian hope is nevertheless not really preoccupied with the predicament of finitude. This is revealed in the very specific social contexts from within which these texts are written. It is only in limit experiences like a serious illness, approaching death or the death of a child that this aspect of Christian hope becomes central.

This tendency is not difficult to account for in a context of relative economic affluence. In such a context, one could scarcely expect people to hope for a dispensation that would be radically discontinuous with the present order. The emphasis of Christian hope is therefore on living this life and coming to terms with the forces that may threaten one's happiness. These may include a sense of social insecurity and the threats of crime and violence. But the most important threats to hope are perceived to come from within. Christian hope should therefore address

82 Ozrovech (1996).

83 Anthonissen (1993, 1994).

84 Botha (1998).

psychological or inter-personal tensions, frustrations and inadequacies.

d) Christian hope as the key to success

How should one come to terms with the limitations of human power and knowledge? Is salvation to be expected through a fruition of immanent forces in which God's presence may be detected? Or is salvation only possible through the intervention of a transcendent God? In response to this question a certain ambiguity in the perceptions of the authors and readers of Lux Verbi's publications may be detected. On the one hand, there is a quietistic and passive response to social threats.

- Ozrovech's considerable oeuvre[85] may, for example, be summarized in terms of the following kerugmatic schema: "We live in difficult times that are often depressing to us. But we may ultimately believe in God's faithfulness to care for us. Let us therefore pray together and put our trust in God. This will bring us some comfort and peace of mind."[86] In this way eschatology remains privatized, individualistic and a-political. "We simply have to rely on God to change a bad situation for the better."[87]

On the other hand, one has to acknowledge that Lux Verbi's readers are not amongst the poor, uneducated and relatively powerless members of South Africa's population. They are at least literate, have sufficient funds to buy books and participate in a culture of reading. One may therefore expect an equally strong reliance on immanent forces to come to terms with social threats. This would include an emphasis on a proper education, a culture of competitiveness from one's early youth, an industrious and entrepreneurial spirit, and ensuring financial security beyond retirement. For these secular concerns one scarcely need the help of an omniscient and omnipotent God – except to provide assistance to cope psychologically with distress and the stringent demands of these pursuits and the inevitable reality of failures.

- Le Roux links Christian hope, based on victory of Christ's resurrection with a successful (business)life – despite difficult times. He gives his readers various guidelines to aim, and achieve, success and satisfaction in this life. In a justification of upper-middle class morality he portrays hope as the key to initiative and enthusiasm.[88]

---

[85] He is one of the most prolific authors of popular Christian literature in Afrikaans. More copies of his diaries are printed and sold than of any other similar publication.

[86] This scheme and keywords such as "difficult times", "changing circumstances", "fear", "anxiety", "uncertainty", the importance of trust in God, God's faithfulness, God's loving care, the need for prayer, comfort and peace of mind – are abundantly present in all Ozrovech's publications. See especially Ozrovech (1998).

[87] Ozrovech (1996: 6 March).

[88] Le Roux (1996:57).

Several authors manage to maintain a balance between a trust in God's faithfulness and human responsibility within this world. Ozrovech, for example, links Christian hope explicitly with the responsibility "to appreciate God's beautiful creation and to preserve it intact." This is only possible through God who empowers us to live purposeful and triumphant Christian lives.[89]

- In a publication entitled, *Brug na môre*, Naude argues that the powerlessness of the cross constitutes the only way in which those Christians who had access to power in the previous dispensation can build a bridge toward the future. Naude's intended readers have been used to years of privilege and power and some have now become disillusioned. They may appreciate that the church does not thrive when it clings to power. It has to be based on the powerlessness of the cross. Only in this way can the cross become a powerful symbol (more so than symbols of national unity) to bridge the isolation caused by apartheid. Only the vulnerability of the cross can help white Christians to come to terms with the past in which they supported apartheid or tacitly enjoyed its privileges. Only the cross can help affluent people to share their bread with the hungry.[90]
- In *Krokus & saffraan* Hester Joubert provides inspiration for those who are trying to come to terms with an experience of loss – of one's dream, loved ones, a job, self-respect, health, youth, a car, or just a purse. She uses Kübler-Ross' analysis of the various phases of mourning to show that any experience of a loss requires time and patience to heal. She concludes with a chapter on hope that is said to be a gift from God; it cannot blossom simply through the power of positive thinking.[91]

These observations indicate that generalizations on the hope expressed in Lux Verbi literature would be inappropriate. There is both a reluctance to engage directly with the apartheid past and some attempts to help pious Afrikaans Christians through a period of transition in order to contribute in a meaningful way to the urgent demands of an emerging South African society. These attempts may facilitate an exposure of the selective justice that continues to characterize much of Afrikaner piety.

---

89 Ozrovech (1998:4).

90 Naude (1994).

91 Joubert (1997).

Part E: A vision of hope for the earth

In the previous two parts (C & D) we followed the trajectories of Christian hope through the centuries. We investigated various manifestations of hope in the twentieth century, also within the South African context. We noted the powers and limitations, the strengths and the weaknesses, the plurality and ambiguity of numerous eschatologies.

This part (E) has to provide the crucial ingredient for the argument of the study as a whole, namely to formulate a systematic vision of hope for the earth. What are Christians entitled to hope for? What is the content of a vision of hope for the earth? Such a vision, we have to remind ourselves, has to meet several requirements. It has to be a vision that can inspire an environmental spirituality, ethos and praxis – especially in the South African context. A vision of hope for the earth should be formulated in clear and accessible images, in language that can be recognized as authentically Christian by Christian communities. At the same time, it cannot simply reiterate a metaphorical wealth of Biblical images without clarifying the meaning and plausibility of these images with reference to the parameters of modern cosmology.

To approach this task, I will follow the earlier argument that any adequate Christian eschatology needs to respond to, but not to conflate and confuse, the three predicaments of evil, (human) finitude and the limitations of human knowledge and power. I maintain that an adequate response to the second and third predicaments should be based on and extrapolated from the soteriological core of the Christian gospel of salvation from sin.

In response to each of the three predicaments, the category of "a theology of life" (World Council of Churches) will be used to express a Christian vision of hope for life amidst the forces of death (Chapter 16), for life beyond death (Chapter 17) and for eternal life with God (Chapter 18).

16. A vision of life amidst the threats of death

16.1 Introduction: The urgency of a response to evil

In the new century, environmental degradation will threaten the flourishing of life on earth. What hope is there, from a Christian perspective, that the earth could be healed from such environmental destruction?

This question has to be put bluntly, in all its concreteness, without hiding an answer behind eschatological abstractions. At the dawn of a new century, Christian eschatology has to confront the powers of death and destruction. It has to address the concrete realities of economic injustice, political and patriarchal oppression, ethnic and religious conflict, and environmental degradation. A Christian vision of hope for the earth can only be meaningful if it focuses directly on the prevailing sense of a looming environmental crisis.[1]

An adequate answer to this question requires a recovery of the soteriological roots of Christian eschatology. Christian hope remains primordially a hope for salvation from sin, liberation from oppression and victory over evil. It has to address both the roots and the evil effects of sin. In the discussion of historical and contemporary manifestations of Christian hope we repeatedly noted the dangers of an independent eschatological curiosity in the predicaments of temporal finitude and spatial limitedness. A preoccupation with the predicament of finitude all too easily leads to rampant speculation and thus remains distant to our everyday concerns. A preoccupation with the limitations of human knowledge and power leads all too easily to an abstract, intellectualist form of eschatology. These dangers can only be avoided if the limitations in space and time are addressed within the context of the effects of sin and the many contemporary manifestations of evil. A world entangled in suffering, guilt and tears cries out for a visible victory over evil.[2]

A recovery of the soteriological roots of Christian eschatology obviously requires an adequate soteriology. Although such a task is clearly beyond the scope of the present study, a few observations will be offered in the next section (16.2). This will provide some parameters to articulate a Christian vision of healing for the earth in the section thereafter (16.3).

16.2 Hoping that the earth will be healed

In the Biblical roots of Christianity, salvation from sin is pictured in a rich array of symbols. These symbols often originated in concrete and specific predicaments from which "salvation" was experienced. These include, for example, experiences such as the following:

---

1 This is of special importance due to the widespread uncertainty caused by apocalyptic images of imminent environmental catastrophes.

2 Pannenberg (1991:164).

- Liberation amidst political oppression and tyranny,
- Liberation from enslavement,
- Release from captivity,
- Feeding in contexts of hunger, deprivation and drought,
- Justice in the context of economic exploitation,
- Safety amidst natural catastrophes,
- Peace and stability amidst political anarchy,
- Military victory in the context of threats to the national security,
- Rest for the weary and burdened,
- Healing from medical and psychological illnesses,
- Cancellation of economic debts,
- Forgiveness in the context of crimes committed against others,
- Sacrifice in the context of an irredeemable past,
- Reconciliation amidst family quarrels,
- Exorcism of evil spirits,
- The provision of ethical guidelines and wisdom to set contours needed for righteous living,
- Embrace in contexts of exclusion,[3]
- Victory over death.

During the centuries of theological reflection on these experiences of salvation especially two necessary, if ambiguous, processes were at work, namely a *generalization* and an *eschatologization* of these soteriological categories.

A degree of generalization and abstraction is inevitable in any theological reflection. In the reflection on the variety of soteriological experiences, this became crucial in the light of the Christian claim that salvation may be obtained through the cross and resurrection of Jesus, the Christ (only). This claim could only be made on the basis of the observation that sin (either one's own sins or the sins of others) is the root cause behind concrete experiences of injustice, oppression, suffering, evil, etc. In Christ, salvation from sin may be obtained. The rich and distinct biblical images of "salvation", "forgiveness", "victory", "healing", and "liberation" were thus fused together to focus on the salvation from sin in Christ.[4] This process of generalization did not prevent the emergence of three dominant theories of salvation, that is, the well-known distinction between, 1) a "classic" notion of salvation as victory over death and evil, 2) the "juridical" notion of the forgiveness of sin (guilt), and 3) the "modern" emphasis on the exemplary life of

---

3 Volf (1996).

4 McClendon (1994:105-122) discusses the same theme but comes to the different conclusion that a semantic process of *catachresis* could be identified here. This entails the "use of language drawn from one sphere in order to indicate something in another sphere that eludes existing speech" (1994:107). While *catachresis* may well have played a role in the New Testament witnesses, my proposal wishes to maintain something of the concreteness of the earlier salvific experiences.

Jesus Christ.

As a result of the dominance of the juridical model in the Western world, salvation from sin came to mean primarily the healing of a broken relationship with God and the benefits that may flow from this. The juridical model diagnoses the root of sin as an estrangement from God. It responds to sin at its very roots through the good news of the justification of *sinners* through God's grace alone (*sola gratia*). The doctrine of justification provides the very foundation of Christian hope, which is based, not on human action or on the power of human hopes, but on God's gracious verdict. The eschatological thrust of justification is equally important. We have to rely on what we hope for if we cannot rely on our own selves. Without this verdict we remain without hope and without God in the world (Eph 2:12).[5] Furthermore, the event of the justification of sinners is itself something final. Bonhoeffer perceived the eschatological dimension of the event of justification vividly: "God's compassion on a sinner must and can be heard only as God's final word; for otherwise it is not heard at all."[6]

The liberating effects of God's forgiveness are experienced through a life of faith. Justification provides the fresh start on the basis of which the sanctification of the lives of believers, the church and the whole earth is based.[7] Through the sanctifying work of the Holy Spirit, the evil effects of sin may be addressed and inverted, if only fragmentarily.[8]

However, justification as a response to the root of sin does not yet imply salvation from the evil effects of sin. We have to come to terms with the problem that salvation in Christ has not yet brought an end to injustice, oppression, and suffering. If our relationship with God is already healed at a personal level, the material benefits of such "salvation" have not yet become concrete and visible. Suffering, pain and death remain prevalent. The earth and its creatures remain under distress. This dilemma is often solved by postponing the final fulfillment of God's promises towards the eschaton. One day, all pain and suffering will come to an end. The eschaton is thus understood as the realization of the salvation that is hoped for. Present experiences of salvation are no more and no less than penultimate signs of the ultimate transformation of the whole created order in the presence of God.[9]

The result of these two processes (generalization and eschatologization) is an understandable hesitation to expect an immediate response to a particular predicament on the basis of the salvation in Christ. We do not necessarily expect a sick person to be healed on the basis of the salvation in Christ. We are often hesitant to link salvation in Christ directly with particular hopes for liberation from

---

5 Bonhoeffer (1995:122).

6 Bonhoeffer (1995:122).

7 See Gilkey (1976:283) and Sauter (1999:167-9) on the priority of the doctrine of justification, also for eschatology.

8 Gilkey (1976:284).

9 De Gruchy (1991:277-281).

oppression, restitution in cases of injustice and victory over evil. To cope with this tension between salvation in Christ and the prevailing reality of evil, salvation is often completely personalized and spiritualized. If the root of sin can be addressed through the justification of sinners, the evil effects of sin (which seem beyond anyone's control) somehow seems less serious. At worst, salvation is understood in an escapist way as salvation *from* the world and not also *of* the world. Granberg-Michaelson uses the apt image of a rescue operation to save the passengers from a burning ship in this regard. The passengers (humanity) is saved from the burning ship (the earth) by a rope (Jesus) hanging from a helicopter (God's Spirit) and brought to safety (heaven). In terms of this image there is little hope for the burning ship itself. However, the cosmic scope of God's salvation implies a loving concern for the burning ship itself.[10]

But what hope is there, in the light of the Christian gospel of salvation in Christ, for a devastated planet? What hope is there that the earth itself may be healed?

An adequate response to this question clearly has to resist the temptations of escapism and a purely spiritual and personalized notion of salvation. The salvation in Christ can only be taken for real if it makes a difference in this world. The Christian hope for salvation from sin therefore has to include a vision of hope for the earth itself. At the same time, a Christian vision of hope for the earth has to maintain the creative tension between the already and the not-yet of the salvation from sin, the liberation from oppression and the victory over evil promised by God.

An emphasis on the not-yet remains crucial precisely because of the reality of evil. Concrete experiences of environmental injustice and degradation continuously remind us that victory over evil has not yet been achieved. An eschatology where the tone of victory is too high will become suspiciously hollow and triumphalist - especially to the victims of (environmental) injustice.

At the same time, an emphasis on the already of God's salvation is also crucial. The Christian hope that victory is indeed assured is based on the promises of God. But Christian hope cannot live from promises that always remain unfulfilled (and therefore empty!). This can only lead to despair. Christian hope is based on the promises of God and strengthened by previous fulfillments of these promises, by previous experiences of salvation and liberation, most notably in the life, ministry, death and resurrection of Jesus, the Christ.[11] The announcement of promises elicits hope only when we can recognize them as promises of the true God whom we know *already*.[12] The *not-yet* of Christian hope only becomes plausible in the light

---

10 Granberg-Michaelson (1982).

11 In his *Theology of Hope*, Moltmann interpreted the incarnation of Jesus Christ also primarily in terms of the category of promise. The resurrection of Christ validates the promises of God, it does not really fulfill it. In this way Moltmann could evade questions about the historicity of the resurrection while emphasizing a futurist consummation of God's promises. See Pannenberg (1998:538).

12 Pannenberg (1998:540).

of salvation *already* experienced.[13] The liturgical community can anticipate the coming Christ only through a celebration of the presence of Christ and through a recollection of the incarnation, cross and resurrection of Jesus, the Christ. Or, to formulate this in explicitly trinitarian language: Christian hope is based on the promises of the God of Abraham, Isaac and Jacob. Our present fellowship with Christ is more than just a promise because it rests on an event of fulfillment that has taken place already. The work of the Spirit is that of a future completion of the salvation that is already guaranteed.[14] The presence of the Spirit provides a proleptic manifestation of this eschatological consummation.

Christian hope may therefore expect salvation also within the parameters of history itself.[15] It awaits the establishment of "justice, peace and the integrity of creation" here on earth. To live with a vision of hope for the earth calls on us to pray for the coming of God's kingdom *on earth*, *now* and not only in heaven, one day. For Christians, the quest for environmental justice is to establish signs of the coming of this kingdom in the face of environmental despair.

In the biblical roots of Christianity, the expectation of salvation from sin, liberation from oppression and victory over evil was expressed in a series of powerful eschatological symbols, for example, a new exodus, a renewed covenant, the year of the Jubilee, a new Davidic ruler, a new Jerusalem, a final verdict and exposure of evil, a festive banquet, and the coming of God's kingdom.[16] In each case a new dispensation was expected where God's all-encompassing *shalom* will prevail.

These eschatological symbols remain influential in Christian communities all over the world. They structure the language in which Christians address experiences of sin, suffering, injustice and evil. They articulate the expectation that God's promises of salvation will be fulfilled anew. In each new historical context there is a need to articulate this vision anew. This also applies to the current context of environmental degradation. Christian hope has to be expressed anew in an appropriate vision that would confront contemporary experiences of sin, suffering and evil directly. It will not be sufficient to imagine that simply any dream will do!

What metaphors and images should guide, inform and inspire the Christian hope for salvation from sin, liberation from oppression, victory over evil and

---

[13] See Moltmann (1979:20f) for a sophisticated discussion of the question whether Christian eschatology should be understood as "the future of what has already come" or as "the presence of what is still to come."

[14] Pannenberg (1998:550-1).

[15] See Moltmann (1996:129f) for a detailed discussion of the historical dimensions of Christian eschatology.

[16] These images provide the focus for what Nürnberger (1992, 1993, 1994, 1997) calls soteriological paradigms. Soteriology expresses the conviction that God intends the comprehensive well-being of the whole creation and the trust that the God of Jesus Christ will indeed establish this in future. Nürnberger traces the historical trajectories of several major soteriological paradigms, for example, the imperial paradigm awaiting the establishment of God's just rule, the patriarchal tradition, the conquest of chaos in the biblical paradigm of creation, and the emergence of the hope for a new heaven and a new earth.

healing from environmental degradation? In an ecumenical context, three articulations of such a vision of hope have become influential, namely the notion of a "sustainable community", the vision for "Justice, Peace and the Integrity of Creation" and the program for a "theology of life". Let us explore the background and content of these proposals in more detail.

16.3 Three ecumenical visions of hope

a) Sustainable community

Hope has been a dominant theme in the ecumenical movement since its inception. The theme of the second assembly of the World Council of Churches at Evanston (1954) was "Christ, the Hope of the World". The theme for the recent seventh assembly in Harare (1998) was again "Turn to God, rejoice in hope." Despite this emphasis on hope, differences in understanding the Christian hope already emerged at the Evanston assembly. Some emphasized the other-worldly dimension of Christian hope while others saw it as a powerful dynamic shaping history and society. The assembly nevertheless maintained the tone of joyful certainty and radiant expectation characterizing a Christian statement of hope.[17]

In the 1970's the WCC's Faith and Order commission began a process of reflecting about and accounting for the hope that is in us. The commission not only engaged in a biblical-theological exposition of Christian hope. It also started a process where groups of Christians, including women and youth, were asked to articulate their hopes as Christians today. This exercise indicated how intensely personal and contextual the language of hope is.[18] Some focused on the basis of Christian hope while others expressed specific desires – to have enough to eat, to have a home, to have a job. In the various expressions of hope there also emerged, as Konrad Raiser observes, a noteworthy "constant transfer of energies of hope from the South to the North, from the poor to the rich, from those without power to those burdened by the responsibility of exercising power, from those who hope against all hope to those who do not know what to hope for because they have everything."[19] The final report of the commission was adopted at the Faith and Order meeting in Bangalore in 1978.

An ecumenical vision of Christian hope, shaping history and society, was concretized at the Nairobi meeting in 1975. In the emphasis on a "Just, Participatory and Sustainable Society" environmental degradation became an important aspect of the social agenda of the World Council of Churches. The introduction of the notion of sustainability expressed the realization of the "limits to growth" which followed the famous report to the Club of Rome in 1972. The assembly also commissioned the continued exploration of "The contribution of faith, science and technology in the struggle for a just and sustainable society."

---

[17] Raiser (1997:77-78).

[18] Raiser (1997:78).

[19] Raiser (1997:79).

This vision gave currency to the notion of "sustainability." Since then, it has been adopted widely in the secular world as well. The concept of "sustainable development" has received widespread currency to express an environmental alternative to the failure of earlier models of development and to the impossibility of unlimited economic growth on a finite planet. Development should be sustainable in terms of the earth's carrying capacity. In its white paper on an *Environmental policy for South Africa* (October 1996), the South African government also adopted a policy of sustainable development, that is, "development that meet the needs of the present while not compromising the needs of future generations."

The value of the notion of sustainable development is that it serves as an important corrective against expansionist notions of economic growth. It reminds us that unlimited economic growth is not sustainable and simply not possible in a world where resources remain limited. However, the notion of sustainable development remains somewhat elusive. Some regard it as a euphemism used by entrepreneurs for "business as usual", that is, economic growth, qualified by a few environmental cautions. When faced with a choice between development and a sustainable environment, the interests of developers and entrepreneurs (who can often provide short-term economic gain in terms of employment) regularly seems to receive a priority.

The abuse of the notion of sustainable development has led many in the ecumenical movement to argue that the notion of *development* itself remains problematic. In response, Rasmussen suggests that the emphasis in many indigenous theologies on community[20] should be linked to the discourse on sustainability

---

20 Numerous indigenous theologians have emphasized a sense of *community* in an attempt to retrieve the ecological wisdom of indigenous peoples, for example from within an American Indian, Latin American, Aboriginal, Philippine, Pacific or African context. These retrievals respond to the economic processes of fragmentation that destroy both indigenous cultures and whole ecosystems. In virtually all these indigenous theologies the harmonious relationship between humanity and nature in pre-industrial cultures is praised and celebrated in songs and legends. There is a sense of wonder for the fecundity of life, for the land and all the creatures that live from it, for the cycles of the seasons. There is an almost overwhelming emphasis on notions of interrelatedness, mutual dependence, reciprocity, ecological balance, wholeness, the integrated web of life, and especially *community*. The world exists as an intricate balance of parts. Human beings must recognize this balance and strive to maintain and stay within this cosmic balance. The earth is regarded as a living being that must be treated with respect and loving care. Everything from hunting to healing is a recognition and affirmation of the sacredness of life.

African contributions to an ecological theology have stressed the importance of an African sense of community, interconnectedness, pan-vitalism, etc. Asante use the concept of "pan-vitalism", Harvey Sindima speaks of the bondedness, sacredness and fecundity of the "community of life", while Gabriel Setiloane celebrates an African biocentric theology and ethos:

> "Reality is inseparable. The African is kin to all creatures - gods, spirits and nature ... The whole of nature must be understood as sacred because it derives its being from the Supreme Being who is the Creator-Animator of the universe" (Emmanuel

and thus proposes a notion of "sustainable community". This echoes earlier work by John Cobb and Herman Daly on sustainability.[21] These authors also emphasized the importance of retrieving a sense of ecological community.

What does such a vision for a *sustainable community* imply? Rasmussen identifies the following characteristics of a sustainable community:

- It is *ecologically sustainable*. Unlimited material growth on a finite planet is simply not possible. We can only survive on this planet if we follow its household rules, not ours. This means that renewable resources are consumed no faster than they can be renewed, that non-renewable resources are consumed no faster than renewable resources can be found and that wastes are discharged at a rate no greater than they can be processed by nature or human devices.[22]
- It provides *sufficient sustenance* for all. While some live in relative luxury, more than a billion people are not able to obtain a calorie-adequate diet (the World Health Organization's definition of the poverty-line). A sustainable community implies that such people should gain access to energy, resources, work and land in order to obtain sufficient sustenance and their fair share of the earth's resources. This calls for a new sense of what is "enough" or satisfactory (*satis* = enough). We need to learn again how to appreciate the simple things in life (which is often for free). We need to adopt a lifestyle based on the virtue of simplicity, of being content with what is sufficient.
- It calls for a *working together in community*. In a sustainable community wealth is defined as the well-being of the whole community. This requires a sense of caring for one another and not just of gaining material prosperity. All economic activity, including paid and unpaid labor, should be conducive to community well-being.
- It requires *participation by all*. This means both the right and responsibility to share in work for the common good of the community. Human dignity requires a dispensation where people will not be excluded from work but will participate in decisions pertaining to their work and to what is best for their community.
- It *respects diversity*. A sense of community does not imply rigid conformity or monotonous identity but calls for an appreciation of community: "Nature depends on diversity, thrives on differences, and perishes in the imbalance of

---

Asante, Ghana, 1985).

"The African idea of community refers to bondedness; the act of sharing and living in the one common symbol – life – which enables people to live in communion and communication with each other and nature. Living in communication allows stories or life experiences of others to become one's own" (Harvey Sindima, Malawi, 1989).

"We Africans sincerely believe that by taking into its fabric these African interpretations and views about the universe, creation and nature, the Christian understanding is enriched rather than impoverished and the image of God becomes more worthy, inspiring greater wonder, love and praise." (Gabriel Setiloane, South Africa 1995).

21 Cobb (1989) and Cobb & Daly (1994).

22 Béguin-Austin (1993:15).

> uniformity. Healthy systems are highly varied and specific to time and place. Nature is not mass-produced."[23]

The urgency and polemic thrust of these notions of sustainability and community cannot be denied. The notion of sustainability provides a clear indication of the social values that are required for a new century. However, the heuristic value of a notion of sustainable community calls for further critical investigation. Where can a model for such a sustainable community be found? Does it not evoke a romantic agrarian dream of a "sweet little village" from a bygone age?

Hans van Hoogstraten questions the idealistic presuppositions of this notion of community. He asks what the basis is for a positive evaluation of the "good community" versus the "bad individual." It seems to be based on the assumption that people live in bio-physical communities and because virtues such as sympathy are dominant communal features, people should follow an economic practice that serves and strengthens the "original" community. The inherent sense of connectedness and relatedness, derived from some features of the biosphere, constitutes the magic formula to retrieve this sense of community.[24]

Van Hoogstraten argues that a sense of "original community" cannot be defended historically. He shows how the Greek *polis* – which Cobb & Daly use as a paradigm – was systematically plagued by the structural inequalities of slavery and patriarchy. Van Hoogstraten concludes:

> We cannot simply reawaken these lost communities; the result will inevitably be either a harmless or harmful idealistic concept. Emancipation, communication, technology, secularization, and the market economy have all contributed to the human community's disappearance as a historical reality. ... Community cannot function as a saving concept, at least not in the sense of an anthropologically or biologically founded postulate.[25]

The retrieval of an African sense of community (or *ubuntu*) is infested by similar caveats. The romanticized memory of a pre-colonial African village can all too easily mask the oppressive impact of authoritarian and patriarchal social structures.

Calls for a retrieval of a sense of community remain appropriate in terms of its polemic thrust against rugged individualism. However, this sense of community may easily degenerate into a subtle manipulation to accept authority and conformity. To escape from the narrow-mindedness of such communities can indeed be a liberating experience. This is also acknowledged (if somewhat hesitantly) by African people who have come to embrace an urban lifestyle.

In addition, the sustainability of pre-industrial societies should not be overestimated. Communities have had an adverse effect on the natural environment since the formation of the first human settlements. It is therefore a fallacy to regard the environmental crisis as a purely modern phenomenon. The shift from hunter-

---

23 Rasmussen (1996:114).

24 Van Hoogstraten (1998).

25 Van Hoogstraten (1998:43).

gatherer to agricultural societies during the neolithic period led to food surpluses, population growth and defined territories with organizational structures. From these settlements the first great civilizations developed. The rise and fall of many of the great civilizations may have been closely linked to environmental factors. Moltmann also comments on this link:

> There are many investigations of the connection between land and civilization which show that, for example, the cultures by the Euphrates and Tigris, the Roman cultures in North Africa, the Maya culture in Yucatan and other collapsed because the land was exploited recklessly and short-sightedly and the fertility of the soil was steadily destroyed. Emigration and the "deportation" of people became necessary, to save both the ground and human beings. It was especially the great empires which exploited their granaries and fertile provinces to feed their great cities and armies and also devastated them through pillaging.[26]

Ingemar Hedström adds in more evocative language: "All the great civilizations of the world began with the felling of the first tree ... the majority of them disappeared with the felling of the last tree."[27]

A notion of a sustainable community can therefore neither be assumed nor be retrieved from a primordial dispensation. It may *become* a regulative vision for the future, an inspiring dream that could install in us a sense of hope. It cannot be paradise regained, but only the promise thereof.[28]

b) Justice, Peace and the Integrity of Creation (JPIC)

The term "Justice, Peace and the Integrity of Creation" emerged at the Vancouver assembly of the World Council of Churches in 1983. However, the roots of the term are situated deep in the history of the ecumenical movement. Indeed, the concerns of JPIC are related to the very meaning of the term ecumenical. Rasmussen explains the links between economy, ecology and the ecumenical movement by referring to the Biblical image of *oikos* (house).

> Creation is pictured as a vast public household. The English words "economics", "ecumenics," and "ecology" all share the same root and reference. "Economics" means providing for the household's material and service needs and managing the household well. But the word also has a theological meaning. One of the classic theological expressions for bringing creation to full health is the unfolding drama of "the divine economy" ... One of the marks of that economy is shared abundance. "Ecumenics" means treating the inhabitants of the household as a single family, human and nonhuman together, and fostering the unity of that family. "Ecology" is knowledge of that systematic interdependence upon which the life of the household depends. And if English had adopted the Greek word for steward (*oikonomos*), we would immediately

26 Moltmann (1989:64-65).

27 Hedström (1990:111).

28 Haught (1993:111f).

recognize the steward as the trustee, the caretaker of creation imaged as *oikos*.[29]

The vision of Christian hope expressed in the notion of "Justice, Peace and the Integrity of Creation" stimulated the so called "conciliar process" in which churches all over the world were asked to commit themselves to this social agenda. This culminated at a World Convocation on JPIC in 1990 in Seoul. Some rather high hopes were expressed for this meeting: to be a "council" at which Christians from all confessions would speak with one voice on urgent problems in such a way that the world would have had to listen. This did not materialize due to some tensions between Christians from the North and from the South. Nevertheless, ten affirmations and four covenants were eventually adopted at this world convocation.

> Affirmation VII speaks of creation as beloved by God and calls on Christians to resist human exploitation of creation, the extinction of species, consumerism, pollution, climate change and policies that would lead to the destruction of life.
> Affirmation VIII states that the earth is the Lord's and claims that human use of land should allow the earth to replenish its life-giving resources and to provide the necessary space for all its creatures.[30]

To concretize these affirmations, the Seoul document called participants to enter into a covenant of solidarity and to commit themselves to building a culture that can live in harmony with creation's integrity.

Since 1983 numerous attempts have been made to clarify the somewhat vague notion of the "integrity of creation." One problem of the use of this term is its association and possible confusion with the notion of a *status integritas*. The term is also perhaps too often linked to a lyrical notion of the overflowing fullness (*pleroma*) or goodness of God's creation. According to Granberg-Michaelson, its vagueness and ambiguity may have been one of its strengths since it seems to invite new ecumenical discussions continuously. There are especially three connotations that contribute to the meaning of this notion:[31]

- It is often emphasized that the whole creation as a one time endowment has its own intrinsic integrity and dignity which has to be acknowledged and protected – like any person's dignity. From a theological perspective the dignity of the whole creation is derived from the confession that the earth is the Lord's. The Christian God is the God not only of the poor, but of all creatures whose integrity is violated.
- Secondly, the integratedness, the wholeness of creation, the mutual dependence and integral functioning of all forms of life and ecosystems as a whole, is of vital importance.

---

29 Rasmussen (1987:116-117). For a similar development of the notion of an ecumenical "household", see Mudge (1998:145f).

30 Preman Niles (1992:173-174).

31 Granberg-Michaelson (1994:102).

- Thirdly, the term suggest the internal relationships between social and environmental justice since creation is at its very roots a shared home for all forms of life. The notion of "integrity of creation" thus portrays a vision of shalom – of a just, equitable and peaceful community of creation.[32]

Jay McDaniel provides a clear summary of the meaning of the phrase "integrity of creation": "It refers to the value of all creatures in themselves, for one another, and for God, and their interconnectedness in a diverse whole that has unique value for God."[33]

c) A "theology of life"

In January 1994, after a process of restructuring, the central committee of the World Council of Churches approved a "Theology of Life" program in Unit III on Justice, Peace, Creation. This program seeks to integrate the concerns of "Justice, Peace and the Integrity of Creation" formulated at the WCC's Vancouver assembly (1983) verbally, thematically and programmatically.

The main concern of the theology of life program was not to fathom the rich philosophical and theological heritage of reflection on the concept of "life". Relatively few contributions have been made from within the context of the World Council of Churches to explain the theological and ethical content of a theology of life.[34] Instead, the program focused on grass roots experiences of the struggle for life. This is exemplified by the *Sokoni* encounter (a Swahili term for an African market place) held in 1996 in Nairobi, Kenya. Here the gift of life was celebrated amidst the stark economic realities on the African continent.[35] In the words of Edna Orteza:

> Long after the last bonfire where Kenyan traditional storyteller Bantu Mwaura had told one of his engaging tales, the spirit of Sokoni remained in the hearts of those who participated in this unprecedented event in the life and world of the World Council of Churches. The beating of the drums, the singing and dancing, the children's poetry, the youth's creative passion, the women's dramatic presentation of their agonies, aspirations and dreams – these, along with symbols, various art forms, traditional costumes colors and sounds have created enduring images for the people who came.[36]

If one subsequently reflects on the pathos of this "theology of life" program the

---

32 See also Rasmussen's (1996:99-107) analysis of six different connotations of this notion of the "integrity of creation."

33 McDaniel & Byrd (1990:165).

34 For literature on the notion of a "theology of life" within the context of the World Council of Churches, see Brinkman (1995), Granberg-Michaelson (1994), Mudge (1998:140-164), Raiser (1996), Rasmussen (1994), Robra (1996), Santa Ana (1995).

35 For a report on this event, see the edition of *Echoes* 97/11.

36 Orteza (1997:3).

following features emerge:

a) The notion of a theology of life should be understood within the context of grass roots experiences of the threats to life, that is, the powers of *death*: violent conflict, injustice and environmental degradation.[37] Unlimited economic growth and unsustainable levels of consumption are, for example, bound to a culture of death that will exhaust the planet's resources and threaten its life systems and integrity. This calls for a Christian praxis of resistance against the powers of death that destroys communities of life for the sake of political and economic power. A theology of life is thus born within the context of a struggle for survival[38] amidst the threats of death. It emerges from the experiences and perspectives of those for whom life is denied and in solidarity with these struggles. It seeks a life that is more than biological existence; life in the sense of self-sufficient, cultural, spiritual, political and economic sustainability.[39] Life is understood here concretely to include land, houses, work, food, health, education, environment, participation in social life, and cultural and religious celebration.[40] The struggles of the helpless for fullness of life in this way exemplify the survival of humanity as a whole and of all life on earth.

b) Within the struggle between life and death, a theology of life affirms faith in the God of life and denounces the idols of death. Or, in the words of Pablo Richard, "Where there is life, God is present; where there is death, there stands idolatry."[41] The vision of God as the Giver and Sustainer of life proclaims an alternative in which all will have life and nature will be whole.[42] Rooted in grass roots experiences of conflict, injustice and degradation, the *theology of life* seeks to offer thanks and praise to God's gracious gift of life in fellowship with all other living creatures. A *life-centered ethos*, based on such a theology of life, needs to reflect not only on a reverence for life (Albert Schweitzer), especially for the weaker, more vulnerable forms of life (an extension of the "preferential option for the

---

[37] See, for example, the contributions from women and indigenous peoples to the 1996/10 edition of *Echoes*.

[38] "Survival" is an important motif in many earlier contributions to an ecological theology. While these contributions speculated on the question whether (human) life on earth will survive, a new emphasis on survival is beginning to emerge, that is, how to survive in a life threatening (economic) system (see, e.g. Antonio 1994). An emphasis on "survival" may challenge an altruistic environmental ethos (while the rich may see beauty and grace in the movement of an animal, the poor may regard it as a source of food). The lives of many people in South Africa are indeed accurately depicted as a basic struggle for survival. Strangely, even the affluent often slip into a mode of "survival" by trying to protect what they have at all costs – amidst the real threats to life, property and employment security.

[39] See George Tinker's contribution to a theology of life (1996:21).

[40] Richard (1994:95).

[41] Richard (1994:95).

[42] Richard (1994:96).

poor"), but also on the material base of creation, that is, the material goods that permit life.[43] A *spirituality of life* perceives in land, health, housing, and work that enhances life, manifestations of God's glory.[44]

c) Precisely in the midst of this struggle for survival, the church as the household (*oikos*) of God may emerge as a sign of new life. If local Christian communities continually receive God's Spirit in fresh ways, they may embody the household rules (economics) that will foster life through the power of forgiveness, solidarity, and hospitality. In this way the local church may share in a mutual upbuilding (*oikodomé*[45]) of the larger, more global household, the household of the entire inhabited earth (*oikumene*).[46]

d) In this task women play a crucial role to give birth, to nurture life and to create the necessary conditions for life in community to flourish. In an African context, Bernadette Mbuy-Beya describes a life-centered spirituality for women in the following words:

> She gives life. Out of the child that she carries in her womb and whom she brings into the world, she tries to make the beginnings of a man or woman. She initiates the child to speech, to the mother tongue, to life in society and to spiritual and cultural values. In traditional society, the task of tilling the field is entrusted to the woman. She holds the secrets of the earth's fertility and develops a spirituality linked to the earth, which is expressed through songs an prayers to God at the beginning of each season. Protectress of life, she also plays the role of mediatrix in her family and her circle. She joins other women to try and ward off death that comes through war or family conflicts. She helps preserve social order by respecting the traditions which favor life.[47]

This notion of a theology of life amidst the forces of death may, in my view, provide an appropriate root metaphor for a contemporary Christian vision of hope for the earth. It may express the Biblical visions of shalom and of the reign of God for a new century. A clarification of the eschatological dimensions of a theology of life may at the same time enhance its theological depth. This task may draw on the rich heritage of philosophical and theological reflection on the notion of "life".[48]

---

43 In his ground-breaking essay on an ethics of life, Rasmussen (1994) identifies two aspects of the material base of life: 1) the need for space, an adequate habitat for life to flourish, and 2) the use and abuse of power in sharing this space with other creatures.

44 Richard (1994:95). Richard refers here to the dictum of Irenaeus "Gloria Dei vivens homo, gloria autem hominis visio Dei." (The glory of God is manifested in the flourishing of human and all other forms of life.)

45 See Müller-Fahrenholz (1995:108f) for a discussion of "ecodomy" as an upbuilding of the house of life.

46 See Mudge (1998:147-8) for a discussion of this household of life as an eschatological paradigm.

47 Mbuy-Beya (1994:73-74).

48 Moltmann (1997:18) lists several important recent contributions to a theology of life,

The more restricted task of this section will be to reflect on the soteriological and kerugmatic dimensions of this assignment.

16.4 Concluding comments: Life, death on earth and judgment

a) A theology of life is able to focus clearly on the predicament of sin and its evil consequences as these are manifested in the numerous contemporary threats to life. In response, it proclaims a vision of life. More specifically it has to affirm that the work of God's Spirit is to bring *new* life amidst the powers of death and destruction. In this way the soteriological roots of Christian eschatology may be affirmed.

The promise of new life will remain a utopian dream (always remaining not-yet) unless it can be rooted in the already of God's salvation. For a trinitarian Christian theology, this may be based on the central affirmations of the Christian faith. A few brief comments in this regard will have to suffice here:

In terms of the doctrine of God, we need to develop a vision of God's love for life, of God's creative, nurturing and corrective love spanning billions of years. God's loving care is not only visible in human history (God is the "hope of Israel" – Jer 14:8), but also in the emergence of life in the universe and more specifically on the earth, our planet. This love is not merely an esoteric, timeless communion, but a story which is lived in the present within the eschatological tension between the already of creation and the not yet of the consummation of all things.

The concept of "life" has rich Christological connotations. Where Jesus is present, there is life, sick people are healed, sad people are comforted, marginalized people are accepted, and demonized people are liberated.[49] In Christ, there is life in abundance (John 6). The mission of Christ is to bring new life, whole life, full life, shared life, unhindered life, everlasting life.[50] However, this new life is only possible within the dialectic between cross and resurrection. Renewed life is not possible without the sacrifice of death.

According to the Nicene Creed, God's Spirit is the "Giver of Life". All things are called into being through God's living breath (Psalm 104). The Spirit is not only the Source of life (*fons vitae*) but also of new life. The Spirit leads the whole creation from the forces of death to new life. It is God's vivifying Spirit who renews the face of the earth (Psalm 104:29f).[51] The sixth assembly of the WCC

---

namely the papal encyclical *Evangelium vitae* issued by Pope John Paul II (30 March 1995), Gustavo Gutiérrez's work *The God of life* (ET 1991), Chung Hyun Kyung's notion of the cosmic Web of Life (see 1994), Moltmann's own work *The Spirit of life* (1992), Michael Welker's *God the Spirit* (1994), and Geiko Müller-Fahrenholz's *God's Spirit transforms a world in crisis* (1995). See also McDaniel (1989) for another example of "a theology of reverence for life".

49 Cf. Moltmann (1997:19). Moltmann (1997:20) significantly adds that: "Jesus didn't bring a new religion into the world. What he brought was new life."

50 Moltmann (1997:19, 1998:61).

51 See Moltmann's (1997:111f) rich meditation on this theme.

therefore expressed the appropriate prayer "Come, Holy Spirit, renew your whole creation." Moltmann adds that hope for the reign of God in this dying world begins with the presence of this vivifying Spirit:[52] "*Missio Dei* is nothing less than the Father's sending of the vivifying Spirit into this world through the Son."[53] Furthermore: "The sending of the Holy Spirit is the revelation of God's indestructible affirmation of life and his marvelous joy in life."[54] From this it follows that the mission of the church is the proclamation of God's love for life and the ministry of bringing new life.

The announcement of the gospel of new life will become shallow and empty without a clear prophetic warning concerning the threats to life. These threats to life have to be spelled out in the clearest possible way. A vision of life without God's judgment on the forces that threaten life will remain hollow and will not be able to sustain an environmental praxis. A prophetic theology of life will only be adequate if it announces the fullness of life *and* denounces the threats to life. A theology of life needs to discern the idols of death.[55] No hope for resurrection is possible without the cross.

This realization that no adequate eschatology can avoid taking God's judgment seriously has important ecological ramifications. A Christian vision of hope for the healing of the earth does not necessarily imply that death and decay will not prematurely end the earth's many fragile ecosystems. The continuation of life is not an automatic (and therefore intrinsically hollow) assurance. The powers of death may still threaten and destroy life.[56] Only a theology of life that allows for the possibility of God's judgment and punishment will be able to survive such destruction.

For the Christian community – and for the earth – God's judgment need not be an expression of fear. In fact, it describes the content of Christian hope. The hope of the earth's victims (including its plants and animals) is that present forces of destruction will be exposed and halted by a just verdict. Only then can justice be served. Only then healing can take place. Only then the alienation between humanity and the earth can be put "right" in the presence of God.

By contrast, the planet's powerful may well fear judgment.[57] Indeed, no civilization built on a legacy of colonialism, slavery, imperialism, capitalism and consumerism will be able to escape God's judgment. History can only be redeemed

52 Moltmann (1998b:55).

53 Moltmann (1998:61).

54 Moltmann (1997:19).

55 Richard (1994:94).

56 Vischer (1993:72).

57 See Moltmann's comment (1996:135): "The person who possesses power is concerned that history should continue to run its course toward the goal he has designed for it. He understands future as the prolongation of his own present, so he swears by economic growth and scientific progress and seeks the increase of the power he already has. ... The person who possesses power fears the end of that power; the person who suffers under it hopes for its end." (Perhaps the exclusivist use of pronouns *is* appropriate here! – EMC.)

if it passes through God's judgment.[58] Israel was only permitted to return to God's land after 70 years of exile. According to Israel's historians the land had to recover because it was denied its Sabbath rest (2 Chron 36:21). Moltmann's warning is therefore appropriate: "If we deny the earth its Sabbath and thus its own spirituality, and exploit it non-stop, it will become desolate and void, and humanity will become extinct, so that the earth can recover from human wickedness."[59]

Judgment may indeed imply punishment. At the very least, the power and authority (in its economic, political, social and military manifestations) of the perpetrators of evil as well as the undue privileges of their beneficiaries[60] will have to come to an end. Of course, the notion that God's punishment may be enacted in the history of a person, a culture, nation or planet is fraught with many theological pitfalls – as the argument about the presumed sins of the blind man in John 9 clearly illustrates. However, this does not invalidate the possibility of punishment – despite the aversion that this may evoke amongst those with liberal sensitivities. James McClendon observes that suffering as deserved punishment may sometimes be painfully welcome: It is easier to suffer when I deserve it than when I do not (i.e. in the form of senseless and inexplicable suffering).[61] If punishment is often indirect and difficult to discern, it remains nevertheless as real as guilt. McClendon is perhaps entitled to add: "That some suffering is punishment is a step toward release for moderns mesmerized by what they take to be a morally empty cosmos."[62]

Perhaps a few further comments at a more personal level are appropriate here. Despite the thrust of this study on hope for the earth, I remain deeply pessimistic about the world that our children's children will inherit from us. I honestly do not think that we will realistically be able to avert some major environmental catastrophes. I do not see the world's affluent reducing their consumption of energy. I do not see the greed of logging and fishing companies being restricted. I do not see an amiable solution to global population problems – resulting in more poverty, hunger, epidemics and social insecurity. I do not see an end to deforestation, desertification and a loss of biodiversity. I do fear that the world will be a much less pleasant place to live in toward the end of the new century.

Christian hope is of course not the same as optimism. It does not necessarily exclude pessimism either. Both optimism and pessimism are dangerous options. Optimism suggests that change will occur naturally and that radical decisions are

---

58 Moltmann (1996:45) comments that the future must be redeemed from the power of history.

59 Moltmann (1997:85).

60 One valid critical observation on the impact of the Truth and Reconciliation Commission (TRC) in South Africa is that it focused too much on the "evil perpetrators" and the "innocent victims" of apartheid. This leaves much unsaid about the many beneficiaries of apartheid, those who tacitly enjoyed, employed and exploited favorable economic conditions and privileges under apartheid legislation.

61 McClendon (1994:175).

62 McClendon (1994:175).

less urgent. Pessimism suggests that change is impossible and that it is futile to try to prevent a disaster.[63] Hope is often born within desperate situations. It calls for resistance and defiance precisely within such contexts – even when no escape appears possible. To hope is to raise children even when disaster looms.

I am often intrigued by the figures of Jeremiah, Jesus and Augustine. All three of them lived in a time just before a major catastrophe was about to occur – the devastation of Jerusalem in 587 BCE, again in 70 CE, and the fall of Rome (from 410 CE). Each of them realized clearly that a crisis is looming in their own lifetimes. They probably sensed that a major catastrophe will not be averted – and history proved them correct. Unlike many contemporary prophets of doom, they took no pleasure in this realization. They knew that it would imply a destruction of most of what was dear to them (the state of Judah, the Roman world of culture and learning). Perhaps they even knew that centuries may have to pass before a new society will emerge from the ashes of the previous one. Again, with historical hindsight we know that this was indeed the case. However, what is most intriguing about these figures is precisely that they did not have the benefit of hindsight. The lives of Jeremiah, Jesus and Augustine provide us with concrete examples of what may be required in such a time. They fearlessly analyzed the roots of the looming crisis, showing the devastating effects of sin and indicating the rottenness from within their own societies. They did not distance themselves self-righteously from their own people, but acted in solidarity with them and stood with the victims who were crushed by the dominant forces in society. And yet, they retained a clear vision of hope, not for a continuation of the status quo, but for the emergence of a new community that would be cleansed from the evil of the old society.

With an environmental crisis looming, we also do not have the benefit of hindsight. We cannot assume that it is already too late.[64] We are not there yet. But we have to face at least the possibility that a major crisis may not be averted. When that time comes, we may draw inspiration from the examples of Jeremiah, Jesus and Augustine.

b) The notion of survival amidst the threats of death provides a clear focus on the predicament of evil. However, an adequate theology of life cannot respond to the predicament of evil only. It has to respond simultaneously to the predicament of finitude, transience and (natural) death. The promise of life will become empty without an acknowledgement of the reality of the death of individual human beings, animals, birds, fish, insects, trees, plants, species, ecosystems and of the

---

63 Ruether (1992:273). Ruether suggests that we need neither optimism nor pessimism but committed love. This committed love can only be empowered by a vision of hope – which Ruether also spells out in terms of a vision of the good society.

64 The presumed end of Western civilization has been debated ever since the publication of Oswald Spengler's *The decline of the West*. For a thorough discussion of the intricacies of this theme, see Körtner (1995). See also Ellul's (1973) assessment of Western culture, which he argues, have marched, step by step, down the road mapped out by Spengler. If Spengler's predictions have not come to pass immediately, they have not been proven false either. The Roman Empire took two centuries to collapse (1973:67-68).

earth itself.

A theology of life will have to recognize the transitoriness and finitude of life.[65] There is no possibility of life without death in any ecosystem. Transitoriness is only amplified by human sin and this manifests itself in the disturbance of the ecological balance. In this sense the result of sin is indeed death (Rom 6:23). A theology of life will therefore celebrate the gift of life amidst the struggle for survival. Life itself is a mystery which, theologically speaking, exists in all its transitoriness in the abundant life of God. This need of a theology of life to respond to the predicament of finitude leads us to the topic of the next chapter.

c) An adequate theology of life also has to reflect on the very possibility and conditions of life. It cannot assume that the flourishing of life on earth is simply a function of life itself. Despite the vast extension of human knowledge and power, we cannot solve the mystery of life itself. As Thomas Berry has often said, human beings cannot make even a blade of grass. But no blade of grass will be left if humans do not do everything in their knowledge and power to reverse the effects of environmental degradation.

A theology of life has to reflect on the origin and destiny of life itself. It has to clarify the notion that the Giver of life is God. And it has to consider the question how eternal life in God's presence may be imagined. It has to clarify the relationship between the reign of God as a reality present and active in history and the reign of God beyond history. This will be the task of Chapter 18.

---

65 Swimme & Berry (1992:244) adds the following provocative comment on death as a natural phenomenon: "While it is true that the various members of the natural community nourish each other, and that the death of the one is the life of the other, this is not ultimately an enmity, it is an intimacy. The total balance of the process is preserved. If there is a taking there is a giving. Without reciprocity the earth could not survive."

17. A vision of life beyond death

17.1 The urgency of a response to finitude

If salvation is understood as life with God, restored fellowship with fellow human beings and with the rest of creation, the faithful may be entitled to pray and hope that this fellowship will continue beyond death. In this way the hope for salvation is extended beyond the boundaries of death. The soteriological response to the predicament of sin is thus extrapolated towards an eschatological response to the predicament of finitude.

But why exactly should a Christian eschatology respond to the predicament of finitude? Will a vision of hope for life on earth free from environmental degradation here and now not suffice to inspire an environmental praxis, ethos, and spirituality?[1] Is the belief in life after death not (as Feuerbach and Marx recognized) a dangerous and egoistic illusion that could only detract us from our responsibility for this life and for this earth? The promise of life after death consoles people in their misery, makes them patient and meek and protects the existing social and political orders. Should we not therefore accept finitude as an integral part of the created order?

Schubert Ogden argues, for example, that the quest for immortality obscures the difference between God and humanity. It implies the rejection of the limitations posed by our creatureliness. It demands to be like God instead of accepting human limitations by living from God's grace alone.[2] John Cobb wonders whether there is not something questionable about "the desire to project this private, isolated sequence of experiences into the indefinite or even infinite future?"[3] Rosemary Radford Ruether concurs that the relentless quest for immortality is related to the unwillingness of the male ego to acknowledge his own limitations. The female body symbolizes corruptible bodiliness that one must flee in order to purify the soul for eternal life. In numerous classical theological texts (Ruether mentions those of Augustine and Thomas Aquinas) female life processes (pregnancy, birth, lactation, indeed female flesh as such) are portrayed as vile and impure and carry with them the taint of decay and death. She says: "The problem of personal immortality is created by an effort to absolutize personal or individual ego as itself everlasting, over against the total community of being."[4] Instead, Ruether suggests that we as human beings should accept our own finitude, our own human scale and accept death as the final relinquishment of individuated ego into the cosmic matrix of matter and energy. The earth is the womb out of which we arise at birth and into

---

1 McFague (1993:197f) and Ruether (1983:214f) focus their discussions on eschatology and ecology on this aspect of hope.

2 Ogden (1975:161).

3 Cobb (1972:12).

4 Ruether (1983:257).

whose womb we are content to return at death.[5] All the component parts of matter and energy that coalesced to make up our individuated self are not lost, but are taken up in the great matrix of being and thus become food for new beings to emerge.[6] Ruether concludes:

> We can do nothing about the 'immortal' dimension of our lives. It is not our calling to be concerned about the eternal meaning of our lives and religion should not make this the focus of its message. Our responsibility is to use our temporal life span to create a just and good community for our generation and for our children. It is in the hand of Holy Wisdom to forge out of our finite struggle truth and meaning for everlasting life. Our agnosticism about what this means is then the expression of our faith, our trust that Holy Wisdom will give transcendent meaning to our work, which is bounded by space and time.[7]

My impression is that a response to the predicament of finitude is nevertheless difficult to avoid. There are especially three reasons for the persistent inclination in Christian eschatology to move beyond the scope of soteriology. Let us look at these three reasons in more detail:[8]

a) Injustice, death and transience

Firstly, an appropriate response to transience in history cannot be avoided. While life endures, the devastating effects of sin can still be reversed. Economic injustice can be overturned through appropriate restitution, alienation between people can be restored through the power of forgiveness[9] and reconciliation, various threats to life can be removed and health can be restored. Ecological devastation can also be repaired, even though this may require hundreds of years.

The process of restoration and healing is not always easy and may in some

---

5 Ruether (1975:211).

6 Ruether 1983:258). She speaks elsewhere in more agnostic terms about the possibility of life beyond death. See Bouma-Prediger (1995:143-5) for an analysis of the development in Ruether's thinking about individual eschatology.

7 Ruether (1983:258). See Ruether (1993:253) for similar formulations. In death, we relinquish our small selves into the great Self in the hope that our creative work will be nourishing to the community of life. See also Moltmann's (1996:276) criticism of Ruether on this point. He argues that Christian hope is thus turned into "a pantheistic omnipresence of the everlasting matrix of life." He adds that "this eulogy on the good earth overlooks the fragility and destructability of the earth's organism and thus the earth's own need of redemption." It cannot take account of the earth's own finitude. Moltmann concludes: "And if we are allegedly in safe keeping in the bosom of the earth and its supposedly eternal cycles, what will happen when the earth dies in cold, or melts in the fierce heat of the sun?" (1996:276). This leaves the earth itself without hope.

8 These reasons again relate to the three aspects of the human predicament. The second aspect will be discussed in more detail in chapter 18.

9 See Hannah Arendt's (1959:212f) classic exposition of the liberating power of forgiveness to reverse the evil effects of previous actions.

cases be virtually impossible. Some forms of injustice are almost irreversible. Consider the lasting injuries caused by rape, physical mutilation, adultery, enslavement or deforestation. Moreover, when death intervenes, restoration becomes impossible in principle. In this way the predicament of finitude becomes a final hurdle thwarting the possibility of victory over evil in this life. This is why death retains its sting, why death remains an ultimate challenge to Christian hope.[10]

But there is more at stake here. Salvation can only have an impact on the continuation of the negative effects of injustice. It cannot undo the traumatic experience itself. Liberating praxis in the present can reduce future suffering but it cannot do anything about past experiences of suffering.[11] Such previous sufferings cannot simply be ameliorated on the basis of future goals. Every moment, every experience, every opportunity in the history of the earth is precious. If any moment is ruined by an experience of trauma this moment can never again be overturned. As Thomas Aquinas realized, even an almighty God cannot undo what has happened in history.[12] God can only respond to the effects of earlier events. If one has lost certain opportunities for good, if one's best years have been ruined through pain or injustice, this can never be given back. There will be a lasting sense of loss for the time that has gone by. Salvation from sin here stumbles against the obstacle of transitoriness.

There is an even deeper dimension to this predicament. In his excellent study on *Exclusion and embrace*, Miroslav Volf reflects on the requirements for reconciliation in contexts of extreme exclusion (e.g. between Jews and Nazis, or Croats and *cetniks*). Let us consider a hypothetical case where soldiers have raped and killed a girl in the presence of her mother. Volf would argue that healing (salvation) requires that the soldiers repent, confess their sins and guilt openly before God and the mother, seek appropriate forms of restitution, etc. Healing for the mother herself is only possible when she forgives them on the basis that God has forgiven them. But what about the lasting effects of the evil deed? How can this be undone? It can, in fact, never be undone. Reconciliation is only possible if the girl is able to forgive them too! Even God's forgiveness of our guilt will not be sufficient. But if the girl is dead, reconciliation again stumbles against the hurdle of finitude.[13]

Two classic possible responses to this problem may be noted here.

1) It is possible to argue that hardship, pain and suffering may be necessary to achieve a vision of a better world in future. We may have to endure negative experiences in order to establish the vision of Justice, Peace and the Integrity of

---

10 See Jeanrond (1995).

11 Volf (1996:134).

12 See Macquarrie (1978:120). He refers to *Summa contra gentiles* II, 25.

13 See Volf (1996). See also Moltmann's earlier comment: "It is not merely guilt, but ultimately death, that makes the past irretrievably past" (1967:267). I am grateful to Professor Volf for a discussion during which he clarified this eschatological dimension of a theology of reconciliation.

Creation. In South Africa many brave people have willingly given their lives in the struggle for political liberation. Some people may willingly suffer injustice for the benefits that others may experience in future. The virtue of such redemptive suffering cannot be denied. However, it should not blind us to confront the problem of the unvindicated suffering of innocent victims of injustice.

Even if the prophetic vision of Justice, Peace and the Integrity of Creation were to be established on earth somewhere in the future, this will not provide solace to the victims of the past. It cannot overturn the lasting effects of injustice to an earlier generation and the sense of loss that this implies. Present experiences of suffering can never be justified on the basis of future goals.[14] Metz therefore maintains that the history of human suffering cannot have any goal, although it can have a future. Eschatology cannot be reduced to teleology. The dynamic of history, Metz argues, "consists of the memory of suffering as a negative consciousness of future freedom and as a stimulus to overcome suffering within the framework of that freedom."[15]

Pannenberg also insists that the hope for the coming reign of God does not expect salvation only for a last generation – since only those who live in it will be able to share in it.[16] It has to be directed towards the transfiguration of all epochs of human history through the fire of divine judgment.[17] Hayes makes a similar observation: "If the meaning of each present moment is finally determined by what it can contribute to the creation of a better earthly future, how is it possible to avoid an ideology of the future in which the future becomes the idol to which each generation must be sacrificed."[18]

For Van de Beek, the establishment of a just society on earth could be a penultimate but never the final aim of creation.[19] The present suffering of innocent victims forms the main obstacle.[20] Such suffering can never be ameliorated by the achievement of future goals. The very reality of present suffering therefore raises the predicament of finitude with an unparalleled acuteness. Van de Beek asks:

> En dan doet zich opnieuw de vraag voor: 'Wat is de zin van dat alles geweest? Wat was de zin van deze kleine planeet en van deze kleine mens op een moment in oneindige ruimte en tijd?' Uiteindelijk kom we dan toch weer terug bij de eenvoudige vraag: Wat is het doel van mijn leven? En wat was het doel van het leven van het kind dat stierf langs de weg van Rwanda naar Zaïre dat bleef liggen omdat zijn ouders hem niet meer dragen konden?[21]

---

14 Van de Beek (1996:208), Pannenberg (1993:631).

15 Metz (1980:108).

16 Pannenberg (1998:586).

17 Pannenberg (1998:631).

18 Hayes (1989:145).

19 Van de Beek (1996:207f).

20 Van de Beek (1996:208-9) also mentions the ambiguities of world history and the anthropocentricism of a just society on earth as the final aim of the history of the cosmos.

21 Van de Beek (1996:210-211).

The goal of achieving a more just society is all too often abused to justify the means of revolution and the suffering of the victims of such a revolution. The romanticism of the "Grand March" (Milan Kundera), the self-congratulation and self-satisfaction for being involved in left-wing struggles for justice, remains a real temptation.[22] Furthermore, history provides ample illustrations of the ambiguities of the new social orders that emerge from previous struggles for justice. It is necessary to insist that no historical concretizing of salvation can (ever) be equated with God's kingdom.[23] This also applies to Constantinian Christendom, medieval Catholicism, Calvin's theocracy, Münzer's apocalyptic kingdom, The German Enlightenment, The French Revolution, 19th century bourgeois culture, a communist classless society in Russia or in China and the American dream of democracy and prosperity. It certainly applies to the "new" South Africa as well.

The reign of God does allow room for the directionality of history. It provides the norm and a lure for achieving penultimate goals in history (Gilkey).[24] It would be bizarre and irresponsible to deny the urgency of the quest to alleviate *future* suffering. However, the completion of the historical process is impossible within this process itself – if the impact of human sin, and therefore the ambiguity of history, is taken seriously. Gilkey argues that eschatological symbols have a double reference. The reign of God has an immediate and immanent reference to the new possibilities of social betterment in the immediate future. In addition, eschatological symbols must also have a transcendent reference beyond every historical possibility in order to function as a critical norm and ultimate goal for history.[25]

The reign of God will not come through sociological evolution or social revolution (left-wing or right-wing). It remains *God's* reign.[26] The predicament of evil can be solved within the parameters of time only by sacrificing past and present generations for the sake of the future. The question about the ultimate significance of every epoch, every species, every human life, every moment in the earth's history will simply have to be faced anew.[27]

2) In the history of the Christian tradition, the problem of unjust suffering was often addressed in terms of the hope for vindication in life after death. If justice is not experienced in this dispensation, consolation may be possible in a next dispensation. Restoration is possible in the life hereafter. In his touching work on a spirituality of hope, Galilea insists that the poor have a right to hope, also those

---

22 Kundera (1984).

23 See Gilkey (1968:53): "This is the besetting spiritual sin of revolutionaries: to interpret their own future eschatologically rather than historically, to raise to the level of religious ultimacy the valid hopes and dreams of a better but not a perfect day."

24 Gilkey (1976:285f).

25 Gilkey (1976:292). Sharon Welch (1990:106f) refers to this transcendent referent as the "eschatological reservation" that liberating praxis cannot be equated with the eschaton. She argues that this inhibits a commitment towards liberating praxis.

26 Küng (1984:213).

27 Wainwright (1988:356).

who will probably die poor. The hope and dignity of the poor cannot be based on human power and aspirations, not on the aspirations of the poor either.[28] It can only be based on God, the hope of the poor.[29] This emphasis on the hope of those who will die poor requires a widening of the scope of eschatology to respond not only to injustice but also to the predicament of finitude. James Cone argues, likewise, that the hope for life after death need not function in an escapist way, but may further the struggle against white supremacy. He says:

> To grasp for the future of God is to know that those who die for freedom have not died in vain; they will see the kingdom of God. This is precisely the meaning of our Lord's resurrection, and why we can fight against overwhelming odds. We believe in the future of God, a future that must become present ... If we really believe that death is not the last word, then we can fight, risking death for human freedom, knowing that the ultimate destiny of humankind is in the hands of God who has called us into being.[30]

Macquarrie maintains that the hope for life beyond death is born from a demand for justice and not simply the longing for a continuation of one's own personal life. Death that cuts short a promising life or strikes down a good person seems to deny a sense of justice (Kant).[31] Moltmann also stresses that the emergence of the belief in the resurrection of the dead was a way of expressing belief in the righteousness of God, which cannot be limited, even by death.[32] Furthermore, the victims of the past demand a just verdict.[33] The history of slavery, colonialism, and apartheid cannot simply be ignored. A sense of justice requires that the wicked should eventually be punished. Without judgment there is no justice. Without resurrection, justice cannot be complete.[34] The Christian hope for a final judgment is born from this sense of justice.[35] At the same time, Christians may hope that the judge will be the God whom we have come to know in Jesus Christ. We may hope that the love

---

28 Academic elites may certainly learn from the accumulated experience of the oppressed. The poor may also be the primary agents to rebuild a spirit of hope (Richard 1994:97). Yet, whatever "epistemological privilege" the poor may have can scarcely imply that the hope of the poor can be hope based on the grassroots movements of the poor themselves.

29 Galilea (1988:36).

30 Cone (1986:141), also (1997:142-145).

31 Macquarrie (1978:22), see also Barbour (1997:216).

32 Moltmann (1974:174).

33 See Van de Beek (1996:212): "De slachtoffers van de wereld vragen om een gericht. Het doel van de schepping kan niet zijn dat zij slechts dienen als het afval van de geschiedenis voor een glorieuze toekomst."

34 Suchocki (1982:177).

35 Pannenberg (1994:173) insists that, "If creation comes to completion only with the world's reconciliation and redemption, then the Creator is allied with us in the battle to overcome *evil* and to reduce and heal suffering in the world. Only the eschatological consummation of the world can definitely *demonstrate the righteousness of* God, and therefore his deity, in the work of creation."

of this God is far greater than we are inclined to desire or able to imagine, that it extends even to the wicked.[36]

Eschatology in this way functions as a form of theodicy: it is a defense of the compatibility of a good God with the evil in the world. It hopes that the unfair suffering of the poor will be compensated, while the wicked will be judged.[37] There is no theodicy without eschatology.

In the discussion below we will return to the relative adequacy of this strategy to deal with the predicaments of sin and finitude.[38]

b) Salvation is from God

There is a second reason why eschatology may be extrapolated beyond its soteriological core. Christian hope for salvation from sin is ultimately a hope in God and not just in human abilities, aspirations, dreams, expectations, or in "the power of positive thinking." Salvation and liberation for creation is not a human achievement. It is a gift from God. Nürnberger correctly insists that the future will be determined not by human achievement but by God's grace.[39] This recognition frees one from the slave master of ambition and competition. It transcends the disillusionment of failed revolutions and transcends our personal failures and limitations. Hope itself is a gift from God.

Two questions follow from this theological assertion.

a) What will the future in the presence of this God entail? Christian eschatology as hope in the God of Jesus Christ cannot easily relinquish a trust in the continued creative love of God.[40] If our future and the future of the earth itself are in God's hands, this requires a response to the predicament of finitude. Indeed, what future is there for the earth with God who transcends the boundaries of the earth's finitude as described in astrophysics?

b) In what way is God the hope of the world? In what way does God act in the world to bring victory over evil? These questions require an appropriate under-

---

36 Migliore (1991:247).

37 Drees (1990:119-120).

38 Pannenberg (1991a:173). Pannenberg curiously adds that: "They (creatures) praise God in their suffering, because this is part of their finitude. As creatures accept the finite existence God has given them, they live it out as an existence that is not grounded in itself but owed to another."

39 Nürnberger (1994:146).

40 See also Pannenberg (1995:81). He says: "... das Vertrauen auf Gott und die Unverbrüchlichkeit des Glaubenden mit dem ewigen Gott (ist) den Kern (die) aller eschatologischen Hoffnung der Christen ausmacht. Hat ein Mensch trotz seiner Endlichkeit und Vergänglichkeit wirkliche Gemeinschaft mit dem ewigen Gott, dann kann solche Gemeinschaft auch mit dem Abbruch unseres irdischen Lebens im Tode nicht enden. Gemeinschaft mit Gott über den Tod hinaus bedeutet aber nicht Auflösung unseres endlichen Daseins in den unendlichen Ozean des göttlichen Lebens."

standing of both God's immanence in the world (to explain that God can actually act within the parameters of history) and of God's transcendence (to explain that it is God who acts). This requires an eschatological response to the predicament of human limitations in space in order to clarify how God transcends our limitations.

These questions are urgent, precisely amidst the struggle for survival amidst the current threats to life. Lukas Vischer argues that the major weakness of the Conciliar process towards Justice, Peace and the Integrity of Creation was that it did not offer a spirituality that could rise above a sense of optimism and pessimism. It did not succeed in speaking convincingly of a hope that is based on God's grace, and independent of fulfillment in history. It therefore remains urgent to clarify the relationship between the reign of God as a reality present and active in history and the reign of God beyond history.[41] If this challenge is not accepted, it can only lead to Christian hope being domesticated into a shallow sense of optimism.

c) Suffering as a result of finitude

The environmental crisis has led to a new urgency to address the predicament of finitude. In Chapter 6 we noted several environmental dimensions of finitude: the death of species and not only of specimens, the disintegration of whole ecosystems, the numerous threats to life on earth and the loss of precious opportunities to reverse environmental degradation. We also noted the planetary and indeed cosmic dimensions of finitude.

Environmental degradation is primarily the product of human sin, of the pervasiveness of evil on earth. However, it is important to acknowledge that suffering, violence, decay, death, and the extinction of species formed an integral part of nature from the very beginning.[42] This assessment is abundantly clear from scientific reconstructions of the evolution of life on earth. Evolutionary science has rendered the assumption of an original cosmic perfection obsolete and unintelligible.[43] Although suffering is amplified by evil, it is an inherent part of God's creation in time.[44] Contrary to the teaching of the dominant trend in the Christian tradition,[45]

---

41 Vischer (1993:73).

42 See Pannenberg (1998:559), Tillich (1957:79) for a discussion of suffering as the result of finitude in distinction from suffering as a result of evil. This emphasis breaks with the dominant tradition from Athanasius who taught that, in spite of the natural corruptibility of our bodily life, we were originally destined to attain immortality through the participation of the soul in the Logos, and it is only because of our separation from God by sin that we were abandoned to the corruptibility of the flesh.

43 Haught (1998b:33). Haught says: "Evolutionary science clearly shows that there was, literally or historically, no original cosmic perfection. If such a notion still has figurative meaning, then nothing is to prevent us from locating this ideal world in the domain of the eschatological future."

44 See Moltmann (1981:50-51): "We cannot say 'if there were no sin, there would be no suffering.' Experience of suffering goes far beyond the experience of guilt and the experience of grace. It has roots in the limitations of created reality itself."

45 See, for example, the insistence of the Constitution *Gaudium et Spes* of the Second

death did not enter the world merely as a result of human sin.[46]

A theological distinction between the environmental effects of sin and the suffering resulting from the finitude of the natural environment is therefore important, if only for the sake of clarity and honesty. We need to acknowledge that there is a "darker side" to God's good, finite creation. There is a need to differentiate natural death from death as the judgment of God.[47] There is inevitably a tragic dimension to the human condition – as the classic Greek playwrights clearly recognized. This implies a need to accept this suffering as an element of finitude with what Tillich called an "ultimate courage."[48]

In the previous chapters we noted several attempts to grapple with such a distinction. Let us recall a few examples. Barth's controversial treatment of the "shadow side" of creation in all its finitude is well-known.[49] Van Ruler argued that the eschaton has to exceed God's good creation if only to make it "fireproof" against sin. Tillich insists that there was no utopia in the past, just as there will be no utopia in the future.[50] For Braaten, mortality is not sinful or evil; it is merely the mark of human finitude.[51] Moltmann's insistence that an eschatological consummation has to be radically new in relation to creation is born from a similar acknowledgement.[52] Pannenberg argues that creation is indeed good but not perfect or infinite (characteristics only applicable to God). The finitude of creation in distinction from an infinite God necessarily implies a degree of imperfection.[53] Haught also insists that creation "in the beginning" was not paradise but only the

---

Vatican Council: "Death is a consequence of sin. The Church's magisterium as authentic interpreter of the affirmations of Scripture and Tradition, teaches that death entered the world on account of man's sin. Even though man's nature is mortal, God has destined him not to die. Death was therefore contrary to the plans of God the Creator, and entered the world as a consequence of sin." (#1008). See Jeanrond (1995:112f) for a critical discussion of this passage.

46 See Moltmann (1981:50f) for a discussion of the causal connection between sin and suffering and death. Moltmann refers to Clement of Alexandria, Origen and Theodore of Mopsuestia who disputed such a causal connection. They taught that death was the result of human finitude. It is not a consequence of sin or a divine punishment.

47 Pannenberg (1998:559).

48 Tillich (1957:70).

49 Barth (*CD* 1.2, 1956:68f; *CD* 3.2, 1960:625f).

50 Tillich (1957:39-44).

51 Braaten (1974:63).

52 For an extensive discussion of this problem see Moltmann (1996:77).

53 See Pannenberg (1994:171): "The deeper reason for the possibility of sin, and therefore for the coming of evil into creation with all its consequences, is that there is an original imperfection in the creature because the creature is ontically limited ... Limitation is a necessary part of creaturehood insofar as every creature is different from God and his perfection." Pannenberg adds that this does not explain the origin of evil in any way. We are to seek the root of evil, rather, in revolt against the limit of finitude, in the refusal to accept one's own finitude, and in the related illusion of being like God (1994:172f).

promise thereof; it is merely a promising first phase in the evolutionary history of the cosmos.[54] This view is echoed by Boff who maintains that, "the earthly paradise does not mean nostalgia for a vanished golden age but the promise of a future that is still to come."[55] Arthur Peacocke comments that there is no evidence that human society was once a perfect society from which it later declined. All the evidence point to the gradual emergence of humanoid species with an increasing capacity for self-consciousness, sensitivity, and eventually moral responsibility.[56]

This observation of the suffering resulting from temporal finitude nevertheless calls for a few important theological qualifications.

a) It may be extremely difficult to discern specific instances where suffering was caused by purely "natural" processes. Indeed, even the destruction that is nowadays caused by the weather may be the result of human interference and therefore of the pervasive contamination of sin. The notion of a "natural" disaster may soon sound like nostalgia for a lost cosmos![57] Christian theology, especially in the Pauline, Augustinian and reformed traditions, has therefore, with valid reasons, retained its focus on the predicament of sin itself. The very question whether suffering and death is part of the created order itself may soon become speculative, purely academic and irrelevant for a world entangled in evil social structures.[58] In fact, such a theological pursuit may be born from a dubious curiosity that can easily distract our attention from the primary problem of sin. A clear focus on the effects of sin (one's own sins and those of others) and the victims of such sins is a prerequisite for a pastoral theology.

b) A clear distinction between suffering as a result of sin and as a result of temporal finitude remains crucial. The temptation to "explain" the emergence of sin, for example as the "inevitable" result of existence (finitude) in time, should be resisted. In this way, the predicaments of sin and of finitude are confused and conflated. The tendency to associate sinfulness with (awareness of) time itself is theologically dubious. This would constitute a denial of the goodness of creation, a depreciation of all that is finite,[59] and would make God (as the Creator) the author of evil. While death may be part of creation in time, sin is not. To err may be human, but

---

54 Haught (1993b:112). See also Hayes (1989:102f): "It is the fearful and painful quality of death that is the result of sin, and not the mere fact of biological death as such."

55 Boff (1997:83).

56 Peacocke (1989:16).

57 See Keller's (1997) observation that ordinary weather reports seemed to have acquired apocalyptic overtones.

58 See the comments by Pannenberg (1998:561): "... it is precisely the sinners' nonacceptance of their finitude that delivers them up to death." Also: "We are to seek the root of evil, rather, in revolt against the limit of finitude, in the refusal to accept one's own finitude, and in the related illusion of being like God (Gen 3:5)" (1991a:171).

59 Welch (1990:111).

to sin is not![60] Sin is not simply the result of human self-consciousness of its own temporality. Sin should not be associated with the process of becoming or evolutionary history.[61] The suffering and death that forms a necessary part of finitude is radicalized by the inexplicable and devastating consequences of the emergence of sin. Sin is the sting of death, not its physical cause.[62] Although an integrated eschatological response to the predicaments of finitude and evil is required, these two predicaments should not be conflated.

c) It is also important to note, as Barth amongst others reminds us, that death, as it actually encounters us, is the sign of God's judgment on us.[63] The finitude of human life stands in fact in the shadow of its guilt. Death is judgment. Death is for Barth the sinister but not intrinsically dark and menacing frontier where, for good or evil, we as human beings must finally meet our God.[64] Barth is quick to add that in death we are not only confronted by death but also by God. At our end, it is not only death, but also God who awaits us.[65]

Taking these important reservations into account, Christian eschatology has to clarify that the eschaton is indeed new in relation to creation. It not only brings salvation from sin and victory over evil. It also consummates the history of creation. At the same time, eschatology has to clarify that it is indeed this creation that will be consummated in the eschaton; it will not be replaced by another one, presumably somewhere in heaven. The continuity between creation and eschaton should indeed be recognizable in order to awaken a sense of hope. This emphasizes yet again the need to balance the eschatological tension between the continuity and discontinuity between creation and eschaton, my present body and my resurrected body, this life and eternal life, this earth and the new earth, *Urzeit* und *Endzeit*, this dispensation and the next.

Let us now look at some possibilities for an adequate response to this problem.

17.2 Hope for life beyond death

In the previous chapter we saw that some eschatological symbols – especially the prophetic vision of shalom and the proclamation of the coming of God's reign –

60 McClendon (1994:124).

61 Haught (1998b:33) argues that "Perfection, evolution helps us to see, lies in the eschatological future. It does lie in the indefinite temporal past, or in an eternal present immune to the travails of becoming." This may be true if imperfection is understood as the result of temporal finitude. However, if imperfection in the "indefinite temporal past" includes the emergence of sin, then sin is the result of creatureliness and God becomes the Creator the origin of sin and evil.

62 Tillich (1957:67-68).

63 Barth (*CD* 3.2, 1960:596).

64 Barth (*CD* 3.2, 1960:632).

65 Barth (*CD* 3.2, 1960:597).

respond primarily to the predicament of sin. A different cluster of eschatological symbols – most notably the resurrection of the dead, the return of Christ, the final judgment, the new Jerusalem, and the new earth – respond not only to the predicament of sin, but also to the predicament of finitude. The tension between continuity and discontinuity has traditionally been discussed in relationship to these eschatological symbols.

Unfortunately, these discussions have been notoriously plagued by a lack of clarity and intelligibility – more so than in the case of the first set of eschatological symbols. If a sense of continuity and of discontinuity becomes difficult to recognize, this will inevitably cloud any form of hope and consolation. Let us briefly look at some of the classic complications that any discussion of these symbols has to confront.

a) The hope for personal life beyond death

Christian hope is sometimes virtually exclusively understood as providing consolation in the face of death – one's own death or the death of loved ones. When our children ask us what happens when someone dies, many have a comforting answer at hand: When I die I will immediately go to heaven and there I will be "safely in the arms of Jesus." The consolation that this image provides is quickly eroded by several difficulties. These difficulties set the agenda to which numerous evangelical eschatologies respond. How can I be in heaven if it is my own recognizable body that is buried? In the past this problem could be solved through the classic distinction between soul and body. The human soul is immortal and returns to God (or descends into hell) immediately after death, while the mortal body remains in the grave. Soul and body will be reunited on the Last Day when the resurrection of the dead (read: of the body) will take place.

Although this image still survives in popular piety, it has been widely discredited in theological debates in the twentieth century.[66] Most theologians are now convinced that the human person cannot be neatly divided, like plywood, into the two or three separate spheres of body, soul and spirit.[67] The human personality is an inseparable psychosomatic unity. A disembodied mind or soul without a brain and cerebral activity is inconceivable.[68] This insight was coupled with the historical awareness that the notion of the immortality of the human soul was derived from Greek philosophy and not primarily from the Biblical roots of Christianity.[69] This brought a new realization that we as human beings are indeed thoroughly mortal in every aspect of our being. This made room for a renewed emphasis on the devastating consequences of sin. No part of the human person can escape death. It strikes us in the very core of our being.

---

66 This view was already held by Herman Bavinck, the influential Dutch reformed theologian (1956:447f). See Berkhof (1967:34-39) for a summary of this emerging consensus.

67 See, for example, Cullmann (1965:24f).

68 Macquarrie (1978:119).

69 See, for example, the classic essay by Cullmann (1965) for a discussion of this contrast.

This shift facilitated a new emphasis on the resurrection of the dead (instead of the immortality of the soul), now understood as the whole dead person, not only the dead body. The contrast is thus no longer between the mortal body and an immortal soul, but between a corruptible body and an incorruptible resurrection body, between creation corrupted by sin and new creation.[70] One problem with this notion is that the resurrection of my own dead body will presumably only take place in the very distant future. How can this provide consolation that I will be with God immediately after my death?[71] This leads to the classic theological question concerning the intermediate state – the position of the dead between death and resurrection. While many theologians have suggested solutions to harmonize the two beliefs,[72] none of these have become integrated in the spirituality of local Christian communities. It is simply regarded as "a difficult problem." The conceptual dissonance is more disturbing than consoling. In times of crisis, many therefore revert to the primary images of the soul being with God, while the belief in resurrection is affirmed but remains somewhat distant. The dualism and otherworldliness of this notion of the immortality of the soul can only serve to denigrate the world of mortal nature. The death of nature is the price that has to be paid for the life of the soul.[73]

The enthusiasm for the notion of the resurrection of the dead is also eroded by its lack of intelligibility within the parameters of modern cosmology. The resurrection of the dead is inconceivable without the coming of a new earth. But how should this image be conceived in the light of the earth's own irreversible finitude?

b) The end of the world

Through the history of the Christian tradition, it has usually been accepted that the world itself, and not only my own life, will eventually come to an end. Images such as the "signs of the time" (earthquakes, wars, famine), the visible appearance of Christ "on the clouds", the destruction of the earth in fire and brimstone, the divine judgment and the resurrection of the dead remain present in the popular imagination. While there is often a degree of vagueness in this regard, the following parameters are usually accepted:

In mainline churches, at least in South Africa, crude and detailed explications of the fulfillment of these images are often rejected – even where apocalyptic texts

---

70 Cullmann (1965:23).

71 Van de Beek (1996:216) comments that the notion that the dead will be "with Christ" immediately after death has been far more influential in Christian piety than the hope for the resurrection of the dead (in the far future?). This calls for a new appreciation of the relationship between eternity (being with God) and the future (the resurrection of the dead, which is predominantly related to the future, it has not yet taken place). See Van de Beek's (1996:217f) notion of death as being "out of time". See also Chapter 18 for a discussion of this relationship between eternity, time and the future.

72 See the detailed discussion by Berkouwer (1972) and the overview by Peters (1995).

73 Haught (1993b:135).

in the Bible are still read as predictions of events leading towards the end of the world. There may be some interest in millennialist, Adventist and dispensationalist debates, but there remains a degree of aversion to predictions of the date of the *parousia*, a reading of contemporary events as the literal fulfillments of biblical promises, and detailed descriptions of the millennium, a period of tribulation or the rapture. In other words: the world will (definitely!) come to an end eventually but we should not speculate too much about it. In the meantime we need to continue with our daily lives as if the End may come any day. While an earlier generation may have emphasized that this life is transitory and that we need to prepare ourselves for eternal life, the present generation is more content to focus on this life. The End will come as an almost rude interruption of our dreams and aspirations for the future. We no longer pray, "Let grace come and the world end" (Didache 10:6). We hope for a continuation of this life as long as this is possible.[74]

This popular belief concerning the end of the world is also confronted by several serious difficulties. Abundant biblical scholarship has shown that apocalyptic texts should not be interpreted as predictions for the long-term future. These texts have to be understood within their own historical contexts, with a distinct message for their own times. Christians simply have no privileged revealed knowledge that could enable them to predict the future.

Even where this insight has dawned there remains some reluctance to accept its implications. The images of the physical return of Christ, the destruction of the earth and the bodily resurrection of the dead have retained a certain tenacity in this regard. In evangelical Christian communities, very few would be willing to give up the conviction that, some time in the future, Jesus will indeed come again in some visible manner.

Yet, there are serious difficulties that simply have to be faced in this regard. We have seen in Chapter 4 that cosmologists suggest a very different picture of the future of the universe. Indeed, human beings will probably disappear from the earth within the next few million years (if not much sooner).[75] But the earth itself will survive the worst catastrophe that human beings can cause. Some form of life on earth may re-emerge beyond any such catastrophe. And the long-term fate of the earth seems sealed: it will be incinerated when the sun becomes a supernova in 5 billion years.

We may maintain the possibility of a radical intervention from God, abruptly bringing an end to the cosmic drama.[76] Jesus may still appear on the clouds some

---

74 Moltmann (1979:18).

75 Some Christians may, on this basis, be inclined to link the return of Christ with the extinction of the human species. This may constitute a more "localized eschatology." See also Pannenberg's (1993:26-7) notion that the Biblical conception of the End of time bears little resemblance to a notion of the end in contemporary cosmology. While a notion of localized eschatology may be helpful, Christian eschatology cannot be reduced to that if God's transcendence over the whole cosmos is to be affirmed and if the cosmic scope of Christian hope is to be retained.

76 This would constitute an "interventionist" form of eschatology. See Russell (1997:213)

time in the future, bringing with him the end of the world (the earth). Indeed, strange things are possible. But it should be acknowledged that this is a highly unlikely and theologically dubious scenario.[77] It is more probable that the human species, the earth and the universe itself will simply continue on its present adventurous journey without any such divine interventions.

Van de Beek comments in this regard that it seems much more difficult to confront what he calls "eschatological creationism" than creationism itself. Creationism assumes that Christians have privileged information on the origin of the universe on the basis of the Biblical creation narratives.[78] But this position is exegetically and theologically increasingly difficult to defend.[79]

If one rejects creationism, the same should apply for "eschatological creationism". We have even less privileged information to predict what will happen towards the end of history (of humanity, the earth and the universe). We simply do not know![80] We also cannot predict on the basis of Biblical evidence that a particular historical event will take place somewhere in the future. We cannot know that Jesus will indeed "come again", if understood as an event at the end of history.[81] Van de Beek concludes that it better to assume that the history of the earth will probably continue on its present adventurous course within the larger history of the cosmos. Perhaps the earth will be affected by some cosmic catastrophes, but even then its history will be governed by the laws of nature, not by some divine intervention in such laws.[82] Christian hope is not based on the possibility of divine intervention, but it may trust that the God of Jesus Christ, who transcends the whole cosmos, holds the future "in his hands."

---

and Peacocke (1993:141f) for a critique of such interventionist notions of God's way of acting in the world.

77 See already Brunner (1954:194) who also questions the direct connection between the end of the cosmos and the end of history.

78 The creation narratives in the Bible do not provide any scientific evidence (although they did make use of the best available "science" of the day). The Bible puts the origin of the universe in an even broader perspective than contemporary science does. It addresses the question how the history of the cosmos relates to whatever may transcend the whole cosmos. The answer of Biblical faith to this question is quite clear: God transcends the origin, history and destiny of the cosmos and continues to "hold the whole world in his hands."

79 Van de Beek (1996:215) notes that the universe may have been created 6000 years ago to seem as if it 15 billion years old, but that very few people would be willing to defend such a position today.

80 See also Robinson (1968:81) and Brunner (1954:198): "We can no more represent to ourselves the end of the world than we can imagine the creation of the world out of nothing."

81 The debate on the *parousia* of Christ remains unresolved and cannot be discussed here in detail. The aim of the observation on eschatological creationism in the text is to guard against any crudely realistic interpretation of the coming of Christ, namely as an event with cosmic scope at the end of (human?) history.

82 Van de Beek (1996:215).

c) The new earth

In the popular imagination the notion of a new earth is still dominated by the eschatological significance of heaven. A purely spiritual understanding of heaven often prevails. For many, heaven is a somewhat uninspiring place where the bodiless souls of the righteous will hover eternally and where choir practices will dominate the agenda. Others may picture quiet lush green fields, typically a beautiful holiday resort, where peace will prevail in the presence of God.[83]

The new appreciation for human bodiliness and the recognition of the theological significance of the resurrection of the body has coincided with an interest in the image of a new earth. Often the image of a new earth is simply regarded as a somewhat more concrete visualization of what heaven may be like. For others the new earth will, in fact, be a continuation of this earth. Heaven will be paradise on earth regained. God will renew and replenish the earth and prepare it for God's people.

This image may have a strong ecological impetus, but it also has to confront several difficulties. Where on earth will the billions of saved ones find enough space to live (on earth)? More importantly, this image denies the earth's own finitude. It simply assumes that the earth (and the sun's energy) will endure forever. But this is difficult to maintain – as we have seen in Chapter 6. If contemporary cosmological parameters are to be acknowledged, Christian hope simply cannot be based on an endless continuation of the earth itself. How, one has to ask, can God's people be said to exist in resurrected bodies in a new heaven and a new earth within a universe in which nothing similar to physical life in our present world will be able to exist?[84] Any contemporary retrieval of the biblical image of a "new earth" will simply have to confront this question directly.

17.3 The destiny of the cosmos remains in God's hands

The discussions here and in Chapter 13 show exactly how difficult it is to maintain the eschatological balance between continuity and discontinuity on the basis of the classic eschatological symbols of the resurrection of the dead, the return of Christ and the new earth. How then, should one understand the continuity and discontinuity between cosmos and eschaton? Let us investigate this question in more detail.

To escape from the difficulties of an intelligible reinterpretation of these eschatological symbols, one may be tempted to emphasize their metaphorical qualities. In Chapter 13 we noted some examples of such attempts to counter a crudely realistic interpretation of these eschatological symbols. Indeed, like all other symbols, metaphors, myths, images, and models, the resurrection of the dead, the return of Christ and the new earth are thoroughly human constructs. Such constructs may be extremely powerful. They may express a vision, for example a vision of Justice, Peace and the Integrity of Creation, that can inspire and stimulate an environmental

---

83 See McDannell & Lang (1988) for a more detailed discussion of various notions of heaven in the history of the Christian tradition.

84 Worthing (1996:184).

praxis. The value of such human constructs cannot be denied – especially to confront the predicament of evil. However, these constructs may also prove to be dangerous. The dream of life beyond death and of a new earth beyond this earth can, as Marx realized, easily function as an opiate. While a utopian vision of liberation from oppression (the predicament of sin) may be inspiring and liberating, visions of life beyond death (the predicament of finitude) may easily become illusionary and escapist. *Clearly, if these images are nothing more than mere human constructs they should either be avoided or be reinterpreted as a response to the predicament of sin only.*

Yet, a belief in the resurrection of the dead, the coming of Christ and the new earth remain alive and vivid in Christian piety. In Christian theology there is also a distinct hesitation to follow the route of abandoning these eschatological symbols altogether. In my view, there is a *theo*logical motivation for this hesitation. It is born from the belief in Godself, from the conviction that God is more than a human construct. Christian *theo*logy is, after all, bold enough to talk about God and not only about human experience, the Bible, the historical Jesus, the Christian tradition, contemporary society or the cosmos.

To believe in the existence of God is to believe that the future is also in God's hands.[85] Christian hope is ultimately a hope in God and not in human abilities, aspirations, dreams, expectations or "the power of positive thinking". Christians are convinced that the God whom they have met in the history of Israel, in the presence of Jesus Christ and through the work of the Spirit will also be there in future – after my death and beyond the death of the earth and of the universe itself. The final victory belongs to God, not to death (1 Cor 15). This conviction must guide any restatement of the meaning of the eschatological symbols in the Bible and the Christian creeds.[86] God will be there even "when the lights have gone out."[87]

The vision of the future which Christian eschatology portrays, is therefore simply the future with God.[88] All eschatological assertions are finally convictions about God.[89] Therefore, as in the beginning, in the end, God.[90] Christian hope is

---

85 See Schillebeeckx (1969:51): "Eschatology is the expression of the belief that history is in God's hands, that the history of the world can reach its fulfillment in communion with God and that it will be brought to this fulfillment in Christ who embodies God's promise."

86 Migliore (1991:239-240).

87 See Worthington (1996:182) for this formulation of the central question for a cosmic eschatology.

88 Gilkey puts this even stronger: Christian hope is concerned with the future *of* God, not only *with* God.

89 Robinson (1968:41). Robinson adds that every statement in eschatology is an inference from some aspect of the doctrine of God and that it must be judged and tested accordingly. False ideas about the "Last things" are the result of inadequate views on the doctrine of God. Robinson neatly takes the argument a step further. Within the Judaeo-Christian understanding of God as a God of history, eschatology is not only the expression of truths about God (the truth of the ultimate). Every statement about God is *ipso facto* an assertion about the end, a truth about eschatology (the ultimacy of the truth).

based on the belief that the world is not an autonomous entity that has its origin, history and destiny in itself.[91] The cosmic dimensions of space and time are transcended by God's presence in eternity. God's eternal presence permeates, embraces and governs the present world. The key to the future of the cosmos remains in God's hands. This theocentric vision provides perhaps the deepest reason why a Christian eschatology has to respond to the predicament of finitude. As Sallie McFague almost hesitantly observes: "And beyond even suffering we live with the hope against hope that defeat and death are not the last word, but that even the least body in the universe, the most insignificant, most vulnerable, most outcast one will participate in the resurrection of the body."[92]

In this way, Christian eschatology responds not only to the predicament of evil, but also to the predicament of the finitude of creation. Remarkably, eschatology also unites the concerns of a theology of salvation and of creation theology. It portrays a vision of God's creative, nurturing and corrective love for the cosmos over billions of years. In this vision, creation theology encompasses the drama of (human) salvation as the brief episode during which the sins of *homo sapiens* threatened the survival of life on this planet. Christian eschatology expresses the hope that, after death and decay, my life and the life of the earth itself will somehow be taken up into the loving presence of God. Christian eschatology as hope in the God of Jesus Christ cannot easily relinquish a trust in the continued creative love of God.

This theocentric focus may provide the key to understand the *theological* continuity between cosmos and eschaton. The continuity is primarily (but not exclusively) a continuity in Godself, a continuity in the creative love of God, in the faithfulness of God to the beloved creation. From this perspective, the notion of creation in the beginning indicates God's original intentions for the world (to achieve the comprehensive well-being of all God's creatures), while the notion of a new creation articulates the hope that these intentions will materialize in the end.[93]

This emphasis on the theological continuity between cosmos and eschaton raises the question whether the continuity is *only* theological. Is there no sense in which "I" will continue to exist in God's presence? Is there some way in which one may recognize this earth in the eschaton? Or, to phrase the question with a cosmic scope: "The question that remains, is whether the anticipated heat death constitutes a sort of cosmic Good Friday, and whether it makes sense to hope that beyond it

---

And further: "What *is* ultimately real *will be* ultimately realized" (1968:47). Unfortunately, Robinson does not develop the Christological and pneumatological dimensions of this insight.

90 See, for example the title of Robinson's book, *In the end God* (1968), and an article with the same title by Moltmann (1998).

91 This discerning phrase is derived from the Faith and Order Study Document, *Confessing the one faith*, produced by the World Council of Churches (1991:35).

92 McFague (1993:201-2).

93 Nürnberger (1994:141). Also Duchrow & Liedke (1987:55f).

lies an Easter for the universe."[94]

I would argue that an adequate reinterpretation of the belief in the resurrection of the body and the new earth is only possible on the basis of a theocentric focus.[95] Its point of departure should be that the ultimate victory belongs to God, not to death.[96] Only with such a theocentric focus will an exposition of these symbols not be obscured by a literalist understanding of the continuity between creation and eschaton. A theocentric vision of the relationship between cosmos and eschaton would require a clear vision of the relationship between God and the world, of God's immanence in and transcendence beyond the cosmos. Since this is the topic of the next chapter, a more detailed and integrated answer to the above questions will have to be postponed. An eschatological response to the predicaments of human limitations in time and in space can only be provided together.

A theocentric understanding of the continuity between creation and eschaton in terms of God's faithfulness, although crucial, remains by itself insufficient. A purely theocentric eschatology will remain somewhat vague, abstract and intellectualist.[97] A specifically *Christian* eschatology will witness to the best available clue to God's presence – the life, ministry and resurrection of Jesus Christ, the crucified.[98] This calls for an appreciation of the link between Christology and eschatology. Indeed, the best available analogy to appreciate the continuity and discontinuity between creation and eschaton is the relation between the incarnation and the resurrection of Jesus, the Christ. This analogy illuminates both the aspect of continuity (the resurrected Christ was recognized by the apostles as Jesus, with a little bit of help, that is) and of discontinuity (the resurrected Christ was no longer mortal and not subject to spatial restrictions). It also puts a vision of hope for the earth in Christological perspective. As Moltmann observes: "(Hope) sees in the resurrection of Christ not the eternity of heaven, but the future of the very earth on which his cross stands."[99]

This Christocentric focus is certainly crucial for a Christian eschatology, but by itself it also remains insufficient. It helps to imagine the discontinuity between creation and eschaton. But how does it help us, especially within the parameters of

---

94 Peters (1988:292).

95 See Moltmann's (1967:209) insistence that the expectation of the resurrection of the dead is not based on either anthropology or cosmology. It is *theo*logically based on the God of promise.

96 This conviction needs to guide any restatement of the meaning of the eschatological symbols of the Bible and the Christian creeds (Migliore 1991:239-240).

97 See McDannell & Lang's (1988:345) criticism of "theocentric minimalism", i.e. the notion of heaven in neo-orthodoxy which allows no images besides a focus on God alone.

98 See Moltmann (1996:261). Moltmann adds that "Cosmic eschatology also belongs within the framework of this remembered hope for Christ: the death and raising of the universe are the prelude to the expected new creation of all things and the 'new heaven and the new earth'."

99 Moltmann (1967:21).

modern cosmology, to appreciate the continuity between creation and eschaton? Van Ruler, for example, insists that the locus of continuity should not be reduced to God's faithfulness or to Christ's presence. He objects against a reduction of the eschaton to Christ as the Eschatos.[100] Whoever wishes to remain loyal to the cosmos cannot be satisfied with the *Eschatos* only! Hope for the earth requires an affirmation of the *eschata* as well. Van Ruler argues that God is not simply the origin and end of creation. This would imply a neo-Platonist view of creation as emanation where the cosmos is simply taken up into God's own being in the eschaton. The evolutionary history would then flow back into its own origin.[101] Christian eschatology, Van Ruler argues, is primarily related to the reign of God and not only to God's own eternal being. The eschaton also has to exist outside God. This allows for a continued existence of the created order distinct from God. Creation is not absolved into salvation. Ontology (and eschatology) cannot be reduced to soteriology.[102] An eschatological response to the predicament of finitude in space and time remains vital.

Schuurman also insists that God and the world must remain distinct in the eschaton. If God and the world are conflated in the eschaton, creatures take on characteristics usually ascribed only to God. The view that in the eschaton there will be God and only God, as before creation, must be rejected. In this way the world is either divinized or annihilated. It leads one to love this world either too much (as that which will become God) or too little (as that which will be annihilated).[103]

For both Van Ruler and Moltmann this requires an appreciation of the importance of pneumatology for eschatology. It is pneumatology that brings Christology and eschatology together.[104] The "life of the age to come" (Nicea) is the work of the Spirit. The biblical vision is not that creation will dissipate into God, but that God will come to dwell in creation, to live amongst us. Moltmann therefore talks about the "coming of God" to creation, the indwelling (*Shekinah*) of God's Spirit in creation. He suggests that a mutual indwelling of the world in God and of God in the world will come into being in the realm of aeonic time (see Chapter 13.4). This implies a reciprocal *perichoresis* where God's salvific presence infuses the world and where the world is taken up and transformed in God's presence.[105]

17.4 A cosmic pilgrimage and a homecoming banquet

A pneumatological focus in Christian eschatology affirms the creaturely continuity

---

[100] Van Ruler (1971:220f).

[101] See Farrow's (1998) critique that Moltmann's systematic contributions to theology reveal a similar neo-Platonist structure. The intention of Moltmann's notion of the protological *zimsum* and eschatological *aevum* may be to guard against emanation but the very need for these categories still reveals an emanationist structure.

[102] Van Ruler (1947:38; 1971:22).

[103] Schuurman (1991:159).

[104] Moltmann (1992:69).

[105] See already Moltmann (1981:157, also 1985:16f, 150f; 1996:307).

of creation and eschaton. However, this affirmation still does not, by itself, provide an adequate way of imagining this continuity. How should the classic Christian symbols of the resurrected *body*, the new *Jerusalem* and the new *earth* be expressed in a context shaped by contemporary cosmology? Let us investigate the power and limits of three alternative images to express this continuity anew, namely the notions of God's memory, a cosmic pilgrimage and the homecoming banquet. It should be kept in mind, though, that the plausibility of these images is dependent on the argument on God's transcendence that will be developed in the next chapter.

a) God's cosmic memory

Several theologians have explored the notion of God's cosmic memory to illuminate the relation between creation and eschaton.

Karl Barth's early emphasis on the qualitative difference between the existence of creation and time and God's existence in eternity remains influential in this regard. In Chapter 13 we already noted Barth's notion that time itself will come to an end. The time will come when the whole created reality will cease to exist, when time as a form of existence will no longer be, when there will be a present without an afterward. Then, Barth argues, everything, all events in history, "every little fly from the time of Hannibal" will return to be simultaneously present with God. Everything will "remain" before God.[106] Barth does not use the image of God's memory explicitly, but one is certainly tempted to ask whether everything will exist "in the mind of God" (only)?

The notion of a "cosmic memory" was developed more explicitly by Whitehead.[107] He introduced the notion of "objective immortality" and argued that whatever has happened in history can never be undone. Death cannot undo what has once occurred. The evil effects of what has happened may be reversed, but once something has occurred, this can never be wiped out from history, not even by an almighty God. It remains inscribed in history. Nothing will ever be able to wipe out the fact that the earth and the human species existed.[108] Furthermore, every event and act in history will make a difference throughout the future. Every present occasion is a selective incarnation of the whole past universe.[109] Every new event

---

[106] See Barth (*CD* 3.3, 1960:99f). Berkouwer (1956:156) paraphrases Barth's intentions in the following way: "God permits nothing to be lost – no hue in deepest ocean depths, no wing beat of an insect that lives but a day, nor the earliest time in earth's history, and certainly nothing in our life. God will not be alone in His eternity, but He will be together with His creature, His creature in its limited duration. Present before God – in this way the creature will be and will remain. This is the way in which it will be unfolded in the great rest of God. This is the preservation, a preservation that is not in addition to or after the preservation in time. This is the mystery of the preservation which must be understood in the light of the expression repeated twenty-six times in Psalm 136, 'For his mercy endureth forever.'" (Berkouwer 1956:164).

[107] Whitehead (1978:523).

[108] Haught (1993b:130).

[109] Cobb & Griffin (1976:23).

is an opportunity to establish new relationships between the building materials established by the past. Even the transition of death (in its personal and planetary dimensions) does not only imply disintegration, but also an opportunity for a wider, more cosmic reintegration. Haught suggests that:

> In this ecological interpretation of death we are released from our narrow relationship to a local frame of reference and given leave to relate more intimately to the whole universe. Death, whose sting is relationlessness, becomes the momentous event of entering finally and decisively into the most intimate relationship with the world and with the God whose compassionate sensitivity always include the world.[110]

In terms of the dipolar understanding of the relationship between God and the world in process thinking, this also means that God is influenced by every single event in history. Everything is inscribed in the "mind" of God. In God's eternal love everything is retrieved that has perished in time.[111] God is receptive and responsive to the history of the cosmos (Pittenger).[112] Our life history is a "book of life" (Hartshorne). When we die, the last page of the book is written, but it will not be destroyed. It remains forever in the memory of God.[113] When the earth itself will perish, it will remain inscribed in God's cosmic memory.[114]

This image of God's cosmic memory was further developed by John Macquarrie,[115] Norman Pittenger,[116] John Haught[117] and others. They argue that this memory is not to be understood as a mere retention or registration of what has happened. God's memory is not analogous to a photocopier or a recording from an omnipresent video camera.[118] The organic memory is not passive but active. It recollects and reorganizes in this recollection process. When something is remembered it comes alive again in the present. The act of remembrance may therefore have causal efficacy.[119] It may become a "dangerous memory" (Metz, Welch),

---

[110] Haught (1993b:139).

[111] Haught (1993b:132).

[112] Pittenger (1980:61-70).

[113] Hartshorne (1963), Pittenger (1980). See also the image used by Drees (1997:235) of a film roll that contains a whole life story (past, present and future) but which as a roll also contains the whole. For a defense of not only objective but also subjective immortality from a process perspective, see Suchocki (1982, 1988:81f).

[114] Haught (1993b:133) deduces from this objective immortality that there is no warrant for a disregard for the planet and its biodiversity. We have to preserve life because it contributes a richness to God's own life that cannot occur if we persist in our present indifference towards nature.

[115] Macquarrie (1978:119f).

[116] Pittenger (1980:61-70).

[117] Haught (1993b:116f, 131).

[118] See Moltmann (1996:70,73,331) for a similar criticism of Whitehead's notion of God's memory.

[119] Pittenger (1980:62).

undermining and healing systemic power imbalances.[120] This also leaves room for a loving memory, a memory that can forgive and that can change the way in which something is remembered. Maybe, there is also room for a God who can forget, who will forgive our iniquities and remember our sins no more (Jer 31:34).[121] The past cannot be undone, but it may be transformed, healed and taken up in the life of Godself.[122] We may therefore pray: "Remember me according to thy great mercy."[123] Evil may be turned upside down. The execution of Jesus on the cross may be remembered as a liberating event.[124] This is possible because the past is recalled through memory and thus becomes present.[125]

One obvious criticism against this image of God's cosmic memory is that it fails to allow for the independence of creation from God. Creation is simply taken up into God's existence. The distinction between Creator and creation thus remains blurred.[126] A "mere remembrance" of what was created only contributes to a filling of the reservoir of divine experience.[127] Geoffrey Wainwright notes that a "mere memorizing" seems to be pale reflection of the power of the risen Christ.[128] John Hick and Wolfhart Pannenberg note that the notion of God's memory assumes that there will be no human *life*, after death, no continuous consciousness, but simply someone else's memory of our lives.[129] James Nash adds that this implicit notion of a God, who saves by memorizing what has been in a flawless memory, is not the suffering servant but a supreme ego. It also begs the question whether God has favorite thoughts. Instead, Nash stresses the need for a retrieval of the Christian hope for resurrection of the dead.[130] Moltmann adds that the Christian hope is that the whole configuration of a person's life, the whole life history, and all the conditions that are meant by his or her name, the whole gestalt

---

[120] See Welch (1990:49-64).

[121] See the controversial suggestion by Volf (1996:131f) on the ambiguous need for "forgetting" for the sake of reconciliation.

[122] Macquarrie (1978:119f).

[123] Moltmann (1996:73).

[124] See Macquarrie (1978:120) and Gustav Aulen's notion of the possibility of a *Gesetz der Umlenkung* in which God uses evil events (e.g. the political census at the birth of Jesus; the death of Jesus) and turns their impact to good effects (e.g. the incarnation; the redemption in Christ).

[125] Macquarrie (1978:123-127) illustrates this with the analogy of observing stars. In this (present!) act we observe quite literally events from the past. It is therefore possible for the past and even the distant past to be present, not just in memory, but in direct perception. The past may therefore in some analogous way still be present to God and alive in God.

[126] Van de Beek (1996:232).

[127] Polkinghorne (1998:23f).

[128] Wainwright (1988:364).

[129] See Pannenberg (1984:132).

[130] Nash (1991:130-131).

will exist before God.[131]

The impact of such criticisms is less serious from within a deliberately panentheist position. If we will exist "only" in the mind of God in the eschaton, it may equally be argued that this is true also of our current existence. God is the one in whom "we live and move and have our being in God (Acts 17:28).[132] We may participate in the life of God now and when we (and the earth) no longer exist, we (and the earth) remain present forever in God's loving memory.[133] We are like the characters in a play who are allowed to develop a life of their own. Once a particular character is introduced by the author, this constrains the author in the way the plot is developed. Authors cannot fully control their own characters – who sometimes seem to prescribe their own subsequent behavior.[134] Likewise, we as human beings participate in the development of the plot of world history. At the end of the play, the whole drama is simultaneously present in God's active memory.[135]

b) A cosmic pilgrimage

The notion of God's cosmic memory may be developed further in terms of the image of a cosmic pilgrimage. This image has been used in the context of creation spirituality by authors such as Brian Swimme and James Conlon.[136] In a more reformed context, the ecological connotations of a "journey to the promised land" have been picked up by Paul Santmire in his well-known study on *The travail of nature*.[137] Let us explore its possible connotations in more detail.

A pilgrimage is a specific kind of journey. No journey is static, it requires an ongoing willingness to adapt to changing circumstances. It requires courage, endurance, and a sense of adventure and exploration.[138] The journey itself is often more important than the destination (which may simply be to return back home).[139] The aim of such a journey is to be enriched by the many experiences along the way. One cannot wait until later to benefit from the journey. One cannot always wait for tomorrow to experience the fullness of life. Every moment of the

---

131 Moltmann (1996:75).

132 See Peacoke (1993:157) for one of his numerous references to this text.

133 Macquarrie (1978:119) acknowledges the danger of reductionism and prefers to speak of "participating in the life of God now and in the eschaton."

134 Peacocke (1993:171).

135 Macquarrie (1978:118).

136 Conlon (1994), Swimme (1996).

137 Santmire (1985:23-25).

138 See the following comment derived from popular wisdom: "A journey is like marriage. The certain way to be wrong is to think that you can control it."

139 See also Robinson's suggestive image that the final move in a game of chess (e.g. check-mate) is not necessarily the decisive move. Though it concludes the game, it may by comparison with earlier moves be quite inconclusive (1968:66). Robinson also adds that, "The picture of the end-time is a representation of the check-mate which *must* follow because in fact it is already contained in the decisive move." (1968:72).

journey is important, although there may be some specifically kairotic experiences. A journey may become a rather lonesome experience if it not shared in good company, especially with a life-long companion. After the journey one may experience a sense of fulfillment, of satisfaction. One may draw inspiration from the recollection of the many good memories, especially if they are shared by others. These memories would be spoilt or even ruined by traumatic experiences, by devastating accidents along the way.

To suggest that a journey assumes the form of a pilgrimage helps to illuminate several other aspects. A pilgrimage is a sacred journey. It takes place on the basis of a calling and with a specific God-given mission. Its goal is not merely self-satisfaction, but to act for the sake of others. It often responds to a need, a predicament, the threat of a specific manifestation of evil. A pilgrimage is an act of love and may require sacrifice. Its ethos and rules are stricter than those of a journey. A pilgrim is continuously reminded of the need to fulfill the mission of the journey. A pilgrimage also requires a willingness to endure a sense of homelessness.[140]

The notion of a journey is a suitable metaphor for a human life lived. Victor Frankl once told the story of an aged couple who were depressed because they realized that the remaining days of their lives were diminishing day by day. Frankl's response was to liken life with a calendar. One may view every day as a page in the calendar that has to be torn out and thrown away once it has transpired. Alternatively, Frankl suggests, one may keep every page to write down some experiences and wisdom gained during that day. Then the focus shifts from the remaining days to the pack of pages, growing day by day. Towards old age this represent the good memories and accumulated wisdom of a lifetime of experience. Old age may thus become an increasingly rich time of recollection.

The evolutionary history of the cosmos may also be viewed as an "immense journey."[141] Haught suggests that we may envisage the entire cosmos as a pilgrimage, as a long story of homeless wandering.[142] The journey of the cosmos itself is again more important than its destination. Haught adds that every moment of the present phase of the cosmic journey is of ecological importance. We are now in a vital stage of the earth's pilgrimage that threatens to disrupt the journey completely. More specifically, it may bring the journey of the human species to a premature end, while other species have already been sacrificed ruthlessly.

The notion of a journey requires a very specific balancing of the temporal tensions between past, present and future. The origin of a journey is the vision of the future destination. It draws its inspiration from the hope to achieve certain (promised) goals. The aim of the journey (after the destination has been reached) is to enjoy the good memories, the wisdom accumulated during the course of the journey, the satisfaction that a particular goal has been achieved. But the focus of

---

140 See Haught's (1990) notion of cosmic homelessness. He suggests that religious homelessness is not foreign to the cosmos or to an ecological ethos because the cosmos itself shares in this indomitable restlessness.

141 Haught (1995:192f).

142 Haught (1993b:62).

the journey is the experience of present joy and fulfillment, to live each moment to the fullest. This is an exceptionally difficult assignment, as is illustrated in the following two excerpts.

Pascal, for example, comments on the malaise of temporality in this way:

> We never keep to the present. We recall the past; we anticipate the future as if we found it too slow in coming and were trying to hurry it up, or we recall the past, as if to stay its too rapid flight. We are so unwise that we wander about in times that do not belong to us, and do not think of the only one that does; so vain that we dream of times that are not and blindly flee the only one that is. The fact is that the present usually hurts .... Thus we never actually live, but hope to live; and, since we are always planning how to be happy, it is inevitable we should never be so.[143]

In *Zen and the art of motorcycle maintenance*, Robert Pirsig explains the same predicament with reference to endurance during mountain climbing. He recalls a pilgrimage of the character Phaedrus to holy Mount Kailas, high in the Himalayas, in the company of a holy man and his adherents. Although Phaedrus had sufficient physical strength and intellectual motivation, he never reached the mountain. After the third day he gave up, exhausted, and the pilgrimage went on without him. Phaedrus acknowledged that he was maybe using the mountain and the pilgrimage for himself, to broaden *his* experience. "He regarded himself as the fixed entity, not the pilgrimage or the mountain ... He speculated that the other pilgrims, the ones who reached the mountain, probably sensed the holiness of the mountain so intensely that each footstep was an act of devotion, an act of submission to this holiness. The holiness of the mountain infused into their own spirits enabled them to endure far more than anything he, with his greater physical strength could take."[144] Pirsig then comments on the need for an integration of past, present and future in the every footstep:

> To the untrained eye ego-climbing and selfless climbing may appear identical. Both kinds of climbers place one foot in front of the other. Both breathe in and out at the same rate. Both stop when tired. Both go forward when rested. But what a difference! The ego-climber is like an instrument that's out of adjustment. He puts his foot down an instant too soon or too late. He's likely to miss a beautiful passage of sunlight through the trees. He goes on when the sloppiness of his step shows he's tired. He rests at odd times. He looks up to the trail trying to see what's ahead even when he knows what's ahead because he just looked a second before. He goes too fast or too slow for the conditions and when he talks his talk is forever about somewhere else, something else. He's here but he's not here. He rejects the here, is unhappy with it, wants to be further up the trail but when he gets there will be just as unhappy because then *it* will be "here." What he's looking for, what he wants, is all around him, but he doesn't want that because it *is* all around him. Every step's an effort, both physically and spiritually, because he imagines his goal to be external and distant.[145]

---

143 Pensées 172. Quoted in Sauter (1999:175).

144 Pirsig (1974:211).

145 Pirsig (1974:211-212). The exclusivist use of male pronouns for ego-climbing is perhaps

To live in the moment, with a vision towards the future and on the basis of a memory of the past is indeed demanding. It requires a certain spirituality, perhaps something like a "spirituality of the road" (David Bosch).[146] In terms of Pirsig's description (with its Zen innuendos), a prerequisite of such a spirituality is to "come into step." To be in step is to appreciate the moment in between footsteps. The moment just before the next foot touches down. It does not help to linger in the past. One has to shift one's body weight with the necessary courage. It also does not help to hasten the movement. This will soon lead to exhaustion. One has to be willing to linger for a moment in the air, in anticipation of touching down and feeling the earth under one's feet anew. Only in this moment of lingering, only through a "rediscovery of slowness" (Stan Nadolny)[147] instead of an ever faster pace, will time be experienced and not merely measured. Only then will one be able to experience the presence of the eternal God in the moment.[148]

This image of a cosmic pilgrimage shares some of the disadvantages of the notion of God's cosmic memory. One of its strengths is that it helps to focus on the journey itself. However, its weakness is that is still does not clarify what happens to the history of the cosmos at the end. Is there any way in which creation remains distinct from God in the eschaton? Is it swallowed up completely in a panentheist notion of God?

c) A homecoming banquet

The legitimate motifs of the images of God's memory and a cosmic pilgrimage may be incorporated in the eschatological image of a homecoming banquet (see Psalm 23:5). If this motif is developed on the basis of the parable of the prodigal son,[149] this may help to internalize and appropriate its message in language and images more familiar to Christian communities.

In the parable of the prodigal son, the journey of the younger son (in this all-male cast) illustrates that a journey may go wrong from its very inception. The journey of this son leads to alienation with family members, to a hazardous waste of limited resources, and to self-destruction. The narrative is subsequently dominated by the need to address the effects of sin, evil, injustice and alienation.

Throughout the journey, the image of the loving and waiting father endures, the father who allows the son the freedom to go directly against the father's own wishes, the father who wants a faithful son and not an unwilling slave in his house. The father is waiting home at the end of the son's journey, calling, as it were, the son towards him through the power of persuasive love. The father is not pushing the narrative from its inception, but drawing the narrative towards its conclu-

---

appropriate! (EMC).

[146] Bosch (1979).

[147] See Moltmann (1998b:41).

[148] Moltmann (1998b:41).

[149] For some of the themes in the exposition of the parable of the prodigal son that is developed below, see the instructive discussion by Bailey (1983:158-206).

sion.[150] The arms of the waiting father remain open and ready to embrace the son.[151] And if the son comes close, the father disrespectfully runs to meet the son, while he is still on the way. He embraces the son and thus ensures that the other villagers do likewise. The son sees and appreciates the father for the first time for the loving parent whom he is.

The climax of the homecoming is a festive banquet for the whole village. The image is not only one of a father reflecting in old age on his son in loving memory. The symbolism of the banquet is concrete, graphic and earthly. It takes place in a spirit of gratitude, hospitality and joy. Everyone may participate in the banquet. Everyone has arrived, except the self-righteous older brother. Even at the feast table there remains unfinished business to be addressed. A comprehensive sense of well-being is only possible on the basis of reconciliation between the brothers, and one may add, with the village and the rest of creation. Even in the eschaton, there remains a lot of "unfinished business" to be done. The festival will not be complete if everybody does not take part.

One may add that, in the celebration of the Eucharist, Christian communities may already participate proleptically in this festive banquet.[152] The Eucharist is quite literally a foretaste, a prefiguration of an everlasting feasting which is to come. "The Eucharist is food for the journey meanwhile," says Geoffrey Wainwright.[153] Thus the church is an interim community, participating in and anticipating the eschatological fulfillment.

This image of a homecoming banquet emphasizes, more than the notion of God's memory and the image of a cosmic pilgrimage, the continued presence of creation in the eschaton. It also realizes the need to address the primary predicament of sin. But it still does not clarify the very possibility of such a homecoming. How should one imagine this in the light of the finitude of my own life, my family life, the earth and the whole cosmos? We will now have to address this crucial question.

---

150 Moltmann (1997:40) also referring to the parable of the prodigal son, comments eloquently: "But the ultimate reason for our hope is not to be found at all in what we want, wish for and wait for; the ultimate reason is that we are wanted, wished for and waited for. What is it that awaits us? Does anything await us at all, or are we alone? Whenever we base our hope on trust in the divine mystery, we feel deep down in our hearts: there is someone who is waiting for you, who is hoping for you, who believes in you. We are waited for as the prodigal son in the parable is waited for by his father." Moltmann (1997:41) concludes with the comment: "God isn't silent. God isn't dead. God is waiting."

151 Volf (1996:156f).

152 See the study by Wainwright (1978) on the relationship between eschatology and the Eucharist.

153 Wainwright (1988:367).

18. A vision of eternal life with God

18.1 The ecological urgency of God's transcendent presence

In previous chapters we noted the quest, most notably in philosophy and the sciences, to extend the frontiers of human knowledge and power (for knowledge is indeed power). We also noted the ecological ambiguity of this quest. In fact, from an ecological point of view it seems far more urgent to accept our human limitations than to extend these limits incessantly. Indeed, an eschatology that promises us that our limited knowledge and power may ultimately be transcended in the presence of God is highly questionable.

Nevertheless, if Christian hope for the earth is ultimately a hope in Godself (as I have argued in the previous chapter), it will be difficult to avoid a discussion of the limitations of human knowledge and power. Hope reaches for a future that is possible, desired, but beyond our own capacity to calculate or control. Hope relies on the God of the future who transcends our limited human power. But how is it possible to recognize this God in the first place – given the limitations of our human knowledge? This introduces the underlying eschatological necessity of reflecting on the very possibility of knowledge of God. The limitations of human knowledge are most poignantly illustrated on the very issue of obtaining trustworthy knowledge of God.

Let us reflect, for a moment, on this question. The following parameters seem to be important in this regard:

- The quest for the knowledge of God forms the epitome of the human quest to extend our knowledge and power. This is well illustrated in the somewhat obscure comments of two of the most well-known physicists of this century. Albert Einstein once said that the ultimate question that drives his scientific inquiry is to understand "how the old One thinks". The concluding sentence of Stephen Hawking's popular, *A brief history of time*, has also become famous: "For then we will be able to know the mind of God."[1] The notion of God that both these scientists assume, is not, of course, the Christian triune God, but a more pantheistic notion of the ultimate mystery of the universe. This mystery can only be known by penetrating deeper and deeper into the hidden secrets of the physical universe.
- In the popular imagination, the problem of obtaining knowledge of God is constituted by the ontological separation between God and the world. This may be born from the legacy of Greek influence on Christian theology or from the obvious acknowledgement that God cannot be observed empirically. The influence of a Newtonian worldview and its deist view of God is also apparent. Knowledge of God can only be obtained if the ontological separation between God and the world is somehow overcome. For some, this may be possible only

---

1 Hawking (1988:191).

through a special (miraculous?) revelation of God, while others may rely on common sense, human religiosity, culture, human conscience or human reason to obtain some knowledge of God (i.e. via a form of natural theology).

- According to the witness of the Hebrew prophets, it is human sin that separated us from God (Is 59:1-2). The apostle Paul insists that sin has alienated us from God's presence (Romans 3). A theist or panentheist notion of God assumes that the transcendent God is also present (immanent) in the world. This presence has not been annulled, but only obscured by the effects of sin. As a result, we cannot, like Jacob (Gen 32:30-31), see God from face to face and live. As God told Moses, no one who sees God's face can live (Ex 33:20). In Isaiah's vision of God in the temple, he has to exclaim: "Woe is me, I am lost, for I am a man of unclean lips, and I have seen the King, the Lord of hosts" (Is 6:5).[2] The problem of obtaining knowledge of God is therefore not due either to an ontological separation between God and the world, or to the limitations of human knowledge.[3] The problem is caused primarily by sin and not by the limitations in space and time which results from our createdness. The Christian kerugma requires from us to discover the power of love in the presence of Jesus Christ instead of a love for power.[4]

This emphasis on the effects of sin indicates yet again the priority of an eschatological response to the predicament of sin. An adequate response to the predicament of human limitations is only possible on the basis of a response to the predicament of sin. Knowledge of God can only be discussed within a soteriological context. In Chapter 16, I argued that any adequate response to sin is based on the promise of God for salvation from sin, liberation from oppression and victory over evil. Salvation is not a human achievement, it is ultimately a gift from God.

Yet, this emphasis on salvation as a gift from God remains insufficient if it not clear who the God is who establishes the victory over evil. Eschatology cannot be reduced to soteriology.[5] Christian eschatology has to return to the doctrine of God. It has to provide a plausible and intelligible clarification of the immanence and the

---

2 Pannenberg (1997:607).

3 See Bonhoeffer's (1971:282) insistence that God is beyond in the midst of our life. In a remarkable formulation, recognizing the boundaries of human knowledge, and in which all three the predicaments are drawn together, Bonhoeffer comments that:

> I should like to speak of God not on the boundaries but at the centre, not in weakness but in strength; and therefore not in death and guilt but in man's life and goodness. As to the boundaries, it seems to me better to be silent and leave the insoluble unsolved. Belief in the resurrection is not the 'solution' to the problem of death. God's 'beyond' is not the beyond of our cognitive faculties. The transcendence of epistemological theory has nothing to do with the transcendence of God. God is beyond in the midst of our life.

4 Nel (1995:75).

5 See especially Van Ruler (1972:109). Van Ruler emphasizes that the drama of human sin and salvation takes place within the wider context of God's love for creation itself. The eschaton therefore relates to creation and not only to sin.

transcendence of God. Let us investigate this need in more detail.

A discussion of God's immanence is crucial to show the very possibility of knowledge of God. Only in this way can it clarify how God interacts with the world to save it from sin. Likewise, a discussion of God's transcendence is equally important to clarify that it is indeed God (and not simply innate material possibilities) who acts in the world to bring victory over evil.

An emphasis on both God's immanence and God's transcendence is also crucial from an ecological point of view. It forms a *sine qua non* for a theological vision of hope for the earth.

Firstly, the immanence of God is crucial for an ecological theology in order to counter the ontological separation between God and the world adopted from neo-Platonic philosophy. The dominance of a deist notion of God in the Western world has had devastating ecological consequences. God kept moving increasingly into the sphere of transcendence, while the world came to be understood in purely immanent and this-worldly terms.[6] As a result, many Christians have been and still are *de facto* deists. This left room for the ruthless exploitation of nature that found religious justification in the notion that human beings are the self-appointed rulers over the world. Moltmann comments: "As God is the lord and owner of the whole world, so human beings must be concerned to become lords and owners of the earth, in order to prove themselves as the image of their God."[7]

Instead, Moltmann proposes a Trinitarian and specifically pneumatological understanding of the *immanence* of "God in creation" (the English title of his major work on creation).[8] The indwelling of God is evident in the whole creation, most notably in the celebration of the Sabbath. Moltmann explains: "If the creative God himself dwells in his creation, then he is making it his own home, "on earth as it is in heaven". All created beings then find in nearness to him the inexhaustible wellspring of their life, and for their part find home and rest in God."[9]

In this emphasis on God's immanence in the world Moltmann has been followed by almost all ecological theologians. Many have adopted an explicitly panentheist notion of God.[10] Sallie McFague's work on *The body of God* provides perhaps the most well-known example.[11] Leonardo Boff and process thinkers like John Haught follow a similar approach.[12] The aim of this emphasis on God's presence in the world is clear. It ensures that the world of nature itself is taken up in God's loving care and creative love.[13]

---

6 Moltmann (1989:54).

7 Moltmann (1989:55).

8 Moltmann (1985:13).

9 Moltmann (1985:5).

10 See Clayton (1997:96f) for a detailed defense of a panentheist position.

11 McFague (1993).

12 Boff (1997:152-4).

13 South African theologian David Field (1996:142) argues, by contrast, that panentheist and pantheist notion's of God cannot do justice to the value and integrity of creation: "In

The pendulum has swung so much from the earlier notion of God's absolute transcendence to an emphasis on God's immanence that Wesley Granberg-Michaelson, in a recent overview of ecological theology, felt the need to ask what the ecological relevance of God's transcendence would be.[14] From an eschatological approach to ecological theology, the answer to this question seems clear. Hope for the earth can ultimately only be based in God. This is not only true in response to environmental degradation and injustice. Any hope to transcend the earth's own finitude can only be in the hands of a God who transcends the evolutionary history of the whole cosmos.

Curiously, it is God's transcendence that thus emerges as the crucial ingredient of an ecological *theo*logy of hope for the earth. This is curious because education, science and technology remain the dominant source of hope, even for pious people. Tragically, when technology fails to provide meaning in life, hope for the future is also shattered and obscured. God's transcendence is invoked only then, apparently as a last resort to fill some missing gaps. This fluctuation between immanent and transcendent sources of hope is hardly adequate towards a vision of hope for the earth. How, then, must we understand God's transcendence? How can we escape from dualist notions of God's transcendence? How can we discern the Transcendent *within* the Immanent? How can we as finite human beings understand something of the infinite mystery that we have learned to name God? How can we transcend the limitations of our knowledge and language to even know that it is God whom we are speaking to? How can we ultimately see God, as if for the first time?

These questions (and thus a response to the predicament of human limitations in space) cannot be avoided for an adequate vision of hope for the earth.

18.2 The dimensions of time and eternity, life and eternal life

On numerous occasions throughout the argument thus far we had to note the importance for eschatology of an adequate understanding of several other doctrines, including sin, salvation, creation, the work of Christ, and the work of God's Spirit. Similarly, we are now confronted with the need for an adequate doctrine of God. More specifically, a Christian eschatology has to clarify something of the mystery of God's transcendence. But how can we begin to comprehend transcendence if it transcends the limits of our knowledge per definition? The refusal to address this question, for example due to an apophatic acknowledgement of this unapproachable mystery, remains short-lived. As Paul Tillich once observed, religion has always trespassed, in poetry and myth, to express this mystery.[15]

There are numerous philosophical and theological models available to account for the possibility of transcendence. A fully developed discussion of God's

---

those understandings creation has value, not by virtue of its own worth, but as a consequence of it being in some sense an extension of the divine, or of the divine being present in it. In the covenantal and trinitarian model creation has worth in and of its self."

14 Granberg-Michaelson (1994:104).

15 Tillich (1963:396).

transcendence is clearly beyond the scope of this chapter. On the basis of the discussion of the contributions by especially Moltmann and Pannenberg in Chapter 13, I would nevertheless like to offer a few tentative observations in this regard. This discussion has at least indicated the need to move beyond a naive spatial or temporal notion of transcendence.

- In the Ptolomaic worldview of the medieval period, God's transcendence was often understood in spatial categories.[16] God was literally viewed, in supra-naturalistic categories, as hovering above the world. The inadequacies of this model became evident with the Copernican revolution. This view of God's transcendence also tends to reduce God to and restrict God within spatial categories. King Solomon already had to realize that even the highest heaven could not contain God (1 Kings 8:27).[17] Curiously, it still dominates Christian piety. When our children ask us, "Where is God?" many of us still point vaguely to the heavens above.
- The popular view of God's presence in eternity as being time without end, focuses on temporal categories, usually assuming a linear notion of time. Eternity is infinite time stretching beyond the finite boundaries of my life, the existence of the earth and of the universe. Eternal life is therefore viewed as a continuation of temporal life after death, not as life that transcends temporality as such.[18] This reduces what is eschatological to what is futuristic.[19] The inadequacies of this model became evident with the emergence of Big Bang cosmology and its emphasis on the time-space continuum.

The contributions by Moltmann and Pannenberg also indicate the need to move beyond purely futuristic notions of God's transcendence (see Chapter 13.4). The debate on God's transcendence has to be relocated within the context of the classic question on the relationship between space-time and eternity. The relation between time and eternity is perhaps, as Pannenberg also observes, *the* crucial problem that has to be addressed in any eschatology.[20] This perplexing question has puzzled many of the great thinkers in and outside the Christian tradition. In this century Barth, Brunner,[21] Althaus, Berkhof,[22] Cullmann,[23] Tillich,[24] Hans Küng, and, more recently, Moltmann, Pannenberg, Paul Helm,[25] Ted Peters,[26] William

16 Van Ruler (1947:35f).

17 Van de Beek (1996:218).

18 Tillich (1963:410).

19 Van Ruler (1947:37).

20 Pannenberg (1998:597).

21 See Brunner (1954:42-56).

22 Berkhof (1967:27-33).

23 See Cullmann (1962).

24 See especially Tillich (1963:394-423).

25 Helm (1988).

Placher,[27] Keith Ward[28] and numerous others have made valuable contributions in this regard. Cosmologists like Stephen Hawking have also investigated the intricacies of time.[29] Few have managed to reach a clarity that transcends the famous words of Augustine: "What then is time? I know well enough what it is, provided that nobody asks me; but if I am asked what it is and try to explain, I am baffled."[30]

Without entering into the detail of this classic debate and at the risk of being naive or presumptuous, I will, in the discussion below simply articulate my own preference for a "dimensional" understanding of God's transcendence.[31]

Augustine argued in his classic exposition that time is a dimension of creation. God created the world together *with* time, not *in* time.[32] Time forms an integral part of the created order. If God is the creator of time, God must exist beyond the finite dimensions of both space and time. This does not imply that eternity is, like for Plato and perhaps Augustine himself, the negation of temporality or that God is unchangeable. Instead, time may be conceived as being incorporated "within" eternity.[33] Eternity is neither timeless identity nor endless time (i.e. permanent change).[34] It has neither the timelessness of absolute identity nor the endlessness of mere process.[35] Eternity encompasses time. There is no time *after* time, but there is eternity *above* time (Tillich).[36] Eternity is the ground and the source of the temporal, standing over time on the one hand and at the end of time on the other

---

26 Peters (1996).

27 Placher (1994:27-52)

28 Ward (1996).

29 Hawking (1988).

30 Augustine, *Confessions* XI, 14.

31 See also the discussions on the notion of dimensions by Karl Heim (1953:146f) and Van den Brom (1993:231-265).

32 In terms of the argument that follows, it may be argued that God created time and space from within God's own eternal time and space. God made room, within the higher dimensional realm of eternal time and space, for a created order to come into being, something that is not Godself. This may or may not be interpreted as an act of God's self-restriction (*zimsum*). See also Van den Brom (1993:268-304).

33 See Moltmann (1996:281), Pannenberg (1991:403f, 1998:595f), Peters (1996:264), Tillich (1963:418). Pannenberg draws on Plotinus who regards eternity as the simultaneous presence of the whole, undivided perfection. Pannenberg suggests that time may be related to the whole or totality of eternity. Since the part (time) can only be experienced, proleptically that is, in terms of the whole (or *Gestalt*: eternity), eternity forms a presupposition for understanding time.

34 Brunner (1954:54); Pannenberg (1984), Tillich (1963:418; 1963b:125); Ward (1996:249f). See also the study by Helm (1988) who argues, to the contrary, that God's eternity does imply timelessness.

35 Tillich (1963:429).

36 Tillich (1963b:125).

(Niebuhr).[37]

How can we conceive of the eternal God as encompassing time?[38] Perhaps God's existence in eternity may be conceived as being in a depth "dimension" beyond the edges of the space-time continuum that we as human beings inhabit. Eternity is according to this dimensional model not simply a very long time that somehow remains open to the future. This would understand the transcendence of eternity above time purely on the basis of time itself. The realm of eternity includes the dimensions of space and time but also transcends these dimensions. More specifically, the relation between time and eternity may be understood as analogous to the relations between length and area, or area and volume, or volume and time. In each case, a qualitatively new dimension is introduced: area is not simply a very long line, volume is not a very large area, and time is not simply very voluminous. It should also be noted that each new dimension includes all the "lower" dimensions.[39] Time implies space; volume implies area; area implies line. The relation between time and eternity is therefore always a relation between time *including space* with eternity.[40] Eternity implies neither timelessness nor spacelessness.[41]

---

37 Niebuhr (1943:299).

38 See Peters (1996:275f) for a discussion of this question. Brunner (1954:54, 56) observes that this question has to be addressed, but that we reach here the limit of what can be expressed in human language. He suggests that to speak about eternity is to speak about God, the transcendence of God in relation to the world, and the divine Lordship over time. Brunner adds that if God is life and if God is love, this can only be expressed in a present that is not vulnerable to the predicament of transitoriness. Our experience of the present constantly crumbles away in that every moment. Only God has "absolute *durée réele*, real undivided, unconquered, indissoluble fullness of life in the present" (1954:55). The Christian hope is to share in this eternal life and love of God. This divine moment holds together past and future in an indivisible unity. The German title of Brunner's book, *Das Ewige als Zukunft und Gegenwart*, indicates that he wished to emphasize (with Barth) the eschatological dimension of the present while maintaining the historical tension between present and future.

39 This observation clearly suggests the panentheist inclination of a dimensional understanding of God's transcendence. Perhaps a form of "Trinitarian panentheism" would describe the position here better. Nevertheless, I am hesitant to solidify this acknowledgement towards a fully developed panentheist position. For a vision of hope for the earth, it remains important to emphasize the distinctness of creation in relation with God. Despite its other limitations, the strength of Moltmann's emphasis on the primordial *zimsum* is its ability to acknowledge this distinctness of creation without losing a sense of God's immanence in the world. This distinctness is not only important to guard against protological and eschatological emanation, but also ensures the possibility of communication between God and the world. In Christian soteriology this kerugmatic communication has to confront the manifestation of evil in the world (not "in" God). Trinitarian theism seems, to me, to be better equipped to address the predicament of evil, while panentheist theologies tend to focus on the predicament of spatial and temporal finitude.

40 Van den Brom (1993:243).

41 See Van den Brom (1993:170f) for a critical discussion of spacelessness as an interpre-

Indeed, as Pannenberg observes, "Time owes its continuity to its connection with space. Without space, time would only be a series of discontinuous moments."[42] This observation also acknowledges the space-time continuum assumed in contemporary science.

This dimensional model of God's transcendence may be further elucidated by a) the well-known story of "Flatland" and b) the diagrams below.

a) The story of "Flatland" is based on the work by Edwin Abbott, *Flatland: A romance of many dimensions*, published in 1884 under the pseudonym "A square." It draws on the development of a non-Euclidian mathematics of space and the recognition that standard plane and solid geometries were only the beginning of a series that engaged more and more dimensions.[43] A freely adapted version of the story of "Flatland" may be told in the following way:

> Once upon a "time", there was country with the name of Flatland. It was inhabited by characters such as Triangle, Circle, Square, Rectangle and Trapezium. The people of Flatland lived happily together even though their world had only two dimensions. Soccer was a favorite sport although they could only kick the ball sideways, not into the air. One day, however, consternation erupted in Flatland when Square came to the marketplace with the mysterious story that she met with a person called Cube from Spaceland. This possibility was dismissed as not only impossible and outrageous but also dangerous for the social security of Flatland. Square ended up in jail. Many years "later" (that is, from our perspective since there is no dimension of time in Flatland), Trapezium called the people of Flatland together to observe the ridiculous people he met from Lineland. Where Flatland had two dimensions, Lineland had only half of that. Everybody was queuing in one single file and had to communicate with the one next to them only. All the people of Flatland laughed long and loud at the simple-mindedness of the people from Lineland. Until they remembered the strange story of Square, still rotting in jail. If a country like Lineland with only one dimension could exist, maybe, just maybe, it is also possible that a different world with three dimensions could exist. Perhaps their minds were far too "flat" to comprehend what life in a country such as Spaceland could involve.

The unstated moral of the story is quite clear: The relation between our existence in space and time and the realms of heaven and eternity is analogous to the relation between "Flatland" and "Spaceland." Although we may not be able to grasp the eschaton or to fathom its depths, we may nevertheless gain a glimpse of this realm and may therefore also be influenced by it. Eternity penetrates, but is not confined to our dimensions of space and time.[44]

b) It is possible, although extremely difficult to sketch the relation between space-

---

tation of God's omnipresence.

42 Pannenberg (1990:89).

43 I am indebted to McClendon (1994:178) for providing helpful historical background to this story that I originally picked up in a daily newspaper.

44 McClendon (1994:178).

time and eternity in a diagram consisting of two dimensions. In a cyclical view of time, eternity is regarded simply as an endless continuation of the rhythmic cycles of days, seasons, harvests, etc.

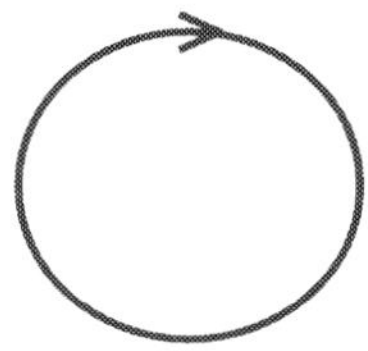

At least since Augustine, this cyclical view of time was replaced by a linear notion of time, indicating a beginning with the creation of the temporal and an ending with the transformation of everything temporal.[45] The inadequacies of a purely linear notion of time have often been discussed in recent literature.[46] Linear notions of time are often reduced to quantitative time, to clock time. It may also suggest linear progression, thus giving credence to optimistic accounts of evolutionary history. Instead, there is a need to acknowledge qualitative time, the emergence of kairotic moments in time, festive time, time for celebration.[47] This is perhaps best done through a narrative notion of time which acknowledges linearity (the storyline), but allows for a rich array of narrative devices (e.g. repetition, acceleration, delay, prolepsis, analepsis) to indicate qualitative time. This form of linearity is ingrained in the storytellers of all traditional societies and is also not foreign to the so-called "arrow of time" described in contemporary thermodynamics. A narrative notion of linear time also needs to acknowledge what Heidegger and Gadamer have called the *Geschichtlichkeit* of human existence is time. In a diagram this may be sketched in the form of an ongoing spiral.

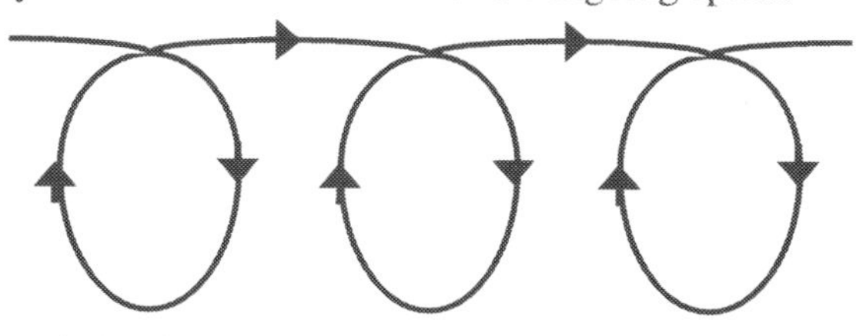

How should the relation between time and eternity be conceived in terms of such a narrative notion of linear time? The following two diagrams represent views that are clearly inadequate.

The first indicates that eternity should be understood as a completely separate realm from the world of space-time (based on a spatial notion of transcendence).

---

45 See Tillich (1963:419) who regards Augustine's contribution in this regard as a "tremendous step".

46 Many of these discussions draw on the work of Gerhard von Rad (e.g. 1965) who argued convincingly that Israel sense of history did not imply a notion of linear time but of kairotic time, the time of festivals, exemplified by the celebration of the Sabbath.

47 See Nolan (1987) and Petersen (1995) for two South African contributions, both emphasizing such a qualitative, kairotic notion of time.

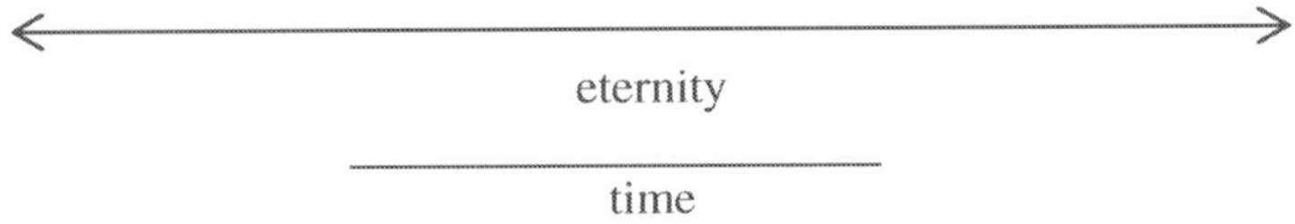

The second diagram indicates that eternity is understood as an infinite extension of time, although not as timelessness (based on a temporal notion of transcendence):[48]

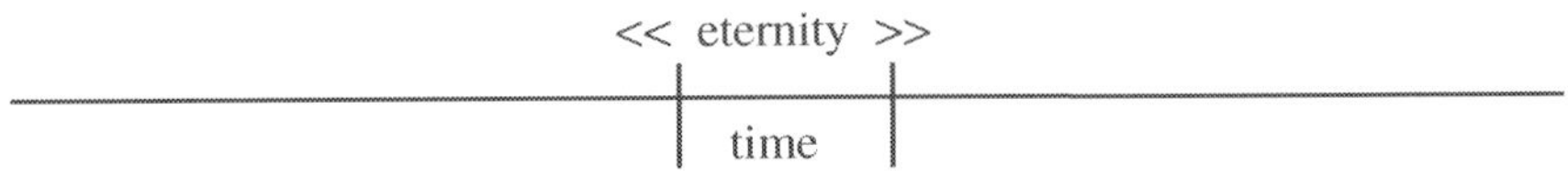

Thomas Aquinas pictured a circle in which time flows along the circumference with God occupying the center. God therefore relates to every temporal point without being part of the timeline itself. Alternatively, Aquinas proposed that God is on something like a high tower (eternity) overlooking a road (time). From this vantage point God can observe every point in time simultaneously while the pilgrims traveling on the road can only observe there fellow travelers.[49]

Paul Tillich suggests a diagram in which the relationship between time and eternity indicates that time is "coming from", "going ahead" and "rising to" eternity. It reaches its deepest point in the existential now (*nunc existentiale*). He also notes that this curve can be drawn in every moment of experienced time.[50] His diagram looks something like the following:

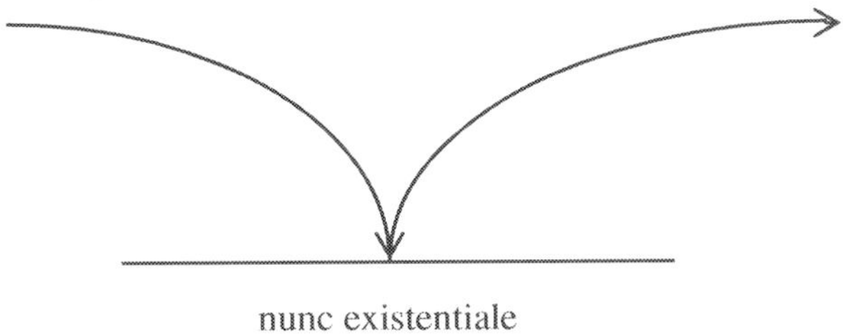

I propose a diagram that would indicate that eternity includes the dimensions of time but that eternity is not simply an extension of time. Time is not linear, but the famous "arrow" of time does give more of a directionality to time than what dialectical theology, for example, tends to acknowledge. This allows for the inherent orientation towards the future of Christian hope.[51]

---

48 See Cullmann (1962) for a similar notion of eternity as an indefinite extension of time.

49 I am indebted to Placher (1994:28-29) for this discussion of the imaged suggested by Thomas Aquinas.

50 Tillich (1963:419-420).

51 See also Rahner (1966:326): "The Christian understanding of the faith and its expression must contain an eschatology which really bears on the future, that which is still to come,

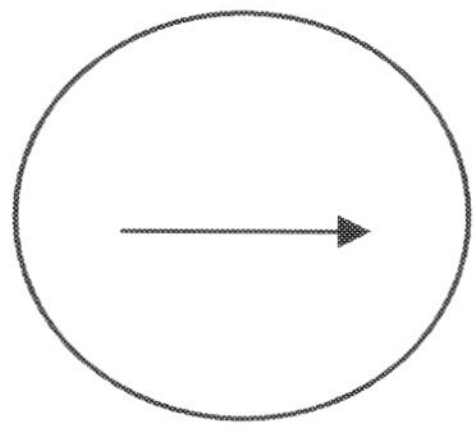

One of the advantages of such a dimensional notion of God's transcendence is that it is indeed conceivable,[52] even mathematically conceivable, but not reductionist. Any higher dimensions can, by definition, never be fully comprehended. Our human minds are simply to "flat" to do so. Higher dimensions would, by definition, be inaccessible for scientific investigation and would therefore transcend any scientific competence – although one may fully acknowledge the limited abilities of science to comprehend the dimensions of space and time.[53] There is even a degree of commonsensical naiveté about the acknowledgement of richer dimensions to reality. To speak of God's existence in dimensions beyond ours, may therefore reaffirm the pious recognition that God is in heaven while we are earthly creatures. Let our words therefore be few! (Eccl 5:2). This affirmation should therefore not lead to any form of speculative theology but is precisely an attempt to guard against it by acknowledging the limitations of human knowledge.

Such a dimensional notion of God's transcendence cannot be called *Christian* (Christians believe in the God of Jesus Christ, not in an abstract notion of eternity) unless it may help us to explain *reflectively* (thus *fides quaerens intellectum*) the cognitive content of God's acts of salvation from sin and liberation from oppression in explicitly Trinitarian language.[54] In my view this is indeed possible.[55] Many

---

in a very ordinary, empirical sense of the word 'time'."

52 Van den Brom (1993:264). See the argument by Drees (1990:198f) that not only the *possibility* but also the *plausibility* of such a dimensional model has to be demonstrated. It should be noted that this plausibility criterion should not be formulated on the basis of what may be plausible to the natural sciences (Van den Brom 1993:299f).

53 See also Van den Brom (1993:247-248). This has important implications for the scenarios of "frying" or "freezing" in astrophysical cosmology. Christian theology, together with contemporary science may accept the ultimate finitude of the universe. Christian hope is not based on an endless continuation of the universe itself. It does not expect to escape death, but can accept finitude as an integral part of creation. Whichever scientific scenario may prove to be more plausible will therefore not falsify eschatological assertions. Christian hope remains ultimately in God who is present in space-time, but who also transcends the dimensions space and time. Christian hope trusts that the whole cosmos will be taken "up" and transformed in this transcendent presence of God. This hope in God cannot be falsified by new scientific theories, precisely because it pertains to "higher" dimensions that are not accessible to the physical sciences.

54 For a similar emphasis, see Peters (1996).

55 See also Pannenberg (1991:407): "If the doctrine of the immanent Trinity is the basis of the idea of plurality in the life totality of the one God which is eternally present to him,

of the classic theological paradoxes seem contradictory only in terms of a reductionist notion of God's transcendence as an aspect or extension of space-time. In a multi-dimensional world God may be transcendent and omnipresent.[56] God's presence, may thus be evident in the Sabbath, in the temple, in the incarnation, and in the church. Christ may be both God and thoroughly human. In the appearance of the resurrected Christ, we gain a glimpse of God's presence in eternity.[57] Christ is coming and is here at the same time.[58] The Spirit may act in the world in and through our actions.[59] The eschaton may be simultaneously present and at the end of time. The dead may be with God even while their dead bodies remain on earth.[60]

A dimensional model of God's transcendence may also provide a thoroughly theocentric vision of the meaning of life that transcends any anthropocentric or cosmocentric visions.[61] Christian faith in God implies the ability to perceive more than the dimensions of space-time, namely to see God's presence in history. Faith and hope is not a form of blindness. It requires not only sight but also insight. It requires an element of seeing and an element of looking deeper into. The viewer needs something like the old stereopticon to see the depth dimension in two

---

the doctrine of the working of the Trinitarian persons in the economy of salvation is the basis of the existence of a plurality of creatures and their incorporation into the life of God for participation in his eternal glory."

56 See Van den Brom (1993:231f) for a similar proposal on God's omnipresence. Van den Brom argues that God may be omnipresent in the sense of being present in a higher dimension that comprehends the four-dimensional space-time continuum (1993:246).

57 Van den Brom (1993:305-307). This calls for an understanding of the resurrection of Christ as an "eschatological" event, that is, an event that transcends but includes the dimensions of space and time. The possibility of a transformation of the dead Jesus has to be located beyond these dimensions. The meaning of the empty tomb is that Christ is not constrained by space or time (see Sauter 1999:46-7). A fuller defense of this assertion is clearly needed, but this would require a major investigation in its own right.

58 See Van de Beek (1996:221f) for a similar exposition of the *parousia* of Christ. The eschaton is the point where time and eternity meets. It is therefore always close to us, to each generation. See also Pannenberg (1998:627): "The coming again of Christ will be the completion of the work of the Spirit that began in the incarnation and with the resurrection of Jesus. From the standpoint of eternity we have here one and the same event because the incarnation is already the inbreaking of the future of God, the entry of eternity into time." Hayes (1989:162) adds: "The parousia is not a return of a Lord who has been absent from the world since the resurrection, but the final breaking through of the victorious presence of divine grace that has been present continuously throughout history, and in a special way since the death and resurrection of Christ."

59 The logical possibility of God's action in the world, and the acknowledgement of the paradox of two agents (Austin Farrer) does not yet solve the question *how* God acts in the world and how the "causal joint" may be conceived. See the many contributions from Clayton, Peacocke, Polkinghorne, Russell, and others in this regard.

60 Pannenberg (1998:606-7).

61 See also Tillich (1963:422).

otherwise flat photographs.[62] In Hebrews 11, the *locus classicus* on Christian faith and hope, faith is described precisely as the visionary ability of Noah, Abraham, Moses and others to see more than what the eye can behold. It does not necessarily attempt to see God directly (in the *visio Dei beatifica*), but envisions God's presence on earth.

Such a dimensional notion of God's transcendence may also provide a model to formulate a clear vision of hope for the earth. More specifically, it may help to envision the relationship between creation, eschaton and God. In this regard, I support the eschatological interest in the relation between time and eternity that is, for example, evident in the mature work of Moltmann and Pannenberg (see Chapter 13.4).

To me, the value of Pannenberg's discussion of eternity in terms of the distinction between the infinite and the finite is precisely his ability to show that the finite is incorporated in the infinite.[63] Logically, the infinite may include the finite, but finite entities cannot be something outside the infinite. An infinite God must encompass a finite creation, so that it is in some or other sense "within" Godself.[64] This implies that, at least in the eschaton, finite time (past, present and future) may participate in infinite eternity. Then it will become evident that time is – and has been all along – a dimension of eternity. Then God will be everything in (or for) everything. In this sense Leopold von Ranke's famous dictum that each moment of time and history is equidistant from eternity is correct. However, this does not allow sufficiently for the directionality of history. Pannenberg is able to maintain a kerygmatic emphasis on the future through his famous argument that wholeness (the eschaton) is as yet incomplete and therefore future, at least for us.

One of the underdeveloped aspects of Pannenberg's emphasis on the distinction between the finite and the infinite is that he acknowledges,[65] but perhaps does not distinguish clearly enough between God and the eschaton. He often speaks of finite creation *participating* in the eternal glory of God, and the *incorporation* of creation into God's eternal present.[66] "Creation will be renewed for participation in the eternity of God."[67] What, then, is the eschatological difference between God and creation if both share the realm of eternity? What characteristics of the infinite (and thus of God) are not applicable to creation if creation participates in God's realm of eternity?

This observation forms the impetus behind Moltmann's somewhat speculative

---

62 McClendon (1994:69).

63 Pannenberg (1991:397f).

64 Clayton (1997:99).

65 See Pannenberg (1991:400): "God gives existence to the finite as that which is different from himself, so that his holiness does not mean the abolition of the distinction between the finite and the infinite."

66 See e.g. Pannenberg (1998:594, 601, 1991:407). Tillich (1963:420f) adopted a similar view that he famously calls "eschatological panentheism". Tillich adds that this being "in" God may indicate creative origin, ontological dependence and ultimate fulfillment.

67 Pannenberg (1991:409).

distinction between absolute eternity (the realm of God) and relative eternity (the *aevum* or *aeon*, the realm of creation in the eschaton). Creation is transformed in the eschaton, but does not become divine. Such a distinction is important in order to guard against a pantheist notion of emanation where, eschatologically, creation is again taken up into God's own being, having been alienated from God protologically.

Although Moltmann's use of a protological *zimsum* and an eschatological *aevum* thus guards against emanation, he does not escape from this (neo-Platonic and Hegelian?) tendency entirely.[68] From within God's absolute eternity (thesis), creation in time (antithesis) emerges and returns to and thus enriches the realm of God (synthesis), although the return is only relative, not absolute (the synthesis is more than the thesis).[69] With both Moltmann and Pannenberg there is a need for greater clarity on how the relation between God and creation should be conceived in the eschaton.[70]

Perhaps Moltmann's own earlier analysis of the duality of heaven and earth may provide an alternative, less speculative, approach to the relation between creation, eschaton and God. In *God in creation* Moltmann argued in favor of the duality of heaven and earth in God's creation.[71] Heaven is a dimension of creation (not of God), a dimension that is open to God, where God dwells and where God's presence may be discerned (e.g. by the angels).[72] Heaven is for Moltmann the relative transcendence of the earth, while the earth is the relative immanence of heaven.[73] In *The coming of God*, Moltmann, significantly, explains the distinction between heaven and earth with the help of the category of aeonic time:

> Whereas for heaven and 'all who dwell in it' there is an aeonic time, for the earth 'and all who dwell in it' there is a transitory time. The differentiation lies in death, which is only earthly, not heavenly.[74]

---

68 See Farrow (1998) for a similar criticism of the circular structure of Moltmann's theology. See also Otto (1992) who maintains that Moltmann cannot escape from a basically Platonic notion of God. He fears that God thus become a little more than a regulative idea that human beings have to create through hope and in historical praxis (1992:132).

69 See, for example, Moltmann (1996:282) where he described creation in time in the typical language of emanation: "In the act of creation, time *emerges* from eternity and *fans out* into before and after, into future, present and past." (emphasis – EMC). See also Pannenberg (1991:408) for a similar Hegelian structure: "The thought of eternity that is not simply opposed to time but positively related to it, embracing it in its totality, offers a paradigmatic illustration and actualization of the structure of the true Infinite which is not just opposed to the finite but also embraces the antithesis."

70 Bouma-Prediger (1995:254).

71 Moltmann (1985:158-184).

72 Pannenberg (1991:402) also suggests that the notion of heaven expresses the thought that all times are present in God's eternity.

73 Moltmann (1985:163).

74 Moltmann (1996:282). Moltmann's further suggestion that aeonic time is somehow

In terms of a dimensional model of transcendence one may argue that heaven is a dimension that transcends, but also include the earth (and indeed the cosmos). However, heaven cannot be equated with God or with the realm of eternity. The dimension of eternity, one may argue, transcends that of heaven. I propose that the relationship between cosmos and eschaton may be imagined on this basis. The eschaton involves a transformation of the cosmos in the realm of the heavenly. Or, in language reminiscent of traditional Christian piety, "The earth and my body, after death and decay, will 'go' to heaven"; that is, it will enter into a new dimension where death and decay will no longer have an effect. It has to be noted that the language of "going" to heaven unfortunately suggests spatial movement and therefore a spatial notion of transcendence and thus of higher dimensions (e.g. the "highest" heavens).[75] This has to be avoided at all costs since such spatial movement can only lead to a form of escapism from the earth. Heaven has to be understood as a transformation of this earth in a "higher" dimension that includes the earth and its dimensions of space and time. The value of the notion of dimensions is precisely that any one dimension includes all the "lower" dimensions.

It is also necessary to be more explicit about the characteristics of the eschaton in distinction from the cosmos and from God. In what way can the cosmos conceivably be transformed and taken "up" into the dimension of the heavenly?[76] How does the transition from time to eternity take place?[77] A few comments in this regard are necessary although the dangers of speculative theology loom large when one enters into such a discussion.

It is important to affirm, with Pannenberg, that the characteristics of the infinite only apply to God. Only God is omnipresent, omniscient and omnipotent. By contrast, creation remains finite, even in the eschaton. However, the problem remains here that the sting of finitude is death. This not only applies to the eventual death of human beings, whole species or the earth. It applies especially to what Whitehead called "perpetual perishing". Existence in time implies an openness to change. Change implies limited duration. Limited duration implies the inevitability of an end – to my life, to the earth, to each century, each year, each moment, each opportunity. Any end implies a sense of loss. It implies that one loses the ability to relate to (and thus to influence and be influenced by) a particular event. This sense of loss accounts for the existential trauma of all the dimensions of finitude in time. As Moltmann puts it:

> In its destructive possibilities, earthly time becomes the time of transience. Chronos then becomes the power of futility, the futility of everything that happens or is done in time.

---

cyclical because it has no beginning and end, no before or after, is perhaps more confusing than helpful (1996:282, 295).

75 This spatial notion of transcendence is fostered by the biblical imagery of the heavenly city of God (e.g. Heb 12:22).

76 The question as formulated by Peters (1996:265).

77 The question as formulated by Tillich (1963:399).

Chronos devours all the children whom he bears.[78]

In response, two traditional strategies may be identified to cope with this predicament. Both of these strategies try to locate the difference between eternity and the finitude that characterizes our existence in time.

The first strategy emphasizes the aspect of simultaneity, the simultaneous presence of what is separated in the sequence of time, the possibility of an "eternal now" (*nunc aeternum*).[79] In Augustine's classic exposition, a degree of simultaneity is experienced already within this life. Through remembrance (*memoria*), the human mind is able to make the past present. Through expectation (*expectatio*) the human mind makes the future present. Through attention (*attentio*) a person can experience the present as immediate presence.[80] This simultaneity in the present constitutes the experience of eternity within time.[81] It is the "eternal now" within the temporal now that stops the flux of time (Tillich).[82] It is an attribute of eternity (Augustine), an "atom of eternity" (Kierkegaard). A sense of simultaneity is crucial and also powerful. The human experience of time is not completely linear in the sense that a point in time is added to another point, each only touching the other. Simultaneity allows for an interaction between past, future and present.[83] Without remembrance and expectation we would not be able to hear a melody or perceive any movement.[84] More importantly, it accounts for the possibility of healing the past through the power of forgiveness and of planning for the future on the basis of promises, covenants and contracts.[85] The eternal now therefore has eschatological significance – as Kierkegaard and Barth[86] clearly recognized. It also has significance for existential decisions, as Bultmann and Tillich recognized.[87]

---

78 Moltmann (1996:284).

79 Moltmann (1996:285, 287); Tillich (1963b).

80 Moltmann (1996:291) adds that there is a mystical "depth-dimension" to this sense of "absolute presence" in the experience of eternity in time.

81 Moltmann (1996:290), Pannenberg (1990:51-2).

82 Tillich (1963b:131).

83 Brunner (1954:44).

84 Pannenberg (1990:82f) observes that this simultaneity of time forms the impetus behind the transcendental philosophy of Kant and the phenomenology of Heidegger. Space and time as transcendental categories provide to the subject an intuition of the infinite whole. However, the unity and of time is no longer provided by the wholeness of eternity, but by the unifying structures of the subject / *Dasein*. Pannenberg argues that, in order to grasp the unity of time, we must have recourse to an infinite unity that rise above the finitude of the subject. The value of Plotinus is, for Pannenberg, that his notion of eternity as an infinite whole includes temporality but also gives a priority to the future because the whole remains not-yet, at least from our human perspective.

85 See the classic exposition by Hannah Arendt (1959) on the power of forgiveness and promise.

86 For an emphasis on eternity as simultaneity, see, i.a. Barth (*CD* 2.1, 1957:608f, 612).

87 See Bultmann's comment: "The meaning in history lies always in the present, and when

However, this simultaneity in the present remains fragmentary. As Pannenberg observes, it is only partially and transitorily that we can retain as a simultaneous unity that which is separated in time.[88] The experience of any "now" has no duration. In the flux of time each now is replaced by another now. The fleeting now of our sense of the present corresponds only remotely to the lasting and abiding Now of his (God's) presence.[89] Pannenberg concludes that, "Hence in the march of time, as Plotinus already realized, we can only seek and hope for the totality of life from a future that will integrate the many moments of life into a unity."[90] Moltmann also articulates this same desire for duration eloquently:

> Because in historical time we experience fulfilled life only in the form of moment-like eternity, we develop a hunger for a wholly and completely unclouded fullness of life, and therefore for the life that is eternal. Out of this experience of present eternity arises the longing for an eternal present in which we can say to the moment, like Goethe's Faust: 'O tarry a while, thou art so fair.'[91]

The second strategy seeks to account for the possibility of the duration that an "eternal now" lacks.[92] In the famous definition of eternity by Boethius both simultaneity and duration is incorporated: eternity is the simultaneous and complete presence of illimitable life" (*aeternitas igitur est interminabilis vitae tota simul et perfecta possessio*).[93] Duration is also decisive to ensure the independent existence of creatures in the eschaton. Only if creatures have duration of their own, can they remain distinct from God and each other.[94] Pannenberg describes duration therefore as a "picture" of "image" of eternity.[95] He says: "Only participation in the eternity of God can overcome the disintegration of human life that are sundered by

---

the present is conceived as the eschatological present by Christian faith the meaning of history is realized ... In every moment slumbers the possibility of being the eschatological moment. You must awaken it." Quoted in Moltmann (1996:293). The reference is to Bultmann's work *History and eschatology* (1957:154).

88 Pannenberg (1991:409) explains: "In contrast to the divine eternity, for which all things are always present, this extension is always divided and scattered, for we are subject to the march of time, and it is only partially and transitorily that we can retain as a simultaneous unity that which is separated in time. Nevertheless, the fact of the time-bridging present and duration in the life of creatures gives us a remote inkling of eternity and a form of participation in it."

89 Pannenberg (1998:598), almost verbatim.

90 Pannenberg (1998:601).

91 Moltmann (1996:291).

92 Pannenberg (1998:596) also sees the need for a clear distinction between simultaneity and duration as characteristics of eternity.

93 See the discussions by Pannenberg (1991:404-5) and Peters (1996:267f) of the legacy of Boethius' definition.

94 Pannenberg (1998:597).

95 Pannenberg (1990:80).

the march of time and integrate such moments into unity and totality."[96]

The predicament of limited duration is that it also limits an ability to heal the past and to structure the future. In a necessarily limited life span, one has to recall the past and imagine the future while living anew in the present. There is simply not enough time to heal the past and to live in the present. The past therefore becomes continuously more complex while the future becomes more limited. This also constitutes the challenge of aging. In response to this predicament, one may simply postulate that eternal life would entail endless duration. This accounts for the popular image of eternity as endless time. However, such a postulation of duration has an inherent tendency towards a notion of eternity as timelessness. This is due to the conceptual difficulties of imagining the possibility of duration including change. Existence in time implies the possibility of change. This remains as crucial as the materiality of our existence, also in the eschaton. A cosmos that is transformed in the eschaton in a way which excludes material change would be completely foreign to us and would provide little hope or comfort. It would deny everything that we treasure in this world. But change necessarily implies limited duration.[97] Change implies an end to a previous state of affairs. Perhaps this dilemma can be avoided if duration is regarded as an endless (?) continuation of opportunity, the new opportunities to consciously engage with the past and the future.

Although the danger of rampant speculation looms large here, one may gather that a dimensional notion of transcendence would include both these aspects of simultaneity and duration. Perhaps one may visualize this possibility through the metaphor of "inscription". The history of the cosmos, this "cosmic pilgrimage", is *inscribed* in the eschaton. Our life history is, moment by moment, written down in the "book of life" (Hartshorne). I imagine this inscription through the analogy of writing on the six sides of a cube. Such an inscription would take place only on the two dimensions of the surface. It has no depth, allowing for these inscriptions to be transformed towards a richer dimension in the eschaton.[98] Once this inscription has taken place it can never be obliterated, not even by an omnipotent God. Eternity does not imply the annihilation of time. Nothing that is past can pass away.[99] It remains forever and therefore has duration. This inscription will be completed when the history of the cosmos finally comes to an end (*finis*). This "objective immortality" (Whitehead) allows for the possibility of duration. Moltmann concurs in more biblical terminology:

> Consequently the direction of hope is not just that God will make all things new. Hope looks also to the future of 'a new time', the 'abiding aeon' of an 'everlasting life (1 John

---

[96] Pannenberg (1998:601).

[97] Moltmann, for example, explains the distinction between aeonic time and earthly time precisely in terms of finitude as a lack of duration. Earthly time is subject to change; aeonic time is time without end.

[98] This transformation would imply the characteristics of duration, simultaneity (in time) and co-presence (in space).

[99] See Moltmann (1996:286) with reference to this eloquent comment by Georg Picht.

1.2) in which chronos will enjoy no more efficacy (Rev 10.6).[100]

It is important to note that such inscriptions also provide (and limit!) the building blocks that would be available to us in the eschaton. Every moment in the earth's journey is therefore not only of ecological, but also of eternal significance. That is why it remains imperative to care for the earth and its creatures and to prevent any catastrophes on this journey. Through caring for the earth now, the building materials for the new earth are now being gathered.[101]

A mere inscription of the history of human pain and suffering would not elicit hope though. It would be a source of fear not joy. It would, in fact, constitute a harrowing, tormenting image of hell.[102] It will give eternal duration to all the evil, suffering and pain of history. What happened in time will also be judged in the broader light of God's eternal presence.[103] The Christian hope is not merely for eternal duration through inscription. The Christian hope is that God's loving and healing presence or indwelling (*Shekinah*) will permeate the cosmos in the eschaton ("on earth as it is in heaven"). This includes the hope that our own life history, the history of the earth and our consciousness of both, will be sanctified in God's holy presence. If this sanctification takes place, not "immediately" (as is often imagined in Christian piety), but through the mediation of our own embodied human consciousness, this would leave an endless (!?) amount of "unfinished business" for the eschaton. The added dimensions of the eschaton, the "many houses" of the father's home (or "ikhaya"[104]) may allow us sufficient room (space) and opportunity for change (time) to address this unfinished business. Thus, lured by God's loving presence, we may have an endless opportunity (thus requiring duration) to address the (now) limited building blocks of our past (thus requiring simultaneity) in order to heal the brokenness of our past and to celebrate the joy of forgiveness, with Christ and together with the community of all creatures in the presence of God.

Christianity should not, as John Polkinghorne observes,[105] lose its nerve to speak about its hope in the God of Jesus Christ and the expectation that we as human beings and the earth itself may find room aplenty within God's eternal love which stretches beyond time and space, a God's whose mercy endures forever.

A specifically Christian vision of hope for the earth is a hope in God the Father

---

[100] Moltmann (1996:284).

[101] Cf. also Hoekema (1978:287).

[102] Moltmann (1996:331f).

[103] See Pannenberg (1998:594) for a similar (Barthian) emphasis on judgment as the legitimate manifestation of an antithesis between time and eternity.

[104] This is a rich Xhosa expression for "home". In traditional villages (the father's home) there are sufficient houses (smaller huts) for everyone to stay in and to enjoy the company and hospitality of the extended family. The extended family may be extended even further to include the company of livestock, pets, birds, vegetation, soil, air, all the brothers and sisters in mother nature.

[105] Polkinghorne (1998:90).

whose love, power and patience stretches beyond our human power and knowledge. It is a hope in the nearness of the Jesus Christ, the Immanuel, who has come (viz. the incarnation), is coming, and will be there to proclaim God's reign, to judge and expose the evil forces of death for what hey are, and to establish Justice, Peace and the Integrity of Creation and to sustain life (viz. the resurrection) amidst the forces of death and destruction (viz. the cross). It is a hope in God's Spirit,[106] the Giver of life from the beginning, who continues to renew the whole creation, and who will create new life, even beyond the boundaries of death.

18.3 The need to respond to the threefold absence of God

This discussion of a dimensional notion of God's transcendence may or may not prove to be relatively adequate. The pursuit for a more adequate theological explication of the cognitive content of Christian hope (*spes quaerens intellectum*) will undoubtedly continue.

Current work on the relationship between time and eternity indicates, in my view, at least that the propositional content of Christian hope no longer needs to be regarded as an intellectual embarrassment. As the story of "Flatland" indicates, a hope based on what transcends the history of the universe is not inconceivable or unreasonable.[107] It is indeed possible to provide a relatively sufficient explication of the cognitive content of the Christian hope for life amidst death, life beyond death, and eternal life. The hope for a new earth no longer needs to be regarded in dualistic or otherworldly categories as a "pie in the sky". Even the gloomy cosmological scenarios on the long-term future of the universe cannot falsify this hope. They merely sketch the radical finitude of the whole creation. The Christian hope is not for an endless continuation of life in the universe, but, quite simply, to be with God, to enjoy God's presence forever.

This assessment, it is now important to add, does not conclude the task of a Christian eschatology. In fact, it only addresses the first of three important tasks.

An explication of the relations between the immanence and transcendence of God – between cosmos, eschaton and God – responds to the intellectual agenda posed by the absence of God in a first sense of the word. Especially in the Western world, the apparent absence of God has traditionally been related to the atheist denial of the existence of God. Atheism maintains that God is absent because God only exists in the constructions of human culture and language. In a still secular world, this remains a pressing agenda for Christian theology. It constitutes a challenge at a cognitive level. The famous question raised by Kant remains: What can I know? Indeed, how can we know God? Christian theology cannot avoid the task of articulating, if only for itself, the plausibility of the Christian belief in a God who created heaven and earth and who will create a new heaven and a new earth.

Although this task often dominates theological agendas, there is a second, even

---

106 See Pannenberg (1998:551) for a similar emphasis on the importance of pneumatology for eschatology.

107 McClendon (1994:178).

more important task for Christian eschatology. Willem Drees observes (as we noted in earlier chapters) that God's absence can also be understood in a different sense of the word. For the world's poor, oppressed, suffering, and dying masses, God's absence is illustrated in concrete experiences of suffering. When confronted with the many contemporary manifestations of evil in the world, the theodicy question soon emerges in all its acuteness: Where, in the midst of such experiences, of evil is God? This question does not imply an atheist denial of God's existence but assumes the possibility of God's presence (an absence crying out for presence).[108] It constitutes a challenge to Christian theology not at a cognitive, but at an ethical level. This agenda should dominate, in my view, any adequate Christian eschatology. We have noted on numerous occasions in previous chapters the need to retrieve the soteriological core of Christian eschatology. In the context of widespread ecological degradation, there is an urgent need to respond primarily and directly to the predicament of evil and its many ecological manifestations. An adequate response to this ethical agenda should not become trapped in the all too cognitive debates on the conceptual intricacies of the theodicy problem. It should retain a kerugmatic focus in which evil (and its many *human* origins) is clearly denounced and where victory over evil is announced. This vision calls for a liberating praxis responding to the concrete needs of society. The famous question raised by Kant remains in all its urgency: What should I do? Indeed, what should we do amidst rampant ecological devastation? In the new century this question will emerge with a frightening urgency.

In his profound work, *Hope in a time of abandonment* (1973), Jacques Ellul identifies a third, far more penetrating, but also deeply disturbing form of God's absence in the world. This is the chilling possibility that we may live in age of abandonment by God. Abandonment here means that God has turned away from us and is leaving us to our fate.[109] Abandonment is more than hiddenness; it is relinquishment. Ellul explains that the whole Old Testament reverberated with this fear: that God would keep quiet, would no longer speak to us, that God would no longer punish us for our transgressions, that God would ignore us, that God would abandon us in dismay, that we will be left alone to the death and decay caused by our own actions. The cry of the Psalmist resounds, "Turn not away from us!", "Cast me not away from thy presence!" This fear of abandonment finds its confirmation and culmination is the cry of Jesus, "My God, my God, why hast thou forsaken me?" (Mark 15:34).[110]

The possibility of abandonment by God cannot be ameliorated by pious assertions that God is love, that God will never abandon those whom God loves, that in Jesus Christ God is and will be with us, forever, that because Jesus was abandoned there can never again be an abandonment, that nothing can separate us from God's love. Once these assertions become abstract truths, independent from a dynamic,

---

[108] Drees (1990:5-6).

[109] Ellul (1973:71). See also Moltmann (1998b:14): "God has concealed his face and is far away from us."

[110] Ellul (1973:119).

living relationship with God, once they are taken for granted, they become idolatrous. Then prophets such as Jeremiah have to announce that God no longer regards Israel with compassion.[111] In an age of abandonment God's nearness may still be experienced by certain individuals.[112] God's Word may still be heard, but it has become as scarce as in day of Eli (1 Sam 3:1).[113]

To be abandoned by God is indeed far worse than to be punished by God. Anger is at least a form of communication. God's wrath, the thundering of the prophets, the threat of condemnation – still indicates that God is speaking to us.[114] When communication itself withers away, the death of a relationship is in sight – as all marriage counselors are acutely aware of. Ellul identifies and discusses numerous signs in contemporary European culture that provide an indication of God's abandonment in that context.[115] The effects of this abandonment are far-reaching. If God chooses to be silent no amount of theology or hermeneutics[116] would be able to retrieve the living Word of God. All forms of cultural expression, all forms of worship, rituals or spirituality, any programs for the upbuilding of congregations, even programs to aid the poor, will become shallow and hollow. Everything will become kitsch. Perhaps the deepest need of a culture abandoned by God is for beauty. Only beauty will redeem the world![117] There is a need to "reassert the value of aesthetic joy against the absolute claim of ethics."[118] This identifies not so much a cognitive challenge or an ethical crisis but an aesthetic[119] and spiritual emptiness (for art remains the closest analogue to religion[120]). The

---

[111] Ellul (1973:72-3).

[112] Ellul (1973:125).

[113] Bonhoeffer (1971:360f) reminds us that the hope for God's presence (see the argument above) has to be related immediately to the motif of God's abandonment. He says: "… the God who is with us is the God who forsakes us … Before God and with God we live without God. God lets himself be pushed out of the world on to the cross. He is weak and powerless in the world, and that is precisely the way, the only way, in which he is with us and helps us."

[114] Ellul (1973:114).

[115] Ellul mentions a perversion of values, the death of the word, the mediocrity of the church, institutional bureaucracy, conformity to the world, etc.

[116] See Ellul (1973:140f) on the futility of hermeneutics in an age of abandonment. He comments sharply: "The truth is that no reading is possible when God is silent" (1973:143); "Hermeneutics is the business of interpreting revelation without revelation" (1973:146).

[117] Metz & Moltmann (1995:106).

[118] Moltmann (1973:iv), in the preface to *Theology and joy*.

[119] Boff (1997:108) quotes the Cuban poet José Roberto Retamar, who writes that, like all human beings, the poor have to basic hungers: one for bread that can satisfied, and another for beauty, which can never be satisfied.

[120] Tracy (1990:43).

problem is not the death of God, but the absence, the silence of God.[121] If God remains silent, one may attempt to elevate human words to the level of the Word of God or to regard the events of history as a continuation of the action of God, but it sooner or later becomes evident that these are only empty pretences, false appearances.[122] The result is a form of despair far more unnerving than any ecological disaster or the "cosmic depths of despair" discussed in earlier chapters. The famous question raised by Kant, now has to be asked in a completely new light: What may I hope for?

Ellul discusses the sources and structure of hope in a time of abandonment in some detail. His constructive proposal is perhaps less valuable and not of immediate importance here.[123] His assessment of European culture certainly does not necessarily apply to other contemporary cultures – although it may help us to raise penetrating questions concerning a culture of affluence and consumerism, also in South Africa.

More importantly, Ellul's study indicates that hope is imbedded in a form of spirituality. The cognitive content of hope cannot be analyzed in abstraction from concrete manifestations of a lived hope. The content and experience of hope[124] remains as inseparable from another as the content and experience of faith (*fides quae creditur* and *fides qua creditur*). An elucidation of the content of Christian hope remains insufficient. No amount of theological exposition will be able to elicit hope. Like virtue, hope cannot be taught.[125] Hope simply begins where hope begins (Downey).[126] Hope itself is a virtue that is born from grace alone; it can only be embodied and lived as a gift, ultimately coming from God.

If hope comes from God, the emergence of hope can only take place through God's revelation. Hope is elicited by a confrontation with the triune God. Human beings come to hope because God is a God of hope. We are inspired to hope because of an encounter with an inspirational God. An exposition of Christian hope therefore has to coincide with an account of the God in whom we believe. Eschatology, like any other appropriate theology, has to proceed in the form of doxology. Likewise, a Christian vision of hope for the earth can only be adequate if it is based on praise to God the Maker of heaven and earth, of all that is seen and unseen, to Jesus through whom all things were made and whose kingdom will have

---

[121] Ellul (1973:110-1).

[122] Ellul (1973:117).

[123] Ellul (1973:192-306). In my view, Ellul's Barthian emphasis does not allow sufficiently for an acknowledgement of God's transcendent immanence in the world. His Protestant emphasis on the verbal and thus auditive character of the gospel does not allow sufficiently for the materiality of signs of new creation emerging already within the context of this world.

[124] See Farley (1996:95-112) for a discussion of the tension between the "subjective" and the "objective" dimensions of hope.

[125] The emergence of a hopeful predisposition is the dominant emphasis in several works on hope and spirituality. See, especially Pieper (1986), Galilea (1988), Downey (1998).

[126] See the title of Downey's study (1998) on the spirituality of hope.

no end, and to the Holy Spirit, the Giver of life, to whom we look for the life of the age to come.

If hope, like faith, is born from the knowledge of God, then hope, in a time of abandonment, is received through the prayers of protest by the faithful before God. Like Job, the faithful may rightfully and with confident certainty lodge an accusation against this God who seems absent and silent amidst so much suffering and evil.[127]

This calls for a further investigation of the integral link between hope, spirituality, morality, and virtues. This is the task of the next chapter.

[127] Ellul (1973:179f).

Part F: To live in hope

19. The social impact of Christian hope

19.1 Introduction

The *content* of Christian hope has been the focus of attention in the previous chapters. The focus now has to be shifted towards the *social impact* of this hope.

The inextricable link between eschatology and ethics has often been highlighted.[1] Faith without love (good works) is dead. But it is hope that empowers us to engage in acts of love. "Hope empowers us to enter into solidarity with the groaning creation and to persist in the struggle for the renewal of all things."[2]

In general terms, the link between eschatology and ethics is constituted by the value-ladedness of the eschaton.[3] Christian eschatological symbols express the values towards which a Christian life is orientated. They indicate a particular vision for society as a whole. They provide a way of seeing the world within an ultimate frame of reference.[4] At the same time, these eschatological symbols elicit in us the will to strive towards the eschaton. Their aesthetic attraction[5] empowers and inspires us to live according to the values of God's reign. The eschatological vision of God's new creation calls for a transformation of the present world in the light of this vision. The vision of God's tomorrow thus becomes not a sedative but a stimulus to earthly action. In this way, it functions proleptically as a present manifestation of what is still to come.[6]

This general observation has to be concretized for three important ethical questions, namely "What is the good life, what is a good society?", "What is

---

1 See Thielicke's (1966:47) comment: "Theological ethics is eschatological or it is nothing." See also the essay by Wilder (1965).

2 Migliore (1991:247).

3 Any adequate eschatology should therefore have an axiological dimension although eschatology cannot be reduced to axiology. Likewise, the eschaton cannot be reduced to a (utopian?) set of moral values or ideas. Any hope for continuity between cosmos and eschaton requires a notion of the eschaton that includes and transcends the whole history of the cosmos in all its material concreteness.

4 McClendon (1994:69f), Hauerwas (1989:88). The primary task of Christian ethics is not to clarify what should be done (the imperative) but how the world should be seen (the indicative). An eschatological vision provides us with a way of perceiving the world.

5 Note the link here between ethics and aesthetics. Without a sense of beauty, eschatological symbols loose their power to inspire. Without this aesthetic attraction, ethics turns into legalism. See also Moltmann (1973:62f).

6 See Peters' (1994b:147-151) emphasis on the proleptic structure of the relationship between eschatology and ethics.

person of good character?" and "What constitutes responsible action in a particular situation?"[7] In environmental ethics, a discussion of the first and third of these questions tend to focus on moral values while a discussion of the second question tends to focus on moral virtues.

The need for appropriate social values has been widely recognized in ecological theology. In the work of James Nash, Larry Rasmussen, and Holmes Rolston the values embodied in the notion of a sustainable society have been discussed in some detail.[8] In Chapter 16 we noted some of these social values that need to be further concretized through "middle axioms" to influence policy making and to aid ethical decision making at the various levels of implementation of environmental programs.[9] One important focus of such contributions is the debate on ecological aspects of human rights, that is, the rights of future generations and biotic (or animal) rights.[10] The quest to formulate appropriate ecological values is also prominent in the current drafting process of an Earth Charter to foster a new global ethos.[11]

The discussion in the rest of this chapter will focus not so much on appropriate ecological *values,* but more on the relationship between eschatology and moral *virtues*. More specifically, the focus will be on the social impact of Christian hope, especially hope for the earth. Again, the analysis of the three human predicaments to which Christian eschatology responds will be used to structure the discussion.

19.2 Hope for victory over evil: inspiration

In Chapter 13 we saw that an emphasis on Christian hope for salvation from sin and evil leads to a typical eschatological tension between the "already" and the

---

7 See Smit (1996) for a discussion of the ethical theory behind this illuminating threefold distinction.

8 Nash (1991:63f) identifies the following values: Sustainability, adaptability, relationality, frugality, equity, solidarity, biodiversity, sufficiency and humility. Rasmussen (1996:142f) identifies a similar list of values: Ecological sustainability, sufficiency or sustenance, community through work, participation by all, respect for diversity. See also Rolston (1988) for a detailed analysis of the need to concretize ecological values.

9 This would respond to an important comment by James Gustafson that the value of a theology of hope for ethical decision is less obvious than is sometimes assumed. Gustafson says: "Only when the object of hope is delineated with enough specificity to make possible the inference of certain achievable moral intentions can it give relatively clear directions to moral action. A general attitude of hope, with its big theological basis and big theological object, is of limited significance, in fact, it is vacuous when particular moral decisions and actions are required" (quoted in Schuurman 1991:10). The reference is to Gustafson's work (1979:215), *Christian ethics and the community* (New York: Pilgrim Press).

10 See, for example, Nash (1991) and Vischer (1990). For bibliographical material on animal rights, see the numerous references in my indexed bibliography (Conradie 1998).

11 See Casey & Morgante (1998) for one of several important recent publications by the *Boston Research Center for the 21st Century* on the Earth Charter process.

"not-yet" of experiences of such salvation. Let us now investigate the social impact of Christian hope if given this content.

The vision of Christian hope for salvation from sin, liberation from oppression and victory over evil is based on the promises of God and is expressed in eschatological images such as the great banquet, peace on earth, the new Jerusalem, the new earth and the coming of God's kingdom. In Chapter 16 we investigated the value of the notion of "sustainable community", the vision for Justice, Peace and the Integrity of Creation and the program towards a theology of life as contemporary expressions of such a vision.

The primary function of the sense of hope expressed in these metaphors and visions is to provide *inspiration* to Christians who believe that something different, something radically new, an *eschaton* in which *God* will renew everything,[12] is indeed possible. The promises of God create an interval of tension between the uttering and the fulfillment of the promise.[13] Christian hope thus incites the imagination to dream new dreams and motivates individuals and societies to fresh efforts to find ways of helping to make and keep the world habitable through culture, science, technology,[14] the arts, in the economy and in politics.[15] Christian hope ignites rather than paralyzes human imagination and action in the direction of God's coming new heaven and new earth.[16]

The inspiration elicited by Christian hope is characterized, not by somberness, but by exalted *joy* and laughter.[17] Christian hope expects, as Moltmann aptly phrases it, "eternal joy in the dance of fellowship with all created being and with the triune God."[18] Indeed, "The laughter of the universe is God's delight."[19] This calls for celebration and an affirmation of life – even amidst poverty, suffering, and degradation. Happiness, fun and games are not the prerogative of those who can afford it only. The festivities of the affluent will always be undermined by the surrounding suffering, starvation, and conflict.[20] However, the celebration of life is not only prevalent amongst the affluent but also in many poorer communities that also engage in joyful celebrations precisely in the midst of deprivation.[21] Such celebrations call for a festive meal. In the midst of scarcity, food and drink are saved for the occasion. As Konrad Raiser observes:

---

12 Cf. Rev 21:5: "Behold, I make all things new."

13 Moltmann (1967:104).

14 Galilea (1988:78) adds that if science and technology does not remain in the service of love, the earth will become less habitable.

15 Migliore (1991:241), Van Ruler (1969:228).

16 Migliore (1991:242).

17 Berkouwer (1972:22f).

18 Moltmann (1997:123).

19 Moltmann (1997:135).

20 See also Moltmann's essay "How can I play in a strange land?" (1973:26-28).

21 Raiser (1997:70).

> In celebration, human beings are able to transcend the scarcities and limitations of everyday life. Joy is the emotion which expresses the experience of overflowing abundance and gratuity of life. Anniversaries and seasonal festivals mark the rhythmic flow of time. They break the dominance of the linear, goal-directed progression of time, and provide moments for recreation and re-generation.[22]

The promise of the renewal of all things also provokes a *critical* dimension, a negation of the negative. What distinguishes a prophetic vision (like Martin Luther King's "I have a dream") from cozy or utopian religious kitsch is this determined rejection of the negative.[23] It denounces as it announces.[24] It functions as a critical reminder that Christians cannot be satisfied with evil, sin, suffering, injustice and oppression. The eschaton calls for a radical and relentless relativizing of any absolutes.[25] Thus it serves as an encouragement for believers to challenge the powers of evil, to work for justice, to establish penultimate signs of the ultimate coming of God's reign.[26] The *promissio* of God thus invokes the *missio* of the church and projects the direction of the *missio Dei*.[27] In the now classic formulation of Jürgen Moltmann:

> That is why faith, wherever it develops into hope, causes not rest but unrest, not patience but impatience. It does not calm the unquiet heart of man. Those who hope in Christ can no longer put up with reality as it is, but begin to suffer under it, to contradict it.[28]

John de Gruchy expresses the same concern within the South African context:

> The eschaton judges our clinging to the past, our attachment to the present status quo, making us dissatisfied with anything less than God's righteousness, justice and peace in the world. It lures us into the future, making us restless with things as they are, it stimulates hope for the fulfillment of God's purpose for the universe.[29]

Simon Maimela expresses the same conviction in explicitly Christological language. He argues that the victorious Christ is the source of hope for Africa because Christ gives humankind new perspectives on life. Maimela concretizes this in the following way:

> The upshot of this claim is that for the believing African the perverted and unjust social relations can no longer be regarded as inevitable and as something Africans must put up

---

22 Raiser (1997:69).

23 Moltmann (1992:75).

24 See Gutiérrez (1973:233) with reference to the revolutionary function of utopia.

25 Ellul (1973:247).

26 See Bonhoeffer (1995:125-142) for a discussion of the relationship between the ultimate compassion of God on sinners and the penultimate preparing of the way.

27 Moltmann (1967:225).

28 Moltmann (1967:21).

29 De Gruchy (1979:199).

> with and tolerate for ever, but instead sin and its social consequences should now be regarded as abhorrent and contradictory to what God has willed for the Africans.[30]

Pannenberg adds that an understanding of reality that is inspired, not by the past, nor by eternal structures, but by the power of the future confronting the present, cannot result in a conservative desire to maintain the established order. It demands change. It assumes that the existing world need not face destruction, but can hope for salvation, but only if it is transformed. At the same time it is also prepared to announce judgment upon a world that rejects the demand for transformation through love.[31]

Christian hope can thus be described as a protest statement; it is a form of *resistance* and defiance against seemingly overwhelming powers, on behalf of the dignity of humanity and in the name of the God who is committed to the well-being of creation.[32] Christian hope is not only receptive, but also productive; it is not only passive, but also militant.[33] A vision of the not-yet in Christian hope has a rebellious and, at times, a revolutionary dimension.[34] It refuses to accept that present suffering need to have the final word. Hope thus fulfills a mobilizing function in history.[35] The eschatological *novum* is a revolutionary principle; it seeks to change the world, not only to understand it. Christian hope is a "resistance movement against fatalism"[36] because the point of departure of Christian faith is the victory achieved in Christ. The element of newness thus discloses itself as a principle of revolutionary life (Brunner).[37] At the very least, hope directs people to active participation in cultural, social and political processes to make the world a better place for all creatures.[38] When hope responds thus to the predicament of evil it becomes exactly the opposite of the compensation for a manco which Marx and Freud duly criticized.

Christian hope is therefore distinctly different from optimism, a "zest for life" (Teilhard), "the power of positive thinking" or the belief that all will turn out well (which may be the best possible formula for ensuring that the worst will happen![39]). Christian hope is not concerned with the future on the basis of the growth, development, maturation or fruition of forces or trends already at work in the present. Eschatology therefore differs fundamentally with the science of futuro-

---

30 Maimela (1992:37).

31 Pannenberg (1969:116).

32 Nürnberger (1994:149). See also Tracy (1987) on hope and resistance.

33 Moltmann (1970:46).

34 Berkhof (1967:21).

35 Gutiérrez (1973:218).

36 This phrase is derived from the 1978 Faith and Order meeting of the World Council of Churches in Bangalore. See Raiser (1997:79).

37 Brunner (1954:61).

38 Hayes (1989:77).

39 Ackermann (1992:67).

logy. It runs counter to both pessimistic and optimistic views of the future.[40] Moltmann expresses this concern in the following way:

> Eschatology is not a doctrine about history's happy end. In the present situation of our world, facile consolation is as fatal as melancholy hopelessness. No one can assure us that the worst will not happen. According to all the laws of experience it will. We can only trust that even the end of the world hides a new beginning if we trust the God who calls into being the things that are not, and out of death creates new life.[41]

Indeed, as a response to the predicament of evil and sin, Christian hope is deeply aware of the prevailing reality of suffering.[42] As John Macquarrie notes:

> True hope lives in the awareness of the world's evils, sufferings and lacks. Hope must remain vulnerable to evidences that count against it, humble in the face of the evils that have to be transformed, and above all, compassionate towards those whose experience has been such that their hopes have grown dim or have been dissolved in despair.[43]

John de Gruchy expresses the same concern within the political realities of the late 1980's in South Africa:

> In proclaiming the political power of confessing guilt and forgiveness, in struggling for justice despite great odds, in risking acts of costly reconciliation, the church keeps hope alive because it is witnessing to possibilities which fly in the face of reality. This is not a false or naive optimism, but a sign that we refuse to surrender to fate or to what is regarded as historically inevitable.[44]

Christian hope often emerges in the midst of suffering and despite this very suffering. Hope is precisely instigated by an unacceptable present, not by the extrapolation of acceptable expectations. This is why Christian hope transcends our "little hopes" for progress in a country,[45] or the end of a war, or a cure for cancer.[46] It can thus endure amidst suffering.[47] In traditional Christian terminolo-

---

40 Berkhof (1967:83).

41 Moltmann (1996:234).

42 Pieper (1986:42) refers to Job 13:15 to indicate this link between hope and suffering: "Although he should slay me, I will trust in him." Job's words question the assumption that Christian hope coincides completely with the fulfillment of material desires.

43 Macquarrie (1978:13).

44 De Gruchy (1988:51).

45 In the South African context, Alan Paton once expressed this "despite" of Christian hope in the following way:

> I say to my fellow South Africans: if you have no hope, you should get out as soon as possible. If you have unbounded hope you should go and see a psychiatrist. If you can't give up hope, if you insist on hoping against all hope, then persist with all the things you have been doing to make this a better country (quoted in De Gruchy 1979:237).

46 Galilea (1988:4).

gy, this endurance amidst suffering calls for a "bearing of one's cross", tribulation or even martyrdom.[48] This hope endures also in predicaments where no solution seems forthcoming, where the power of evil seems overwhelming, beyond the locus of control of the one who hopes.[49] Denise Ackermann therefore sees a link between hope, expectation and *waiting* (and not only impatience):[50]

> Hope means that we must learn to wait. This requires patience and endurance and is the opposite of resignation. It means acknowledging moments of despair but moving beyond doubt and anger in order to wait expectingly.[51]

Indeed, hope is purified through waiting.[52] In an age where the advertising culture promises immediate satisfaction, there is a need to wait patiently and expectantly for the fulfillment of Yahweh's promise of salvation (Psalm 130). This does not imply a passive waiting where Christians may lounge in lackadaisical boredom until the door of the waiting room is opened. Christian hope is an expectant, even militant waiting (Metz).[53] Hope is waiting with an agenda for change.[54] Tillich adds that we are stronger when we wait in silence than when we possess:

> If we wait in hope and patience, the power of that for which we hope is already effective in us. He who waits in absolute seriousness is already grasped by that for which he waits. He who waits in patience has already received the power of that for which he waits. He who waits passionately is already an active power himself, the greatest power of transformation in personal and historical life. We are stronger when we wait than when we possess.[55]

John Haught sees in this aspect of hope as patient waiting an apophatic dimension. It requires a willingness to let go of the present and to anticipate patiently the arrival of God's future: "This willingness to wait is clear evidence of a mature hope's openness to the graciousness, extravagance and unexpectedness of revelation."[56] Hope requires its own kind of asceticism in the form of a painful

---

47 Galilea (1988:15) notes the paradox that bad times, more than good times, are often times of hope.

48 Berkouwer (1972:116) see in such suffering a concrete manifestation of the "not-yet" of salvation.

49 See Hentz (1997:2,7) for this emphasis on hoping as the reach for what is beyond our own capacity to calculate and control

50 See also Haught (1993b:93, 176).

51 Ackermann (1992:67).

52 Galilea (1988:115).

53 Metz (1969:95).

54 Farley (1996:100).

55 Quoted in Haught (1993a:177). The reference is to Tillich's work (1948:55), *The shaking of the foundations* (New York: Charles Scribner's Sons).

56 Haught (1993b:93).

willingness to abandon the present, to cease clinging to the way things are. It lets go of the present in order to receive the open, surprising, and inexhaustible reality of the future.[57] Waiting is therefore further qualified by *vigilance*. Watchfulness is required when a startling and unpredictable coming is to be expected, something than cannot simply be deduced from the already.[58]

In his classic analysis, Josef Pieper identifies two possible aberrations from this tension between patient waiting and impatient resistance in Christian hope, namely presumption and despair. Presumption is a premature, self-willed anticipation of the fulfillment of what we hope for from God. Despair is the premature, arbitrary anticipation of the non-fulfillment of what we hope for from God. Both presumption and despair demand impatiently that God's promises should be fulfilled now already or not at all.[59] Moltmann adds that presumption, symbolized by the heroic image of Prometheus, was typical of German idealism in the 19th century whereas despair, symbolized by the tragic figure of Sisyphus, was typical of existentialism in the middle of the 20th century.[60]

John Cobb relates these virtues of hope as inspiration, critical confrontation, expectation and waiting explicitly to an environmental praxis. He comments that those who maintain a vision of hope can view environmental threats unflinchingly: "They do not deny its seriousness either in their thoughts or in their feelings. Yet their hope is the refusal of despair. Those who hope seek openings, assume responsibility, endure failure after failure, and still seek new openings for fresh efforts."[61]

In the discussion thus far, four traits of Christian hope in response to the predicament of evil were mentioned. The role of eschatological visions and symbols to provide *inspiration* and joy amidst an unacceptable present was emphasized. A vision of the eschaton also has a *critical* function, namely to warn believers not to acquiesce in evil, sin, decay or suffering. At the same time, the tension between an already and the not-yet implies both a "holy *impatience*" with evil and a willingness to wait, to *endure* suffering in the trust that God's promises will be fulfilled. Hope calls us to be active in the world, to challenge the power of the powerful, to confront suffering, to unmask ideology (Moltmann).

These positive traits of Christian hope can easily become distorted if the eschatological tension between an already and the not yet is not maintained. Such distortions will inevitably lead either to *resignation* or to *utopian fabrication* instead

---

57 Haught (1993b:93).

58 Sauter (1999:59).

59 Pieper (1986). See also Brunner's (1954:91) comments on a hurried existence without hope: "The believer may wait in hope; he who has no hope must hurry. The gate threatens to close - then all is over. For ever. This anxious impatience to scramble for as much as possible and pack it into life affects not only the scramble for material goods, for fortune, and for pleasure, but applies equally to the attempt to establish an order of justice and humanity. Here lies the true source of utopianism ..."

60 Moltmann (1967:23-24).

61 Cobb (1992:123).

of inspiration. One may describe this tension in terms of an eschatological arch.

If exclusive emphasis is put on realized eschatology, this can only result in resignation. The claim that victory over evil has already been achieved will necessarily be contrasted with experiences of persisting or increasing suffering, conflict, injustice and degradation. If the promised salvation is presumably already realized and little change could be expected in future, this will soon lead to hopelessness in such contexts. A denial of the possibility of something new will soon lead to despair.

Alternatively, if one enjoys a position of relative power, a sense of realized eschatology may easily lead to various forms of triumphalism where the evil effects of sin in the world is dangerously underestimated. This is evident in the ecclesial triumphalism of the medieval *corpus Christianum*, the evolutionary optimism amongst colonial powers in Europe in the nineteenth century, the educational elitism of Western civilization, and the technocratic optimism of those dominating the current global economy – to name only a few examples.

In a culture of affluence, a realized eschatology may lead to a sense of self-satisfaction. As Hans Küng observes, the younger generations in affluent societies are exhibiting a tremendous self-centeredness and a lack of readiness for commitment. A "culture of Narcissism" (Christopher Lasch) may well be the product when the eschatological tension between the already and a not-yet is not maintained. In such a culture there is little responsibility for society as a whole, no commitment to family, calling, marriage, still less to work, to party, to state or church.[62]

In the light of these distortions it remains crucial to emphasize the not-yet of salvation from sin, liberation from oppression and victory over evil. Van Ruler, for example, insists that salvation cannot be understood only in terms of the tension between what is hidden and what is revealed. The realization of the eschaton has to be more than a revelation of the victory that has already been achieved. The groaning creation is not only in need of revelation, but of cleaning up.[63]

By contrast, if exclusive emphasis is put on future salvation, this will result in wishful thinking, to utopian fantasies, to ill-founded, illusionary forms of hope. If the promises of God are never fulfilled, always remaining provisional, never concrete, these promises will soon become empty and distant. Without present, admittedly provisional experiences of salvation, the promise of future salvation will remain shallow. If the future seems empty, if no significant change can be expected, this will in the end lead to disillusionment. Galilea therefore sees the need for hope to be educated and nourished. He mentions the word of God, the sacraments of the church, the testimony of the saints, as "privileged signs of hope". But also the gestures of self-denial and solidarity we see in others, the unity of families, the selfless defense of the weak and oppressed, gratuitous service given to human suffering, peace and equanimity in adversity, a capacity for reconciliation without arrogance, these are for Galilea signs that hope has already begun to be realized

---

62 Küng (1984:192).

63 See Van Ruler (1971:223f) for an illuminating discussion of an appreciation of the earthly life as the implication of eschatology.

among us.[64] De Gruchy adds that ...

> The church is called ... to become signs of hope for the world. To live by hope means that we become signs of hope. What keeps hope alive in many situations throughout the world is not necessarily the big signs that make us optimistic, but the love and commitment of people who really care for others, and who, even in the most depressing circumstances remain faithful.[65]

At the same time, as Moltmann often points out, the "not-yet" of expectation surpasses every fulfillment that is already taking place now. Experiences of salvation already taking place now, becomes a point of departure for the confirmation, exposition and liberation of a greater hope. Once the hope, longing and desire of human beings are awakened by the promises of God, it stretches further than any fulfillment that can be conceived or experienced.[66]

Most Christian eschatologies therefore strive to maintain a balance between the already and the not yet. In the discussion above we have seen that this does not preclude a whole spectrum of eschatological emphases. John de Gruchy neatly captures the need to maintain a creative tension in this regard:

> Hope is not false optimism, it is not a denial of the awful reality that surrounds us, nor is it believing that everything will simply change for the good without God's judgement in history being worked out, without pain and struggle. ... But hope is living life today, fully cognisant of reality, yet refusing to accept it as the last word. Hope is living now beyond apartheid, living in the light of the resurrection. ... it anticipates surprises, look for signs of hope amidst the realities that make others despair. So our little or large penultimate, proximate victories, those moments when justice is done and reconciliation becomes a reality, becomes pointers to the ultimate judgement and redemption of God. This we celebrate now; this we will celebrate even more when apartheid has finally ended; but all of this is only in anticipation of the great celebration of the coming of the Lord.[67]

An account of the content of Christian hope for salvation from sin may therefore be tested in terms of its social impact, hovering in an "eschatological arch" between resignation / triumphalism, inspiration and utopian fabrication. Furthermore, if the reality of sin is simply avoided this can only lead to a form of evolutionary optimism, to *false hope*.

19.3 Hope for life beyond death: preparation

In Chapter 13 we saw that an emphasis on Christian hope for life beyond death is expressed in personal images such as the resurrection of the dead, in historical

---

64 Galilea (1988:45), almost verbatim.

65 De Gruchy (1992:122).

66 Moltmann (1967:106).

67 De Gruchy (1992:122).

images such as the *parousia* of Christ, and in cosmic images such as the new earth. This leads to a typical eschatological tension between the continuity and discontinuity of this dispensation and the next. What is the social impact of Christian hope if given this content?[68] Again, one may describe this tension between continuity and discontinuity in terms of an eschatological arch.

One way of describing this arch is in terms of the tension between an evolutionary and a revolutionary ethos. An emphasis on the continuity between creation and eschaton (a repristination of creation) may lead to a view of the social order as static and fixed and therefore to conservative norms for social life. If the eschaton is already realized, this may also lead to the danger of ecclesial triumphalism. An emphasis on the discontinuity of creation and eschaton (the annihilation of creation) may, on the other hand, lead to revolutionary social norms.[69] This tension is indeed appropriate in terms of the ethical implications of the relationship between creation and eschaton. However, it is not as clear in what way this would be related to the predicament of personal, societal and cosmic finitude.

Another way of describing this eschatological arch is in terms of the tension between a world-affirming and a world-denying ethos. The sense of continuity is crucial for an ecological ethos to clarify that it is indeed this earth that has to be sanctified.[70] This tension is also applicable to an eschatological response to the predicament of human limitedness in space (see 19.4 below).

Yet another point of departure for construing this arch is the danger of escapism in a Christian hope for life beyond death. An emphasis on the discontinuity between creation and eschaton can indeed lead to escapism. A radically discontinuous eschaton creates the difficulty of relating the eschatological future to the historical future of creation. This can only lead to an ineffective or a world-denying ethic.[71] When the expectation of a new earth is denied or relativized, the meaning

---

68 See the helpful discussion of this question by Schuurman (1995) in conversation with Volf (1995).

69 Schuurman (1991:3f). Schuurman (1991:168) adds that although creation has sometimes been used to provide warrant for a conservative acceptance of the status quo, and although eschatology has been used to provide warrant for a revolutionary rejection of it, this need not necessarily be the social impact of these doctrines.

70 See Van Ruler (1971:116-223) for an emphasis on the eschatological significance of sanctification. The eschaton will not only imply the redemption from sin, but also the sanctification of the earthly. What is expected in the eschaton also provides a vision and calling for the present: to prepare the earth for its future sanctification.

71 See Schuurman (1987:50f) who argues that Moltmann's creation-annihilating conception of the eschaton leads to a world-denying ethic. He states: "My chief objection to Moltmann's eschatology and ethics is that his vision of the eschaton includes an unwarranted annihilation of creation, resulting in an ethic that is inadequate with respect to valuations and moral directives that affirm creational life" (1987:43). Whatever other constructive moral guidance Moltmann offers, is not based on his eschatology (Schuurman (1987:59). Schuurman adds that such a world-denying ethic does not necessarily imply a disavowal of social responsibility or ascetic valuations of the world or culture, but rather that it leads to a negative form of social responsibility that defines Christian

of life on this earth breaks down.[72]

A Christian hope for life beyond death has often been criticized as escapist. Believers are promised a proverbial "pie in the sky when they die" to escape from an unacceptable present. This provides "opium" for the masses, soothing them into acceptance of oppressive suffering. Instead, we are called to confront oppressive powers, to work for justice here on earth, in this dispensation. The danger of an exclusive emphasis on the discontinuity between cosmos and eschaton is that hope may function as a dangerous illusion that could only detract us from our responsibility for this life and for this earth.

The ambiguities of an emphasis on discontinuity are especially evident in apocalyptic portrayals of the end of the world. In the history of Christianity millennialist expectations of an imminent end to the world has incited a wide range of haphazard ethical responses. Some simply stopped working. Some sold all their possessions. Others desperately tried to ensure their place in heaven through good deeds. Very few have followed Luther's sound ecological advice to plant a tree![73] The same tendency is prevalent is some ascetic movements. Walter Rauschenbusch once commented that: "Ascetic Christianity called the world evil and left it. Humanity is waiting for a revolutionary Christianity which will call the world evil and change it."[74]

Van Ruler, perhaps more than any other Christian theologian, insists that it is this world that has to be saved. It is this earth which is destined to become the new earth. An emphasis on radical discontinuity between creation and eschaton can only lead to a shallow idealism and romanticism. Van Ruler therefore calls for an appreciation and a sanctification of the earthly life. Furthermore, if this earth is God's earth and if the reign of God is to be established here on this earth, Van Ruler even sees the need to retrieve the classic theocratic ideal.[75]

On the other hand, an emphasis on the enjoyment of this sensuous life may be world-affirming, but can also lead to a serious distortion of Christian hope.[76] It may degenerate into triumphalism, hedonism and consumerism, leading to a lack of commitment and responsibility for society as a whole.

Like an emphasis on the already of salvation from sin, an emphasis on this world may also lead to either *triumphalism* or *resignation*, depending on one's present position of power. Furthermore, a denial of life beyond death may not encourage lofty ideals and ethical visions but the far more mundane caricatures of

---

moral action primarily in terms of being critical of existing social institutions. Schuurman concludes that Moltmann's concept of the eschaton as radically new generates a social ethic that can only be critical of, and never constructive toward, social structures (1987:66).

72 Berkouwer (1972:227).

73 See Stackhouse (1997) for a similar range of responses to an expectation of an imminent end to the world.

74 Rauschenbusch (1965:91).

75 Van Ruler (1971:19-29).

76 See Bavinck (1956:544) for a similar assessment.

hedonism and consumerism[77] – the quest for meaning and happiness in work, possessions, profits, careers, prestige, sport and pleasure.[78] It may encourage a hedonistic spirit of "Eat, drink and be merry, because tomorrow we're dead!" Hans Küng comments that this constitutes a religion of prosperity and progress, with the "gods" of sex, car and career operating as a holy Trinity for conformists.[79] The shopping center, and not the home or the work place, has become the locus for finding one's self-identity.[80] Ted Peters observes that the insatiable demands of the affluent leads to the habit of "moving sponge like through life, sopping up one experience after another, soaking in rich food, exciting travel, thrilling risks, sexual pleasure, and even religious ecstasy."[81] Since such extravagance cannot ultimately provide happiness or security, there emerges a new curiosity in what Galilea calls the "superstitions of hope": horoscopes, telling the future, charms that should protect the house, a false confidence in technology and the sciences, in the power of psychology and the medical sciences to provide healing, in the substitutes of political ideologies, etc.[82] A far more serious effect of a culture of affluence is the way in which the over-consumption of the affluent leads to global injustice, poverty and hunger and to a squandering of the world's limited resources.

Brian Swimme argues that consumerism is providing a new cosmology and that those working in the advertising industry are the high priests maintaining this cosmology. The following eloquent excerpts indicate the gist of his argument:

> The fact that consumerism has become the dominant world-faith is largely invisible to us, so it is helpful to understand clearly that to hand our children over to the consumer culture is to place them in the care of the planet's most sophisticated religious preachers.[83]
>
> ... what we need to confront is the power of the advertiser to promulgate a world-view, a mini-cosmology, that is based upon dissatisfaction and craving. One of the cliches for how to construct an ad captures the point succinctly: 'An ad's job is to make them unhappy with what they have.'[84]
>
> Advertisements are where our children receive their cosmology, their basic grasp of the world's meaning, which amounts to their primary religious faith, though unrecognized as such.[85]

---

77 See also Küng (1984:189).

78 Küng (1992:188).

79 Küng (1984:189).

80 Peters (1980:35).

81 Peters (1980:32)

82 Galilea (1988:32).

83 Swimme (1996:14).

84 Swimme (1996:16). See also the comments by Peters (1978:75) on the logic of the advertising industry. When the average consumer already has the basic things they need (food and shelter) advertisements motivate them to buy something that they do not actually need simply because it is new.

85 Swimme (1996:17).

> In the propaganda of the ad the ideal people, the fully human humans, are relaxed and carefree – drinking pepsis around a pool – unencumbered by powerful ideas concerning the nature of goodness, undisturbed by visions of suffering that could be alleviated if humans were committed to justice. None of that ever appears. In the religion of the ad the task of civilization is much simpler. The ultimate meaning for human existence is getting all that stuff. That's paradise. And the meaning of the Earth? Premanufactured consumer stuff![86]

Tragically, the whole "global village" has come under the spell of the "American dream" of the pursuit of happiness here and now. Consumerism has become the dominant global culture, also in Africa. And, as Richard Foster once commented about the love of money: "Those who have it the least, love it the most."

In response to this disturbing situation, Moltmann insists that the newness of the eschaton breaks open new possibilities in this world. The radically new and different eschaton breaks the paramount power of this closed future and crushes disabling despair by opening new possibilities. Moltmann says:

> It sees reality and mankind in the hand of him whose voice calls into history from its end, saying, 'Behold, I make all things new," and from hearing this word of promise it acquires the freedom to renew life here and to change the face of the world.[87]

Indeed, a strong emphasis on otherworldly hope does not necessarily function in an escapist way. In fact, it may have a powerful critical function. It can question the alleged self-sufficiency of the secular world. It denounces the illusions of a secular belief in the attainability of a perfect happiness in this world and any political pretensions that justice and peace can be fully achieved in secular society.[88] It can also withstand the seductive technocratic notion that the future can somehow be controlled and manipulated and maintains, instead, a spirit of openness to the secrets of the future.[89] Moreover, it is only when we lose hope in a transcendent future that we seek to cling to the securities of the present or find refuge in a world to come.[90] By contrast, the longing for another world may become a stimulant to action instead of a sedative. It does not necessarily lead to withdrawal from the world but to more realistic and unpretentious involvement in the world. James Cone argues that for enslaved Americans the radical contrast between God's future heaven and present oppression provokes criticism and action:

> The partly revealed future of God, as disclosed in the cross and resurrection of Christ, made black people resist the condition of enslavement. Indeed, if the Kingdom was truly present in their midst, and if it was really ultimate, then they *had* to disobey all values that hindered their obedience to the coming Kingdom. Heaven then did not mean passi-

---

86 Swimme (1996:18).

87 Moltmann (1967:26).

88 See Pannenberg (1984:123-4).

89 Sauter (1999:92).

90 Peters (1980:111).

> vity but revolution against the present order. Against overwhelming odds, black people fought the structures of slavery and affirmed their membership in a "city whose builder and maker was God."[91]

An eschatological balance between the continuity and the discontinuity of creation and eschaton is exceptionally difficult to formulate.[92] Likewise, the ethical implications of the eschaton have to be balanced with the proton. Miroslav Volf observes that we remain part of the present world infested by sin into which the eschaton has broken. We do not yet live in the eschaton. Ethical reflection will therefore always have to ask: To what extent can the ultimate intention of God for creation be realized under the present conditions?[93] Perhaps the classic Christian category of *preparation*, of "preparing for the coming of the Lord", may provide the heuristic key to an adequate ethical response to this eschatological tension. A vision for the future needs to provide both inspiration and a sense of commitment to this life. As Van Ruler insists, it is this earth that must be prepared for God's coming glory.[94]

This notion of preparation should, not be understood on a temporal axis only. Barth's polemic against the idea of a continuation of this life after death is, to my mind, entirely appropriate.[95] We are not being freed from the limitations of this life for a life beyond death. The notion of preparation should be understood as preparation for God's eternal glory.[96] This life serves as a preparation for the homecoming banquet.[97] This gives an ethical sense of urgency to *this* life.[98] It also requires the classic virtues of patience, vigilance, perseverance, and courage.[99] Each and every moment in the cosmic pilgrimage is important.[100] The journey is as important as

---

91 Cone (1986:11).

92 See Schuurman (1995:154f) for a more detailed discussion of the social and ethical impact of this tension of the continuity and discontinuity between creation and eschaton.

93 Volf (1995:138).

94 This notion of preparation may be contrasted with the classic position of *gratia nont destruit, sed praesuponit et perfecit naturam*. See Moltmann's (1985:7) similar suggestion, also using the category of "preparation": *gratia non perfecit, sed praeparat naturam ad gloriam aeternum*. See also Küng's (1984:197) notion of *love for life* which includes this life and future life.

95 Barth (*CD* 3.2, 1960:633).

96 See also Bonhoeffer's (1995:133f) notion of "the preparing of the way", more specifically, preparing the way for the word."

97 See Barth (1956:98f) on this motif of preparation for and anticipation of the wedding banquet of the coming bridegroom.

98 Barth returns to this subject in his treatment of ethics (*CD* 3.4, section 56) where he emphasizes the "once and for all" character of any opportunity.

99 See Galilea (1998:63) & Hentz (1997:10f) on the importance for Christian hope of the virtue of vigilance.

100 McFague (1997:176) argues that an orientation on the present may be more helpful for an environmental ethos than a preoccupation with final goals. She says:

the destination. Every moment of the journey prepares us to reach the destination. At the same time, the winking destination incites us to prepare for (the remaining leg of) the journey. This notion of preparation may be deepened by an understanding of the relationship between time and eternity where eternity is not simply (but indeed *also*) a continuation of time. The significance of every moment of this life is reinterpreted within the context of the dimensions of eternity.

The notion of preparation incorporates many of the classic features associated with eschatological proclamation. An eschatological vision calls for repentance, conversion, existential decision (Bultmann), a moment of truth (kairos).[101] The radical otherness of the eschaton provides both consolation and a stern warning. It calls on us to prepare ourselves to meet our God![102] And since the earth is the venue for this meeting, it has to be prepared and sanctified for God's coming glory. More specifically, in a time of environmental degradation, *preparation* clearly also requires *reparation* and, in a context of economic injustice, also restitution.

Perhaps one may imagine the conceptual language of preparation in terms of preparing for a joyous banquet, a wedding feast, or even better, preparing for the festive celebration of the weekly Sabbath, the Sabbath year and the year of Jubilee in anticipation of the wedding banquet of the Lamb that was slain, of the eschatological feast that we do not need to prepare because God has prepared it for us.[103]

More specifically, one may focus on the preparations for a coming celebration amongst poor communities and amidst scarcity, suffering, and degradation. In the midst of scarcity, food and drink are saved for the occasion. We have to prepare for the time when the whole household (= *oikos*) of God will gather to celebrate God's presence in joyful anticipation, with much laughter, singing and dancing – precisely in the face of scarcity, poverty, suffering, and degradation.[104] Jesus Christ will

---

> Nor is there any assurance that if we do act on the basis of a conversion to the earth our planet will be saved. We can certainly hope that our actions will have an effect, but Christians do not love the earth in order to save the planet. We should love nature for the same reason we should love God and our neighbor: because it is valuable in itself and deserves our love. The end of things is not in our hands and focusing on global outcomes can lead to despair.

[101] Berkouwer (1972:113f), Galilea (1988:63f).

[102] See Müller (1985) on the eschatological dimensions of Christian preaching.

[103] See Bonhoeffer's (1995:140) incisive comments in this regard:

> The end of all preparation of the way for Christ must lie precisely in perceiving that we ourselves can never prepare the way ... Preparation of the way is a way from the ultimate to the penultimate. Christ is coming of His own will, by His own strength, and out of His own love ... He is the preparer of His own way; it is this, and really only this, that makes us the preparers of His way ... We await Christ; we know that He is coming; that alone is why we prepare His way.

[104] See also Bonhoeffer's description of the task of "preparing the way". This implies immense responsibilities for all those who know of the coming of Christ: "The hungry man needs bread and the homeless man needs a roof; the dispossessed need justice and the lonely needs fellowship; the undisciplined need order and the slave need freedom." (Bonhoeffer 1995:136). This is not ultimately a question of the reform of earthly condi-

be the host for this gathering and the invitation is open for all. This calls for several immediate responsibilities that we have to attend to in the power of God's Spirit: planting and harvesting sufficient food, using the available resources frugally, helping the needy, ensuring everyone's good health, fixing the roof, adding more "houses" (rooms) to the father's home ("ikhaya"), cleaning the house, doing the dirty laundry, sending out invitations, setting the table, cooking and sampling the food, and enjoying all the aromas that are beginning to fill the house.

An account of the content of Christian hope for life beyond death may therefore be tested in terms of its social impact, hovering in an eschatological arch between triumphalism (or resignation), preparation and escapism. Furthermore, if the reality of finitude is simply avoided, this can only lead to a limited sense hope, to hope for this or the next moment only.

19.4 Responsibility in the presence of God

In Chapter 13 we investigated the Christian hope for the knowledge and presence of God that transcends the limitations of human knowledge and power. This emphasis leads to a typical eschatological tension between God and the world, between time and eternity, between God's immanence and God's transcendence. What is the social impact of Christian hope if given this content?

A Christian hope to transcend the limitations of human knowledge and power has often been criticized as other-worldly. In many Christian traditions this has fostered a sense of *contemptus mundi*, of world-denial instead of world-affirmation. These criticisms are closely related to the charge of escapism leveled against the Christian hope for life beyond death.[105] Escapism is indeed characteristic of a longing to leave this world behind in order to enter into the presence of God. Likewise, a one-dimensional world-affirmation can easily degenerate into hedonism and consumerism.

In addition to these dangers of hedonism and escapism, there is a further aspect to the social impact of the eschatological tension between God's immanence and God's transcendence. This may be described in terms of an eschatological arch ranging from activism to quietism.

If Christian hope is entirely related to God's transcendence, then such hope has to expect everything from God alone. God's grace may become so overwhelming that it negates any need for human action. Human power and knowledge remains utterly insignificant compared to God's omniscience and omnipotence. Hope can come from God alone. Within such a framework, Christian hope soon degenerates into a submissive acceptance of one's destiny. One just has to hope for the best. Since things are no longer under one's own locus of control, one can do nothing but to hope that God is somehow still in control. "We live in difficult times, but if we pray to God and trust in God, somehow God will help us." Such a spirit of

---

tions but of preparing for the coming of Christ (Bonhoeffer 1995:137).

105 This is hardly surprising in the light of a notion of eternity that transcends both the dimensions of space and time.

quietism expects everything from God without taking responsibility for the effects of human power and knowledge. At worst, the material world is denounced as evil and beyond redemption. Hope can come from God alone in a realm beyond this earth.[106] If, on the other hand, this expectation is disappointed, this soon leads to secularism and a plunge into nihilism.

By contrast, a Christian hope that minimizes God's transcendence will lead to the opposite extreme of activism. We have to take responsibility for the creation of a new world order into our own hands. We have to establish a utopia through our own actions, revolutionary if necessary.[107] Since God is radically immanent in the world, God's presence should also be evident in human knowledge and power. Accordingly, human beings should be able to control their own destinies. We cannot rely on God to intervene in this world. An emphasis on the indicative of God's grace is thus replaced by an emphasis on the imperative of good works. An exclusive emphasis on God's immanence implies the need to rely on material forces and innate human abilities for the future. Again, this may encourage either *triumphalism* (activism) or *resignation*, depending on one's present position of power. Tragically, when the realization dawns that suffering (the predicament of evil) and death (the predicament of finitude) is indeed beyond the control of finite human beings, such imperatives leave many with a sense of disillusionment and disempowerment. Responsibility without any grounds for hope is a burden too great to bear. It cannot motivate the change of attitude and praxis that is needed.[108]

How can a distortion of this eschatological tension between God's immanence and God's transcendence be prevented? In the history of Christianity an answer to this question often referred to the notion of *responsibility*. The mission and responsibility of the church is to proclaim the gospel faithfully and practise its message with steadfastness, through its kerugma, diakonia, koinonia and leitourgia. This link between hope and responsibility indicates the appropriateness of the metaphor of stewardship (despite its managerial and androcentric inadequacies). Christian are indeed responsible for "tending the garden", for caring for creation.

There is no need to spell out the practical implications of such an environmental responsibility here. Literature on this theme abounds. Within the tension between God's immanence and transcendence it is perhaps more important to comment on the source of a sense of responsibility. This need is illustrated by one of the anomalies and impasses of an environmental awareness. We have witnessed more than three decades of environmental conscientizing, outcries, statistics, analyses, programs and movements. Despite this huge effort, we have not been able to turn the tide of consumption, pollution, increasing population, deforestation and the exploitation of non-renewable resources. The problem has not been a lack of information or planning. It is less a problem of know-what or know-how than of know-why and know-wherefore. The problem is not ignorance (the predicament of limited human knowledge), but sin (the predicament of evil). Good Christian

---

106 See De Gruchy (1999:68).

107 See De Gruchy (1999:68).

108 Cobb & Griffin (1976:157).

people know that they need to love their neighbors, but still find themselves unable to do so. The problem is not a lack of good intentions; it is a result of the bondage of the human will. The repetition of calls for environmental responsibility is important but will not by itself provide the impetus to change destructive patterns.[109]

From the point of view of Christian faith, a sense of *responsibility* is only possible when human beings are compelled by God's grace (e.g. through Word and sacrament) to *respond* to God's love by fostering bonds of love in this world. Christian hope is something that carries us, not something that we have to carry. Or, to express this in typically reformed language: An appropriate response to God's gracious presence is a life of prayer[110] and *gratitude*. It *retrospectively* recognizes God's activity in the world and offers a prayer of thanksgiving for God's grace.

Grace is indeed a crucial feature of Christian hope. The reign of God is not the product of ethical activity, but the rule of God that is prior to any human activity. In an essay on "The liberating feast" Moltmann comments on the aesthetic dimension of grace:

> Christian eschatology has never presented this end of history as the result of historical struggles or the goal of human moral efforts. It has regarded it as the end of the history of domination and work, and described it in aesthetic categories – as a song of endless joy, the dance of the redeemed, with infinitely varied patterns ...[111]

What, then, is the link between hope and responsibility? Carl Braaten explains that a Christian ethos can only anticipate the coming rule of God proleptically:

> The kingdom of God which is really future retains its futurity in the very historical events which anticipate it in the present. Christian ethics is not to be understood as the means of producing the future kingdom of God, but only as annunciation, anticipation, and approximation, let us say as 'signs of the coming kingdom.'... Such ethical actions

---

109 See Cobb (1992:12) who also argues that moral exhortation is of little use since the structures of an industrial society thwart any noble attempts to follow a simple lifestyle.

110 See Galilea (1988:115f) and Pieper (1986:36) for the link between prayer and hope. Prayer and hope are naturally ordered to each other. Prayer is the expression and proclamation of hope. Hope itself speaks through prayer. For prayer, in its original form as a prayer of petition, is nothing than the voicing of hope. One who despairs does not petition because she assumes that her prayers will not be granted. One who is presumptuous petitions, indeed, but his petition is not genuine because he fully anticipates its fulfillment (Pieper 1986:70). Prayer is thus a prolonged act of hope (Galilea 1988).

Prayer, one may add, is directly related to the predicament of the limitations of human knowledge and power. In prayer, one gives expression in the presence of God, to aspects of life that are precisely beyond one's own locus of control. This implies to prayers of gratitude and petition alike. To pray for things that are within one's own power to address, will often result in soliloquy. Ellul (1973:189) adds that hope is for this very reason hope in God alone. Why hope for something that one can (and should!) do oneself?

111 Metz & Moltmann (1995:105).

> do not realize the kingdom; rather, the kingdom reveals itself through actions that prefigure its coming.[112]

It is especially in contexts of radical despair, where environmental degradation seems to have the final word, where injustice and oppression prevails, where the poor know that they and their children will probably die poor, where death intervenes that Christian hope can no longer *trust in human abilities* only. Hope then becomes more than the equivalent of a way to inspire people to achieve certain visions and desirable goals. Hope frees us from the slave masters of ambition and competition in the rat race of industrial capitalism, which "whips us into action and leaves us in frustration."[113] It transcends the disillusionment of frustrated revolutions and personal failures. Migliore explains the difference between Christian hope and utopian thinking clearly:

> Authentic Christian hope will certainly stand in opposition to present injustice and to every effort to absolutize the status quo. However, in the struggle for justice, equality, and human rights, Christians will always insist on something more, something greater than what is ever achievable by human effort alone, a hope beyond hope. Utopian hope finds in humanity itself the resources and capacities to remove all suffering, establish universal justice, and complete history. A Christian theology of hope, by contrast, knows that the fulfillment we seek is an incalculable gift of God.[114]

Migliore continues:

> In the midst of our struggle for a renewed world in which life flourishes and the forces of evil, death, and destruction are overcome, we learn the meaning of hoping in God rather than in our own abilities and achievements.[115]

Hope therefore has a *theocentric dimension* and not merely an *anthropological basis*: it is in this sense a trust in God alone. What Christians hope for, only God can establish. It is finally God who will create the "new heavens and a new earth".[116] Hope as trust in Godself can therefore endure *despite* present experiences of God, despite situations where God seems to have abandoned people completely (when war, rape, the death of a child, the murder of innocent people, the extinction of a species, ruthless exploitation is precisely *not* averted – despite a sincere trust in God).[117] Christian hope can therefore be a "hope against hope", a hope that often flies in the face of reality because it is based on a faithfulness of the

---

[112] Braaten (1974:110-111).

[113] Nürnberger (1994:149).

[114] Migliore (1991:241).

[115] Migliore 1991:249).

[116] De Gruchy (1999:73).

[117] According to Van de Beek (1987:44), this is exactly what we often experience of God. We experience powerlessness, chaos, broken lives, sickness, abuse. Van de Beek asks: Does God have nothing to do with such experience – and only with compassion and aid?

God who continuously surprises us.[118]

This hope in God is itself a gift from God.[119] It is only discovered through discipleship, when it is realized that Christian hope offers no guarantee of quick or easy solutions, where suffering prevails, when liberation proves beyond the sphere of influence of the one who hopes, when it is understood that there is a human hurt for which no social or political cure exists (Schillebeeckx).[120]

This hope in God alone is born from the unnerving realization that human beings cannot transcend the boundaries of finitude in space and time. Faced with the awareness that injustice and untimely death will often have the final word in this life, Christian hope expresses a trust in a God who transcends these dimensions of finitude. In the language of numerous Psalms, it raises a vehement complaint against this God to urgently respond to our suffering here and now. It asks the question "How long?" on the basis of earlier experiences of the already of God's presence.

It is this feature, as we have repeatedly noted in previous chapters, that calls for an extrapolation of Christian eschatology to address the predicament of finitude (and not only sin).

An account of the content of Christian hope for eternal life with God may therefore be tested in terms of its social impact, ranging in an eschatological arch between activism and triumphalism (or resignation), responsibility and quietism. Moreover, if the limitations of human knowledge and power are simply avoided, this would lead to unfounded, futile hope, to hope based on human potential alone.

19.5 Maintaining an eschatological dialectic

One further remarkable feature of the social impact of Christian hope should be noted here. The different eschatological tensions do not call for a neat balancing of the tension somewhere in the safe middle ground. Instead, it produces a creative tension that requires a dialectic where both poles are given their full weight. This implies that a focus on the not-yet, on the hereafter and on God – which is often seen as world-denying – is in fact crucial for a world-affirming ecological ethos. Barth already perceived that daily hope can persist only when it is itself eternal hope. Where there is this "great hope", there will necessarily be small hopes for the immediate future.[121]

- A full acknowledgment of the "not yet" is necessary precisely to provide inspiration to resist the forces of evil now. Without the possibility of a *novum*, a spirit of despair will become inevitable. To proclaim the not-yet does not necessarily deny, but may precisely affirm the here and the now.

---

118 De Gruchy (1999:75).

119 See Pieper (1986:33): "But the very habit of hope, by virtue of which one expects happiness, stems not from merit, but solely from grace."

120 Quoted in Migliore (1991:250). The reference is to the work by Schillebeeckx (1977:624), *Jesus: An experiment in Christology*, (New York: Seabury Press).

121 Barth (*CD* 4.1, 1956:119-121).

- An acknowledgment of the discontinuity of the hereafter is important to put the present life into the broader perspective of eternal life[122] and thus to empower and encourage a commitment towards this life.[123] Therefore, as we live on this earth, we are preparing the earth for the life of the new earth.[124] Without a vision of heaven, we will become obsessed with overcoming our anxieties about our own existence, with accumulating material possessions, with fruitless crusades and with frantic pleasure seeking.[125] To proclaim life beyond death does not necessarily deny, but may precisely affirm this life.
- A full recognition of God's transcendence is important in order to acknowledge and to accept responsibility for both the limitations and the potential of human power and knowledge.[126] We are most loyal to the earth when our ultimate loyalty is to God alone.[127] It is only when we behold the love of God mirrored in Jesus Christ that we are able to look at the earth with new eyes.[128] To proclaim God's transcendence does not necessarily deny but may precisely affirm this world.

This dialectic is also important for an ecological ethos. Christian hope is a trust that the future is ultimately in God's hands, not in our own. This calls for an acceptance of the limited ability of human beings to conquer evil. It calls for an acceptance of

---

[122] See Moltmann (1998b:41): "A person who is certain of eternal life has a great deal of time. We linger then in the moment, and open ourselves up to the intensive experience of life. We experience eternity in the moment (*Augenblick*) that is lived utterly and completely."

[123] Pannenberg (1995). CS Lewis came to a similar conclusion that Christians who are no longer concerned with the heavenly will become powerless in their witness. Lewis says:

> But a constant longing for eternity is not, as some people reckon, a form of escapism. If one reads history, then one will notice that those Christians who did most in the here and now were also the people who longed most for the hereafter. Quoted in Cilliers (1997, meditation for 5 June).

[124] Cf. Hoekema (1978:287).

[125] See Conyer (1992:164). Conyer provides a sustained argument for the earthly importance of God's transcendence (hope in the world beyond) and warns against the eclipse of heaven in contemporary Christianity. Moltmann (1997:107), likewise, senses that there is a link between a fear of death and greed for life. The fear of death finds expression in an unbridled hunger for power, for pleasure and for possessions, and in a thirst for recognition through success and admiration.

[126] Pannenberg (1969:61f, 111f). Pannenberg argues that a Christian ethical failure is closely related to an inadequate doctrine of God. An otherworldly notion of God may be important to gain a critical distance from the present and to kindle an enthusiasm for the transformation of the present. However, this will lead to escapism if this is not coupled with an affirmation of the world, e.g. by regarding the Creator also as the future of the world. A notion of transcendence is therefore necessary that is engaged in the dynamics of this world (Pannenberg 1969:114).

[127] Migliore (1991:250).

[128] Nel (1995:63).

our inability to transcend human finitude or to acquire infinite power and knowledge. This acceptance creates the necessary room for the following features that are crucial to a life of hope to emerge:

- The trust that it is God (not we) who will indeed establish the reign of God, on earth, as it is in heaven;
- The conviction that, after death and decay, my life and the whole history of the earth itself will be taken up in the loving presence of God;
- The belief that this loving presence of a transcendent God has already become manifest in God's love for and presence in the whole of creation – and that this is exemplified in Jesus Christ and through the Spirit of God.

20. Stories of hope for the earth

20.1 Introduction

The Christian vision of *shalom*, of "Justice, Peace and the Integrity of Creation" has inspired numerous Christian individuals and local Christian communities to establish signs of hope amidst ecological despair. It has challenged them to resist environmental degradation and injustice and the ideologies supporting the status quo. They embody the virtues of living in hope. They provide concrete examples of what it means to live with a vision of hope for the earth, many of them in a traditional African context.

In this chapter we will look at some of the practical ways in which Christian communities have responded to environmental degradation. These stories have been collected from various sources inside and outside South Africa.

20.2 Stories of hope from within South Africa

The Khanya Programme

The Khanya Programme is a ministry designed by the Methodist Church of Southern Africa for rural people. It has sought to develop a church-based development model in the rural communities of the Eastern Cape. Based on the presupposition that Christian ministry involves serving both the spiritual and material needs of people it has attempted to address the development needs of poverty stricken communities. It uses available church land for the benefit of the poor by way of empowering people to overcome unemployment and hunger. The local Methodist churches have become centers for development initiatives directed toward the whole community. The development program is multifaceted and includes the following:

- People's need for food is met through training them to grow their own fruit and vegetables making use of permaculture techniques.
- The Khanya Programme provides poor people with domesticated animals and training in animal care. These animals benefit their owners in a number of ways. They provide manure for the vegetable gardens and food for their tables. Recipients of animals pledge to "pass on the gift" by giving the first female offspring to another family with no animals.
- Solar power plants have been installed in remote areas that have no access to electricity. People are then encouraged to purchase a package which includes a 12 volt battery, wiring, a fluorescent light and a plug point.
- Micro-industries have been established. At the present most of these are small bakeries.
- Appropriate housing: The Khanya Programme seeks to equip the people to build affordable, yet attractive and durable houses of mud bricks.

The center of all these projects is the revitalization of corporate worship. In the blessing of the seeds ceremony, people are reminded of the time for planting and about our responsibility for our own food production. They take part in this ceremony by bringing their seeds and also by reading a pledge that commits them to planting and caring for their gardens. For the first fruit ceremonies, they offer thanks for God's act of leading our country away from apartheid while marking our responsibility to shape our country and our future (Deut 26:1-11). During the harvest festivals, people are encouraged to celebrate God's provisions and to commit ourselves again to making use of the gardens. The final liturgical activity consists of 'combined worship with animals, land produce and people,' with the goal of linking worship of God with the lives of the rural people, their animals and gardens.[1] In the words of one of the participants in this program:

> Practising permaculture in my garden has been a relief to me as I am a man who is unemployed with children and grandchildren who need good food in order to grow healthy. Having been given two goats by the Joseph Project, I can see that even the complexion of my family has changed to light which is a sign of a well nourished family. I am expecting two kids which means not only more milk but beneficiaries by way of passing-on of gifts. Health complaints now decrease remarkably. I have a happy family. (Mhlope Kini, Mzwini).[2]

The Goldfields Faith and Earthkeeping project

The Faith & Earthkeeping Project was founded in 1995 under the auspices of the World Wide Fund for Nature (SA) and is managed as a project within the context of the Research Institute for Theology and Religion at the University of South Africa.

The principal aim of the project is to help conscientize, empower and support communities and individuals at a grassroots level to create and implement their own activities and policies for local, regional and national environmental protection, conservation and sustainable resource use, with a view to help improve their quality of life. This is done through the promotion of a religious engagement in ecological and development issues.

It supports a number of local organizations towards projects for tree planting, the preservation of water resources, veld management and land use, cleaning-up operations, urban greening and agriculture, nurseries and recycling projects. Several successful community projects have been initiated by Faith & Earthkeeping in seven of the nine provinces in South Africa, for example in Mamelodi, Attridgeville, Soshanguve (multi-dimensional urban projects), Winterveld, Rust de Winter, Qwa-Qwa, Seakha (rural sustainable agriculture projects), Delmas (semi-urban agriculture and greening projects).[3]

---

1 I am grateful to Welile Sigabi for his inputs to this case study.

2 *Khanya Programme Newsletter* 5:1, 4, Winter 1997.

3 I am grateful to Victor Molobi for his inputs to this case study.

The struggle against toxic waste near Philadelphia

In August 1994 a large waste disposal company investigated the possibility of a hazardous waste dump (baptized "gifgat", "poison hole") two kilometers from the small rural town of Philadelphia, off the N7 near Cape Town. The company offered a huge amount to an absentee farmer in the area for a suitable piece of land and promised employment for many workers. The farming community was soon up in arms about the dangers of highly toxic waste infiltrating into the groundwater system of the area. One semi-employed farm worker responded to the offer of a well-paid job: "No, not if this will bring death to my children."

The local DRC congregation facilitated a series of meetings and a long and intricate battle ensued. The Department of Environmental Affairs, legal experts, environmental monitoring groups and the local newspapers soon got involved in the process. The company used everything in its considerable power to push its plans through – from bribery to clandestine scare tactics. After numerous meetings, telephone calls, peacemaking efforts and prayers, the owner of the land unexpectedly withdrew his offer to sell the land. David had managed to deter the mighty Goliath.

Abalimi Bezekhaya ("Planters of the home")

This organization promotes an urban agriculture and greening program. Its aim is to provide opportunities for the poor, especially women, in the townships of the Cape Flats, to support each other, to grow food for themselves and their families and to gain self-respect by creating home food security. Low-cost resources and skills training are the means by which this support is offered. More than 10 000 people are already involved as small-scale vegetable farmers in this project.

The associated Cape Flats Tree Project promotes the greening of local neighborhoods, schools and public parks. It establishes well-maintained models to inspire others to follow. By establishing these models, a greater environmental awareness and understanding of biological organic methods for the healing of both the earth and her people is encouraged. Abalimi Bezekhaya is a non-denominational organization, is independently managed and funded but remains affiliated to the Catholic Welfare and Development.

"Wikkel, Woeker, Werk": A recycling project

A congregation of the Gereformeerde Kerk in Alberton-West started in 1991 with a project to collect iron, tin, aluminium, glass, paper and plastics for reuse and recycling. Enormous quantities of material have been collected since then. In this way the congregation helped to clean the environment, manage waste, gave young and old in the congregation a sense of purpose, encouraged a spirit of community and cooperation and also earned a considerable income for the congregation. They also published two booklets giving advice to other congregations on how to manage such a project.

The Diocese of Umzimvubu

The rural regions of the Eastern Cape face numerous environmental challenges. Many of these are a legacy of the homeland system. The Anglican Diocese of Umzimvubu, under the leadership of Bishop Geoff Davies, has attempted to address some of these issues as well as to raise the church's consciousness of environmental issues. This work is symbolized in the development of the Glenthorn Training Center outside Kokstad. The Glenthorn farm, the residence of the Bishop of Umzimvubu, is in the process of being transformed. Efforts are being made to reverse the ecological degradation that has taken place in the past. Part of the estate is being set aside and developed as a nature reserve. A training center has been set up where various conferences and training courses are held within the context of an awareness of the goodness of God's creation.

The work of the diocese is not confined to Glenthorn. The diocese appointed an agricultural officer, Bob Thelin, to teach and equip farmers within the diocese to engage in sustainable agriculture. It is envisaged that this project will not only contribute to providing food for many poverty stricken families, but will also counter the effects of the ecological degradation of the past.

The Diocese also acted as a voice for the community in recent debates concerning the development of a toll road and holiday resorts along the Wild Coast. While the project was abandoned for financial reasons, Bishop Davies had become a spokesperson for the groups' opposition to the development due to its environmentally destructive character and its failure to empower and develop the local communities.

20.3 Examples from the Southern African region

The following examples of church-based environmental projects were collected during a tour of the region in which I was fortunate to participate in 1997. They are therefore not representative or in any way comprehensive.

Tree-planting Eucharists in Zimbabwe

The tree-planting initiatives of African Independent Churches in Zimbabwe have become quite famous throughout the world. Since the formation in 1988 of ZIRRCON (Zimbabwe Institute of Religious Research and Ecological Conservation), churches in the country have been challenged on the basis of their Christian faith to engage in tree planting activities. In 1991 the Association of African Earthkeeping Churches (AAEC) was established. These organizations promote massive programs for afforestation, wildlife conservation and the protection of water resources. Several nurseries have been established from where trees are planted for fuel-wood, for nutrition (fruit trees), for commercial use and building operations (e.g. blue gums), to protect and clothe the soil and for coming generations (e.g. red mahogany).

Tree planting ceremonies are often linked to Eucharistic services. These innovative liturgies are introduced to integrate environmental ethics and church praxis.

In this way Christians are "proclaiming a widening message of salvation which encompasses all of creation, and in their services of worship they are dancing out a new rhythm which, in its footwork, spells hope for the ravaged earth" (Marthinus Daneel).[4]

Projects for sustainable agriculture in Zambia

a) The Christian Council of Zambia is involved in numerous development projects all over Zambia. In some respects, it seems to provide infrastructure and training where the government is unable to fulfill its responsibility. One of these projects is based on a 100 acres farm in Lusaka West which serves as a model and training center for sustainable agriculture. On this farm a system of rainwater harvesting and the building of small water tanks or wells have been developed. Other activities include fish farming, a nursery for tree planting, the use of indigenous plants for fertilization and pesticides, etc. This project serves as an example to the government and local villages of what could be done towards food security and sustainable farming with limited resources.

b) In Madzimoyo, the Reformed Church in Zambia has established a Church Lay Training Center. The emphasis of this lay training center has shifted from a predominant emphasis on spiritual training to a more holistic approach. One of the projects is a demonstration plant to provide a model of sustainable agriculture to local farmers, to provide in basic needs for nutrition (also for the training center), and to earn some additional income through the surplus produce. This project encourages the use of natural forms of fertilization and pesticides. This is not only environmentally more sustainable but also reduces expenditure and financial risks.

A Center for Appropriate Technology at Mindolo

The Mindolo Ecumenical Foundation is located at Kitwe, in the Cobberbelt region of Zambia. It provides training programmes towards self-employment to students from all over Africa. This includes a Center for Appropriate Technology (with an emphasis on carpentry and metal work), a Pottery School and a Small Holdings Farm. The emphasis in these courses falls on community based self-employment which would be sustainable within a rural context. This requires less sophisticated forms of technology that would not be expensive to acquire or maintain. The farming project enables the Mindolo Community to feed itself. In these ways a self-sustaining use of water, energy and food is encouraged.

The heritage of the mission in Zambia

Since the 1890's mission stations were built all over Zambia by the Catholic

---

4 For more detail on this remarkable movement, see the many contributions by Daneel (e.g. 1991, 1994).

Church, the London Missionary Society and the Dutch Reformed Church, often due to requests from the local (Ngoni) chiefs. The early missionaries set an example of enhancing the fertility of the land by their water projects, the planting of numerous fruit trees and various small-scale agricultural projects. These examples still encourage people in local villages to plant and protect trees, to care for the environment and to create a source of nutritional food in the process.

An animal orphanage at Mua in Malawi

Deforestation has taken place on an enormous scale in Malawi. One of the consequences of this process is that the natural habitat of a large number of animals has been destroyed. At the Catholic mission at Mua, near lake Malawi, an animal orphanage has been started to provide shelter for a wide variety of these homeless animals. This has helped local parishioners to develop a relationship with these animals instead of viewing them only as a source of meat.

Mua is best known for the Kungoni Arts and Crafts Center that was developed there under the leadership of the local priest, father Boucher. This center explores the relationship between Christian symbols and traditional symbols in the Chewa, Yao, and Kungoni cultures. The creation stories in these cultures are told through art in order to draw attention to the intrinsic link between culture and the environment and the threat of human insensitivity to the preservation of natural resources.

20.4 Examples from elsewhere in the world

Among the numerous examples of Christian earthkeeping from elsewhere in the world, the following few stories may be mentioned here:

The "one grain of rice" movement in India and Pakistan

In parts of India and Pakistan, Christian women's groups have started the "one grain of rice" movement. Women were powerless because of poverty and because they had no control over the land. They have formed groups and encourage each other to put aside one grain of rice a day, no matter how hungry they or their families are. These grains of rice are pooled, and as soon as they have collected a few hundred grams, the rice is sold and the money put away in the women's bank. Gradually a sum of money is accumulated, enough to buy or lease land that is eroded and abandoned unfit for growing crops. By working on this land together, the women terrace it, plant trees, and gradually bring the land back into cultivation. In this way women have become decision-makers about the land and have gained some power over their own lives.[5]

The Living Churchyard project

This project in Britain offers advice and encouragement to enable individual

5 Breuilly & Palmer (1992:112-3).

churches to manage their churchyards in an ecologically sound way, whether they are rural or inner city parishes.[6]

The Ormylia project

This project was established by the Greek Orthodox Church in 1990. It began as an organic farming and recycling project on the monastery's lands, in an area affected by environmentally destructive practices such as extensive pesticide use. They recruited a team of experts to advise it on organic agriculture on the monastery's land – its farm, plantations of pears, olives and almonds and its herds of sheep, cows and chickens. It has become a model for surrounding farms and attracts thousands of annual visitors.[7]

Human scale farming

Groups like the Hutterites, Amish and Mennonites have traditionally based their lifestyles on sustainable farming practices. By relying on family and community help, and using horses instead of tractors, farms are kept to what one Amish farmer described as "a human scale". Farms are no bigger than what one family can take care of.[8]

20.5 Eschatological perspectives on sustainable communities

These case studies provide examples of how an environmental praxis and spirituality can be concretized within an urban and rural African context. They embody a vision of hope for the earth. They indicate that the church itself may set an example of a sustainable community. Perhaps they also provide a new vision for the church. They help us to visualize what it means for the church to be the eschatological new creation amidst the brokenness of the present creation. The church is here indeed a sign of the new creation, a community of hope, the place where the world becomes conscious of its destiny in God's reign, the prolepsis of a new world.[9]

Let us look briefly at some of the ways in which traditional eschatological images of the church receive a fresh content in the experience and practices of these case studies.[10]

a) In the biblical image of the church as the "first fruits" of the new creation, it is

---

6 Breuilly & Palmer (1992:112-3).

7 Breuilly & Palmer (1992:112-3).

8 Breuilly & Palmer (1992:112-3).

9 See Braaten (1969:109) for an exploration of these themes.

10 These reflections have emerged from a detailed discussion with David Field. His many inputs are gratefully acknowledged.

portrayed as the first installment of the renewal of creation. In the exuberant harvest celebrations of numerous sustainable agriculture projects this image receives a new content. The first fruits of the vegetable gardens are presented before God in gratitude for the harvest and for a new avenue towards self-sustenance and human dignity. The church thus becomes the first fruits (and vegetables!) of the new creation.

To identify the church as the first fruits of the new creation is to confess not only that the redemption that has begun with the church will extend to the entire earth, but also that through the church the earth will be sanctified and cleansed. It is the presence of the Spirit who constitutes the church as the first fruits of the new creation. The Spirit empowers and equips the church to engage in a praxis of transformation as it looks forward in hope to the redemption of all things. The fruit of the Spirit (Gal 5:22f) does not come from us but from God. As Jürgen Moltmann insists, we cannot make the fruit of the Spirit, nor can it be learnt. We have to wait expectantly for it, and let it grow, as fruit ripen on a tree.[11] When this does happen, for example when churches and other Christian groups become involved in the struggle for eco-justice, as is seen in the case studies that are mentioned above, they are giving expression to the nature of the church as the first fruits of the new creation.

b) In 1 Corinthians 15:20 Christ is described in as the first born of a new dispensation. This image may be extrapolated to the church as the body of Christ and the first born of the new creation. The image of the first born has a rich heritage in the Bible. All believers participate as newborn people in a new creation. Those who have received a cow or a goat through the Khanya Programme – and thus a new livelihood for themselves – pledge to give the first female offspring to someone else in need. In this way concrete and visible signs of the new creation are established on earth.

c) The eschatological vision of Isaiah 11 projects peace between God and animals, and not only between human beings and God. In the envisaged sanctuary of the Khanya Programme (where a kraal for animals forms one of the three circles in the building structure) something of this harmonious co-existence between God, humanity and the animals becomes visible and concrete. The animals may also come into God's presence.

d) A further image of some potential is that of the church as a tree of life. Tree planting is a crucial aspect in the work of the Association of African Earthkeeping Churches, Abalimi Bezekhaya and numerous other NGO's. Especially in rural areas this forms a crucial of earthkeeping in the light of the problems of deforestation and the daily task of collecting ever-scarcer firewood. In biblical imagery trees are a symbol of the good life that God intended for creation in the beginning (the tree of life). The tree of life also appears as an eschatological symbol in the last

11 Moltmann (1997:53).

chapter of Revelation where it bears fruit 12 months on the year and where leaves of the tree brings healing for the nations. This rich imagery is concretized in the praxis of tree planting Eucharists. The church is a tree planting community and therefore functions as a "tree" (source) of life for the whole creation.

There are numerous other eschatological symbols for the church that may be explored in a similar way (e.g. the church as the communion of the saints, the river of life, a banquet for the poor, etc). The direction is clear. The earthkeeping practices of these African case studies help to concretize and renew the meaning of these eschatological symbols for the church. They provide an example of what the church as an agent of new creation could look like in the midst of the injustice, deprivation and degradation of the world in which it is situated.

These case studies not only provide examples of a hope-infested environmental praxis in an African context. They also illuminate what an environmental spirituality may embody. The importance of a worshipping community is evident in many of these case studies. The models provided by the Khanya Program and the tree planting Eucharists of the African Initiated Churches in Zimbabwe are particularly suggestive with regard to the centrality of revitalized worship. In both cases responses to issues of eco-justice are integrated into a renewal of worship and thus into the heart of the life of the church. This renewed worship becomes the center and dynamo for the praxis of eco-justice. The exclusive focus on God and God's transcendence in worship functions as a critique of other absolutes and illuminates the contrast to the brokenness, suffering and degradation in the context surrounding the worshipping community. It also inspires them to engage in small, but meaningful actions towards a transformation of these realities.

The church celebrates God's presence in the midst of creation and together with the rest of nature. It therefore examines ways in which the whole of creation can be included in worship, in anticipation of the eschatological worship of "every creature in heaven and on earth and under the earth and in the sea and all that is in them" (Rev. 5:13).

Bibliography

Abraham, KC 1994. A theological response to the ecological crisis. In: Hallman, DG (ed) 1994. *Ecotheology. Voices from South and North*, 65-78. Geneva: World Council of Churches.

Ackermann, DM & Joyner, T 1996. Earth-healing in South Africa. Challenges to church and mosque. In: Ruether, RR (ed) 1996. *Women healing earth. Third world women on ecology, feminism and religion*, 121-134. Maryknoll: Orbis Books.

Ackermann, DM 1992. A time to hope. *Journal of Theology for Southern Africa* 81, 66-70.

Alberts, L & Chikane, F 1991. *The road to Rustenburg. The church looking forward to a new South Africa*. Cape Town: Struik Christian Books.

Albright, Carol & Haugen, J (eds) 1997. *Beginning with the end. God science and Wolfhart Pannenberg*. Chicago & LaSalle, Ill: Open Court.

Alves, R 1969. *A theology of human hope*. St. Meinrad: Abbey Press.

Anthonissen, K 1993. *Dansend na die lig*. Kaapstad: Lux Verbi.

Anthonissen, K 1994. *Die aand is vol lig*. Kaapstad: Lux Verbi.

Antonio, EP 1994. Letting people decide: Towards an ethic of ecological survival in Africa. In: Hallman, DG (ed) 1994. *Ecotheology. Voices from South and North*, 227-234. Geneva: World Council of Churches.

Arendse, RA 1998. The historical Jesus, eschatology and hope for the earth? *Scriptura* 66, 245-268.

Arendt, H 1959. *The human condition. A study of the central dilemmas facing man*. Garden City: Doubleday.

Asante, E 1985. Ecology: untapped resource of pan-vitalism in Africa. *AFER: African Ecclesial Review* 27, 289-293.

Augustine, A 1907. *Confessions*. Translated by E.B. Pusey. London: J.M. Dent & Sons.

Aune, DE 1992. Biblical eschatology. In: Freedman, DN (ed) 1992. *The Anchor Bible Dictionary* 2, 575-609. New York: Doubleday.

Bailey, KE 1983. *Poet & peasant. Through peasant eyes*. Grand Rapids: WB Eerdmans.

Barbour, IG 1997. *Religion and science. Historical and contemporary issues*. San Francisco: Harper & Row.

Barns, I 1998. Eschatological hope and ecological justice. *Ecotheology* 5 & 6, 173-184.

Barth, K 1928. *The Word of God and the word of man*. New York: Harper & Row.

Barth, K 1933. *The Epistle to the Romans*.[2] Oxford University Press.

Barth, K 1956. *Church Dogmatics 1.2*. Edinburgh: T. & T. Clark.

Barth, K 1957. *Church Dogmatics 2.1*. Edinburgh: T. & T. Clark.

Barth, K 1960. *Church Dogmatics 3.2*. Edinburgh: T. & T. Clark.

Barth, K 1960. *Church Dogmatics 3.3*. Edinburgh: T. & T. Clark.

Bavinck, H 1956. *Our reasonable faith*. Grand Rapids: Baker Book House.

Béguin-Austin, M (ed) 1993. *Sustainable growth - contradiction in terms?* Geneva: The Ecumenical Institute.

Behrens, G 1999. Healthy, wealthy and unhappy. *Time* 19/7/1999, 60.

Beker, JC 1994. *Suffering and hope. The Biblical vision and the human predicament*. Grand Rapids: WB Eerdmans.

Bellah, R 1989. Christian faithfulness in a pluralist world. In: Burnham, FB (ed) 1989. *Postmodern theology. Christian faith in a pluralist world*, 74-91. San Francisco: Harper & Row.

Berger, PL & Luckmann, T 1967. *The social construction of reality: a treatise in die sociology of knowledge*. New York: Penguin Press.

Berkhof, H 1967. *Gegronde verwachting. Schets van een Christelijke toekomstleer*. Nijkerk: GF Callenbach.

Berkhof, H 1981. *Bruggen en bruggehoofden*. Nijkerk: GF Callenbach.

Berkhof, H 1985. *Christelijk geloof. Een inleiding tot de geloofsleer*. Nijkerk: GF Callenbach.

Berkouwer, GC & Van der Woude, AS (eds) 1969. *In gesprek met Van Ruler*. Nijkerk: Callenbach.

Berkouwer, GC 1956. *The triumph of grace in the theology of Karl Barth*. Grand Rapids: WB Eerdmans.

Berkouwer, GC 1972. *The return of Christ*. Grand Rapids: WB Eerdmans.

Berry, T 1988. *The dream of the earth*. San Francisco: Sierra Club Books.

Berry, T 1991. *Befriending the earth: a theology of reconciliation between humans and the land*. Mystic, Co: Twentythird Publications.

Beyerhaus, P 1969. An approach to the African Independent Church Movement. *Ministry* 9, 78f.

Boesak, A 1977. Zwarte theologie, hoop en versoening. In: *Afscheid van de onschuld*. Kampen: JH Kok.

Boff, L & Elizondo, V (eds) 1995. *Ecology and poverty. Cry of the earth, cry of the poor. Concilium* 1995/5. London: SCM Press.

Boff, L 1995. *Ecology and liberation*. Maryknoll: Orbis Books.

Boff, L 1997. *Cry of the earth, cry of the poor*. Maryknoll: Orbis Books.

Bonhoeffer, D 1971. *Letters and papers from prison*. London: SCM Press.

Bonhoeffer, D 1995. *Ethics*. Translated from the sixth German edition. New York: Simon & Schuster.

Bonner, G 1994. Augustine's thoughts on this world and hope for the next. *Princeton Seminary Bulletin,* Supplementary Issue 3, 85-103.

Bosch, DJ 1979. *A spirituality of the road*. Sotdale: Herald Press.

Bosch, DJ 1984. The roots and fruits of Afrikaner civil religion. In: Hofmeyer, JW & Vorster, WS (eds): *New faces of Africa*, 14-35. Pretoria: UNISA.

Botha, F 1998. *Die lewe na die dood*. Kaapstad: Lux Verbi.

Bouma-Prediger, S 1995. *The greening of theology. The ecological models of Rosemary Radford Ruether, Joseph Sittler, and Jürgen Moltmann*. Atlanta: Scholars Press.

Bouma-Prediger, S 1997. Creation as the home of God: The doctrine of creation in the theology of Jürgen Moltmann. *Calvin Theological Journal* 32, 73-90.

Braaten, CE 1969. *The future of God. The revolutionary dynamics of hope*. New York: Harper & Row.

Braaten, CE 1972. The significance of the future. In: Cousins, EH (ed) 1972. *Hope and the future of man*. Philadelphia: Fortress Press.

Braaten, CE 1974. *Eschatology and ethics*. Minneapolis: Augsburg Press

Braaten, CE 1985. The kingdom of God and life everlasting. In: Hodgson, PC & King, RH (eds) 1985. *Christian theology. An introduction to its traditions and tasks*. Philadelphia: Fortress Press.

Breuilly, E & Palmer, M (eds) 1992. *Christianity and ecology*. London: Cassell Publishers.

Bridger, F 1990. Ecology and eschatology: a neglected dimension. *Tyndale Bulletin* 41:2, 290-301.

Brinkman, ME 1995. A theology of life: Open questions. *Exchange* 24, 176-183.

Brown, D 1981. *To set at liberty. Christian faith and human freedom*. Maryknoll: Orbis Books.

Brueggemann, W 1977. *The land. Place as gift, promise and challenge in Biblical faith*. Philadelphia: Fortress Press.

Brueggemann, W 1993. Trajectories in Old Testament literature and the sociology of ancient

Israel. In: Gottwald, NK & Horsley, RA 1993. *The Bible and liberation. Political and social hermeneutics*. Maryknoll: Orbis Books.

Brunner, E 1954. *Eternal hope*. Philadelphia: Westminster Press.

Bultmann, R 1957. *History and eschatology*. Edinburgh: Edinburgh University Press.

Burger, CW 1994. *Storie vir ons tyd*. Kaapstad: Lux Verbi.

Caldecott, S 1988. Cosmology, eschatology, ecology: Some reflections on *Sollicitudo rei socialis*. *Communio: International Catholic Review* 15, 305-318.

Capps, WH (ed) 1970. *The future of hope*. Philadelphia: Fortress Press.

Casey, HM & Morgante, A (eds) 1998. *Human rights environmental law and the Earth Charter*. Boston: Boston Research Center for the 21st century.

Chial, DL 1996. The ecological crisis: A survey of the WCC's recent responses. *Ecumenical Review* 48:1, 53-62.

Chilton, B (ed) 1984. *The kingdom of God in the teaching of Jesus*. Philadelphia: Fortress Press.

Cilliers, J 1997. *Dié dag is vol genade*. Kaapstad: Lux Verbi.

Cilliers, P 1998. *Complexity and postmodernism. Understanding complex systems*. London & New York: Routledge.

Clayton, P 1997. *God and contemporary science*. Edinburgh University Press.

Clayton, P 1998. Metaphysics can be a hard mistress. *CTNS Bulletin* 18:1, 15-19.

Cobb, JB & Daly, HE 1994. *For the Common Good: Redirecting the Economy toward Community, the Environment, and a Sustainable Future*.[2] Boston: Beacon.

Cobb, JB & Griffin, DR 1976. *Process theology: An introductory exposition*. Philadelphia: Westminster Press.

Cobb, JB 1972. What is the future? A process perspective. In: Cousins, EH (ed) 1972. *Hope and the future of man*. Philadelphia: Fortress Press.

Cobb, JB 1992. *Sustainability. Economics, ecology & justice*. Maryknoll: Orbis Books.

Cochrane, J 1999. Reading the signs of the millennium. *Journal of Theology for Southern Africa* 105, 29-41.

Cochrane, J & West, GO 1993. War, remembrance and reconstruction. *Journal of Theology for Southern Africa* 84, 25-40.

Cochrane, J, De Gruchy, JW & Petersen, RM 1991. *In word and deed. Towards a practical theology of social transformation*. Pietermartizburg: Cluster Publications.

Cock, J & Koch, E (eds) 1991. *Going green. People, politics and the environment in South Africa*. Cape Town: Oxford University Press.

Cock, J 1994. Christian witness and ecology. *International Review of Mission* 83:328, 89-92.

Comstock, GL 1987. Two types of narrative theology. *Journal of the American Academy of Religion* 55:4, 687-717.

Concerned Evangelicals 1986. *Evangelical Witness in South Africa*. Grand Rapids: WB Eerdmans.

Cone, JH 1986. *A black theology of liberation*.[2] Maryknoll: Orbis Books.

Cone, JH 1997. *God of the oppressed*. Maryknoll: Orbis Books.

Conlon, J 1994. *Earth story, sacred story*. Mystic, Co: Twenty-Third Publications.

Conradie, EM 1996. *Rus vir die hele aarde*. Kaapstad: Lux Verbi.

Conradie, EM 1997. Reconstructing an ecological cosmology: A South African contribution. *Scriptura* 61, 213-230.

Conradie, EM 1998. 'Hope for the earth?' Discerning the cosmic depths of despair. *Scriptura* 66, 279-308.

Conradie, EM 1998. *Christian theology and ecology. An indexed bibliography*. Study Guides on Religion and Theology 2. Bellville: University of the Western Cape.

Conradie, EM 1998. Extrapolating the Biblical trajectories on 'Hope for the earth'. *Scriptura*

66, 173-188.

Conradie, EM 1999. In search of a clear vision of hope for a new century. *Journal of Religion & Society* 1, par 1-58 (http://www.creighton.edu/JRS).

Conradie, EM 1999. *Towards a Christian ecological theology: An overview of current debates and South African contributions.* Stellenbosch: EFSA. (forthcoming)

Conyers, AJ 1992. *The eclipse of heaven.* Downers Grove: Intervarsity Press.

Cooper, T 1990. *Green Christianity.* London: Hodder & Stoughton.

Cousins, EH (ed) 1972. *Hope and the future of man.* Philadelphia: Fortress Press.

Cowdin, DM 1994. Toward an environmental ethic. In: Irwin, KW & Pelligrino, ED (eds) 1994. *Preserving the creation: Environmental theology and ethics.* Washington: Georgetown University Press.

Crutchfield, JP et al 1995. Chaos. In: Russell, RJ, Murphy, N & Peacocke, AR (eds) 1995. *Chaos and complexity. Scientific perspectives on divine action.* Vatican Observatory Publications.

Cullmann, O 1962. *Christ and time.* London: SCM Press.

Cullmann, O 1965. Immortality of the soul or resurrection of the dead? In: Stendahl, K (ed) 1965. *Immortality and resurrection,* 9-53. New York: Macmillan.

Cullmann, O 1967. *Salvation in history.* London: SCM Press.

Daneel, ML 1983. Black Messianism: Corruption or contextualisation. *Theologia Viatorum* 11:1, 1-25.

Daneel, ML 1987. *Quest for belonging.*Introduction to a study of African Independent Churches. Harare: Mambo Press.

Daneel, ML 1994. African Christian theology and the challenge of earthkeeping. In: Mouton, J & Lategan, BC (eds) 1994. *The relevance of theolgy for the 1990's,* 435-476. Pretoria: Human Sciences Research Council.

Daneel, ML 1994. African Independent Churches face the challenge of environmental ethics. In: Hallman, DG (ed): *Ecotheology. Voices from South and North,* 248-263. Geneva: World Council of Churches.

David Philip Publishers 1992. *A book of hope.* Cape Town & Johannesburg: David Philip.

Davies, P 1994. *The last three minutes of the universe.* London: Phoenix.

De Gruchy, JW 1979. The hope of the kingdom. In: *The church struggle in South Africa.* Cape Town: David Philip.

De Gruchy, JW 1986. *Cry justice. Prayers, meditations and readings from South Africa.* London: Collins Liturgical Publications.

De Gruchy, JW 1988. The struggle for justice and ministry of reconciliation. *Journal of Theology for Southern Africa* 62, 43-52.

De Gruchy, JW 1991. *Liberating reformed theology. A South African contribution to an ecumenical debate.* Grand Rapids: WB Eerdmans.

De Gruchy, JW 1992. Is there any hope for South Africa? In: *Faith for a time like this. South African sermons.* Rondebosch United Church.

De Gruchy, JW 1999. A new heaven and a new earth. *Journal of Theology for Southern Africa* 105, 65-74.

De Klerk, JJ 1994. *Op ver paaie.* Kaapstad: Lux Verbi.

Deist, FE 1994. *Hemelpastei en navolging.* Kaapstad: Lux Verbi.

Dodd, CH 1961. *The parables of the kingdom.*[2] New York: Charles Scribner's Sons.

Downey, M 1998. *Hope begins where hope begins.* Maryknoll: Orbis Books.

Drees, WB 1990. *Beyond the Big Bang. Quantum cosmologies and God.* La Salle: Open Court.

Drees, WB 1995. Gaps for God? In: Russell, RJ, Murphy, N & Peacocke, AR (eds) 1995. *Chaos and complexity. Scientific perspectives on divine action.* Vatican Observatory Publications.

Drees, WB 1997. Contingency, time and the theological ambiguity of science. In: Albright, Carol & Haugen, J (eds) 1997. *Beginning with the end. God, science and Wolfhart Pannenberg*, 217-247. Chicago & LaSalle, Ill: Open Court.

Duchrow, U & Liedke, G 1987. *Shalom. Biblical perspectives on creation, justice & peace*. Geneva: WCC Publications.

Durand, JJF 1982. *Skepping, mens, voorsienigheid*. Pretoria: N.G. Kerkboekhandel.

Durand, JJF 1985. Afrikaner piety and dissent. In: Villa-Vicencio, C & De Gruchy, JW (eds): *Resistance and hope*, 39-51. Cape Town: David Philip.

Durning, A 1990. *Apartheid's environmental toll*. Worldwatch Paper 95.

Dyson, FJ 1979. Time without end. *Reviews of Modern Physics* 51.

Edwards, D 1995. The discovery of chaos and the retrieval of the Trinity. In: Russell, RJ, Murphy, N & Peacocke, AR (eds) 1995. *Chaos and complexity. Scientific perspectives on divine action*. Vatican Observatory Publications.

Ellis, GFR & Murphy, N 1996. *On the moral nature of the universe*. Philadelphia: Fortress Press.

Ellul, J 1973. *Hope in a time of abandonment*. New York: The Seabury Press.

Faith and Order Study Document 1991. *Confessing the one faith*. Geneva: World Council of Churches.

Farley, E 1996. *Deep symbols: their postmodern effacement and reclamation*. Valley Forge: Trinity Press International.

Farrow, D 1998. In the end is the beginning: A review of Jürgen Moltmann's systematic contributions. *Modern Theology* 14:3, 425-447.

Ferguson, D 1997. Eschatology. In: Gunton, CE (ed) 1997. *The Cambridge companion to Christian doctrine*, 226-244. Cambridge: Cambridge University Press.

Field, DN 1996. Reformed theology, modernity and the environmental crisis. Doctoral dissertation. University of Cape Town.

Ford, L 1972. Response to Johannes Metz. In: Cousins, EH (ed) 1972. *Hope and the future of man*. Philadelphia: Fortress Press.

Freyne, S & Lash, N (eds) 1998. *Is the world ending? Concilium* 1998/4. London: SCM Press. / Maryknoll: Orbis Books.

Galilea, S 1988. *Spirituality of hope*. Maryknoll: Orbis Books.

Gilkey, L 1968. The contribution of culture to the reign of God. In: Muckenhirn, M (ed) 1968. *The future as the presence of shared hope*, 34-58. New York: Sheed and Ward.

Gilkey, L 1970. Eschatology and time. In: Herzog, F 1970. *The future of hope. Theology as eschatology*. New York: Herder & Herder.

Gilkey, L 1976. *Reaping the whirlwind. A Christian interpretation of history*. New York: Seabury Press.

Gillies, F 1980. The Bantu concept of time. *Religion* 10, 16-30.

Govender, S 1987. The road ahead. In: *The road ahead*. Documentation on the confessing church debate. Cape Town: The Belydende Kring.

Govender, S 1995. Life in between the times: The South African renaissance. In: Villa-Vicencio, C & Niehaus, C (eds): *Many cultures, one nation*, 131-145. Cape Town: Human & Rousseau.

Gowan, DE 1986. *Eschatology in the Old Testament*. Philadelphia: Fortress Press.

Granberg-Michaelson, W (ed) 1987. *Tending the garden: essays on the gospel and the earth*. Michigan: WB Eerdmans.

Granberg-Michaelson, W 1982. Earthkeeping: a theology for global sanctification. *Sojourners* 11, 21-24.

Granberg-Michaelson, W 1990. Renewing the whole creation. Constructing a theology of relationship. *Sojourners* 19:2, 10-14.

Granberg-Michaelson, W 1994. Creation in ecumenical theology. In: Hallman, DG (ed)

1994. *Ecotheology. Voices from South and North*, 96-106. Geneva: World Council of Churches.

Granberg-Michaelson, W 1994. Towards a theology of life. *Reformed World* 44, 99-110.

Gudynas, E 1995. Ecology from the viewpoint of the poor. In: Boff, L & Elizondo, V (eds) 1995. *Ecology and poverty. Cry of the earth, cry of the poor. Concilium* 1995/5, 106-114. London: SCM Press.

Gustafson, JM 1994. *A sense of the divine. The natural environment from a theocentric perspective*. Edinburgh: T & T Clark.

Gutiérrez, G 1973. *A theology of liberation*. Maryknoll: Orbis Books.

Hall, DJ 1990. *The steward: a biblical symbol come of age*. New York: Friendship Press.

Hall, DJ 1996. *Confessing the faith. Christian theology in a North American context*. Minneapolis: Fortress Press.

Hallman, DG (ed) 1994. *Ecotheology. Voices from South and North*. Risk Book Series. Geneva: World Council of Churches.

Hauerwas, S & Willimon, WH 1989. *Resident aliens*. Nashville: Abingdon Press.

Haught, JF 1990. Religious and cosmic homelessness: some environmental implications. In: Birch, C, Eakin, W & McDaniel, JB (eds): *Liberating life: contemporary approaches to ecological theology*, 159-181. Maryknoll: Orbis Books.

Haught, JF 1990. Religious and cosmic homelessness: some environmental implications. In: Birch, C, Eakin, W & McDaniel, JB (eds) 1990. *Liberating life: contemporary approaches to ecological theology*, 159-181. Maryknoll: Orbis Books.

Haught, JF 1993. *Mystery and promise. A theology of revelation*. Collegeville: The Liturgical Press.

Haught, JF 1993. *The promise of nature: Ecology and cosmic purpose*. Mahwah, NJ: Paulist Press.

Haught, JF 1995. *Science and religion: From conflict to conversation*. New York: Paulist Press.

Haught, JF 1996. Ecology and eschatology. In: Christiansen, D & Grazen, W (eds) 1996. *And God says that it was good. Catholic theology and the environment*, 47-64. Washington: United States Catholic Conference.

Haught, JF 1998a. Evolution, information and cosmic purpose. *CTNS Bulletin* 18:1, 26-37.

Haught, JF 1998b. Evolution, tragedy, hope. In: Peters, T (ed) 1998. *Science and theology: The new consonance*. Westfield Press.

Haught, JF 1998c. Science, religion and the role of metaphysics. *CTNS Bulletin* 18:1, 1-19.

Hawking, S 1988. *A brief history of time: From the Big Bang to black holes*. New York: Bantam Books.

Hayes, Z 1983. *What are they saying about the end of the world?* New York: Paulist Press.

Hayes, Z 1989. *Visions of the future. A study of Christian eschatology*. Wilmington: Michael Grazier.

Hebblethwaite, B 1984. *The Christian hope*. Grand Rapids: WB Eerdmans.

Hedström, I 1990. Latin America and the need for a life-liberating theology. In: Birch, C, Eakin, W & McDaniel, JB (eds): *Liberating life: contemporary approaches to ecological theology*, 111-124. Maryknoll: Orbis Books.

Hellwig, MK 1991. Eschatology. In: Schüssler Firoenza, F & Galvin, JP (eds) 1991. *Systematic theology. Roman Catholic Perspectives*, 349-372. Minneapolis: Fortress Press.

Helm, P 1988. *Eternal God. A study of God without time*. Oxford: Clarendon Press.

Hentz, O 1997. *The hope of the Christian*. Collegeville: The Liturgical Press.

Hessel, DT (ed) 1992. *After nature's revolt. Eco-justice and theology*. Philadelphia: Fortress Press.

Hoekema, AA 1978. *The Bible and the future*. Exeter: Paternoster Press.

Hubbard, DA 1983. Hope in the Old Testament. *Tyndale Bulletin* 34, 33-59.

Institute for Contextual Theology 1985. *Speaking for ourselves.* African Independent Churches. Braamfontein: ICT.

Institute for Contextual Theology 1986. *The Kairos Document. Challenge to the church.*[2] Johannesburg: ICT.

Jeanrond, W 1995. "Death where is your sting?" Death as the ultimate challenge to Christian hope. In: Junker-Kenny, M (ed) 1995. *Christian resources of hope.* Collegeville: The Liturgical Press.

Johanson, B 1975. *The church in South Africa - today and tomorrow.* Johannesburg: SACC.

Jonker, LC 1998. Hope beyond the pre-exilic period: The interrelationship of the creation and the temple / Zion traditions during the monarchical and exilic periods. *Scriptura* 66, 199-216.

Joubert, H 1997. *Krokus & saffraan.* Kaapstad: Lux Verbi.

Kato, BH 1975. *Theological pitfalls in Africa.* Kisum: Evangel Publishinng House.

Keller, C 1994. Chosen personas and the green ecumenacy: A possible Christian response to the population apocalypse. In: Hallman, DG (ed) 1994. *Ecotheology. Voices from South and North*, 300-311. Geneva: World Council of Churches.

Keller, C 1994. Eschatology, ecology and a green ecumenacy. In: Chopp, RS & Taylor, ML (eds) 1994. *Reconstructing Christian theology.* Minneapolis: Fortress Press.

Keller, C 1996. *Apocalypse now and then. A feminist guide to the end of the world.* Boston: Beacon Press.

Keller, C 1997. Eschatology, ecology, and a green ecumenacy. *Ecotheology* 2, 84-99.

Khem, GH 1992. The new story. Redemption as fulfillment of creation. In: Hessel, DT (ed): *After nature's revolt. Eco-justice and theology.* Minneapolis: Fortress Press.

Kinghorn, J (ed) 1986. *Die NG Kerk en apartheid.* Johannesburg: Macmillan

Klink, WH 1994. Ecology and eschatology: Science and theological modeling. *Zygon* 29:4, 529-546.

König, A 1989. *The eclipse of Christ in eschatology: Toward a Christ-centered approach.* Grand Rapids: WB Eerdmans.

Körtner, UHJ 1995. *The end of the world. A theological interpretation.* Westminster: John Knox Press.

Kreck, W 1961. *Die Zukunft des Gekommenen. Grundprobleme der Eschatologie.* München.

Kroh, W 1991. Foundations and perspectives for an ecological ethics: the problem of responsibility. In: Metz, J and Schillebeeckx, E (eds) 1991. *No heaven without earth. Concilium* 1991;4, 79-93.

Kuitert, H 1993. *I have my doubts. How to become a Christian without being a fundamentalist.* London: SCM Press.

Kundera, M 1984. *The unbearable lightness of being.* New York: Harper & Row.

Küng, H 1984. *Eternal life?* London: Collins.

Küng, H 1992. *Credo.* London: SCM Press.

Küppers, B-O 1995. Understanding complexity. In: Russell, RJ, Murphy, N & Peacocke, AR (eds) 1995. *Chaos and complexity. Scientific perspectives on divine action.* Vatican Observatory Publications.

Kyung, CH 1994. Ecology, feminism and African and Asian spirituality: Towards an spirituality of eco-feminism. In: Hallman, DG (ed) 1994. *Ecotheology. Voices from South and North*, 175-178. Geneva: World Council of Churches.

Landes, GM 1984. Creation and liberation. In Anderson, BW (ed) 1984. *Creation in the Old Testament*, 135-151. Philadelphia: Fortress Press.

Lane, D 1996. *Keeping hope alive. Stirrings in Christian theology.* New York: Paulist Press.

Lawson, L 1991. The ghetto and the greenbelt. In: Cock, J & Koch, E (eds) 1991. *Going green. People, politics and the environment in South Africa*, 46-63. Cape Town: Oxford University Press.

Le Roux, J 1996. *Fokus en floreer*. Kaapstad: Lux Verbi.

Lindbeck, GA 1984. *The nature of doctrine: religion and theology in a post-liberal age*. Philadelphia: Westminster Press.

Lindbeck, GA 1989. The church's mission to a post-modern culture. In: Burnham, FB (ed) 1989. *Postmodern theology. Christian faith in a pluralist world*, 37-55. San Francisco: Harper & Row.

Lindsey, H 1970. *The late great planet earth*. Grand Rapids: Zondervan.

Livingstone, DN 1991. Evolution, eschatology, and the privatization of providence. *Science and Christian Belief* 2:2, 117-130.

Lodahl, ME 1992. *Shekinah / Spirit. Divine presence in Jewish and Christian religion*. New York: Paulist Press.

Lombaard, C 1983. Kontinuïteit en diskontinuïteit in die denke van A.A. van Ruler – 'n kritiese gesprek met P. van Hoof oor die aktualiteit van die "Intermezzo". M.Th. tesis. Universiteit van Wes-Kaapland.

Loubser, B 1996. *'n Mooier toekoms wag*. Kaapstad: Lux Verbi.

Macquarrie, J 1978. *Christian hope*. London: Mowbrays.

Maimela, S 1986. Current themes and emphasese in black theology. In: Mosala, IJ & Thlagale, B (eds) 1986. *The unquestionable right to be free*. Johannesburg: Skotaville Publishers.

Maimela, S 1992. Jesus Christ: The liberator and hope of oppressed Africa. In Pobee, J (ed) 1992. *Exploring Afro-Christology. Studies in the intercultural history of Christianity* 79, 31-41. Frankfurt am Main: Peter Lang.

Makhubu, P 1988. *Who are the independent churches?* Johannesburg: Skotaville.

Mangum, JM (ed) 1989. *The new faith - science debate. Probing cosmology, technology and theology*. Minneapolis: Fortress Press.

Martin, ML 1964. *The biblical concept of messianism and messianism in South Africa*. Morija: Morija Sesuto Book Depot.

Mbiti, J 1969. *African religions and philosophy*. London.

Mbiti, J 1971. Eschatology. In: Dickson, KA & Ellingworth, P (eds) 1971. *Biblical revelation and African beliefs*. London: Lutterworth Press.

Mbiti, J 1971. *New Testament eschatology in an African background*. London: Oxford University Press.

Mbiti, J 1975. *Introduction to African religion*. London: Heinemann.

Mbuy-Beya, B 1994. African spirituality: A cry for life. In: Abraham, KC & Mbuy-Beya, B (eds) 1994. *Spirituality of the Third World*. Maryknoll: Orbis Books.

McClendon, JW 1994. *Doctrine. Systematic theology*. Nashville: Abingdon Press.

McDaniel, JB & Byrd, J 1990. *Earth, sky, Gods, mortals. Developing an ecological spirituality*. Mystic, Co: Twenty-Third Publications.

McDaniel, JB 1989. *Of God and pelicans: A theology of reverence for life*. Westminster: John Knox Press.

McDannell, C & Lang, B 1988. *Heaven - A history*. New haven: Yale University Press.

McDonagh, S 1986. *To care for the earth*. London: Geoffrey Chapman.

McDonagh, S 1994. *Passion for the earth*. London: Geoffrey Chapman.

McFague, S 1991. Cosmology and Christianity: implications of the common creation story for theology. In: Davaney, S (ed) 1991. *Theology at the end of modernity*, 19-40. Philadelphia: Trinity Press International.

McFague, S 1993. *The body of God. An ecological theology*. London: SCM Press.

McFague, S 1997. *Super, natural Christians*. Philadelphia: Fortress Press.

McGrath, AE 1994. *Christian theology. An introduction*. Oxford: Basil Blackwell.

McKibben, B 1989. *The end of nature*. New York: Random House.

McKim, DK 1988. *Theological turning points. Major issues in Christian thought*. Westminster: John Knox Press.

Metz, JB & Moltmann, J 1995. *Faith and the future. Essays on theology, solidarity, and modernity.* Maryknoll: Orbis Books.

Metz, JB 1969. *A theology of the world.* London: Burns & Oates / Herder & Herder.

Metz, JB 1970. Religion and society in light of a political theology. In: Capps, WH (ed) 1970. *The future of hope*, 136-154. Philadelphia: Fortress Press.

Metz, JB 1972. The future *ex memoria passionis.* In: Cousins, EH (ed) 1972. *Hope and the future of man.* Philadelphia: Fortress Press.

Metz, JB 1980. *Faith in history and society. Toward a practical fundamental theology.* New York: The Seabury Press.

Migliore, DL 1991. *Faith seeking understanding.* Grand Rapids: WB Eerdmans.

Míguez-Bonino, J 1975. *Doing theology in a revolutionary situation.* Philadelphia: Fortress Press.

Molia, MP 1990. God's kingdom and political commitment. *Journal of Theology for Southern Africa* 71, 18-28.

Moltmann, J 1967. *Theology of hope.* London: SCM Press.

Moltmann, J 1968. "Behold, I make all things new": The category of the new in Christian theology. In: Muckenhirn, M (ed) 1968. *The future as the presence of shared hope*, 9-33. New York: Sheed and Ward.

Moltmann, J 1970. Religion, revolution, and the future. In: Capps, WH (ed) 1970. *The future of hope*, 102-126. Philadelphia: Fortress Press.

Moltmann, J 1972. Response to the opening presentations. In: Cousins, EH (ed) 1972. *Hope and the future of man.* Philadelphia: Fortress Press.

Moltmann, J 1973. *Theology and joy.* London: SCM Press.

Moltmann, J 1975. *The experiment hope.* Philadelphia: Fortress Press.

Moltmann, J 1977. *The church in the power of the Spirit.* New York: Harper & Row.

Moltmann, J 1979. *The future of creation.* London: SCM Press.

Moltmann, J 1980. *Experiences of God.* London: SCM Press.

Moltmann, J 1981. *The Trinity and the kingdom.* San Francisco: Harper & Row.

Moltmann, J 1985. *God in creation: An ecological doctrine of creation.* London: SCM Press.

Moltmann, J 1989. *Creating a just future: the politics of peace and the ethics of creation in a threatened world.* London: SCM Press.

Moltmann, J 1992. *The Spirit of life. A universal affirmation.* Philadelphia: Fortress Press.

Moltmann, J 1996. *The coming of God. Christian eschatology.* Philadelphia: Fortress Press.

Moltmann, J 1997. *The source of life. The Holy Spirit and the theology of life.* Philadelphia: Fortress Press.

Moltmann, J 1998. In the end - God. In: Freyne, S & Lash, N (eds) 1998. *Is the world ending? Concilium* 1998/4, 116-125. London: SCM Press. / Maryknoll: Orbis Books.

Moltmann, J, Wolterstorff, N & Charry, ET 1998b. *A passion for God's reign. Theology, Christian learning and the Christian self.* Edited by M. Volf. Grand Rapids: WB Eerdmans.

Mudge, LS 1998. *The church as moral community. Ecclesiology and ethics in ecumenical debate.* New York: Continuum.

Müller, BA 1985. Eskatologiese prediking. In: Burger, CW, Müller, BA & Smit, DJ 1985. *Riglyne vir eskatologiese prediking.* Kaapstad: Lux Verbi.

Müller-Fahrenholz, G 1995. *God's Spirit transforming a world in crisis.* New York: Continuum.

Nash, JA 1991. *Loving nature: Ecological integrity and Christian responsibility.* Abingdon Press.

Naude, CFB & Sölle, D 1985. *Hope for faith. A conversation.* Geneva: World Council of

Churches.
Naude, P 1994. *Brug na môre*. Kaapstad: Lux Verbi.
Ndegwa, P & Green, RH 1994. *Africa to 2000 and beyond. Imperative political and economic agenda*. Nairobi: East Africa Educational Publishers.
Ndungane, N 1998. Discipleship in a local context. The assembly theme as inspiraton for mission. *Ecumenical Review* 50:4, 217-226.
Nel, A (ed) 1995. *God maak sin*. Kaapstad: Lux Verbi.
Niebuhr, HR 1937. *The kingdom of God in America*. New York: Harper & Brothers.
Niebuhr, R 1932. *Moral man and immoral society*. New York: Charles Scribner's Sons.
Niebuhr, R 1943. *The nature and destiny of man. A Christian interpretation*. New York: Charles Scribner's Sons.
Niehaus, C 1993. *Fighting for hope*. Cape Town: Human & Rosseau.
Niles, D Preman (ed) 1992. *Between the flood and the rainbow*. Geneva: World Council of Churches.
Niles, D Preman 1989. *Resisting the threats to life: Covenanting for justice, peace and the integrity of creation*. Geneva: WCC Publications.
Nolan, A 1986. Theology in a prophetic mode. In: Thlagale, B & Mosala, I (eds) 1986. *Hammering swords into ploughshares*. Johannesburg: Skotaville Publishers.
Nolan, A 1987. The eschatology of the Kairos Document. *Missionalia* 15:2, 61-69.
Noordmans, O 1979. Herschepping. In: *Verzamelde Werken* 2, 214-322. Kampen: JH Kok.
Nürnberger, K 1992. The royal-imperial paradigm in the Bible and the modern demand for democracy. *Journal of Theology for Southern Africa* 81, 16-34.
Nürnberger, K 1993. The God of Abraham, Isaac and Jacob: The trajectory of a soteriological paradigm in Biblical times. *Scriptura* 46, 1-23.
Nürnberger, K 1994. Towards a new heaven and a new earth. In: De Gruchy, JW & Villa-Vicencio, C (eds) 1994. *Doing theology in context. South African perspectives*, 139-151. Cape Town: David Philip.
Nürnberger, K 1997. The conquest of chaos: The Biblical paradigm of creation and its contemporary relevance. *Journal of Theology for Southern Africa* 98, 45-63.
Oberman, HA 1986. *The dawn of the reformation*. Edinburgh: T. & T. Clark.
Ogden, S 1975. The meaning of Christian hope. *Union Seminary Quarterly Review* 30, 153-164.
Olivier, DF 1989. The role of eschatology and futurology in the quest for a future in the light of the ecological crisis. *Theologia Evangelica* 22:1, 24-33.
Oosthuizen, GC 1968. *Post-Christianity in Africa - A theological and anthropological study*. London: C. Hurst & Co.
Oosthuizen, GC 1976. *The theology of a South African Messiah*. Leiden: EJ Brill.
Ortega, O 1989. Celebrating hope. *Ecumenical Review* 41:4, 522-526.
Orteza, E 1997. The Sokoni, a story. *Echoes. Justice, Peace and Creation News* 1997/11.
Osborn, L 1993. *Guardians of creation. Nature in theology and the Christian life*. Leicester: Apollos.
Otto, RE 1992. The eschatological nature of Moltmann's theology. *Westminster Theological Journal* 54, 115-133.
Ozrovech, S 1996. *Op vlerke van geloof*. Kaapstad: Lux Verbi.
Ozrovech, S 1998. *Hoop*. Kaapstad: Lux Verbi.
Pannenberg 1970. Can Christianity do without an eschatology? In: Caird, GB et al 1970. *The Christian hope*, 25-34. London: SPCK.
Pannenberg, W 1969. *Theology and the kingdom of God*. Philadelphia: The Westminster Press.
Pannenberg, W 1973. Eschatology and the experience of meaning. In: *Basic Questions in theology, Volume Three*, 192-210. London: SCM Press.

Pannenberg, W 1984. Constructive and critical functions of Christian eschatology. *Harvard Theological Review* 77:2, 119-139.

Pannenberg, W 1990. *Metaphysics and the idea of God.* Grand Rapids: WB Eerdmans.

Pannenberg, W 1991. *An introduction to systematic theology.* Grand Rapids: WB Eerdmans.

Pannenberg, W 1991. *Systematic Theology. Volume 1.* Grand Rapids: WB Eerdmans.

Pannenberg, W 1993. *Toward a theology of nature. Essays on science and faith.* Westminster: John Knox Press.

Pannenberg, W 1994. *Systematic Theology. Volume 2.* Grand Rapids: WB Eerdmans.

Pannenberg, W 1995. Die Aufgabe christlicher Eschatologie. *Zeitschrift für Theologie und Kirche* 92:1, 71-82.

Pannenberg, W 1997. Theological appropriation of scientific understandings: Responses to Hefner, Wicken, Eaves, and Tipler. In: Albright, Carol & Haugen, J (eds) 1997. *Beginning with the end. God science and Wolfhart Pannenberg*, 427-445. Chicago & LaSalle, Ill: Open Court.

Pannenberg, W 1998. *Systematic Theology. Volume 3.* Grand Rapids: WB Eerdmans.

Pascal, B 1932. *Pensées.* Translated by WF Trotter. London: JM Dent & Sons.

Peacocke, AR 1979. *Creation and the world of science.* Oxford: Clarendon Press.

Peacocke, AR 1989. The challenge of science to theology and the church. In: Mangum, JM (ed) 1989. *The new faith - science debate. Probing cosmology, technology and theology*, 10-22. Minneapolis: Fortress Press.

Peacocke, AR 1993. *Theology for a scientific age: Being and becoming - natural, divine, and human.* Minneapolis: Fortress Press.

Peters, TF (ed) 1989. *Cosmos as creation. Theology and science in consonance.* Nashville: Abingdon Press.

Peters, TF 1978. *Futures - human and divine.* Atlanta: John Knox Press.

Peters, TF 1980. *Fear, faith and the future.* Minneapolis: Augsburg Publishing House.

Peters, TF 1984. Creation, consummation, and the ethical imagination. In: Joranson, PN & Butigan, K (eds) 1984. *Cry of the environment: rebuilding the Christian creation tradition.* Santa Fe: Bear and Co.

Peters, TF 1990. Hope and eschatology. *CTNS Bulletin* 10, 27-29.

Peters, TF 1992. *God - The world's future. Systematic theology for a postmodern era.* Minneapolis: Fortress Press.

Peters, TF 1993. Pannenberg on theology and natural science. In: Pannenberg, W 1993. *Toward a theology of nature. Essays on science and faith.* Edited by Ted Peters. Westminster: John Knox Press.

Peters, TF 1994. *Sin. Radical evil in soul and society.* Grand Rapids: WB Eerdmans.

Peters, TF 1994b. Eschatological sanctions and Christian ethics. *Princeton Seminary Bulletin* Supplementary issue 3, 129-152.

Peters, TF 1995. The physical body of immortality. *CTNS Bulletin* 15:2, 1-20.

Peters, TF 1996. The trinity in and beyond time. In: Russell, RJ, Murphy, N & Isham, CJ (eds) 1996. *Quantum cosmology and the laws of nature. Scientific perspectives of divine action.*[2] Vatican City: Vatican Observatory & The Center for Theology and the Natural Sciences.

Peters, TF 1998. Revolution and Christian hope: A response to John Haught. *CTNS Bulletin* 18:1, 22-25.

Petersen, RM 1995. *Time, resistance and reconstruction. A theology of the prophetic and the popular.* Dissertation. University of Chicago.

Pieper, J 1986. *On hope.* San Francisco: Ignatius Press.

Pieterse, HJC 1994. *Met die draai van die gety.* Kaapstad: Lux Verbi.

Pirsig, RM 1974. *Zen and the art of motorcycle maintenance.* London: Corgi Books.

Pittenger, N 1980. *After death – Life in God.* New York: Seabury Press.

Pityana, B 1995. A theology of life. In: Koegelenberg, R (ed) 1995. *The Reconstruction and Development Programme (RDP): The role of the church, civil society and NGO's*, 67-76. Stellenbosch: EFSA.

Placher, WC 1994. The eternal God. In: *Narratives of a vulnerable God. Christ, theology, and Scripture*, 27-52. Westminster: John Knox Press.

Polkinghorne, J 1994. *Science and Christian belief. Theological reflections of a bottom-up thinker.* London: SPCK.

Polkinghorne, J 1998. *Belief in God in an age of science.* New haven: Yale University Press.

Pretorius, HL 1987. The new Jerusalem: Eschatological perspectives in African Indigenous Churches. *Missionalia* 15:1, 31-41.

Rahner, K 1966. The hermeneutics of eschatological assertions. In: *Theological investigations IV*, 323-346. London: Darton, Longman & Todd.

Raiser, K 1997. *To be the church. Challenges and hopes for a new millennium.* Geneva: World Council of Churches.

Ramphele, M & McDowell, C (eds) 1991. *Restoring the land: Environment and change in post-apartheid South Africa.* London: Panos.

Rasmussen, LL 1975. The future isn't what it used to be: "Limits to growth" and Christian ethics. *Lutheran Quarterly* 27, 101-111.

Rasmussen, LL 1987. Creation, church and Christian responsibility. In: Granberg-Michaelson, W (ed) 1987. *Tending the garden: essays on the gospel and the earth*, 114-131. Michigan: WB Eerdmans.

Rasmussen, LL 1991/11/18. Honoring creation's integrity. The ecocrisis: a question of ethics and cosmology. *Christianity and Crisis*, 354-358.

Rasmussen, LL 1994. Cosmology and ethics. In: Tucker, ME & Grimm, JA (eds) 1994. *Worldviews and ecology. Religion, philosophy, and the environment*, 173-180. Maryknoll: Orbis Books.

Rasmussen, LL 1994. Theology of life and ecumenical ethics. In: Hallman, DG (ed) 1994. *Ecotheology. Voices from South and North*, 112-129. Geneva: World Council of Churches.

Rasmussen, LL 1996. *Earth community. Earth ethics.* Maryknoll: Orbis Books.

Rast, T 1970. Eschatologie. In: Van der Gucht, R & Vorgrimler, H (eds) 1970. *Bilan de la Théologie du XXe Siècle*, 501-519. Tournai-Paris: Casterman.

Rauschenbusch, W 1991. *Christianity and the social crisis.* Louisville: John Knox Press.

Ray, B 1972. Recent studies on African religions. *History of Religions* 12:1.

Richard, P 1994. A theology of life: Rebuilding hope from the perspective of the South. In: Abraham, KC & Mbuy-Beya, B (eds) 1994. *Spirituality of the Third World.* Maryknoll: Orbis Books.

Robinson, JAT 1968. *In the end God.* London: Collins.

Robra, M 1996. Theology of life - Justice, peace, creation: An ecumenical study. *Ecumenical Review* 48:1, 28-37.

Rolston, H (III) 1988. *Environmental ethics: Duties to and values in the natural world.* Philadelphia: Temple University Press.

Rolston, H 1987. *Science and religion. A critical survey.* Orlando: Harcourt Brace & Company.

Roux, A (ed) 1997. *Business futures 1997.* University of Stellenbosch: Institute for Futures Research (restricted access).

Ruether, RR 1975. *New woman / New earth: Sexist ideologies and human liberation.* New York: Seabury Press.

Ruether, RR 1983. *Sexism and God-talk. Toward a feminist theology.* London: SCM Press.

Ruether, RR 1992. *Gaia & God: An ecofeminist theology of earth healing.* Harper & Collins

Publishers.

Runia, K 1997. Eschatology in the second half of the twentieth century. *Calvin Theological Journal* 32, 105-135.

Russell, RJ 1986. How does a scientific cosmology shape a theology of nature? *CTNS Bulletin* 6:1, 1-11.

Russell, RJ 1989. Cosmology, creation, and contingency. In: Peters, TF (ed) 1989. *Cosmos as creation. Theology and science in consonance*, 177-210. Nashville: Abingdon Press.

Russell, RJ 1994. Cosmology from Alpha to Omega. *Zygon* 29:4, 557-577.

Russell, RJ 1997. Cosmology and eschatology: The implications of Tipler's 'Omega point' theory to Pannenberg's theological programme. In: Albright, Carol & Haugen, J (eds) 1997. *Beginning with the end. God, science and Wolfhart Pannenberg*, 195-216. Chicago & LaSalle, Ill: Open Court.

Russell, RJ 1997. Does "the God who acts" really act? New approaches to divine action in light of science. *Theology Today* 54, 43-65.

Russell, RJ, Murphy, N & Peacocke, AR (eds) 1995. *Chaos and complexity. Scientific perspectives on divine action.* Vatican Observatory Publications.

Santa Ana, J de 1995. Elements for a theology of life. *Exchange* 24, 159-175.

Santmire, HP 1985. *The travail of nature*. Philadelphia: Fortress Press.

Santmire, HP 1989. The future of the cosmos and the renewal of the church's life with nature. In: Peters, T (ed) 1989. *Cosmos as creation. Theology and science in consonance*, 265-282. Nashville: Abingdon Press.

Sauter, G 1999. *What dare we hope? Reconsidering eschatology*. Harrisburg: Trinity Press International.

Scharper, SB & Cunningham, H 1993. *The green Bible.* Maryknoll: Orbis Books.

Schillebeeckx, E 1969. *God the future of man.* London: Sheed and Ward.

Schillebeeckx, E 1969. Some thoughts on the interpretation of eschatology. In: Schillebeeckx, E 1995. *The language of faith*, 43-54. Maryknoll: Orbis Books.

Scholder, K 1990. *The birth of modern critical theology*. London: SCM Press.

Schuurman, DJ 1987. Creation, eschaton, and ethics: an analysis of theology and ethics in Jürgen Moltmann. *Calvin Theological Journal* 22:1, 42-68.

Schuurman, DJ 1991. *Creation, eschaton, and ethics: The ethical significance of the creation-eschaton relation in the thought of Emil Brunner and Jürgen Moltmann.* New York: Peter Lang.

Schuurman, DJ 1995. Creation, eschaton, and social ethics: A response to Volf. *Calvin Theological Journal* 30, 130-143.

Schwarz, H 1984. Eschatology. In: Braaten, CE & Jenson, RW (eds) 1984. *Christian dogmatics*, 471-588. Philadelphia: Fortress Press.

Schweitzer, A 1910. *The quest for the historical Jesus*. London.

Setiloane, G 1995. Towards a biocentric theology and ethic - via Africa. *Journal of Black Theology* 9:1, 52-66.

Siegwalt, G 1975. Inwiefern betreffen die Umweltfragen unser christliches Denken? *Kerygma und Dogma* 21, 225-238.

Sindima, H 1989. Community of life. *The Ecumenical Review* 41:4, 537-551.

Smit, DJ 1996. Reformed ethics and economic justice. *Ned Geref Teologiese Tydskrif* 37:3, 438-455.

Smit, N 1994. *Deur die oë van 'n vrou.* Kaapstad: Lux Verbi.

Stackhouse, R 1997. *The end of the world. A new look at an old belief.* New York: Paulist Press.

Suchocki, M 1988. *The end of evil. Process eschatology in historical context.* New York: State University of New York Press.

Suchocki, MH 1982. *God Christ church. A practical guide to process theology*. New York:

Crossroad.

Sundkler, B 1961. *Bantu prophets in South Africa*. London: Oxford University Press.

Sundkler, B 1976. *Zulu Zion and some Swazi Zionists*. London: Oxford University Press.

Swimme, B 1988. The cosmic creation story. In: Griffin, D (ed) 1988. *The reenchantment of science: Postmodern proposals*. Albany: State University of New York Press.

Swimme, B & Berry, T 1992. *The universe story*. San Francisco: Harper & Row.

Swimme, B 1996. *The hidden heart of the cosmos*. Maryknoll: Orbis Books.

Teilhard de Chardin, P 1959. *The phenomenon of man*. New York: Harper Colophon Books.

Teilhard de Chardin, P 1960. *The divine milieu*. San Francisco: Harper & Row.

Templeton, JM & Herrmann, RL 1989. *The God who would be known*. San Francisco: Harper & Row.

Theron, PF 1978. *Die ekklesia as kosmies-eskatologiese teken. Die eenheid van die kerk as 'profesie' van die eskatologiese vrede*. Pretoria: N.G. Kerkboekhandel.

Thielicke, H 1966. *Theological ethics. Volume I*. Philadelphia: Fortress Press.

Thompson, D 1996. *The end of time. Faith and fear in the shadow of the millennium*. London: Sinclair-Stevenson.

Tillich, P 1936. Eschatology and history. In: *The interpretation of history*, 266-284. New York: Charles Scribner's Sons.

Tillich, P 1951. *Systematic Theology. Volume one*. Chicago: University of Chicago Press.

Tillich, P 1952. *The courage to be*. New Haven: Yale University Press.

Tillich, P 1957. *Systematic Theology. Volume two*. Chicago: University of Chicago Press.

Tillich, P 1963. *Systematic Theology. Volume three*. Chicago: University of Chicago Press.

Tillich, P 1963b. *The eternal now*. New York: Charles Scribner's Sons.

Tinker, GE 1996. Creation as beloved by God. Eco-justice, sovereignty and a theology of liberation. *Echoes. Justice, Peace and Creation News* 1996/10, 19-22.

Tipler, F 1988. The Omgea point theory: A model of an evolving God. In: Russell, RJ, Stoeger, W & Coyne, G (eds) 1988. *Physics, philosophy, and theology*. Vatican City: Vatican Observatory.

Tipler, F 1994. *The physics of immortality*. New York: Doubleday.

Tipler, F 1997. The Omega point as eschaton: Answers to Pannenberg's questions to scientists. In: Albright, Carol & Haugen, J (eds) 1997. *Beginning with the end. God, science and Wolfhart Pannenberg*, 156-193. Chicago & LaSalle, Ill: Open Court.

Torrance, AJ 1996. *Creatio ex nihilo* and the spatio-temporal dimensions with special reference to Jürgen Moltmann and D.C. Williams. In: Gunton, CE (ed) 1996. *The doctrine of creation*. Edinburgh: T & T Clark.

Toulmin, S 1982. *The return to cosmology. Postmodern science and the theology of nature*. Berkeley: University of California Press.

Toulmin, S 1990. *Cosmopolis. The hidden agenda of modernity*. New York: The Free Press.

Tracy, DW & Lash, N (eds) 1983. *Cosmology and theology*. Edinburgh: T & T Clark.

Tracy, DW 1987. *Plurality and ambiguity: Hermeneutics, religion, hope*. San Francisco: Harper & Row.

Tracy, DW 1990. *Dialogue with the Other: The interreligious dialogue*. Grand Rapids: Michigan.

Tracy, DW 1994. *On naming the present. God, hermeneutics, and Church*. Maryknoll: Orbis Books.

Trost, LA 1998. Pannenberg's metaphysics and Haught's proposal for "evolution's God. *CTNS Bulletin* 18:1, 19-22.

Truesdale, A 1994. Last things first: The impact of eschatology on ecology. *Perspectives on Science and Christian Faith* 46, 116-122.

Tshishiku, TT 1983. Eschatology and cosmology. In: Tracy, DW & Lash, N (eds) 1983. *Cosmology and theology*, 36-43. Edinburgh: T & T Clark.

Turner, HW 1979. *Religious innovation in Africa*. Boston: Hall.

Tutu, DM 1983. *Hope and suffering. Sermons and speeches*. Grand Rapids: WB Eerdmans.

Van de Beek, A 1989. Rust is ver te zoeken. In: Van Erkelens, H (ed) 1989. *Van utopie naar werkelijkheid. Gebrokenheid dan der schepping. Kernvragen van het concilair proces*, 42-52. Kampen: JH Kok.

Van de Beek, A 1996. *Schepping. De wereld als voorspel voor de eeuwigheid*. Baarn: Callenbach.

Van den Brom, LJ 1993. *Divine presence in the world. A critical analysis of the notion of divine omnipresence*. Kampen: Kok Pharos.

Van Hoogstraten, HD 1999. *Deep economy. Caring for ecology, humanity, and theology*. New Jersey: Humanities Press. (forthcoming)

Van Niekerk, AA 1994. *Tussen wanhoop en vreugde*. Kaapstad: Lux Verbi.

Van Ruler, AA 1947. *De vervulling van de wet*. Nijkerk: Callenbach.

Van Ruler, AA 1969. *Theologisch werk. Deel I*. Nijkerk: Callenbach.

Van Ruler, AA 1971. *Theologisch werk. Deel II*. Nijkerk: Callenbach.

Van Ruler, AA 1972. *Theologisch werk. Deel IV*. Nijkerk: Callenbach.

Van Zyl, DC 1998. From survival to domination: Hope in the pre-monarchical until the early monarchical period of Israel. *Scriptura* 66, 189-198.

Villa-Vicencio, C & De Gruchy, JW (eds) 1985. *Resistance and hope. South African essays in honour of Beyers Naudé*. Cape Town: David Philip.

Villa-Vicencio, C 1993. *The spirit of hope. Conversations on politics, religion and values*. Johannesburg: Skotaville Publishers.

Vischer, L (ed) 1990. *Rights of future generations, rights of nature. Proposal for enlarging the Universal Declaration of Human Rights*. Studies from the World Alliance of Reformed Churches 19. Geneva: World Alliance of Reformed Churches.

Vischer, L 1993. Koinonia in a time of threats to life. In: Best, TF & Granberg-Michaelson, W (eds) 1993. *Koinonia and Justice, Peace and Creation: Costly unity*. Geneva: World Council of Churches.

Volf, M 1995. Eschaton, creation, and social ethics [reply to book review by L. Hardy]. *Calvin Theological Journal* 30, 130-143.

Volf, M 1996. *Exclusion and embrace: A theological exploration of identity, otherness, and reconciliation*. Nashville: Abingdon Press.

Von Rad, G 1965. Israel's ideas about time and history, and the prophetic eschatology. In: *Old Testament Theology. Volume Two*, 99-125. London: SCM Press.

Vorster, WS (ed) 1987. *Are we killing God's earth*? Pretoria: University of South Africa.

Wainwright, G 1971. *Eucharist and eschatology*. London: Epworth Press.

Wainwright, G 1988. The last things. In: Wainwright, G (ed) 1988. *keeping the faith. Essays to mark the centenary of Lux Mundi*, 341-370. Philadelphia: Fortress Press.

Walsh, B 1987. Theology of hope and the doctrine of creation: An appraisal of Jürgen Moltmann. *The Evangelical Quarterly* 59.

Ward, K 1996. God as a principle of cosmological explanation. In: Russell, RJ, Murphy, N & Isham, CJ (eds) 1996. *Quantum cosmology and the laws of nature. Scientific perspectives of divine action.*[2] Vatican City: Vatican Observatory & The Center for Theology and the Natural Sciences.

Ward, K 1998. *God, faith & the new millennium*. Oxford: One World.

Weinberg, S 1977. *The first three minutes*. New York: Basic Books.

Welch, S 1990. *A feminist ethic of risk*. Philadelphia: Fortress Press.

Welker, M 1994. *God the Spirit*. Philadelphia: Fortress Press.

Wessels, GF 1988. Early Catholocism in Collosians and Ephesians? D.Th. Dissertation. University of Stellenbosch.

White, L 1967. The historical roots of our ecological crisis. *Science* 155, 1203-7.

Whitehead, AN 1978. *Process and reality*. Edited by Griffin, DR & Sherburne, DW. New York: The Free Press.

Wilder, AN 1965. *Kerygma, eschatology, and social ethics*. Philadelphia: Fortress Press.

Wildiers, M 1982. *The theologian and his universe: Theology and cosmology from the middle ages to the present*. Translated by P Dunphy. New York: Seabury Press.

Wildiers, NM 1973. *Wereldbeeld en theologie. Van de middeleeuwen tot vandag*. Antwerpen: Standaard Wetenschaplijke Uitgeverij.

Wildman, WJ & Russell, RJ 1995. Chaos: a mathematical introduction with philosophical reflections. In: Russell, RJ, Murphy, N & Peacocke, AR (eds) 1995. *Chaos and complexity. Scientific perspectives on divine action*. Vatican Observatory Publications.

Wilkinson, L (ed) 1991. *Earthkeeping in the '90s. Stewardship of creation*. Grand Rapids: WB Eerdmans.

Worsnip, M & Van der Water, D (eds) 1991. *We shall overcome. Spirituality for liberation*. Pietermartizburg: Cluster Publications.

Worthing, MW 1996. *God, creation and contemporary physics*. Minneapolis: Fortress Press.

Wright, NG & Kill, DG 1993. *Ecological healing. A Christian vision*. Maryknoll: Orbis Books.

29794343R00210

Printed in Great
Britain
by Amazon